The Picture Bible DICTIONARY

Berkeley and Alvera Mickelsen

Chariot Books™
David C. Cook Publishing Co.

Dedicated to

Dr. Berkeley Mickelson,

whose love and dedication to studying the Bible
has earned him the title of
a true scholar of the Word.

Chariot Books™ is an imprint of David C. Cook Publishing Co.
David C. Cook Publishing Co., Elgin, Illinois 60120
David C. Cook Publishing Co., Weston, Ontario
Nova Distribution Ltd., Newton Abbot, England

THE PICTURE BIBLE DICTIONARY

Book and cover design by Nancy Haskins
Illustrations by Andre Le Blanc and David Barnett
Edited by Jeannie Harmon

Photo credits: Bettman Archives, page 41; Ewing Galloway, pages 34, 114; Matson Photo Service, pages 32, 67, 103, 140, 195; Metropolitan Museum of Art, 209; Religious News Service, page 101, 286; Paul Schrock, page 100, 289; Toronto Star Syndicate, pages 26, 29, 35, 73, 134, 137, 155, 181, 182, 225, 247, 249, 268, 332, 348, 354, 362.

The biblical scholars who participated in reading and checking of the material were: Dr. George R. Beasley-Murray of Southern Baptist Theological Seminary, Louisville, Kentucky; Dr. David Scholer of Fuller Theological Seminary, Pasadena, California; Assoc. Professor Kermit Ecklebarger of Denver Theological Seminary, Denver, Colorado; and Dr. Gerald Hawthorne of Wheaton College, Wheaton, Illinois.

First Printing, 1993
Printed in the United States of America
97 96 95 94 93 5 4 3 2

Library of Congress Cataloging-in-Publication Data

Mickelsen, A. Berkeley.
        The picture Bible dictionary / Berkeley and Alvera Mickelsen.
        p.   cm.
        ISBN 0-7814-0133-X
        1. Bible—Dictionaries. I. Mickelsen, Alvera. I. Title.
BS440.M445 1993
220.3--dc20
                                                                                                93-8472
                                                                                                CIP

Preface

The Picture Bible Dictionary has been created for one purpose—to help children and other readers enjoy and understand the most important book in the world, God's Word—the Bible.

The Bible shows us real people and events in history. But its history and culture may sometimes seem far removed from us. *The Picture Bible Dictionary* will help all readers—children and adults alike—to understand both the likenesses and differences of the Bible from our world today, and help us better understand God's will and work in our lives.

To help young readers put the information in the context of today's world, locations are given in terms of current geography as well as ancient geography. For example, "Ephesus was the capital city of the Roman province called Asia (now a part of Turkey)."

Arranged alphabetically, *The Picture Bible Dictionary* includes significant persons, places, and terms mentioned in *The Picture Bible*, plus many other religious terms and concepts not mentioned specifically, such as *Advent, Dead Sea Scrolls,* and *forgiveness.* In addition, there is a short summary of every book in the Bible. Entries answer the basic Bible questions of young readers without going into complex issues.

We pray that the young people who use this volume will catch the excitement and growth that comes from understanding God's Word in greater depth.

Aaron was a better speaker than his brother Moses, especially when they had to face the pharaoh.

AARON *(AIR-run)*

was Israel's first high priest. He was three years older than his brother, Moses, and was a good speaker and leader.

When God told Moses to lead the Hebrew people out of their slavery in Egypt, Moses said he was afraid because he was not a good speaker. God reminded him that his brother Aaron was a good speaker and that Aaron would help him (Exod. 4:14-16). Together Aaron and Moses tried to convince the pharaoh (king) of Egypt to let the Hebrews go. After God sent ten terrible plagues, Pharaoh finally agreed.

Aaron was Moses' helper all through the forty years the Hebrews spent in the wilderness before they entered the promised land(Exod. 5—15). While Moses was on the mountain receiving the Ten Commandments, Aaron committed a terrible sin. He helped the people make a

AARON'S ROD

Aaron and his four sons were anointed with oil.

golden calf, an idol to worship (Exod. 32).

However, God forgave Aaron, and later Aaron did some heroic things. Once a large group of Israelites revolted against the two brothers. God sent a terrible disease as a judgment, and many people died. Aaron took a container with fire and incense from the tabernacle altar and ran among the people so God would forgive them. God stopped the disease. See Numbers 16.

Aaron and his four sons became the first priests to serve in the tabernacle (Lev. 8—9). They were given beautiful robes and were anointed with holy oils—a symbol that God had specially appointed them to His holy work.

Aaron died at age 123 before the Hebrew people entered the promised land.

AARON'S ROD *(AIR-run's rod)*

was probably a straight piece of wood made from an almond tree. It was a sign of authority; God sometimes told Aaron to use it to work miracles (Exod. 7:8-10,

19-22; 8:16-18). It turned into a serpent when he threw it down before Pharaoh; it changed the rivers and lakes of Egypt into blood; and it brought plagues of frogs, then lice.

Later, when some people rebelled against Aaron's authority as high priest, his rod became part of a test to show that Aaron was God's choice. Twelve rods (one for each tribe of Israel) were placed in the tabernacle. The next morning, only Aaron's rod had buds, blossoms, and ripe almonds. See Numbers 17:1-11.

Aaron's rod was then placed permanently either in front of or inside the ark of the covenant (the text isn't clear). See Numbers 17:10; Hebrews 9:4.

ABBA *(AB-uh)*

is the Aramaic *(AIR-uh-MAY-ick)* word like "Daddy"—it's what a child called his father. (Aramaic was the language spoken by Jesus and the Jews of His time.) Abba appears in Mark 14:36, Romans 8:15, and Galatians 4:6. Each time it shows the loving relationship Christ had with God, His Father. If we are believers we may have the same closeness with God, our Father.

ABEL *(AY-bul)*

the second son of Adam and Eve, was the first person in the Bible to die. He was murdered by his older brother, Cain. Abel was a shepherd and had brought to God an offerings—a lamb from his flock. Cain, a farmer, had brought some vegetables he had grown.

God was pleased with Abel's offering but not with Cain's. The Bible does not say why, but it may have been because Abel's life pleased God and Cain's did not. First John 3:12 says Cain's "deeds were evil and his brother's righteous."

Cain was angry. He urged Abel to go out into a field with him, and there he killed him. See Genesis 4.

ABIATHAR *(uh-BY-uh-thar)*

was the only survivor of eighty-six priests from Nob whom King Saul ordered to be killed. Saul was angry because Abiathar's father, Ahimelech, the high priest, had helped his enemy, David. The priest had given David some of the bread from the tabernacle altar. He had also given him the sword David used to kill Goliath several years before. See I Samuel 22:20-23.

When Abiathar escaped, he brought David an ephod, a special garment worn by priests (I Sam. 23:6-14). David apparently thought the ephod had some power to reveal the future or God's will.

Later David asked Abiathar to help carry the ark back to Jerusalem (I Chron. 15:11-28). When David's son Absalom led a rebellion against his father, Abiathar stayed loyal to David (II Sam. 15:24-37).

Shortly before David's death, a struggle grew between Adonijah, David's oldest living son, and Solomon over who would be the next king. Abiathar was on Adonijah's side (I Kings 1:5-7). Even after Solomon became king, Abiathar favored

ABIGAIL *(AB-uh-gale)*

was the intelligent, charming wife of a very rich sheepherder named Nabal, a mean and stingy man. Abigail's wise acts as a peacemaker saved her community from disaster.

Abigail got to David and apologized just in time.

Nabal's sheep grazed in a place where David and his men had been hiding. They had protected Nabal's men. When David heard that Nabal was having a feast, he sent his men to ask for an invitation. Nabal said no and insulted them. David was so angry about this that he threatened to kill Nabal and his men.

When Abigail heard what her husband had done, she quickly gathered a large amount of food and took it to David. David was so impressed by her graciousness that he canceled the raid.

The next morning, when Abigail told Nabal how close he had come to disaster, the Bible says "his heart died within him"—in other words, he probably had a stroke that paralyzed him. Ten days later, he died.

Abigail later became the third wife of David. They had one son, Chileah. See I Samuel 25.

Adonijah, and because of this, Solomon made him leave Jerusalem and stop being a priest (I Kings 2:26, 27).

Jesus mentioned Abiathar in Mark 2:26.

ABIHU *(uh-BY-who)*

was the second of Aaron's four sons. He became one of the first priests of Israel (Exod. 28:1).

Abihu, his father, brother, and seventy elders went with Moses part way up the mountain to receive the Ten Commandments (Exod. 24:1-13).

Abihu died after he and his brother Nadab offered "strange fire" before God (Lev. 10:1-7). We aren't sure what was wrong with their offering, but it must have been contrary to God's command.

"Whose spear and water jar are these, Abner?"

ABIMELECH *(uh-BIM-ih-leck)*

is the name of several persons in the Old Testament, including two kings of the Philistines.

1. One was the king of Gerar, a Philistine city. Abraham and Sarah were afraid of him, and when Abimelech wanted to make Sarah one of his wives, Abraham pretended that she was his sister. Later God appeared to Abimelech in a dream and told him to give Sarah back to Abraham, so he did. Abraham later made a covenant (agreement) with Abimelech after their servants argued about who owned a certain well. See Genesis 20:1-18; 21:22-32.

2. A second King Abimelech took Isaac's wife (similar to case of Abraham). This story also includes an argument over a well. See Genesis 26:1-33.

3. Abimelech the son of Gideon led a revolt that killed all of his brothers except Jotham, the youngest. Abimelech then became king of Shechem. But the people revolted against him twice. The first revolt, when he had been king three years, he put down cruelly. In the second revolt, a woman threw a grindstone from a roof and hit Abimelech in the head. He was dying yet he didn't want people to say a woman had killed him, so he asked his young armor-bearer to kill him instead with his sword. See Judges 9.

4. A priest named Abimelech was the son of Abiathar and served during the time of David. See I Chronicles 18:16.

ABINADAB *(uh-BIN-uh-dab)*

lived on a hill in Kiriath-jearim. The ark of God was suddenly left at his house after many people had died because they disobeyed God by looking into the ark. The ark stayed in his house for twenty years until David took it to Jerusalem. See I Samuel 6:19—7:2; II Samuel 6:1-15.

ABNER (AB-ner)

was Saul's cousin and commander of Saul's army. When David defeated the giant Goliath, Abner brought David back to meet Saul.

Later, when Saul was trying to kill David, Abner helped Saul look for David and stayed close to Saul to protect him. After David got into Saul's camp one night and took his sword and jug of water as proof, David shouted from across the valley about Abner's failure to protect Saul.

After Saul's death, Abner helped make lsh-bosheth, son of Saul, the king. This brought two years of war between David's men and those following Ish-bosheth.

Abner later decided to help unify Israel under David's rule. He tried to convince Saul's followers to transfer their loyalty to David. After meeting with David to make an agreement, Abner started home.

But Joab, commander of David's forces, had heard about the meeting and was angry. He thought Abner was a spy. So, without David's knowledge, he followed Abner and killed him.

When David found out, he proclaimed a curse on Joab. David's sincere mourning and fasting for Abner, whom he described as "a prince and a great man," convinced Abner's followers that David had nothing to do with his death. This kept further war from breaking out. See II Samuel 2:8—3:39.

ABRAHAM (AY-bruh-ham)

is called the father of the Israelites or Hebrew people. He is the spiritual father

When Abraham and his family moved, they made up quite a caravan.

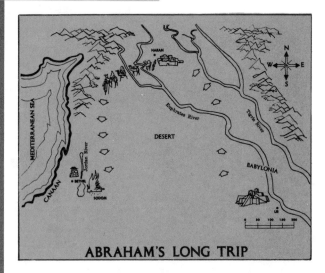

ABRAHAM'S LONG TRIP

of all Christians because of his deep faith in God. His story is told in Genesis 12—25. (See also Rom. 4; Gal. 3:6-29.)

In the beginning, his name was Abram. His family lived in the city of Ur. Then the whole clan moved nearly 800 miles northwest to Haran. They probably traveled by foot and camel. See Gen. 12:1-9.

At Haran, God called Abram to go to Canaan. He took his wife, Sarai, and his nephew, Lot, with him. They lived in Canaan until a famine forced them to move to Egypt, about 750 miles from Haran (Gen. 12:10—13:1).

The ruler there, the pharaoh, tried to take Sarai into his harem. But God sent diseases on the house of the pharaoh, and she was released. Then Abram and his family left Egypt and went back to Bethel in Canaan.

Abram and his nephew, Lot, were both growing rich; each had many cattle and herdsmen. But there was not enough grass to graze all the cattle, and Lot's workers argued with Abram's. Knowing they must separate, Abram took Lot up on a hill. He told Lot to choose either the land to the east or to the west, and Abram would take the opposite. Lot saw the fer-

tile valleys of the Jordan River to the east and chose that land—and much trouble (Gen. 13:2-18). (See *Lot*.)

At that time, Abram had no children. But God appeared to him and said that someday he would have as many descendants as the stars in heaven (Gen. 15). When Sarai still did not have children, Sarai suggested that Abram and a servant woman named Hagar have a child. (This was a common custom in that day.) A son, Ishmael, was born when Abram was eighty-six (Gen. 16).

Thirteen years later, God changed their names from Abram to Abraham and from Sarai to Sarah (Gen. 17:1—18:15). He again promised that they would have a son. They knew this would be a miracle because they were much too old to have children. But when Abraham was 100 years old, a son, Isaac, was born! (See Gen. 21:1-7).

God tested Abraham's faith by telling him to offer his son as a sacrifice. Abraham followed God's directions. But at the last moment, God stopped him from killing his son as a sacrifice. God said He only wanted to see how much Abraham trusted Him (Gen. 22).

When Abraham was 140 years old, Sarah died (Gen. 23). After her death, Abraham married Keturah and had six more children (Gen. 25:1-10). However, all of the Hebrew people, the nation of Israel, are Abraham's and Sarah's descendants.

ABSALOM (see box at right)

ABSTAIN, ABSTINENCE
(ab-STAIN, AB-sti-nens)

means "to stay away from." They are used to guide Christians away from sins and actions that offend other people.

ABSALOM *(AB-suh-lum)*

was the third son of King David. He was handsome and had long, beautiful hair. He planned the murder of his older brother Amnon. He then had to get away from his father's anger and stayed away for three years. Finally he returned, and David forgave him.

However, in a few years, Absalom turned the loyalty of many Israelites away from King David to himself. In a terrible battle between Absalom's men and those of King David, Absalom was riding a mule, and his long hair caught in the branches of a tree. The mule ran off and left Absalom hanging there. Some of David's men found him and killed him,

Absalom liked to impress people with his chariot.

even though David had forbidden them to hurt Absalom. This caused David great grief. See II Samuel 13—18.

ACACIA (see *Plants*)

ACCURSED *(uh-CURST)*

means to be condemned or cut off from God.

ACHAIA *(uh-KAY-uh)*

was a Roman province in what is now the southern half of Greece. Corinth was the capital, although Athens may have been a more important city. Paul visited this area on two of his three missionary journeys.

ACHAN *(AY-kun)*

was an Israelite who disobeyed God and brought defeat to his nation's army. At the battle of Jericho, God commanded the warriors to take no loot for themselves. Everything made of metal (gold, silver, bronze, iron) was to be devoted to God; everything else was to be destroyed. But Achan took some clothing, gold, and sil-

ver for himself and buried it beneath his tent.

Because of his disobedience, God let the Israelites be badly defeated in the battle for the city of Ai. Then He told Joshua there was sin among his men. God also told him how to identify the guilty person. Achan finally confessed. Achan and his family were put to death for the sin. (In ancient Israel, the family was considered a unit, and what the father did involved everyone in his family.) See Joshua 7:1-26.

ACHISH *(AY-kish)*

was a king of the Philistines. David ran to his city once when he was running from Saul, but the soldiers there didn't trust him. So David pretended he was insane so he could escape (I Sam. 21:10—22: 1).

Later, David with his 600 warriors returned to the kingdom of Achish. This time Achish trusted him and even invited

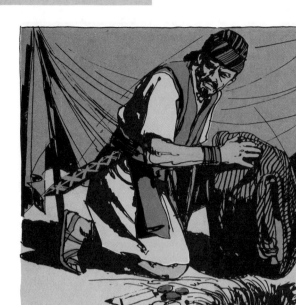

Achan's secret loot didn't stay secret for long.

him and his men to join his army in a war against Israel and King Saul. David agreed, but the Philistine commanders objected, saying that in battle David and his men might turn against them. Reluctantly, Achish sent David and his men away (I Sam. 29:1-11).

ACRE (see *Measures*)

ACTS OF THE APOSTLES
(uh-PAH-suls)

is the fifth book in the New Testament. It was probably written by Luke, the doctor who went with Paul on parts of his second and third missionary journeys. He probably wrote it about A.D. 61 or 62.

Acts shows how the church grew from a small group of frightened believers who huddled in one room to a courageous, growing church spread across the Roman Empire.

Acts centers mostly on the work of two men—Peter and Paul. Peter is the main

person until the end of chapter 12. Beginning in chapter 13, Paul becomes the main character.

The most important happening in the early part of the book is the Day of Pentecost, when the Holy Spirit came on the believers in Jerusalem. From that time on, the Church began to grow. At first, the growth was just in Jerusalem itself, but beginning in chapter 8, the Church spread to the rest of Judea and Samaria and then to Antioch and other places.

Beginning in chapter 13, Paul's missionary journeys are traced as the Gospel is told in Asia Minor, Greece, and Rome. The letters of Paul in the New Testament are written to some of the churches he started while on those journeys or to pastors and Christian workers in those churches.

The story in Acts also shows some of the problems that came when the Christian faith became separate from the Jewish faith. Most of the very early Christians were Jews, and it was hard to bring them together with non-Jews in one church. But Acts shows that the gospel of Christ and the Holy Spirit break down barriers that divide people so that all can become part of the "Body of Christ"— His church.

ADAM *(AD-um)*

is the name of the first person God created (Gen. 1:26—2:7). The name Adam also sometimes means all people or mankind. It is used this way in Genesis 5:2.

Genesis 1:27 says that God created the first man and the first woman. He told them to take care of all He had created, a beautiful world in the garden of Eden,

rich with fruits, vegetables, and animals. See Genesis 2:19-25.

The Bible does not say how long Adam and Eve lived in the beautiful garden before they sinned by eating the fruit of the one tree God had said they were to leave alone (Gen. 3:1-7). When Adam and Eve disobeyed God, sin, with all its ugliness, entered the world.

After that, Adam and Eve no longer had a good, open feeling toward God. Their harmony with nature and with each other was also destroyed. God told them they must leave the garden of Eden and that they would die (Gen. 3:8-24).

From that time on, every person born into the world would, like Adam and Eve, choose the way of sin. Only the coming of Jesus Christ, God's Son, could remove the barriers between people and God. Jesus is called the "second Adam" in Romans 5:14-21 and in I Corinthians 15:22, 45.

After Adam and Eve left the garden of Eden, they had many children (Gen. 4:1-2, 25), but the best known are Cain and Abel. Adam lived to be 930 years old.

ADAR (see *Calendar*)

ADDER (see *Animals*)

ADONIJAH
(AD-oh-NY-juh))
was the handsome, spoiled fourth son of King David. His three older brothers died while they were young men, leaving Adonijah the oldest at the time of David's death. He wanted to become king, even though he knew his younger brother Solomon had been chosen by God to be the next king. When David was old, Adonijah convinced some of David's right-hand men to help make him king.

Adonijah planned a great feast where he would be crowned. He was careful, of course, not to invite Solomon or those who still supported David.

When Nathan, a prophet loyal to David, heard about the plan, he told Solomon's mother, Bathsheba. She told David that Adonijah was proclaiming himself king. David immediately ordered Solomon to ride upon the king's mule and be anointed king. In this way Solomon was pro-claimed king.

When the news came to Adonijah at his feast that Solomon already had been anointed, Adonijah's supporters ran away. Adonijah knew his life was now in danger because he had tried to take the throne. He ran to the altar in the tabernacle, where fugitives were protected from harm.

Solomon forgave Adonijah, and he returned to Jerusalem. But after David's death, Adonijah asked his brother for permission to marry Abishag, who was David's companion during his last illness. In the eyes of the people, this could have been interpreted as meaning Adonijah was the rightful heir to all that had belonged to David. Solomon was angry at the request and ordered Adonijah to be put to death. See I Kings 1:1—2:25.

ADOPTION *(uh-DOP-shun)*
describes how a person can become a member of a family even though he or she was not born into it. The word is used by Paul to explain how people who are naturally sinners can by "adoption" become children of God, with many privileges and joys. In Ephesians 1:3-5, Christians are adopted into God's family through Jesus Christ, God's Son.

Paul shows the difference between being a slave and being a son in Galatians 4:1-7. He says Christ came to redeem those who were slaves (of sin) so they could receive the adoption of sons.

In Romans 8:14-17, Paul says the Holy Spirit is the witness that we are now sons of God. He may have been referring to the Roman law requiring witnesses to an adoption.

Christians are children of God, not simply because He created them, but

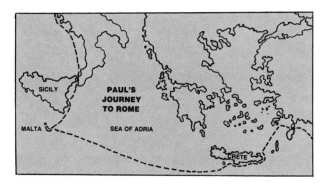

because they have been adopted into God's family.

ADRIA *(AY-dree-uh)*

was the part of the Mediterranean Sea between the island of Crete and the island of Sicily. Paul was shipwrecked in this sea on his voyage to Rome and finally landed on the island of Malta, south of Sicily (Acts 27:27—28:1).

ADULTERY *(uh-DUL-ter-ee)*

refers to sexual intercourse between a man and a woman when either of them is married to someone else. Another term, *fornication*, means sexual intercourse between any man and woman who are not married to each other. Both adultery and fornication are wrong according to the Bible.

The term *adultery* is also used as a figure of speech meaning "idolatry." In the Old Testament, the Jewish people are referred to as the "wife" of God, and when they turned from God to idols, they were said to be "committing adultery."

See Exodus 20:14; Matthew 15:19; Jeremiah 3:9.

ADVENT *(AD-vent)*

means the coming of Christ. The term *Advent Season* means the four Sundays before Christmas—the time of getting ready to celebrate the coming of Christ. It is a time when Christians think about Christ's birth and what it means.

AGABUS *(AG-uh-bus)*

was a New Testament prophet from Jerusalem who went to the Christians at Antioch and foretold a famine (Acts 11:27-30). After hearing his prophecy, the Antioch Christians decided to send Paul and Barnabas to Judea with help for the believers there. Agabus appeared again many years later, where he foretold that Paul would be arrested if he went to Jerusalem (Acts 21:10, 11).

AGRICULTURE, *or farming*

is the oldest occupation in the world. It began in the garden of Eden when Adam and Eve were told to care for the garden. Cain, their oldest child, was a farmer; Abel, their second son, was a herdsman. Most people in the ancient world farmed or raised cattle and sheep.

Farming the land that is now Israel was never easy. The land was very stony, and the first job of every farmer was to pick up the rocks, usually using them to build fences or dividers. The land was also hilly; farmers often had to build terraces to raise crops.

The climate made farming difficult. Every year there was a five-month summer season without rain and sometimes with hot, searing winds. While the farmer knew there would be a hot, dry season from May to October, the rainy season (the rest of the year) was unpredictable. If it did not rain often from November through April, he knew the summer would bring famine.

Farmers in Bible times tried to prepare for dry seasons by building storage places

15

Plowing the field

Planting the seed

Gleaning the grain

Winnowing at harvesttime

for the water that fell during the rainy season. Archaeologists have dug up these cisterns all over Israel. Farmers also carried water from streams or springs.

In addition to problems of rocky land and not enough water, farmers struggled with plant diseases and insects. Locusts, a kind of grasshopper, were a constant threat. A plague of locusts could eat everything green in a few days, leaving only dry stubble. The Book of Joel was written about a locust plague.

Common crops were grapes, olives, wheat, and barley. However, the Bible says people also grew figs, pomegranates, onions, leeks, beans, and garlic.

The farmer of Bible times had few tools. He plowed with oxen pulling a wooden stick with a small metal point. He cut grain by holding the stalks in his hand and cutting them off close to the ground with a large curved knife called a sickle.

To separate the kernels of grain from the stalks, the farmer might beat the grain with a stick or drive his cattle around on piled-up stalks until their hoofs trampled out the grain. Or he might drag some heavy instrument or sledge over the grain.

When the grain had been threshed (kernels separated from stalks), it had to be winnowed. The farmer threw the grain into the air when the wind was blowing. The wind would blow away the lighter chaff, and the heavier seeds would fall to the ground.

During harvest times, every healthy person worked in the fields—owners and slaves, women and children. At night, many men would stay in their fields to guard their threshed grain or their ripening crops from robbers or animals.

The religious life of the Hebrew people centered in part around the harvest periods. They gave a tithe (one tenth) of their seed to God. The first sheep born into a flock would be sacrificed to God. At the time of the Passover Feast, usually in April, the fields were just beginning to bear barley, and the people brought to God an offering of the first stalks of grain, "the sheaf of first fruits."

Fifty days later, at the Feast of Pentecost, the wheat would be ripe, and the Jewish people brought two loaves of fresh bread as an offering to the Lord. Later on, the Feast of booths marked the end of the harvest and lasted eight days. (See *Feasts*)

AGRIPPA *(uh-GRIP-uh)*

was the name of two rulers in the time of Paul.

1. Herod Agrippa I began ruling a small territory in A.D. 37 and ruled all of Israel from A.D. 40 to 44. The Bible simply calls him "Herod." Acts 12:1, 2 tells that he had James, the brother of John, put to death "to please the Jews." He also had Peter arrested. He died suddenly at age 54 after he permitted his followers to say he was a god (Acts 12:1-23).

2. Herod Agrippa II, the son of Herod Agrippa I, is called "Agrippa" in the Bible. He was the ruler before whom Paul gave a speech defending himself. After the speech, Agrippa said Paul did not deserve to be in prison (Acts 25: 23—26: 32).

AHAB *(AY-hab)*

was the seventh and most evil king Israel ever had. He was a strong political and military leader who defeated Syria twice. He reigned from about 874 to 853 B.C.

He married Jezebel, who was not an Israelite. She brought her pagan gods to Israel and led the people to worship them. She persecuted the prophets of God and killed many of them.

Ahab was king during the famous conflict between the prophet Elijah and the prophets of Baal on Mount Carmel, when God sent fire to consume Elijah's offering (I Kings 18:1—19:1).

Although Ahab was very rich, he always wanted more. Next to his place was a vineyard that belonged to a man named Naboth. Ahab offered to buy it, but Naboth did not want to sell, because the land had belonged to his ancestors. Ahab pouted and refused to eat. To get the vineyard for Ahab, Jezebel lied and accused Naboth of crimes for which he was put to death. For this sin, Ahab lost his life in the next battle with Syria (I Kings 21; I Kings 22: 1-28).

AHASUERUS *(uh-HAZ-oo-EAR-us)*

was a powerful king of the Medes and the Persians. He is probably the same person known in secular history as Xerxes I, who reigned from about 486 to 465 B.C.

He became angry with his queen, Vashti, when she refused to appear at a huge banquet of many drunken men. So he got rid of her and later chose Esther, the cousin of Mordecai, to be the new queen.

At the request of Haman, his chief officer, Ahasuerus ordered that all Jews were to be killed on a certain day. Esther went to the king about it, and eventually Ahasuerus ordered Haman to be hung in the very place Haman had built for Mordecai. The Jews were allowed to protect themselves from harm.

Later, Ahasuerus made Mordecai his

AHIJAH

Elijah said, "You did not obey God's commandments."

chief officer.

See the Book of Esther.

AHIJAH *(uh-HI-juh)*

was the name of seven men in the Bible, two of whom were important.

1. One was the great-grandson of Eli. This Ahijah served as priest in the days of Saul, about 1025 B.C. In a battle between the Israelites and the Philistines, Saul commanded Ahijah to bring the ark to the scene. The Israelites eventually won. See I Samuel 14:1-23.

2. Another Ahijah was a prophet from Shiloh who met Jeroboam on a road going out of Jerusalem. Ahijah said God would make Jeroboam ruler of the ten northern tribes of Israel. He dramatized his prophecy by tearing his clothes into twelve pieces and giving ten of them to Jeroboam. This all came true about 930 B.C. Ahijah later foretold the fall of Jeroboam's family and the death of his son. See I Kings 11:29-40; 14:1-17.

AHITHOPHEL
(uh-HITH-uh-fel)

was one of David's advisers when he first became king. For reasons not stated in the Bible, Ahithophel joined Absalom (David's son) in rebelling against David. Both David and Absalom considered Ahithophel to be a very wise man. Ahithophel urged Absalom to gather

ALABASTER
(AL-uh-BAS-ter)

was a soft, creamy-colored stone often used for making perfume flasks and boxes for fragrant salves or creams. Alabaster had streaks of varying shades and colors.

12,000 men and attack while David and his army were tired and discouraged.

However, Absalom also asked another man, Hushai (who was a counterspy—pretending to serve Absalom, but really on David's side). He suggested that Absalom postpone the battle until he could gather a larger army. Absalom took Hushai's advice instead of Ahithophel's, and the extra time gave David and his men a chance to escape.

When Ahithophel saw that his advice was not followed, he went home and hanged himself.

See II Sam. 15:12, 31; 16:15-23; 17:1-23.

AI *(AY-eye)*

was an old city in central Israel. After Joshua and his army conquered Jericho, Ai was the next city to be attacked. Joshua sent spies to check it out, and they came back saying that the city was small and unprotected; 2,000—3,000 men could easily defeat it.

Joshua sent 3,000 men, but they were beaten by the men of Ai. In despair, Joshua prayed, and God said they were defeated because some Israelites had sinned in the Battle of Jericho by keeping

some of the treasures of the city. After the sin was found, the Israelites returned to the battle, using a clever ambush to draw the warriors out of Ai. The city was destroyed and burned.

It was apparently rebuilt in later years (after the Book of Joshua was written), because some men of Ai were among those who returned from captivity in Babylon.

See Joshua 7: 1—8: 29; Ezra 2:28; Nehemiah 7:32.

ALEXANDER THE GREAT
(AL-eg-ZAN-der)

is not mentioned in the Bible, but his life is important in understanding the New Testament. The greatest military general of many centuries, he conquered almost all of the then-known world for Greece. In 334 B.C., he crossed from Greece into Asia Minor (now Turkey) and conquered the armies of the Medes and Persians;

The famous general, Alexander the Great.

then he went as far south as Egypt, which he took without a battle. There he founded Alexandria, today the second largest city of Egypt. He traveled across Israel to Babylonia and all the way to India.

His army refused to go any farther, and he was forced to stop. He died at age 32 of a fever. He was said to have wept because there were no more worlds for him to conquer.

As the result of his campaigns, Greek became the common language in most of the known world. This was important in the spread of the Gospel after Christ's death and resurrection. Most scholars think the "king of Greece" in Daniel 8:5-8 and 11:34 was Alexander the Great.

ALEXANDRIA (AL-eg-ZAN-dree-uh)

is the second most important city in Egypt (Cairo is first). It was also important in New Testament times, although it is mentioned only four times. Stephen, in Acts 6:9, debated with men from the synagogue of the Alexandrians; twice "ships of Alexandria" are mentioned in Paul's journeys. Apollos, who became a leader of the church at Ephesus, came from Alexandria.

Alexandria was founded by Alexander the Great in 332 B.C. From its beginning it was a city famous for its learning—art, literature, poetry, medicine, mathematics, and astronomy. Many Jews lived in Alexandria, and in this city, Jewish scholars first translated the Old Testament from Hebrew into Greek, working from about 250 to 150 B.C. Their translation was known as the Septuagint, and it became the Bible of the early church.

ALLEGORY (AL-luh-gore-ree)

is a kind of story in which objects or people represent something else to teach a particular lesson. The Bible has many allegories. One is found in Psalm 80:8-16, where the Jewish nation is pictured as a vine that came out of Egypt and was planted in other ground, but has been destroyed.

John 15:1-10 is another allegory, in which Christ is pictured as a vine; believers are branches on the vine, and God the Father is pictured as the farmer who takes care of the vine and its branches. The allegory teaches two lessons—it is important for believers to keep close to Christ; and God wants Christians to be "fruitful," showing their faith by their lives.

ALLELUIA (see Hallelujah)

ALLIANCE (uh-LY-unce)

is an agreement between persons or nations, usually to help each other. Most alliances in the Bible involved military help. King Ahaz made an alliance with the king of Assyria to get help in a war against the king of Syria (II Kings 16:5-9). Other alliances were for business purposes. When Solomon was building the temple, he made an alliance with Hiram, king of Tyre, to trade cedar and cypress wood for wheat and oil.

The Hebrews were warned not to make alliances with other countries but to trust in God alone (Exod. 23:32; 34:12-16). The rulers of Israel often disobeyed that command.

ALMIGHTY (all-MIGHT-ee)

is a name of God that appears forty-eight times in the Old Testament and nine times in the New Testament. The Hebrew word means "with great strength," the Greek word for means "all-powerful."

ALMS *(ahmz)*

are acts of kindness to those who need food, shelter, or other help. Usually it refers to giving money or food to the poor. Jesus taught His followers to give alms and do it quietly, without letting others know. See Luke 12:33; Matt. 6:24.

ALPHA and OMEGA
(AL-fuh and oh-MAY-guh)

are the first and last letters of the Greek alphabet. When the two are used together, it usually means completeness. In Revelation 1:8, God calls Himself "Alpha and Omega, the beginning and the ending." These words are also used of Christ in Revelation 22:13.

ALTAR (see box below)

AMALEKITES *(uh-MAL-uh-kites)*

were a fierce, warlike tribe of nomads who descended from one of the sons of Esau. They seemed to wander from what is now the Sinai desert to Israel. From the time the Israelites came out of Egypt (about 1450 B.C.) to the time of King Hezekiah (about 700 B.C.), the Amalekites always seemed to be Israel's enemy

The Amalekites first attacked the Israelites as they were coming out of Egypt (Exod. 17:8-16). In that famous battle, the Israelites kept winning as long as Aaron and Hur held up the arms of Moses. God told Moses at that time, "I will utterly blot out the remembrance of Amalek from under heaven."

In Judges 6:3, the Amalekites appear as a people who swept down upon settlements and took food, animals, and other possessions (Judg. 6:3-5).

While David and his men were gone from their village of Ziklag, the Amalekites burned it, capturing their wives and children (I Sam. 30:1-26). David later organized a raiding party and rescued the wives and children from the Amalekites.

Saul was told to destroy the Amalekites, but he did not do it completely. They continued to harass the Israelites until the time of Hezekiah, when they were finally destroyed.

ALTAR *(AWL-ter)*

is a structure made of stone, wood, marble, brick, or other materials; it is used in worship. Altars were common in pagan religions as well as in Judaism. Some altars were very simple; others were fancy. The first altar mentioned in the Bible was built by Noah.

The Jewish tabernacle had two altars. One was the altar of burnt offering, where sacrifices to God were burned. The other was an altar of incense, sometimes called

Animals were offered to God on altars

a golden altar. Incense was burned on this altar twice each day to symbolize believers' prayers (see *Offerings*).

AMEN (ay-MEN)

means roughly "It is true." It often appears at the end of important truths such as in Romans 11:36. The word *Amen* is applied to Christ in Revelation 3:14, perhaps emphasizing Christ as the truth. *Amen* was part of the Jewish synagogue worship and has been carried over into the Christian church.

AMETHYST (AM-uh-thist)

is a rare gem ranging in color from purple to blue-violet. It was one of the gems sewn into the breastpiece worn by the high priest in the Old Testament (Exod. 28:15-20). The amethyst is also mentioned as one of the jewels in the foundation of the Holy City (Rev. 21:19, 20).

AMMON, AMMONITES
(AM-un, AM-uh-nites)

Ammon was a son of Lot; he became the ancestor of the Ammonites. God told Moses not to make war on them when the Israelites left Egypt for Canaan (Deut. 2:19).

Many years later, however, the Ammonites became persistent enemies of the Israelites. The Ammonites were brutal and fierce. They worshiped idols and sometimes sacrificed humans to the god Molech. Saul once fought and defeated them (I Sam. 11:1-11).

During short periods, they were friendly to David. Solomon had some Ammonite women among his harem (I Kings 11:1-8). But the Ammonites remained enemies of the Hebrews for nearly a thousand years. When Nehemiah came back from exile to rebuild the walls of Jerusalem about 444 B.C., one of those who opposed him was Tobiah the Ammonite. The Ammorites apparently survived until about 100 B.C..

AMORITES (AM-uh-rites)

were a very large and powerful group of people who once lived in Mesopotamia, later in Babylon, and still later in Israel. They were living in Canaan when Joshua was fighting for the land, and he subdued them. They were apparently a very wicked people. See Genesis 15:16; Joshua 10:1—11:14.

AMOS (AY-mus)

was a sheepherder and grower of fig trees who became an Old Testament prophet. He lived in Tekoa, a few miles south of Jerusalem in Judah. His preaching and prophesying, however, were mostly in Samaria, the capital city of Israel, the northern kingdom.

In his prophecy, he insisted that people should be treated fairly. He said Israel (Samaria) had become very prosperous under King Jeroboam II. These newly rich people should have used their wealth to help the poor. Instead, they used their power to make poor people even poorer.

Amos said that religious feasts, holy days, and offerings to God only made God angry if the people were not being fair and honest with each other.

Amos pointed out that the Lord is the Creator of the world and He also keeps it running. God decides whether there will be famine or good crops.

We don't know whether the people listened and responded to Amos's prophecy. In the end, he was told by the priest of Israel, Amaziah, to go home to his own land (Judah) and do his prophesying there!

His book of prophecy, like many other parts of the Old Testament, is written in Hebrew poetic style. Although Amos was a sheepherder, his use of words to paint

The priest said, "Go on back to Judah, Amos!"

vivid pictures shows that he was a man of great spiritual, moral, and mental strength.

See Amos 4:4-13; 5:10-13; 6:4-7.

ANANIAS *(an-uh-NI-us)*

is the name of three important people in the New Testament. All appear in the Book of Acts.

1. Ananias and Sapphira were husband and wife; they sold a piece of their land and pretended they were giving the church all the money they received from it. They were actually keeping part of it. When Ananias came to present the gift to the apostles, Peter faced him with his lie, and Ananias fell down dead.

Later Sapphira appeared, repeated the same lie—and she too died. The story shows that their sin was in lying to the Holy Spirit rather than in keeping part of the money. See Acts 5:1-11.

2. Another Ananias was a devout Jewish Christian who lived at Damascus. After Saul's conversion on the road to Damascus, he became blind and was led into the city. Three days later, God spoke to Ananias, telling him where to find Saul and saying that he should lay his hands on Saul so that his eyesight would be restored. Ananias was afraid because he had heard that Saul persecuted Christians. However, he obeyed God, and Saul was healed. See Acts 9:10-19.

3. Ananias was also the name of the high priest before whom Paul was brought for trial in Jerusalem. Ananias was so angry at Paul that he ordered those near him to slap Paul's mouth. Paul answered back in anger, but then apologized. This same Ananias later went to Caesarea, the capital of Judea, to accuse Paul before the Roman governor. See Acts 23:1-5; 24:1.

ANDREW

was one of Jesus' twelve apostles. He and

Andrew was one of the fishermen Jesus called.

his brother, Peter, were both fishermen.

Andrew was first a disciple of John the Baptist. But one day John pointed to Jesus and said, "Behold, the Lamb of God!" (See John 1:35-44.) Andrew then became a follower of Jesus and also brought his brother to Jesus.

When Jesus wanted to feed 5,000 people with five loaves and two fish, it was Andrew who found the boy with his lunch (John 6:8-13). Andrew was one of the four disciples who questioned Jesus about what would happen in the future (Mark 13:34).

After Acts 1:13, Andrew is not mentioned again in the New Testament. However, tradition says he became a martyr for Christ in Achaia (present-day Greece), where he was crucified on an X-shaped cross. That shape is now known as Saint Andrew's cross.

ANGELS

are supernatural being—thousands and thousands of them (Rev. 5:11)—created by God before He created man. Angels appear many times in the Old and New Testaments. Jesus said they do not marry; they also never die (Luke 20:34-36). But they are not to be worshiped (Col. 2:18).

What do angels do? They worship God (Heb. 1:6). They also serve as His messengers. For example, angels told Abraham that Sarah would have a son (Gen. 18:1—19:1).

Angels guide God's people. An angel told Philip to go to a certain road where he met an Ethiopian official (Acts 8:26). An angel opened prison doors for the disciples (Acts 5:19).

Sometimes an angel brings encouragement to people who need it, as one did for Paul on a boat about to be shipwrecked (Acts 27:23, 24).

Angels protect God's people in many circumstances (Ps. 91:11; Heb. 1:14).

Angels had a special ministry in the life of Christ. They announced His birth to Mary, Joseph, and the shepherds (Matt. 1:20-24; 2:13-15; Luke 1:26-38; 2:8-15). Angels helped Christ after His temptation (Matt. 4:11); they strengthened Him before the crucifixion (Luke 22:43); they rolled the stone away from His tomb (Matt. 28:2-7); and they were with Him at His ascension (Acts 1:11).

Apparently some angels, before the creation of man, decided not to serve God and "fell." See II Peter 2:4; Jude 6. What has happened and will happen to them? Evil angels are to be sent to eternal fire (Matt. 25:41), while good angels will go on serving God throughout eternity.

ANGER

is a feeling both in people and in God. People may become angry for many reasons, making them often want to quarrel or fight. But when the Bible says God is angry, it is always because of people's sin, injustice, wrongdoing, or unbelief. See Psalm 79:5, 6; 86:15; 103:8-12.

ANIMALS OF THE BIBLE

Since many of the people in the Bible were farmers or sheepherders, animals are often mentioned. Many of the animals are very similar to animals of the same name today. Others are quite different.

Although cows, pigs, horses, sheep, and dogs were tamed, they were rarely used as pets. Cats are never mentioned in the Bible, and dogs, although mentioned about forty times, are nearly always seen as snarling, dirty, undesirable creatures.

A man's riches were counted mostly by how many sheep, oxen, camels, cows, and horses he owned. A person's animals were so much a part of his life that when the Israelites were told to destroy cities in Canaan, they were often told to destroy all the animals as well.

Because animals were so important to people of that day, it is not surprising that they were sometimes thought to be sacred. Idols and images were often made to look like animals. When Moses stayed a long time on the mountain getting the Ten Commandments, the Israelites made a golden calf to worship—probably similar to the images they had seen worshiped in Egypt.

The list below does not include all animals mentioned in the Bible, but it includes the most important ones and

The angels rejoiced at the coming of the Christ child.

A shepherd and his flock of sheep near Bethlehem.

also those that are unfamiliar to most of us, or are different from animals we know by the same name.

Apes are mentioned in I Kings 10:22 as part of the valuable cargo the ships of King Solomon brought to Israel. They were probably more like our rhesus monkeys than our present-day apes.

Adders or **Asps** were poisonous snakes, probably similar to cobras. They are mentioned in Isaiah and in Romans 3:13.

Ants are mentioned in Proverbs 6:6-8 and 30:25 as an example of hard work and planning for the future. Ants store up their food in the summer so they won't be hungry in the winter.

Antelopes (*AN-tuh-lopes*) are something like deer, except they do not shed their horns every year. The **gazelle** is one kind of antelope. The antelope is mentioned in Deuteronomy 14:5, where the King James Version calls it a "wild ox." An antelope is also mentioned in Isaiah 51:20, but the King James Version calls it a "wild bull."

Asses are part of the horse family and are mentioned 150 times in the Bible. They are the same as our modern donkey. They were used for heavy farm work and were also ridden with a saddle. Rulers and great men usually rode asses when they were on a peaceful journey. Horses were used in war. When Jesus rode into Jerusalem on an ass, it was a symbol that He was coming in peace, not as a rebel to overthrow the government.

Badger skins are mentioned in Exodus 25:5 and 26:14 (in the King James Version) as being used to cover the upper part of the tabernacle. However, other translations say "goatskins" or "sealskins" or "leather" for this word. Our present kinds of badgers are not now found in Bible lands.

Bats, probably similar to modern-day bats, are mentioned in Leviticus 11:19

and Deuteronomy 14:18 as "unclean"—not to be eaten.

Bears are mentioned 14 times in the Old Testament, always as fierce, threatening animals. They were probably Syrian brown bears, which are still found in modern Lebanon. David is said to have fought and killed a bear while guarding his sheep. The story is told in I Samuel 17:34-37.

Behemoth (*buh-HE-muth*) is described in Job 40:15-24 as a powerful creature. Most scholars think the animal was a hippopotamus, although some think it might have been an elephant.

Boar is mentioned in Psalm 80:13 and was probably a wild pig.

Bulls, bullocks are male cattle, usually mentioned in the Bible as sacrificial animals. To be used for sacrifice, a young bull had to be at least eight days old; in some cases it had to be a year old; in other cases, three years old or seven years old. Bulls were used as sacrifices on many important occasions and feast days such as the consecration of priests, dedication of the altar, the Passover, and the Feast of booths. Some of the rules are given in Leviticus 9:2-4 and 22:27.

Calf, calves are mentioned in the Bible as meat for special festive occasions. When the prodigal son came home, the father killed the fatted calf. Usually only the wealthy could afford such special foods. Calves, like bulls, were also used as sacrifices.

Camels are mentioned more than 60 times in the Bible. They were important in the Middle East, because they are very hardy and can live 40 to 50 years. They are cud-chewing vegetarians and have a three-part stomach that can store three days' water supply. They carry heavy bur-dens and travel long distances. The Hebrews were not permitted to eat camel meat, but Arabs often ate it. Camel hair was used in making cloth. Job had 3,000 camels before his troubles began, and later in life he had 6,000. To own camels was a sign of wealth.

Cattle were a sign of wealth among the Israelites and other people in Bible times. The term usually means larger animals such as oxen, asses, horses, and cows rather than sheep and goats. However, sometimes *cattle* refers to all domesticated animals. Because cattle were so important to the life of the Israelites, the Law of Moses said they should be permitted to rest on the sabbath just like people.

Cattle were used in sacrifices, for food (milk and meat)—and sometimes images of them were made and worshiped.

Cattle were considered part of the loot

Camels' broad two-toed feet keep them from sinking in the desert sand. Camels can go many days without water because of the fat stored in their humps. The fat turns into energy, which produces water. Their nostril-slits can be closed during a sandstorm to keep out the sand.

27

or bounty of war. A conquering army often took the cattle of the people they had defeated.

Chamois (*SHAM-ee*), mentioned in Deuteronomy 14:4-6 as an animal the Israelites could eat, was a mountain sheep, small and sure-footed.

Colts are either young camels, horses, or donkeys (asses). According to John 12:15, Jesus rode into Jerusalem the Sunday before Easter on the colt of an ass.

Dogs are mentioned forty-one times in the Bible, and in most instances they are considered undesirable. They were scavengers and disease carriers. Although they were used to guard sheep, they were not considered pets or companions. Only in the story of a Syrophenician woman in Matthew 15:26, 27 is there any suggestion of a dog as a pet.

Elephants are not mentioned in the Bible. However, *ivory* is mentioned, so elephants must have been somewhere in the area. Records other than the Bible show that elephants were common in Syria.

Foxes are mentioned nine times in the Bible. They were probably similar to the red fox in America.

Gazelles (*guh-ZELLS*) were small, swift antelopes that usually lived in hot, barren areas.

Goats are mentioned at least 130 times in the Bible and were important sources for milk and meat. They were also used in sacrifices. Their hair was made into clothing and their skins into containers for water and wine.

Harts (male) and **hinds** (female) were large, fast deer, a bit smaller than American elks.

Heifers (*HEF-ferz*) are young cows. A perfect (unblemished) red heifer was used for an important purification ceremony described in Numbers 19.

Horses have been tamed for thousands of years. In Bible times, horses were used mostly for war. They pulled chariots and were sometimes ridden—especially by kings and important people. In the story of Esther, Mordecai was honored by riding the king's horse around the capital city.

The Israelites were told in Deuteronomy 17:16 that they were *not* "to multiply horses." However, Absalom disobeyed this command, and so did Solomon and some later kings.

Jackals (*JACK-ulz*) are a kind of wild dog, smaller than a wolf. Jackals move around in packs, usually at night. They eat other small animals, poultry, fruit, vegetables, and garbage. They have a distinctive wailing howl.

Kids are young goats. Kids were used for food on special occasions, and sometimes as sacrifices. In Exodus 23:19, the Jews were told, "You shall not boil a kid in its mother's milk." This command is why many Jews still do not eat meat and milk at the same meal.

Lambs were the animals most frequently used as a Jewish sacrifice. They were used at the Passover feast, in the morning and evening burnt offerings in the tabernacle, and for many other sacrifices. For the Israelites, the lamb was a symbol of innocence and gentleness.

Leopards of Bible times were similar to modern leopards or cheetahs. They were fierce animals, feared by the people.

Leviathan (*lev-EYE-uh-thun*) appears several times in the Old Testament as some kind of monster. Some scholars think the term refers to a crocodile; others think it is a make-believe creature.

A wild goat, *or ibex, in the wilderness of Judea.*

In Israel today, young Bedouins use donkeys to carry things. In the background is this family's flock of goats.

Lions were well known to the Hebrews, but they are now extinct in the Middle East. They were feared as killers, as in the story of Daniel. Lions were respected for their strength and majestic beauty. Jesus is called the "Lion of the tribe of Judah" (Revelation 5:5).

Mice were apparently common in Israel, and the term seems to include small and medium-sized rats.

Mules are a cross between male donkeys and female horses. Kings and officers often rode mules. David's son Absalom was riding a mule when his hair got caught in branches, leaving him hanging there as the mule went on. He was found and killed as a result.

Oxen are bulls with their sex glands removed. Because they were strong, they were usually used to pull wagons, plows, and other farm implements. Almost every Hebrew farmer had an ox. Oxen were also frequently used as sacrificial animals.

Rams are mature male sheep, often used for sacrifices, but also used for meat. Their skins were used as coverings in the tabernacle, and their horns were commonly used for trumpets.

Roe, roebuck (*ROW-buck*) is a small deer. It is mentioned in Deuteronomy 14:5 as an animal the Israelites were permitted to eat.

Sheep are mentioned more often in the Bible than any other animal. The earliest mention is in Genesis 4:2, where Abel, the son of Adam and Eve, "was a keeper of sheep."

Sheep were kept more for their milk and wool than for their meat. The needs of the sheep kept many of the Hebrews and Arabs living as nomads. The sheep needed pasture and water, so the shepherd and his household moved with the sheep from place to place. Sheep needed constant care. The picture of God as the Good Shepherd in Psalm 23 was based on

Gabriel told Mary that she would have a son.

the well-known habits of shepherds in caring for their sheep.

Swine is the Bible name for pigs and hogs. They were declared "unclean" animals; Hebrews could not eat them. The Hebrews did not raise pigs, but Gentiles in Israel and surrounding areas did.

Unicorns were probably wild oxen or antelopes.

Weasels (*WEE-sulz*) in the Bible are like today's weasel—small animal somewhat larger than a mouse. It eats other animals. Israelites were forbidden to eat weasels in Leviticus 11:29.

Whales mentioned in the Bible are not necessarily the same species as we know today. They could be any of several large, warm-blooded, air-breathing sea mammals. The "great fish" of the story of Jonah might have been some other large marine animal or dolphin.

Wolves are well known in Israel, although most of the biblical references to wolves are in word pictures comparing them to people. For example, Jesus said false prophets and false teachers were like "ravenous wolves" (Matt. 7:15).

Vipers were poisonous snakes.

ANNA *(ANN-uh)*

was an eighty-four-year-old prophetess in the temple when Jesus was brought to be dedicated. She recognized Him as the Messiah (Luke 2:36-38).

ANNAS *(ANN-us)*

was the high priest in Jerusalem from A.D. 6 to A.D. 15, during the time when John the Baptist began to preach in the wilderness. Annas was the father-in-law of Caiaphas, who was high priest when Jesus was crucified. Annas still had great influence even after the governor of

Judea forced him from his position. When Jesus was arrested, He was taken to Annas before He was sent for actual trial before Caiaphas. See Luke 3:1-3; John 18:13-24.

ANNUNCIATION

(uh-NONE-see-AY-shun)

is the word used to describe the angel Gabriel's visit to Mary, telling her that she would have a son who would be called Jesus (Luke 1:26-38).

ANOINT *(uh-NOINT)*

means to apply oil to a person or a thing. The Bible mentions anointing with oil in three ways:

1. As part of everyday life. People used scented oils as perfume or as a treatment for dry skin. A gracious host always anointed his guests. Anointing was also God. The tabernacle and its furniture were anointed. Prophets, priests, and kings were anointed as a sign that God had chosen them for special work. The word *Messiah* means "the anointed one."

3. In the Book of James, Christians are told to pray for the sick and to anoint them with oil in the name of the Lord (Jas. 5:14). The New Testament also speaks of Christians being anointed by the Holy Spirit as a sign of God's presence with them (I John 2:20). Jesus was said to be anointed by the Spirit of God (Luke 4:18).

ANTICHRIST *(AN-tih-christ)*

means an enemy of Christ or one who takes over Christ's name and tries to grab power that really belongs to Christ. Jesus warned His listeners in Matthew 24:24

Young David was anointed by Samuel to be king.

The city of Antioch (in Syria) as it looks today.

against "false Christs and false prophets" who would try to deceive Christians.

In I John 2:18, 22, and 4:3, the readers are told to expect that antichrists have and will come to deny Jesus.

ANTIOCH *(AN-tee-ock)*

was the name of sixteen cities founded by Alexander the Great in memory of his father, Antiochus. Two are mentioned in the Bible.

1. Antioch of Pisidia (*pih-SID-ee-uh*). This one was called Antioch near (or of) Pisidia, which was another city nearby. It was on an important trading route in Asia Minor (now Turkey). Paul and Barnabas preached in the synagogue in Antioch on their first journey, and many people were interested in the Gospel. Acts 13:44 says, "The next sabbath almost the whole city gathered together to hear the word of God." But some Jews became jealous of Paul's success and stirred up hatred, so Paul and Barnabas had to leave. Paul may also have stopped there on his second and third missionary journeys.

2. Antioch in Syria was the city where believers were first called Christians, according to Acts 11:19-26. It was 15 miles from the Mediterranean Sea, with the Orontes River leading to the sea. It was a business center with many caravan routes going through it. In the time of Paul, it may have had a population of 500,000.

Antioch had the first Christian church that was made up mostly of Gentiles rather than Jews. When the church at Antioch began to grow, the church at Jerusalem sent Barnabas to help the new Christians. He, in turn, sent for Paul to help him.

This church sent Paul on his missionary journeys, and between journeys he returned to the Antioch church to tell what had happened.

This city still exists today and is now called Antakiyeh, with a population of about 42,000.

APOLLOS *(uh-PAHL-us)*

was a Christian Jew who came from Alexandria, Egypt. He was well-educated, had an excellent knowledge of the Old Testament, and knew the story of Christ. However, he did not know about the Holy Spirit or about Christian baptism.

When he came to the Christians at Ephesus, he met Priscilla and Aquila, who were Paul's fellow workers there. They taught him more about the way of God.

Later Apollos went to Achaia (now Greece), where he became a leader in the church at Corinth and other churches there. When he arrived, he was a great help to the Christians by debating with the Jews in public, showing by the Scriptures that the Christ was Jesus.

Many scholars believe that Apollos was the author of the Letter to the Hebrews.
See Acts 18:24-28.

APOSTLES *(uh-PAH-suls)*

usually refers to the twelve men chosen by Jesus as His special disciples. These twelve were with him during His three years of teaching, traveling, and healing. They were with Him before His crucifixion, and they saw Him after His resurrection.

The list of the apostles included Peter, Andrew, James the son of Zebedee, John, Philip, Bartholomew, Thomas, Matthew, James the son of Alphaeus, Simon the Zealot, Thaddeus, and Judas Iscariot, who betrayed Jesus. After Judas committed suicide, Matthias replaced him.

The Romans built the Appian Way so well that parts of it are still used today.

The word *apostle* means "one chosen and sent" and is also applied to Paul and, in a more general sense, to some of the other leaders of the early church.

Although the original twelve apostles were the closest followers of Jesus, they did not really understand His mission until after the resurrection. In spite of what Jesus told them, they expected Jesus to become an earthly ruler who would conquer the current Roman rule. They were frightened and disappointed when He was crucified. They did not expect Him to rise again, but after He did and after the Holy Spirit came, the apostles became leaders and teachers of the early church. According to tradition, most of them were killed as martyrs for Christ.

APPEAL TO CAESAR (SEE-zur)

In New Testament times, the Roman government permitted the Jews mostly to rule themselves. If a Jew were accused of a crime, however, and thought he might get a fairer trial from the Romans, he could ask to be tried by the courts of Rome rather than by the Jewish courts— if he held Roman citizenship. This is what Paul did in Acts 25:11 when he said, "I appeal unto Caesar."

The Jewish courts, however, could not put anyone to death; this always had to be approved by Roman authorities.

APPIAN WAY (AP-ee-un way)

was the oldest of the Roman roads. It was begun in 312 B.C. and ran from Rome south to Naples. Parts of it are still in use today. Paul no doubt traveled to Rome on this road.

APRON

in the Bible means a cloth belt. It was usually a square yard of cloth folded into a triangle, then folded into a sash five to eight inches wide, and tied around the waist. People carried small objects or money in its folds.

AQUILA (see *Priscilla*)

ARABIA (*uh-RAY-bee-uh*)

was the area roughly the same as what is now Saudi Arabia, a large, dry peninsula between Egypt and the Persian Gulf. It is first mentioned in the Bible when the kings of Arabia brought gold and spices to Solomon. Arabians are mentioned several times in the Old Testament as paying tribute, selling cattle, or being judged by God. See I Kings 10:15; Galatians 1:17; 4:25.

ARAMAIC (*air-uh-MAY-ik*)

the language Jesus spoke, was the common language of Israel during the time of Christ. It is something like Hebrew. Some parts of Daniel and Ezra were written in Aramaic, and there are a few Aramaic expressions in the New Testament.

ARARAT (*AIR-uh-rat*)

is the name of a country in biblical times that is now a part of Turkey. It is also the name of a mountain in Turkey. Some modern explorers believe Noah's ark is still buried in the ice on this mountain. Genesis 8:4 says, "The ark came to rest on the mountains of Ararat," meaning one of the mountains in the country of Ararat.

ARCHAEOLOGY
(*ARK-ay-OLL-uh-jee*)

and geology both involve a lot of digging into the earth. Geologists dig to find out how the rocks, minerals, and land were formed. Archaeologists dig to find out how people lived thousands of years ago. They look for old pots, clay tablets, coins, and tools. They keep track of the exact location where they find them. By doing this, archaeologists can learn about the history and life of people who lived long ago.

Archaeology helps us understand the Bible. Archaeologists have also found writings by Egyptians, Assyrians, and others. These add to our information about the people living near the Hebrews and help fill in many details not given in the Bible.

The findings of archaeology also help us understand many biblical customs that seem strange to us. For example, when

Archaeologists put back together some of the pieces of this synagogue at Capernaum, where Jesus taught.

Rachel became the wife of Jacob and was leaving with him to go back to Canaan, she stole her father's household gods (small images) and hid them in her camel's saddle. The Bible does not explain why Rachel did this. But other evidence found by archaeologists shows that people in that time considered the household gods to be the real owners of the property, and whoever had the gods was therefore the owner of the family property.

Many cities mentioned in the Bible no longer exist. However, the remains of many of them have been located under small hills called *tells*. Most of the cities were quite small, with houses close together. Many cities had walls to protect the people from wandering robbers or from enemies who wanted to conquer them. Individual cities often had their own kings and their own armies and would try to take over nearby cities.

As a result of these frequent battles, cities were often conquered, destroyed, and later rebuilt on the same location. People would level off the rubble and stones left from previous buildings and build a new city on top. Archaeologists can sometimes identify as many as ten cities that were erected on one hill. By comparing the pots or tools or old coins found on one layer with those in layers above or below, or with layers found in other tells, archaeologists can estimate how many thousands of years ago that particular layer represents and how people lived at that time.

Many of these findings support information in the Bible.

Archaeology is one of the most popular studies in Israel today. Excavations (called "digs") are carefully controlled by the government and assigned only to highly skilled persons and groups. If you visit Israel, you will see many digs and partial uncoverings of old cities.

ARCHANGEL (ark-AYN-jull)

is a term applied to the angel Michael in Jude 9. It seems to mean the highest rank among the angels. First Thessalonians 4:16 says that the dead who believe in Christ will rise at the call of the archangel.

ARCHER (see *Occupations*)

ARK OF NOAH (see *Noah's Ark*)

ARK OF THE COVENANT
(KUV-un-unt)

was a wooden chest about 4 feet long, 2-1/2 feet wide, and 2-1/2 feet high. God told Moses how it should be built (Exod. 25:10-22). It was to be covered with gold inside and outside. It was to be carried on poles pushed through four golden rings on the corners. On top were two golden cherubim (winged creatures that looked both animal and human). Inside the ark were the Ten Commandments written on tablets of stone. There was also a pot of manna and Aaron's rod that budded.

The ark was placed in the Tabernacle. God promised to meet and talk with Moses where it was placed.

The people of Israel carried the ark for their forty years in the wilderness. When the priests carried it across the Jordan River into the Promised Land, the waters rolled back and all the people passed over on dry land. At the Battle of Jericho, the priests carried the ark around the outside of the city before the walls fell down (Josh. 6).

After the resurrection, Jesus ascended up into heaven.

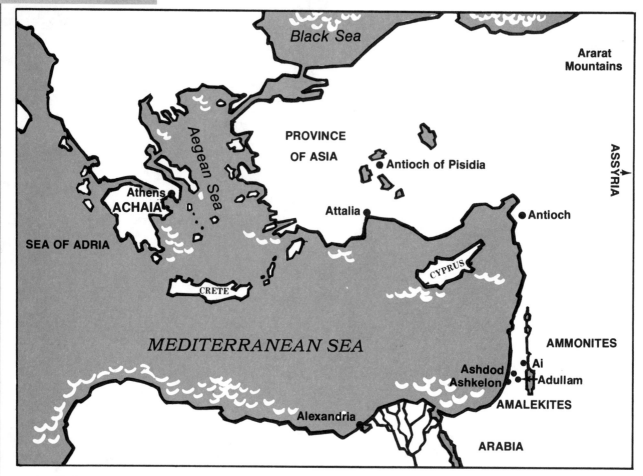

churches in several of its cities, including Ephesus. The Book of Revelation is written to churches in Asia.

ASSYRIA *(uh-SEAR-ee-uh)*

was an old and powerful empire north and east of Israel. It was an enemy of the Israelites for many years, and finally in 722 B.C. it overran the northern kingdom (Israel) and took many of its people into captivity. More than 27,000 upper-class Israelites (the wealthy and the leaders) were forced to move to Assyria, and many Assyrians were sent to live in Israel instead. This was a common wartime custom to keep a conquered country from rebelling.

The Assyrians who moved into Israel eventually married Israelites and became the Samaritans mentioned in the New Testament—a people who were looked down upon by the pure Jews who lived around them.

The most important cities of the Assyrian Empire were Nineveh, Assur, and Calah. The Assyrians worshiped idols and had temples to their gods in many cities. The king of Assyria was also his country's religious leader and commander of its huge army.

Assyria is mentioned often in the Bible as a threat or enemy in war. Many of the kings of Israel and Judah paid tribute (money, gifts) to the kings of Assyria to keep them from attacking their country. King Hezekiah gave Sennacherib, the king of Assyria, all the silver in the house of the Lord as well as all the silver he had in his own house (II Kings 18:13-16). He even stripped the gold from the doors and door posts of the temple to give to the Assyrians.

Still, Sennacherib was not satisfied and announced that he was going to capture Jerusalem. However, God did not let him do it. One night, the angel of the Lord killed 185,000 sleeping Assyrians in their camp (II Kings 19:35-37). Sennacherib was killed by one of his own sons soon after he returned home.

After that, the Assyrian Empire grew weaker and was conquered by Babylonia. It was never again a great power.

ASTROLOGERS
(as-TRAWL-uh-jers)
are those who try to tell the future from looking at the positions of stars and moon. They are said to be like magicians and wizards, who practice superstitions instead of seeking help directly from God.

They are mentioned in Daniel 2:27; 4:7; 5:7, 11; and Isaiah 47:13.

ASTRONOMY (see *Stars*)

ATHALIAH *(ATH-uh-LY-uh)*
was the only woman to reign over Judah. She was the daughter of wicked Ahab, king of Israel, and Jezebel, his Baal-worshiping wife. After her son, King Ahaziah, was killed by an arrow, she came into power. She was an evil ruler. Normally, one of Ahaziah's sons should have been the next ruler, but Athaliah ordered all of them killed.

However, one infant son, Joash, escaped

ATHENS *(ATH-enz)*
has been an important city for about 3,000 years. It is now the capital of Greece. Its ancient architecture and ruins of old buildings (the Parthenon and several ancient temples) show what a beautiful city it was hundreds of years before the time of Christ. It was the center of Greek art, science, and philosophy and was the most important university city of the ancient world. Its time of greatest glory was 459 to 431 B.C. Later it was defeated in war by the Spartans, then by the Romans, later by the Goths and the Turks.

Paul visited the city on his second missionary journey and spoke to a group of people. In the sermon, he called attention to an altar marked "To an Unknown

God" that he had seen in the city.

Although some became Christians during his visit, there is no record of Paul beginning a church in Athens.

See Acts 17:15-34.

with the help of his aunt, who was the wife of the priest. His aunt and uncle hid him for seven years in the temple. Then his uncle, the priest, arranged for the young Joash to be secretly crowned king of Judah.

At the time of the coronation, Athaliah heard crowds gathering, and she went into the temple, arriving just after Joash was crowned. "Treason! Treason!" she screamed, but the crowd wanted young Joash. At the order of the priest, she was killed as soon as she left the temple. She had reigned six years.

See II Chronicles 22—23.

ATONEMENT (uh-TONE-ment)

means making up for a wrong act. In the Bible, it usually means to become friends with God after sin has separated us from Him.

Because all of us sin, we are all separated from God. Atonement is the way to bridge that separation. In the Old Testament, the Israelites were told to bring sacrifices to atone for their sins. On the Day of Atonement (once a year), the high priest offered a bull and a goat as a sacrifice for himself, his family, and the tabernacle.

He also took a live goat and confessed over it all the sins of the people. The goat was then led into the wilderness (Lev. 16:15-22) and left there as a symbol that the sins of the people had been carried away. We now see this as a picture of Christ's carrying away the believer's sins forever.

The New Testament teaches that the death of Jesus Christ is our atonement (Rom. 5:11; Titus 2:14). Because Christ was perfect and never sinned, He could be a substitute for sinners. He could "pay the price" or "make up" for our sins. Christ did this willingly—Titus 2:14 says He "gave himself for us to redeem us from all iniquity."

The word *atonement* appears many times in the Old Testament in connection with sacrifices. In the New Testament it is used in the King James Version in Romans 5:11. The newer translations often use the word *reconciliation* instead of *atonement*.

ATONEMENT, DAY OF
(see *Day of Atonement*)

AUGUSTUS CAESAR
(uh-GUS-tus SEE-zur)

was the ruler of the Roman Empire at the time Jesus was born. He was the grand-nephew of Julius Caesar. See Luke 2:1.

AUTHOR

when used in the Bible, refers to God as the Creator or the cause or source of something. In the King James Version, Hebrews 5:9 speaks of Christ as the "author of eternal salvation unto all them that obey him." This means that Christ is the cause of eternal salvation. In Hebrews 12:2, Jesus is said to be the "author and finisher of our faith." Here it means that Christ is the founder of our faith as well as the one who completes it.

AUTHORIZED VERSION
(AWE-thor-eyezd)

also known as the King James Version, was published in England in 1611. King James I of England wanted a translation that would show the best work of the finest scholars at Oxford and Cambridge universities. He appointed fifty-four men to work on it. They were formed into committees, each responsible for translating a part of the Bible. They then turned in their work to the other committees for approval. They worked for more than two years without pay.

The men were chosen because they knew Greek and Hebrew (the languages of the first writings), but they also used parts of other translations that had been made earlier. The result was a translation so beautiful and accurate that it is still used today, even though the language is now old-fashioned and the meanings of some words have changed. It has been the most popular translation in America since the beginning of the country.

AX

was a common tool in Bible times. It was somewhat similar to axes in our day, except that the head was probably made of bronze or stone.

Axes are often mentioned in the Bible for cutting trees, for shaping things of wood, or as weapons of war. When an

Fifty-four men worked more than two years on the King James Version of the Bible.

army overran a city, the soldiers used their axes to destroy buildings and walls.

A story in the Bible shows that people in Bible times had a hard time fastening axheads securely to the handles. In the story, the head fell off the handle and into the Jordan River. Elisha, the prophet, performed a miracle when he threw a stick into the river where the axhead had sunk—-and it floated to the top.

See II Kings 6:1-7.

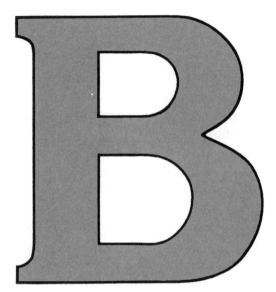

*Baal, the pagan god of the Canaanites,
was often pictured as a warrior
with thunderbolt spears.*

44

BAAL *(bale)*

was the name of many gods worshiped by
the people of Canaan. They thought the
Baal gods ruled their land, crops, and animals. Gradually *Baal* became a proper
name for the chief Canaanite god. The
Canaanites believed that each year Baal
had a battle with the sea and rivers, bringing them under his power. Baal then
made it rain on the fields for a good crop.

The Canaanites made images or idols of
Baal. He was pictured as a warrior holding
a thunderbolt spear in one hand and a
shield in the other. His helmet was decorated with bull horns.

In worship, the Canaanite priests cut
themselves with knives (I Kings 18:17-
29). Even children were sacrificed to Baal
(Jer. 19:5). And in the temples, evil sexual
practices were carried on.

The Hebrews were often tempted to
worship Baal. Many prophets warned
them against believing in false gods. Two
evil queens, Jezebel and her daughter
Athaliah, murdered some of the Hebrew

BABEL *(BAY-bul)*, TOWER OF

was a place where people began speaking different languages after God was displeased with them.

The people tried to build a tower with "its top in the heavens." Scholars think their idea was to make a ziggurat—a series of levels, one on top of the other, each smaller than the one below it. At the top of such ziggurats was usually a shrine to a god.

But God "confused their languages" so they could no longer understand one another. The people had no choice but to

The tower of Babel was probably a ziggurat like this.

stop working on the tower.

Many scholars believe the tower of Babel was in Babylon, located in what is now the country of Iraq.

See Genesis 11:1-9.

prophets and priests for not worshiping Baal (II Kings 11:1-21; II Chron. 22:2-3).

Finally, on Mount Carmel, the prophet Elijah called Baal's prophets to a test to show who the true God really was (I Kings 18:17-40). Baal lost.

BABYLON *(BAB-uh-lun)*

the capital city of Babylonia, built near the Euphrates River, was probably the largest and richest city in the ancient world. It's mentioned in Genesis 11 as the place where the tower of Babel was built.

Babylon reached its full glory when Nebuchadnezzar was king (605-562 B.C.). The people of Judah were captured and taken to live in Babylon during this time (II Kings 24:10-16). Daniel and his three friends lived in Nebuchadnezzar's courts (Dan. 1:1-16).

Babylon was attacked, destroyed, and rebuilt again and again throughout its history. Now Babylon is only a series of mounds near the Euphrates River.

In the New Testament, *Babylon* is used

as a word picture for a government that is an enemy of God (Rev. 16:19; 17:5; 18:10, 21). When *Babylon* is used in I Peter and Revelation, it probably refers to the city of Rome, the capital of the Roman Empire. Some scholars believe the word also refers to a final world empire like Rome.

BACKSLIDING *(back-SLY-ding)*

describes Israel's turning away from God to other gods or religions. See Isaiah 57:17; Jeremiah 8:5; Hosea 11:7. Today, Christians can also slip back into old

Babylon today is only a field of ruins.

habits or sins, not caring about God. See Mark 4:16, 17; Galatians 1:6, 7; I Timothy 5:15.

BANQUET *(BAN-kwit)*

is a big party or feast (much like our Thanksgiving) with lots to eat and wine to drink. The Hebrews held banquets for religious sacrifices, marriages, birthdays, funerals, and many other occasions. People wore bright-colored robes and strings of flowers. Singers, dancers, musicians, and jesters entertained the guests, who sat or lounged at long tables. The most important people sat at the head of the table. The not-so-important people sat farther down. See I Samuel 9:22-24; Esther 7:3, 5, 9.

BAKING

was done over an open fire or in a clay oven. To heat the clay ovens, grass, straw, dung, or thorns were set on fire inside the oven or under it. Then bread dough or other foods were laid inside the oven until cooked.

See Isaiah 44:15, 19; Ezekiel 4:12.

BALAAM *(BAY-lum)*

was a Midianite prophet in the land of Moab (now called Jordan). When the Israelites camped near Moab, King Balak offered Balaam a reward if he would curse the Israelites (Num. 22—24).

On the way to King Balak's city, an angel of the Lord blocked Balaam's path. This caused his frightened donkey to speak out loud. Balaam was warned to speak nothing but the Lord's words.

To King Balak's surprise, Balaam didn't curse Israel, but blessed it three times. Balaam went home to Peor and helped cause the Israelites to sin. When Israel went to war against Moab and Midian, Balaam was killed (Num. 31:8, 16).

In the New Testament, Balaam is an example of a false teacher who leads Christians away from truth (II Pet. 2:15).

BAPTISM *(BAP-tiz-um)*

In Moses' day, baptism simply meant washing (Exod. 30:17-21). But when John the Baptist called the crowds to be baptized, he was asking them to be washed inside and outside (Matt. 3:1-6). The outside washing showed that the person wanted to be changed on the inside. Baptism meant he was asking God to forgive his sins.

Jesus was baptized in the Jordan River by John (Matt. 3:13-17; John 7:29-34). He had not done anything wrong, but He wanted to show that His work of preaching, teaching, healing, and saving had begun.

Today baptism is a way to show that we are followers of Jesus. Being baptized is a picture of Jesus dying, being buried, and rising again to life. Paul says the sinful part of us has died and been buried with Jesus. Christians begin a new life by expressing faith in Christ.

See Romans 6:3-5; Galatians 3:26-29; Titus 3:5; I Peter 3:21, 22.

BARABBAS *(buh-RAB-us)*

was a robber who was in prison for murder and rioting when Jesus was arrested. At the Jewish feast of Passover, the Roman governor Pilate usually set one prisoner free. Pilate asked the people if they would rather have Jesus or Barabbas. Priests standing in the crowd began screaming, "Barabbas! Barabbas!" Pilate asked the crowd what he should do with Jesus, who had done nothing wrong. The crowd yelled, "Crucify Him!" So Barabbas, the criminal, was set free. See Matthew 27:15-26; Mark 15:6-15; Luke 23:18-25; John 18:39, 40.

BARAK *(BEAR-uk)*

was a military leader of the Israelites. When Deborah was judge of Israel, the people were being oppressed by the Canaanites, who robbed their farms. Deborah told Barak that God wanted him to bring together an army of 10,000 men to fight the Canaanites. Barak said he would do it only if Deborah went along into battle with him. She agreed to go.

Although the Canaanites had 900 war chariots and the Israelites had none, the Canaanites were defeated. Their commander, Sisera, ran from the battle, and Barak followed him. Sisera hid in the tent of a woman named Jael, but while he slept, she killed him. When Barak reached the tent, Sisera was already dead. See Judges 4.

After the great victory, Deborah and Barak sang a song of victory that is recorded in Judges 5. Barak is mentioned among the people of faith in Hebrews 11:32.

BARLEY (see *Plants*)

BARNABAS *(BAR-nuh-bus)*

was the nickname of a follower of Jesus. His real name was Joseph, but the apostles called him Barnabas, which means "son of encouragement." He was always helping people as a preacher, teacher, and missionary. When the new Christians at Jerusalem needed food, Barnabas sold a field and gave the money to the apostles (Acts 4:36, 37).

Barnabas and Paul were good friends. It was Barnabas who spoke up for Paul when the apostles still feared him (Acts 9:27). He and Paul together taught the Christians in the church at Antioch. When a famine struck Jerusalem, the new Christians at Antioch sent money with Paul and Barnabas to help the Christians who were without food in Jerusalem (Acts 11:22-30).

Jesus showed how important baptism is by being baptized Himself.

Soon after coming back to Antioch, Paul and Barnabas went on a missionary trip (Acts 13:2—14:28). Barnabas's young cousin, John Mark, went with them. At Iconium, some people tried to kill them. At Lystra, the townspeople tried to worship them as gods when they healed a crippled man (Acts 14:14).

Paul and Barnabas disagreed when planning their second missionary trip. Barnabas wanted to take John Mark along again. Paul didn't, because John Mark had not finished the first trip. He had gone home. Finally, Paul and Barnabas chose separate trips. Barnabas took John Mark and sailed to Cyprus (Barnabas's old home). Paul chose another companion (Acts 15:22-41), Silas, and went to Asia Minor (now called Turkey).

Some scholars think Barnabas wrote Hebrews, though no one knows for sure.

BARRENNESS (BEAR-un-ness)

means that a husband and wife cannot have any children. In Bible times, most men and women were very sad and ashamed when this happened. They thought God was punishing them.

Rachel, for example, didn't have any children, and her sister had many. Rachel was so jealous she cried, "Give me children or I shall die!" (See Gen. 30:1). This was how many barren women felt. If the Lord healed barrenness, there was much rejoicing. See I Samuel 1:5; Psalm 113:9; Luke 1:25.

BARTHOLOMEW
(bar-THOL-uh-mew)

was one of the twelve apostles, but nothing else is written in the Bible about him. We do not know what work he did or what kind of person he was. Some people think Bartholomew and Nathanael are the same person, but the Bible does not say for sure. See Matthew 10:3; Mark 3:18; Luke 6:14; John 1:45, 46; Acts 1:13.

BARTIMAEUS (bar-tuh-MAY-us)

was a blind man who sat along the road outside of Jericho begging for money. When Jesus and His disciples walked by, Bartimaeus called Jesus' name (Mark 10:46-52).

When Jesus asked what He wanted, Bartimaeus said, "My sight."

Jesus answered, "Go. Your faith has healed you." Immediately, Bartimaeus could see, so he joined the crowd and followed Jesus.

BARUCH (BEAR-uk)

came from a noble family in Jerusalem (Jer. 32:12, 16). He could have been a powerful friend of the king. Instead he chose to be the friend and assistant of the prophet Jeremiah. He wrote down Jeremiah's words and read them to the people.

Together, Baruch and Jeremiah faced lots of trouble. Once King Jehoiakim threw Jeremiah's writings in the fire. He ordered Baruch and Jeremiah arrested, but they escaped. Baruch rewrote the burned prophecy and added more of Jeremiah's words (Jer. 36:27-32). They were thrown into prison, accused of being traitors. Both Jeremiah and Baruch went to Egypt (Jer. 43:6, 7) when Jerusalem was taken over (586 B.C.). They probably died there.

BASKETS (BASS-kets)

in the Old Testament were made from reeds, twigs, or ropes. They were used for carrying fruit, bread, or clay. They were

*Barnabas traveled by ship several times
while preaching the Gospel.*

carried by hand, on the head or shoulders, or attached to a pole, depending on their size. See Genesis 40:17: Exodus 29:2, 3; Deuteronomy 26:2.

In the New Testament, two kinds of baskets are mentioned. One was like a small backpack. The other was a large, sturdy basket that could hold a person.

See Matthew 16:9, 10, John 6:13; Acts 9:25.

BAT (see *Animals*)

BATHSHEBA *(bath-SHE-buh)*

was a beautiful woman. She and her husband, Uriah the Hittite, lived near King David's palace. Uriah was a soldier in David's army.

One spring day, when all of his army was off fighting, King David wandered up on his palace roof. From there he saw Bathsheba bathing. Sending for her, he committed adultery with her. Bathsheba later told David she was pregnant.

David sent for Uriah and gave him a vacation. David hoped he would go home and have sexual relations with his wife, so he would think the child was his. When Uriah didn't go home, David gave orders that in the next battle Uriah was to fight where the danger was greatest. Uriah was killed. See II Sam. 11.

After Uriah's death, David made Bathsheba one of his wives. Her first child died, but they had four more sons (I Chron. 3:5), one of whom was Solomon.

When David grew old, another of his sons, Adonijah, decided to claim kingship (I Kings 1). Bathsheba and the prophet Nathan defeated Adonijah's plot, reminding David of his promise to make Solomon the next king.

Solomon was one of Jesus' ancestors (Matt. 1:6).

Jesus cured the blind beggar, Bartimaeus, of his blindness.

BEARDS

were a sign of manhood to the Jews. The Egyptians shaved their faces and their heads, but if a Jew was shaved, it was considered shameful. The Israelites were forbidden to shave the "corners of their beards." Some people think the "corners" were sideburns.

A man plucked out his beard to show great sorrow. During times of extreme trouble, the Jews let their beards get uneven and ratty.

Like a handshake today, a beard was used in greeting. One man grasped another man's beard to pull him gently forward for a kiss or hug.

See Leviticus 17:27;21:5; II Samuel 19:24; 20:9; Jeremiah 48:37.

BEATITUDES *(bee-AT-uh-toods)*

are short sayings beginning with the word *blessed* or *happy* that describe actions or thoughts that will give a person joy and peace. In the Old Testament, beatitudes were written by psalmists and prophets. Psalm 1:1-3 gives a beatitude: "Blessed is the man who walks not in the counsel of the wicked . . .but his delight is in the law of the Lord. . . . In all that he does, he prospers." The Old Testament beatitudes often promise blessings of health, peace, prosperity, a family. But most of all they promise that God will be near to a righteous person. See Psalm 41:1; 65:4; 84:5; 106:3; Proverbs 8:32, 34; Isaiah 32:20.

The beatitudes in the New Testament have one big difference from those in the Old Testament. They stress the joy of belonging to God's Kingdom. In the Sermon on the Mount Jesus says the poor in spirit, those who weep, and those who are persecuted are blessed because they belong to God and enjoy being close to

At Abraham's well in Beersheba, you can still see the grooves worn into the rock by ropes lowering and raising water buckets for many centuries of time.

Him. See Matthew 5:1-11; Luke 6: 20-22.

BEAUTIFUL GATE

was probably the eastern gate to the temple in Jerusalem. It was beautifully crafted of Corinthian bronze, and it opened into the temple's Court of Women. Peter and John healed a paralyzed man outside the Beautiful Gate (Acts 3:2-10).

BED

was sometimes nothing more than the ground, for those who were very poor. They would use their thin coats as blankets. Most people used a mat or rug in the house. But the rich had beds made of ivory, iron, gold, or silver. See Deuteronomy 3:11; Esther 1:6; Amos 6:4.

BEERSHEBA *(beer-SHE-buh)*

is the town farthest south in Judah. The phrase *from Dan to Beersheba* meant the entire country of Israel and Judah from north to south.

The history of Beersheba's name, "well of the oath," is told in Genesis 21:22-34. Jacob had a vision at Beersheba as he traveled to Egypt to join his son Joseph.

See Genesis 46:1, 2; II Samuel 3:10.

BELSHAZZAR *(bell-SHAZ-ur)*

was the last king of Babylon. He was a descendant of King Nebuchadnezzar.

Belshazzar did not worship God. At one

of his feasts in 539 B.C., he praised the idols of gold, silver, bronze, and iron because he was drinking from cups made of those materials. The cups had been stolen from the Jerusalem temple.

As Belshazzar drank with his thousand guests, a hand appeared on the wall and wrote strange words. Belshazzar was afraid and cried for his wise men to explain the writing. No one could.

Finally, Daniel was called. His explanation is found in Daniel 5:24-28.

That very night, the writing came true. Belshazzar was killed, and his kingdom was taken over by the Medes and Persians. See Daniel 5.

BENJAMIN (see box below)

BETHANY (BETH-uh-nee)

was a village two miles southeast of Jerusalem, near the Mount of Olives.

Jesus' friends Simon the leper, Martha, Mary, and Lazarus (whom Jesus raised from the dead) lived in Bethany (Matt. 26:6-13; John 11:1-44). Jesus rose into heaven near Bethany. A town is still there today (Luke 24:50, 51).

BETHEL (BETH-ul)

was a town twelve miles north of Jerusalem. When Jacob was traveling to find a wife, he camped for the night near a Canaanite town called Luz. He slept on the ground with his head on a rock.

There, Jacob had an amazing dream (Gen. 28:10-19). When he awoke, he called the place Bethel, which means "house of God," because he had met with God. He later built an altar there.

After the Israelites entered Canaan, the ark of the covenant was kept at Bethel (Judg. 20:26-28).

When the country split into the north-

BENJAMIN (BEN-juh-min)

was the youngest son of Jacob. His mother, Rachel, died when he was born. Her last word was "Benoni" ("son of my sorrow") which became his name. Later Jacob changed his name to Benjamin, meaning "son of the right hand." Jacob loved him as dearly as he had loved Rachel (Gen. 35:16-21).

When the entire family came to live in Egypt with Joseph, the sons of Jacob and their families became the twelve tribes of Israel (Gen. 42: 1—45: 15).

In Canaan, the tribe of Benjamin was given land twenty-six miles long by twelve miles wide. The tribe of Judah was to the south, and the tribe of

When Benjamin was brought to see his older brother Joseph in Egypt, it was a happy reunion.

Ephraim to the north. When the country split, the tribe of Benjamin joined the southern kingdom of Judah.

King Saul (I Sam. 9:1) and the apostle Paul (Phil. 3:5) were both from the tribe of Benjamin.

ern and southern kingdoms, wicked King Jeroboam chose Bethel as a place to set up his golden calves (I Kings 12:26-30). The wickedness in Bethel caused the prophet Hosea to call it Bethaven, which means "house of idols." King Josiah finally destroyed the idols (II Kings 23:15-23).

BETHESDA (see *Pool of Bethesda*)

BETHLEHEM *(BETH-luh-hem)*

is best known as the place of Jesus' birth. The Old Testament prophet Micah predicted the Messiah would be born in Bethlehem (Mic. 5:2). The angels announced Jesus' birth to the shepherds outside the town (Luke 2:8-15). All male babies two years old or younger around Bethlehem were sentenced to death by jealous King Herod, who wanted to kill the new king of the Jews (Matt. 2:16-18).

Bethlehem is called the "city of David" in Luke 2:11 because David grew up there. His father Jesse, his grandfather Obed, and his great-grandparents Boaz and Ruth all lived in Bethlehem.

BETHSAIDA *(beth-SAY-uh-duh)*

was a fishing village on the northwestern shores of Lake Galilee. Andrew, Peter, and Philip were from Bethsaida. Jesus healed a blind man there, but He also scolded the people of Bethsaida for their unbelief. See Matthew 11:20-24; John 1:44; 12:21.

BIRDS

Of the 360 to 400 kinds of birds that live in Israel, twenty-six kinds can be found only in Israel and nowhere else. The Bible mentions about fifty kinds of birds altogether.

Chickens are like our barnyard chickens. The male, called a cock or rooster, crows at dawn. This signal reminded Peter of Jesus' words that he would deny he knew his Lord. Jesus said He wanted to care for the people of Jerusalem as a hen gathers her chicks under her wings. See Matthew 23:37; 26:74.

Cocks are the male of any bird. At the time of Jesus' trial, He said Peter would deny Him three times before the cock crowed. The term "cock crow" in Mark 13:35 refers to the hours between midnight and 3:00 A.M.

Doves look like the pigeons we see today in parks and city streets. Noah sent out a dove to find dry land. A dove's soft cooing often sounds like crying. Jesus told His disciples to be harmless as doves. The Spirit of God descended on Jesus like a dove. Doves were sold in the temple for purification rituals. See Genesis 8:8-12; Matthew 3:16; 10:16; 21:12.

Eagles were called unclean by God. They were unfit for the Jews to eat. The eagle is large and hawklike with powerful wings and a wingspread of four feet. Many word pictures about eagles appear in the Bible. The Lord renews a person's spiritual strength, so they mount up with wings like eagles. An eagle is swift in flight, like death and life. Riches are said to be like eagles, which swiftly disappear or fly away. See Leviticus 11:13; II Samuel 1:23; Job 9:26; Proverbs 23:4, 5; Isaiah 40:31.

Falcons are hawks, with long, pointed wings and tail. They could not be eaten, as commanded in Leviticus 11:16.

Fowl is a name for all flying birds and bats. Many fowls were used as sacrifices. In God's eyes, people are worth more than many fowls. See Genesis 1:20; Leviticus 1:14; 11:13-19; Luke 12: 24.

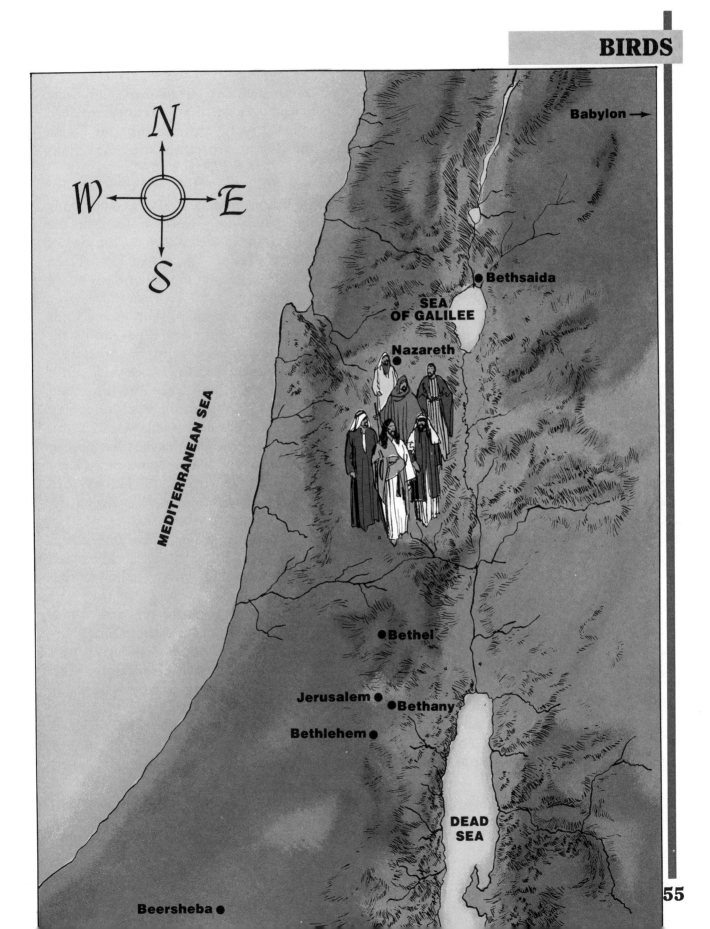

Babylon →

● Bethsaida

SEA
OF GALILEE

Nazareth

MEDITERRANEAN SEA

● Bethel

Jerusalem ●   ● Bethany

Bethlehem ●

DEAD
SEA

Beersheba ●

Kite is probably a different name for the vulture or falcon. A kite is called unclean in Leviticus 11:13-19.

Night Hawks are small-beaked and eat winged insects; they are called unclean in Leviticus 11:16.

Ospreys (*AH-sprees*) are fish-eating hawks that have rough pads on their feet to hold slippery fish. Ospreys are said to be unclean.

Ostriches (*AH-strich-es*) are the largest living birds. Job 39:13-18 describes ostriches. They can run as fast as 40 miles per hour. Lamentations 4:3 says they are cruel.

Ossifrage (see *Vulture*)

Owls—little owl and great owl—were unfit to eat. They hunt at night for rats and other animals. They reminded the Israelites of ruined cities. The great owl is similar to the American great horned owl, about 22 inches long. See Leviticus 11:17; Deuteronomy 14:16; Isaiah 34:15.

Partridges are good for eating. David said he felt like a hunted partridge when Saul was after him. Partridges supposedly steal other birds' eggs and hatch them—a good example of getting rich dishonestly. See I Samuel 26:20; Jeremiah 17:11.

Peacocks are beautiful birds that strutted about Solomon's courts.

Pelicans have webs between their toes for swimming while catching fish. Leviticus 11:18 calls them unclean.

Pigeons were common rock doves. They were used by the poor for sacrifices since they were so numerous. See Genesis 15:9; Luke 2:24.

Quail are good for eating. They live on the ground and scratch for food. In Bible lands, quail migrate in huge flocks, flying only a few feet off the ground. See Exodus 16:13; Numbers 11:31.

Ravens look like large crows. They were unclean because they sometimes eat dead bodies. But ravens also brought Elijah food during a drought. See Leviticus 11:15; I Kings 17:4; Job 38:41.

Sea gulls are web-footed birds who eat fish, worms, insects, bird eggs, and young birds. Their noisy calls are heard on the Mediterranean coasts and on the Sea of Galilee. (Deut. 14:15 and Lev. 11:16 include sea gulls in the list of birds not to be eaten.)

Sparrows are small, seed-eating birds like American sparrows. They busily flit about and chirp constantly. Sparrows were so cheap that when four were sold, a fifth sparrow was added free. But Jesus said that God knows about each one. See Psalm 84:3; Matthew 10:29. 31.

Storks feed in the marshes but nest in the trees (as Ps. 104:17 points out). They have powerful wings, and they migrate each year. See Jeremiah 8:7; Zechariah 5:9.

Swallows are quick fliers and have a piercing call. In Isaiah 38:14, Hezekiah said he was as uneasy as a swallow during his illness.

Turtledoves are wild pigeons, which often sing early in the spring. Since turtledoves were cheap and plentiful, the poor used them for sacrifices. See Genesis 15:9; Song of Solomon 2:12; Luke 2: 24.

Vultures are birds that feed on dead animals and even dead people. Vultures fly high and far. The ossifrage is called "the bearded vulture." Leviticus 11:13 calls them unclean or unfit to eat. See Job 28:7; Isaiah 34:15.

Water hens could have been horned owls. Leviticus 11:17 calls them unclean, so they probably ate flesh.

VULTURE

RAVEN

PEACOCK

TURTLEDOVE

QUAIL

PARTRIDGE

BIRTHRIGHT *(BURTH-rite)*

was the blessing and double share of wealth a father gave to his oldest son. Esau carelessly sold his birthright for a bowl of soup. See Genesis 25:29-34; Hebrews 12:16.

BLASPHEMY *(BLAS-fuh-me)*

means speaking against God, using careless, dirty, or wicked words. Exodus 20:7 says blasphemy is a sin. The Jews punished blasphemers by stoning them to death. Jesus and Stephen were falsely accused of blasphemy (Matt. 9:3; 26:65, 66; Acts 6:11).

When people said Jesus' miracles were done by Satan's power, they blasphemed against the Holy Spirit (Mark 3:28-30).

BLESSING

in the Old Testament meant a gift of something good, given by God. A blessing was usually something material, such as more cattle, sheep, children, or wealth.

See Proverbs 3:16.

A father often announced a blessing for his sons. An example of this is Isaac's blessing to Jacob (Gen. 27:28-29), "May God give you . . . the fatness of the earth, and plenty of grain and wine."

In the New Testament, Jesus brought a different blessing from God to people. He brought them forgiveness, freedom, and salvation (Eph. 1:3).

BLINDNESS (see box on pg. 58)

BLOOD

in the Bible is considered to be the basis of life, both in people and in animals. Therefore God commanded the Israelites (Lev. 17:10-14): "No person among you shall eat blood." Meat was to be drained of its blood before it could be cooked or eaten.

Blood represented life, according to Leviticus 17:11, and therefore it was needed for forgiveness (Heb. 9:18-28).

57

BLINDNESS

means not being able to see. A person may be born blind (John 9:1). Diseases like smallpox can cause blindness. Old age sometimes brings partial or complete blindness (Gen. 27:1; I Kings 14:4).

The Philistines, Assyrians, Babylonians, and other evil people often blinded the captives they took in war. Samson lost his eyesight this way (Judg. 16:20-22).

Since a blind person had to beg for money to live, the Law instructed the Jews to lovingly care for the blind (Lev. 19:14; Deut. 27:18).

A special sign of the Messiah was that He would "open the eyes of the blind." See Isaiah 29:18. Jesus healed many blind people.

When Jesus healed one blind man, He sent him first to wash his eyes in the pool of Siloam.

The Israelites offered animal sacrifices to God as He commanded. But when Jesus Christ died, He became the final sacrifice for our sins. Jesus said, "This is my blood of the covenant, which is poured out . . . for the forgiveness of sins."

The phrases *blood of Jesus*, *blood of Christ*, and *blood of the Lamb* all refer to Christ giving His life so that our sins can be forgiven and we can be saved. See Matthew 26:28; I Corinthians 10:16; Ephesians 2:13; I Peter 1:2, 19; I John 1:7.

BODY OF CHRIST

has three meanings in the New Testament:

1. It means Christ's human body. He became a man with flesh and blood like other people. His physical body actually died. This was part of His offering of Himself for us. Hebrews 10:10 says, "We have been sanctified through the offering of the body of Jesus Christ once for all." People who said Jesus didn't have a human body were called antichrists in I John 4:2, 3.

2. Another meaning is found in Jesus' words at the Last Supper. He took bread, broke it in pieces, blessed it, and gave it to His disciples. He said, "Take, eat; this is my body." This is a word picture of Jesus' death on the cross. His body was "broken" on the cross to bring forgiveness and salvation. See Matthew 26: 26; Mark 14:22; Luke 22:19; I Corinthians 11:24.

3. The Body of Christ also refers to the total church. All true believers through all time are members of Jesus Christ. The church is called "His Body," and Jesus Christ is called "the head." This shows how much Christians and Christ are a part of each other. See Ephesians 1:22, 23; 4:15, 16; Colossians 1:18.

BORROWING and **LOANING** were much the same in Bible times as they are now. In the Old Testament, the Hebrews could lend money to foreigners with interest—an extra amount of money the borrower paid to be able to use the money. But they could not charge each other interest. Though there were many guidelines for lending and borrowing, the people who owed money were often treated badly (Deut. 15:1-6; 23:19, 20; 24:10-13).

In the New Testament, the Jews lived under the Roman system of banking, which included tax collectors, bankers, and the money lenders who charged interest. Jesus said to show mercy to people who owed money (Matt. 18:23-35; Luke 6:34-36). He even said His followers should lend without expecting interest. Another Bible word for interest is *usury*.

BRAMBLE (see *Plants*)

BRANCH

is a name the prophets Jeremiah and Zechariah gave to the coming Messiah, because He would be part of David's family tree. The Messiah would be a king, peace-bringer, and Savior. See Jeremiah 23:5, 6; 33:15; Zechariah 3:8; 6:12.

BREAD

in Bible times was made from wheat flour that was leavened (raised by yeast). Then the dough was shaped into loaves and baked.

The night of the Passover, the Israelites ate unleavened bread because of their hurry to leave Egypt. Unleavened bread has no yeast, doesn't have to rise, and comes out hard and flat. Many churches today use it in Communion.

Poor people made their bread from barley. The boy with five barley loaves in John 6:9 was probably from a poor family. Times of famine caused everyone to eat barley bread. Ezekiel 4:9-17 describes

For a while God gave His people miracle food called manna, to gather each morning,

Jesus once stopped a funeral procession—so He could raise the dead man back to life!

baking in famine times.

Jesus called Himself "the Bread of Life" (John 6:35-59). Bread symbolizes the food all people need to live. Just as people need food to live a healthy physical life, so Jesus said He was the source of spiritual life. See Genesis 3:19; Exodus 12; Matthew 6:11.

BROTHERS OF OUR LORD

Matthew 1:25 says that Jesus was born when Mary was a virgin. Since God, not Joseph, was Jesus' father, the other sons born later to Mary and Joseph were Jesus' half brothers. Mark 6:3 gives their names: James, Joses, Juda, and Simon.

During the first part of Jesus' ministry, His brothers didn't believe in Him (John 7:1-10), but later some of them did. James became a leader of the first church in Jerusalem (Acts 15: 13; 21: 18). Most likely, the letters of James and Jude in the New Testament were written by two brothers of Jesus. Nothing is known about Joses and Simon.

BROTHERS or BRETHREN

can describe several different relation-ships. The most common meaning of *brother* is the relationship of a son to other sons or daughters of the same parents (Gen. 27:6; 28:2; Judg. 8:19). *Brother* can also mean a man from the same country (Exod. 2:11), a member of the same tribe (II Sam. 19:12), an ally (Amos 1: 9), or any member of the human race (Matt. 7:3-5).

In the New Testament, the Christians called each other "brother" because they were all in God's family and they deeply loved one another (Matt. 23:8; Rom. 1:13). Christians are even called brothers of Jesus (Heb. 2:10-13).

BUCKLER (see *Weapons*)

BULRUSH (see *Plants*)

BURIAL *(BEAR-ee-ul)*

is placing a dead body in a grave or tomb. The Israelites usually buried their dead in caves, for two reasons: first, Israel has a lot of caves; and second, the ground there is mostly rock with only a small layer of soil, so digging is difficult.

Long before the Israelites took over the land of Canaan, Sarah (Gen. 23), Jacob (Gen. 49:29-32), Joseph (Josh. 24:32-33), and others were buried in a cave at Hebron.

In Jesus' day, the dead bodies were wrapped in clean linen with fragrant spices and ointments. When a death occurred, friends (usually women) hurried to the house and cried loudly. Mourners were often hired to add to the noise (Jer. 9:17; Mark 5:38). See also Matthew 27:57-61; Luke 23:53-56.

C

Calvary was the hill where Jesus was killed.

CAESAR *(SEE-zur)*

was at first the family name of Julius Caesar. Later the name *Caesar* was added to the name of each of the Roman emperors, so it became a title like *emperor* or *king.* Instead of "Emperor Tiberius," he was called "Tiberius Caesar." "Caesar Augustus" meant the same as Emperor Augustus.

CAESAREA *(SES-uh-REE-uh)*

was a city on the Mediterranean Sea named in honor of Caesar Augustus. It was about sixty-five miles northwest of Jerusalem. During the time of Christ and the early church, it was the official capital of Israel. It had beautiful palaces, an open-air stadium, a large arena, and a temple dedicated to Caesar.

Caesarea was the military headquarters for the Roman army in the area. The first time Peter preached to Gentiles was in Caesarea in the house of Cornelius, a Roman soldier (Acts 10).

Caesarea was also the home of Philip the evangelist and his four daughters who prophesied (Acts 21:8, 9). Paul stayed in Philip's home on his third missionary journey.

After Paul was arrested in Jerusalem, he spent two years in Caesarea as a prisoner. While a prisoner, Paul preached to three Roman officials: Felix, Festus, and King Agrippa (Acts 23:23—26:32).

CAESAREA PHILIPPI
(SES-uh-REE-uh FILL-uh-pie)

was an ancient town in northern Israel. There Herod the Great built a temple in honor of Augustus Caesar. Herod's son, Philip, enlarged the town and named it Caesarea Philippi so it would not be confused with another Caesarea, the larger city on the coast. See Matt. 16:13-28; Mark 8:27-37.

CAIAPHAS (KAY-uh-fuss)

was high priest from about A.D. 18 to 36, during the life and death of Christ and the beginning of the early church. He was the son-in-law of Annas and seemed to work closely with him.

After Jesus raised Lazarus from the dead, Caiaphas and others were eager to kill Jesus (John 11:45-53). They said He was "stirring up the people." Caiaphas was involved in the trial of Jesus (John 18:13-28). He is also mentioned in the arrest of Peter and John (Acts 4:5-22).

CAIN

was the first son of Adam and Eve—the first person born by a natural birth. He was a farmer who brought an offering of vegetables to God. His brother Abel brought a lamb. God was not pleased with Cain's offering. The Bible does not explain why, but I John 3:12 does say that Cain "was of the evil one."

Cain was so jealous of his brother that he killed him. He was punished by having to leave his parents and become a wanderer, always in fear of being killed. God promised him protection from being killed by his enemies.

Cain went to a country east of Eden where he married and had a son, Enoch.

See Genesis 4:1-17.

CALEB (see page 64)

CALENDARS (CAL-un-ders)

have been based since Bible times on the appearance and disappearance of the moon in cycles of 29-30 days. The first day of a new month on the Jewish calendar began when the thin sliver of the new moon could be seen at sunset. The Jews had two separate calendars—the sacred calendar that began in the spring, and the government calendar that began in the fall. Usually, the months were spoken of by number ("the third day of the second month") but sometimes by name. The names changed over the years. In Exodus 13:4, the first month is called Abib; in Esther 3:7, the first month is called Nisan. The same is true of other months. We do not know the early names of all the months. See chart on page 65.

The months of the Jewish calendar didn't begin on the same days that ours do today.

Cain grew angry when God accepted Abel's offering of a lamb and did not accept his offering of fruits and vegetables.

Caleb and the others brought back huge clusters of grapes from Canaan.

CALEB *(KAY-lub)*

was one of the twelve men sent by Moses to spy out the land of Canaan (Num. 13:1—14:38). The spies spent 40 days in Canaan, observing the land, cities, crops, and people. When they returned, they told the people it was a rich land, but it had walled cities and people who were big like giants. The Israelites were afraid and feared defeat. Caleb and another spy named Joshua reassured the people that God would be with them and help them take the land. Despite their efforts, the people of Israel wept and wanted to go back to Egypt. The Lord grew angry and said that none of the adults except Caleb and Joshua would ever enter Canaan. All would die in the wilderness.

Forty years later, their children did enter Canaan, led by Joshua, who replaced Moses. Caleb was the only other man of the original group still alive. He asked to settle near Hebron where the giantlike people lived who had frightened the other spies! Even though Caleb was old, he directed the battle against these people and drove them out (Josh. 14:6-15; 15:13, 14).

CALVARY *(KAL-vuh-ree)*

is where Jesus was crucified. The name comes from a Latin word meaning "skull." It may have been called that because it was a place where criminals were executed and skulls were found there, or because the hill itself looked like a skull.

We don't know the exact location of Calvary. Two places have been suggested. One is where the Church of the Holy Sepulchre now stands in Jerusalem; the other is a hill known as "Gordon's Calvary." On Gordon's Calvary there are holes in the rocky side of the hill that resemble the eyes and nose of a skull.

The Bible says nothing about location except that it was near Jerusalem and that it was near a garden with a new tomb.

See Matthew 27:33; Luke 23: 33; John 19:41.

CAMP

refers to a group of tents set up for temporary living.

The Israelites camped for forty years in the wilderness (Num. 2—3). They moved from one site to another, waiting for the time they could enter the promised land. God gave exact instructions about how their camp was to be set up—the tabernacle in the center, the tents of the priests and the Levites around the sides, and further back those of the twelve tribes—each assigned a certain position.

After the Israelites entered Canaan, armies camped when they were at war (I Sam. 25:13). During battles, often some warriors remained behind to guard the camp.

CANA *(KAY-nuh)*

was a village in Galilee mentioned four times in the Gospel of John. We don't know its exact location, but it was probably west of the lake of Galilee.

Jesus performed His first miracle in this town—turning the water at a wedding into wine (John 2:1-11). It is also the place where Jesus met the nobleman whose son was dying, and Jesus told him his son would live (John 4:46-54).

CANAAN *(KAY-nun)*

was the name of a man and the name of a place.

1. Canaan was the grandson of Noah and the son of Ham. He was the ancestor of the people who later lived in the land of Canaan, which was named after him.

2. Canaan was one of the old names for Palestine (now Israel). The people who

Jewish Calendar

Month Sacred	Month Gov't.	Early Name	Later Name	Mentioned in Bible	Our Calendar	Festivals
1	7	Abib	Nisan	Exodus 12:2; Esther 3:7	March-April	Passover Unleavened Bread First Fruits
2	8	Ziv	Iyyar	I Kings 6:1, 37	April-May	Later Passover
3	9		Sivan	Esther 8:9	May-June	Pentecost Feast of Weeks
4	10		Tammuz		June-July	
5	11		Ab		July-August	
6	12		Elul	Nehemiah 6:15	August-September	
7	1	Ethanim	Tishri	I Kings 8:2	September-October Day of Atonement	Trumpets
						Tabernacles Solemn Assembly
8	2	Bul	Heshvan	I Kings 6:38	October-November	
9	3		Chislev	Nehemiah 1:1	November-December	Dedication
10	4		Tebeth	Esther 2:16	December-January	
11	5		Shebat	Zechariah 1:7	January-February	
12	6		Adar	Ezra 6:15	February-March	

lived there before the Israelites conquered it were called Canaanites.

See Genesis 9:18; Exodus 6:4.

CANAANITES *(KAY-nuh-nites)*

were the people living in Canaan when the Israelites came into the land after wandering forty years in the wilderness.

They were descendants of Canaan, the son of Ham, and included tribes of the Hittites, Jebusites, Amorites, Hivites, and others. They lived in well-developed cities, each with its own king, army, and taxes. The city-kingdoms often battled each other.

The Canaanites had many gods and goddesses. Many temples to Baal, Dagon, Astarte, and Asherah have been found by archaeologists.

The Israelites had to conquer the Canaanites before they could live in peace in the promised land. But the Israelites never completely conquered them.

CANDACE *(KAN-duh-see)*

was the title of the queens of Ethiopia. One of these queens had a treasurer who became a Christian after he met Philip the evangelist (Acts 8:26-40).

CAPERNAUM *(kuh-PURR-nay-um)*

was a large town on the northwest shore

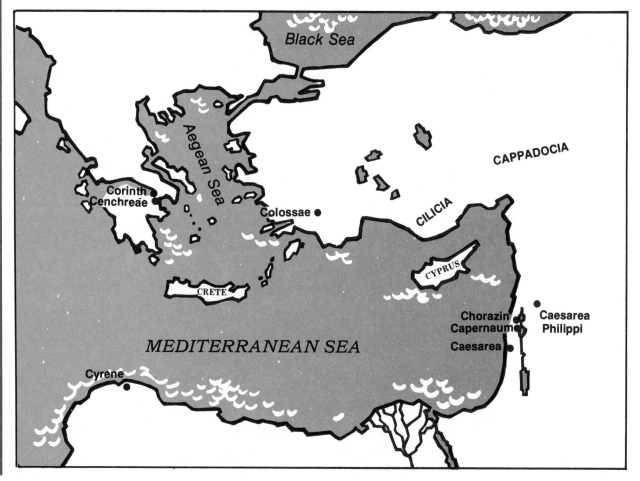

Even today in the Middle East, caravans of camels move across the deserts.

of the Sea of Galilee. Jesus made this town His headquarters during his work in Galilee. He performed many miracles at Capernaum, including the healings of a centurion's servant and a nobleman's son (Matt. 8:5-13; Luke 7:1-10; John 4:46-54). Many of His important teachings were spoken there. Because the people did not respond, Jesus predicted the city would be destroyed (Matt. 11:23-24). His prediction was so completely fulfilled that today no one is sure where the town was.

CAPTIVITY (see *Exile*)

CARAVAN (*CARE-uh-van*)

is a group of people traveling together for protection. In Bible times, travelers in the deserts or foreign lands went in groups to protect each other from robbers, wild animals, or accidents. When families moved, they went in caravans; traders also traveled in caravans.

CAVES

are openings in the earth. In Israel, where the hills are largely limestone or chalk, there are many large caves that are quite safe from cave-ins. Some are large enough to be used for homes. Lot and his two daughters lived in a cave after Sodom was destroyed (Gen. 19:30). Some of the prophets hid in caves when Jezebel was trying to kill them (I Kings 18:4).

Caves were also used for storage and as burial places.

CEDAR (see *Plants*)

CENSUS (*SEN-sus*)

is the counting of the number of people in an area. A census was taken soon after the Israelites left Egypt (Num. 1:2). Another was taken near the end of the forty years in the wilderness (Num. 26:2). David also made a census when he was king, and the Bible says that David dis-pleased God by doing it. See I Chronicles 21:1-7.

These census reports counted only men twenty years and older so that they could find out how strong (in number) the army could be.

The New Testament says Caesar Augustus once ordered a census. Because each person had to be counted in the place of his birth, Joseph and Mary had to go to Bethlehem. While they were there, Jesus was born (Luke 2:1-7).

CENTURION (see *Occupations*)

CEPHAS *(SEE-fus)*

means rock or stone. It was the name Jesus gave to the apostle Peter (see Peter). See John 1:42; I Corinthians 1:12; Galatians 1:18.

CHAFF

is the dry, worthless parts of grain the farmers of Bible times got rid of by throwing the grain into the air on a windy day. This useless stuff blew away, and the heavier kernels of grain fell back where they could be gathered.

CHARIOTS *(CHAIR-ee-uts)*

were two-wheeled carts pulled by horses. In ancient times, they were used mainly for war, but also for races and important processions by kings or other high officials. Usually two men rode in a chariot—a driver and a warrior. In some countries, a third man with a shield also rode along.

Joseph rode in Pharaoh's second chariot in Egypt (Gen. 41:43). When the people of Israel left Egypt, Pharaoh's warriors went after them with chariots and got bogged down in the Red Sea (Exod. 14:21-29).

When the Israelites were trying to conquer Canaan, the Canaanites had chariots "with iron," and the Israelites had none. However, the chariots were not so useful in hilly areas, so the Israelites won more battles there (Judg. 1:19).

Both David and Solomon added chariots to their armies.

CHARITY (see *Love*)

CHERUBIM *(CHAIR-uh-bim)*

are heavenly creatures described in Ezekiel 10 as having wings and also some human features. Each cherub had four faces: man, lion, ox, eagle. Cherubim and a flaming sword were placed east of the garden of Eden to keep Adam and Eve from coming back after they sinned.

Pictures of cherubim were embroidered on the curtains of the tabernacle (Exod. 26:1); carvings of cherubim were on the walls of the temple (I Kings 6:23-29). Cherubim made of gold were on the mercy seat of the ark of the covenant (Exod. 25:18-22).

CHIEF PRIEST (see *High Priest*)

CHRIST (see *Jesus Christ*)

CHRISTIANS *(KRIS-chuns)*

means "Christ's ones." The term was first used by non-Christians in Antioch to point out those who were following Jesus Christ's teachings. The word appears only three times in the New Testament. The believers in New Testament times usually spoke of themselves as brethren, *believers, saints, disciples,* or *the church.* See Acts 11:26; 26:28; I Peter 4:16.

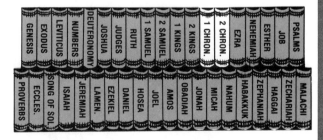

CHRONICLES, I and II
(KRON-uh-culls)

are two books in the Old Testament that tell the history of Israel. They cover some of the same things as II Samuel and I and II Kings. But the Chronicles concentrate more on the southern kingdom, Judah, than on the northern kingdom, Israel.

New Jewish believers shared what they had with others.

The books do not tell who wrote them, but many scholars think they were written by Ezra, the priest and scribe. The people of Judah had been taken into Babylonia when the southern kingdom was conquered in 586 B.C. Ezra wanted the people to know about their own history and the importance of the reign of David and Solomon. He wanted them to understand temple worship so that when Cyrus, king of Persia, allowed them to return home, they could rebuild the city of Jerusalem and begin worshiping again in the temple.

The first nine chapters of I Chronicles is almost all "begats." It tells who was the father of whom—all the way from Adam to King Saul.

I Chronicles 1—29 is about the kingdom of David and how it developed.

II Chronicles 1—9 tells about Solomon, the temple he built, and the worship there.

II Chronicles 1—36 gives the history of the southern kingdom, Judah, and points out its religious reforms and its military victories.

Chronicles was originally written as one book. It was divided into I and II Chronicles about 150 B.C. In the Jewish Bible, the Chronicles are the last books in the Old Testament.

When Jesus spoke in Luke 11:50-51 of the "blood of all the prophets . . . from Abel to Zechariah," He was speaking of the first martyr, Abel, and Zechariah, the last one in the Jewish Old Testament. His story appears in II Chronicles 24—the last book of the Jewish Bible.

CHURCH

is a group of believers in Jesus Christ. The "local church" means the believers in a certain city or area. The word *church* also refers to believers anywhere in the world, from the time of Christ to today. This is the "universal church." Every local church is part of the universal Church because it is a part of Christ.

Jesus said the church was "His church." He is the head of the church, the one who brought the church and all creation into being (Col. 1:18-20).

The church began to grow rapidly soon after the resurrection of Christ and the Day of Pentecost. New Jewish believers in Jerusalem gathered to pray, sing, and encourage each other. Later, in other cities, many non-Jews became Christians and met together to form fellowships or churches, usually meeting in the homes of Christians.

Paul knew it was important for the new churches to understand how much they were tied to other churches. This is one reason he suggested that some churches send money to the church at Jerusalem, where members were very poor. Paul (I Cor. 16:1-4) risked his life by personally carrying the gifts of money to Jerusalem.

Many of the books of the New Testament are letters written by Paul or other apostles to the young churches.

See also Ephesians 5:19-20 and I Corinthians 12—14.

CIRCUMCISION
(SIR-kum-SIH-zhun)
is an operation to cut away the foreskin, an unneeded flap of skin on the penis. It is usually done when the baby boy is only a few days old.

Among the Hebrews this was a sign of their covenant (or agreement) with God that they had a special relationship with Him. If they faithfully worshiped God and obeyed Him, He would be their God and they would be a special nation. See Genesis 17:9-14.

In the early church, some people thought that all Christians had to be circumcised to become a part of God's people (this was essential for the Jews. according to the Law of Moses). The apostle Paul argued against this idea, and the leaders of the early church agreed with Paul (Acts 15:1-35).

CISTERN *(SIS-turn)*
is a covered tank or hole dug in the earth or hollowed out of rock to collect and store water. There were many cisterns in Israel, because the summers were usually long and dry and water was scarce. The water in cisterns usually came from rainwater collected through gutters and pipes. Some cisterns were 100 feet deep.

Empty cisterns were sometimes used as prisons. Jeremiah was kept in one for a while (Jer. 38:6).

CITIZENSHIP *(SIT-uh-zen-ship)*
means belonging to a certain country and having certain rights and responsibilities. For example, Paul was a citizen of Rome and also a citizen of Tarsus, where he was born. To be a citizen of Rome was a special privilege not given to everyone who lived in lands ruled by Rome.

A Roman citizen could not be punished without a trial, he was not to be tied up or beaten, and he had the right to "appeal to Caesar"—to have his trial moved to Rome. Paul's Roman citizenship helped him in his work as a special messenger of the Gospel to Gentiles (non-Jews). See Acts 16:37-39.

CITY

Ancient cities differ from modern cities.

1. A city always had a high wall around it several feet thick and made of rocks. The wall protected the people from enemy armies and from robbers.

2. Cities had gates. Some cities had only one gate; large cities might have up to twelve. The gates were closed and barred at night.

3. The marketplace was an open area just inside the main gate. Here the people carried on business, held court, assembled for meetings, and visited one another.

4. The tower was an inner fort usually just inside the wall. People could run there for protection if the rest of the city was conquered by an enemy.

5. Streets in the city were narrow and winding, without any fixed plan.

Ancient cities were usually built to give protection to the farmers who worked in surrounding fields. The people went out to their fields in the daytime and returned at night to sleep. Most cities were built on hills because the people could see approaching enemies better. Cities were often built around a spring or a well because water was scarce in Israel.

Small villages were often built outside the city, but these people knew they could go to the city for protection.

CITY OF DAVID

has three meanings.

1. Bethlehem was called "the city of David" because it was his hometown. See I Samuel 17:12-15; Luke 2:4.

2. A part of the city of Jerusalem was known as "the city of David." It was captured by David from the Jebusites. David

Jesus called Matthew from his tax booth in the city gate..

CITY GATES

were important in ancient times. The gates were the opening in the walls of the city that were always closed and barred at night.

The gates were usually double doors plated with metal. Most of the important functions of a city took place in the broad, open area just inside the city gates. People bought and sold things there, listened to reading of the Law, and held courts of justice.

When enemies conquered a city, they were said to "possess the gates."

See Ruth 4:1-12; Psalm 107:16.

later made this part his royal home when he became king. See II Samuel 5:5-7.

3. The entire city of Jerusalem. Later writers often used the term *city of David* to refer to the entire walled city of Jerusalem. See Isaiah 22:9.

CLOTHING

in Bible times was quite different from ours. Men and women dressed somewhat alike except for colors and differences in embroidery or needlework. Women's garments were usually more colorful than men's.

Except in hot weather, both men and women wore long white cotton undershirts that might reach to the knees or even to the ankles.

In hot weather, men and women wore rather close-fitting tunics, with either short or long sleeves. They were usually made of wool and often lined with white cotton material so they wouldn't scratch the skin when the undershirt was not worn. Although the tunic usually came to the ankles, hard-working men sometimes wore shorter tunics.

People tied their tunics at the waist with a wide sash called a girdle. The girdle was usually a square yard of woolen, linen, or silk cloth. It was folded first into a triangle and then folded into a sashlike belt five to eight inches wide. This girdle not only held the tunic in place but also formed pockets in the folds where men and women could carry small articles or money. When a person was "girded," he was ready to work or travel.

The outer garment was a cloak or mantle. This was used as a coat during the colder seasons of the year and also as a blanket to wrap up in at night. The cloaks were usually made of wool, goat

Arab men still wear head scarves today.

hair, or camel hair.

Men used three kinds of headwear.

1. Cotton or wool caps, similar to skullcaps, were worn by poor men.

2. Turbans were also common. These were long pieces of thick linen material wound around the head with the ends tucked under.

3. Head scarves were a square yard of colored cotton, wool, or silk folded into a triangle and draped around the man's head with the point of the triangle falling down the middle of the back. The man held it in place with a silk or a woolen cord coiled around his head.

Women wore headscarves or shawls. These were often pinned over a cap made of stiff material and decorated with pearls, silver, gold, or other ornaments. Sometimes they were used to form a veil that covered at least part of a woman's face and upper body.

Both men and women wore jewelry including earrings, nose rings, and rings on toes, ankles, and wrists.

See Isaiah 3:18-24.

COCK (see *Birds*)

COLOSSAE (*kuh-LAH-see*)
was an important city for more than a thousand years—from 500 B.C. to A.D. 600. It was located in the southwestern part of what is now Turkey. Originally it was on the main road from Ephesus to the east, but the Romans changed the road, and the city became less important.

What was left of the city was destroyed by the Turks in the twelfth century A.D. No one lives there now, but archaeologists have uncovered some of its ruins.

The church at Colossae probably was begun by Epaphras (Col. 1:7, 4:12-13), a friend of Paul's, while Paul was living at Ephesus during his third missionary journey. Probably Philemon and Onesimus were also members of the church at Colossae, and it apparently met in Philemon's home (Philem. 1, 2). Most of the Christians at Colossae were Gentiles.

COLOSSIANS (*kuh-LAH-shuns*)
is a letter written by the apostle Paul to the church in Colossae, a city in the southwestern part of what is now Turkey. Paul was probably in prison in Rome when he wrote this letter about the year A.D. 61.

Epaphras, who had helped begin the church at Colossae, had visited Paul and told him of some of the wrong ideas being taught there. Paul wrote this letter to help the Christians at Colossae get their ideas straightened out.

He sent the letter with two men. One was Tychicus and the other was Onesimus, a runaway slave who had become a Christian through Paul. Onesimus lived in Colossae, and Paul sent another letter along with him to his owner, Philemon.

The letter to the Colossians shows that some of the Christians there were letting wrong ideas interfere with their worship of Christ.

1. They were worshiping angels—giving more importance to angels than to Christ. Paul reminded them that Christ is the Creator of the universe, the Lord of heaven and earth, stronger than any other powers.

2. They were worrying too much about certain things they should do and should not do—observing holy days, fasting, not eating certain foods, or touching certain things. Paul reminded them that becoming strong Christians did not depend nearly so much on these things as on loving Christ and trying to do what pleases Him.

3. They were too impressed with the fancy language and knowledge of some false teachers. Paul said that real knowledge about Christ comes to every person who truly gives himself to Christ.

Paul included practical advice in this letter to the Christians about how to live for Christ in the society of their day. He also added many greetings to individuals he knew in the church.

COLT (see *Animals*)

COMMANDMENT
(kuh-MAND-ment)
means a rule, a teaching that has authori-

ty. Jesus summarized the commandments of God as being "to love God" and "to love your neighbor as yourself." See Matthew 22:35-40.

COMMUNION *(kuh-MEWN-yun)*
means sharing fellowship, having a close relationship, or being a part of something. The word is also used by the church to mean the Lord's Supper. When we eat the bread and drink the wine, we commune with Christ and show our close relationship with Him (I Cor. 10:14,22).

CONDEMN, CONDEMNATION
(kun-DEM, kon-dem-NAY-shun)
are words that refer to judging something wrong, or judging someone who is guilty of doing wrong and pronouncing punishment.

In the Old Testament, God often condemns those who do wrong, but He will not condemn those who trust Him (Ps. 34:21, 22).

The New Testament says that all of us are sinners and therefore are under the judgment or condemnation of God. However, there is "no condemnation for those who are in Christ Jesus." John 3:17, 18 tells us that God did not send Christ into the world to condemn the world, but that the world through Him might be saved.

Final condemnation is a judgment that will not be changed (Rom. 8:1).

CONFESSION *(kun-FEH-shun)*
means to admit or declare something. Confession sometimes means telling God our sins. Confession also may mean to state publicly our faith in Christ. We "confess Christ."

Confessing our sins to God and confessing our faith to others are both important things for Christians to do. See Romans 10:9; I John 1:9.

CONSCIENCE *(KON-shuns)*

is an inner sense of what is right or wrong. Our conscience depends on what

Cooking meant a lot more work in Bible times.

COOKING *(KUK-ing)* AND COOKING UTENSILS

Women did most of the cooking in Bible times, except in wealthy homes where servants did it. The evening meal was the most important meal of the day. For poor people, it was the only meal.

Bread was the most important food. Poor people made their bread of barley. The rich made theirs of wheat. Each family ground its own grain and baked its own bread, although some large cities had public bakeries where women could take their bread to be baked.

Families also used wheat or barley to eat as hot cereal. They grew and stored dried

beans and lentils to eat. Many people ate locusts. Food was seasoned with salt, onions, garlic, and sometimes with dill, anise, coriander, mint, and thyme. Nuts of all kinds were important in the diet of the Hebrews.

Most Hebrews ate very little meat—it was too expensive. On special occasions when common people ate meat, they usually had lamb or goat. Since there was no way to preserve meat or keep it cold, a family had to cook and eat the whole animal the same day they killed it. They cooked meat over an open fire on a spit, or boiled it in water, or cooked it in oil. They broiled fish over coals.

Ovens were usually outside to protect the house from fire. They were made of clay mixed with stones or pottery fragments. Often ovens were shaped like huge bowls two or three feet wide and turned upside down with the bottom missing. The cook placed large stones in the oven among the charcoal. When the fire was only embers, the women brushed off the stones and placed the food on the stones or around the walls of the oven. Most people used cooking utensils made of pottery, although some wealthy people had kettles and pans made of copper.

Families usually cooked with wide shallow pots. Most families had a small-mouthed piece of pottery for heating water. They stored grain, flour, and oil in pottery designed especially for these foods.

we understand to be right or wrong. It reminds us when we don't live the way we think we should. The Bible says that all people have consciences and that each Christian should make sure he/she has a clear conscience (Rom. 2:15; I Tim. 1:19).

CONVERSION *(kun-VER-zhun)*

means "turning," and usually describes a person turning away from sin and selfishness to become a person who worships and serves the true God.

There are many examples of conversion in the Bible. The most dramatic is that of Paul on the road to Damascus, when he was struck by a bright light as he was going to persecute Christians (Acts 9:1-20). The Philippian jailer also had a dramatic turning to God (Acts 16:25-34).

Other examples in the Bible tell of more gradual conversions. Timothy apparently came to know and trust God over a period of time. The disciples learned little by little what it meant to be followers of Christ (Acts 16:1-3; II Tim. 3:15).

COOKING (see box on page 76)

CORINTH *(KORE-inth)*

was the capital of Achaia (now southern Greece) and an important seaport in New Testament times. It was known for its luxury but also for its low morals.

Most of the 700,000 people who lived in Corinth were Greeks or Romans, but there were also some Jews. More than half the people in Corinth were slaves.

One reason for the low moral standards of the Corinthians was their worship of Aphrodite, the goddess of love. In the large and magnificent temple to this goddess, worship included immoral acts.

When Paul visited Corinth on his second missionary journey, he began, as usual, by preaching in the synagogue to Jews. When the Jews refused his message about Christ, another man, Titus Justus, invited Paul to use his house next door to the synagogue.

Justus and many others who heard Paul preach became Christians. Paul stayed in Corinth for a while with Aquila and Priscilla, a Christian Jewish couple.

The new church included Jewish Christians, slaves who had been converted to Christ, pagans who used to worship the goddess of Corinth, and some people from the upper social classes. It was hard for this group of people to understand each other and to live in harmony together. Paul's two letters to this church show some of the problems the church faced.

In the years after the New Testament period, Corinth was destroyed and rebuilt several times. In 1858 an earthquake destroyed most of the city, so another city named Corinth was built a few miles away from the old location. The new Corinth had a destructive earthquake in 1928. But the city was rebuilt.

CORINTHIANS, I and II

(KORE-inth-enz)

are two New Testament letters that the apostle Paul wrote to the church at Corinth (in what is now southern Greece). Paul wrote the letters during his third missionary journey around A.D. 55 or 56.

In the first letter, Paul answered some questions he had received in a letter from the Christians in Corinth. First Corinthians 7:1 begins, "Now concerning the matters about which you wrote."

The church at Corinth had many problems. The Christians favored different teachers. They had problems with suing each other in the courts, problems of immorality and marriage, and eating meat offered to idols.

Paul reminded the Corinthians that Christ alone was their Master and that everything they had should be used to glorify God. He also told the Corinthians how they should worship.

The second letter to the Corinthians was written during Paul's third missionary journey, and was a personal message to the church. Paul shared the trials he had been facing. He told them about his illness and how he accepted the fact that God did not heal him. He also told them about some of his God-given visions.

He also reminded the people of their responsibility to contribute money for the poor Christians in Jerusalem.

CORNELIUS *(kor-NEEL-yus)*

was a centurion (commander of 100 men) in the Roman army stationed at Caesarea. He was a Gentile who had become interested in the Jewish religion. He prayed to God and gave money to the poor.

God told Cornelius in a vision to send men to the house of Simon the tanner in the city of Joppa and to ask for a man named Peter.

Cornelius did as he was told. In the meantime, God sent a vision to Peter. A sheet seemed to come down from heaven holding animals that Jews were not permitted to eat. In the vision, Peter was told to kill and eat them. Peter refused, saying that they were "unclean." But God told him that what God had cleansed, Peter must not call unclean.

While Peter was trying to figure out what the vision meant, the men from Cornelius came to the door. They told him their master, a God-fearing Gentile, wanted Peter to come and visit him.

Until that time, Peter had not tried to preach the Gospel to anyone but Jews, and he had only lived and eaten with Jewish people who ate "clean" foods.

Peter went with the men to Cornelius's house. He and Cornelius told each other about their visions. Peter understood, probably for the first time, that the good news about Jesus Christ was not only for Jewish people but for the whole world.

He told Cornelius and his family and servants how Christ had come to earth to die for their sins so they could be forgiven. While Peter was still preaching, the Holy Spirit came to those who were listening. Peter saw that God was at work, and he said they should be baptized as believers. Peter stayed with them for several days.

All this was important to the early church because it showed clearly that Gentiles did not have to keep the Jewish

God gave Peter a rather shocking vision.

COURT OF THE WOMEN

COURT OF THE PRIESTS

COURT OF THE GENTILES

COURT OF ISRAEL

laws in order to become Christians.

See Acts 10:1—11:18.

COUNCIL (KOWN-sul)

is a group of persons who have been given certain responsibilities to govern or give advice. In ancient times there were religious councils and also government councils.

In the New Testament, the word *council* often refers to the Sanhedrin, the ruling group of Jews in Israel. It had seventy members (see *Sanhedrin*).

See Matthew 10:17; Acts 5:34; 25:12.

COUNSELOR (KOWN-sell-or)

means one who gives advice or help. God gives counsel to those who serve Him.

In the Old Testament, kings often had counselors help them make decisions.

In the New Testament, the Holy Spirit is called the counselor of the Christians.

See II Chronicles 25:16; Psalm 16:7; 33:11; John 14:16 (RSV).

COURT, COURTYARD
(KORT-yard)

was an enclosed place in a building. It had no roof, but it was surrounded by other parts of the house and was therefore private. Homes in Israel often had enclosed courts.

The temple of Solomon and the temple of the New Testament (Herod's temple) had four courts:

A. Court of the Gentiles (GEN-tiles)

was the largest open area in Herod's temple. Anyone could enter this section, and people often used it as a shortcut across the templ. It was larger than a football field. In this area, scribes debated each other and held schools. Merchants sold animals for sacrifices and changed money from Roman coins to the required temple money. It was in this court that Jesus drove out the money changers and overturned their tables (Matt. 21:12; Mark 11:15-17.

B. Court of Israel

was the inner court in the temple where only Jewish males were permitted.

C. Court of the Priests

was the part of the temple to which only priests were allowed— except during the Feast of Tabernacles, when all Jewish men could enter. The altar for burnt offerings was in this section.

D. Court of the Women

was a small court in the inner section of the temple. Both Jewish men and Jewish women could enter the women's court, but women were not permitted in the men's court, called the Court of Israel. Jesus often taught in the Court of Women.

In the women's court were thirteen chests that were shaped like trumpets. Offerings were placed in them. See Mark 12:41-44.

COVENANT (KUV-uh-nunt)

means an agreement. The word appears often in the Bible, especially in the Old Testament.

Sometimes covenants are made between people; both sides decide what the agreement shall be. This was the kind of friendship covenant Jonathan and David made in I Samuel 18:3.

More often in the Bible, *covenant* means an agreement between God and people. However, in God's covenants, God decides what shall be done, and people accept and live by the covenant.

Some of the covenants of God mentioned in the Old Testament include:

1. God's covenant never again to destroy the earth by flood (Gen. 9:12-17).

2. God's covenant with Abraham to make his family a great nation (Gen. 17:2-7).

3. God's covenant with Israel to make them His special people (Exod. 6:4-7; 24:7, 8). This covenant demanded that the people show they accepted the covenant by doing certain things. One of these acts was circumcision. Another was to serve only God and not idols.

The New Testament speaks of a "new covenant" that came through Jesus. He said His blood was the "blood of the covenant, which is poured out for many for the forgiveness of sins" (Matt. 26:28). The New Covenant makes it possible for every person who believes in Christ to become a member of the family of God (Heb. 9:15-22; 8:8-13; 10:15-18).

CREATION (see box on page 81)

CRETE (kreet)

is a mountainous island in the Mediterranean Sea. It is about 156 miles long and varies from seven to thirty-five miles wide. Paul's ship stopped there when he was on his way to Rome as a prisoner. After he was released from prison in Rome, Paul visited Crete again and left Titus, one of his helpers, to be in charge of the believers.

The people in Crete (Cretans) had a reputation for being lazy and for telling lies. The Letter to Titus was written by Paul while Titus was working in Crete. See Acts 27:7-13; Titus 1:5, 12.

CROSS

in the Bible has three meanings.

1. The wooden frame for torturing criminals to death. Jesus was crucified on a Roman cross. Four kinds of crosses were used (see diagram). Christ probably died

CREATION *(KREE-ay-shun)*

is God's work of beginning all new things. Usually *creation* refers to the beginning of the universe and life on earth.

Genesis 1 and 2 tell that God created everything. They do not tell us how God created. He spoke it into existence and the Bible says, "And it was so."

The Genesis account gives us the order of God's creative acts:

Day 1   Light
Day 2   Firmament (sky)
Day 3   Seas, land, vegetation
Day 4   Sun, moon, stars
Day 5   Birds
Day 6   Fish, animals, and people

The story in Genesis talks of "days."

The word *day* has several meanings in the Bible. Sometimes it means a twenty-four-hour period; other times it means a long period of time; sometimes it means a time of judgment. Some people believe that the days in Genesis aretwenty-four-hour periods; others think they represent periods of time, or that the pattern of days shows that God created everything in an orderly way. The story of Creation in Genesis does not emphasize *how* God created the world, but that He *did*. The important thing is that God did the creating.

Genesis shows that God is not the same as nature. God is different from the things He made. People who know this do not worship trees, animals, or other people.

The Creation account in Genesis also shows that men and women are supposed to manage the universe for its owner, God. They are to be responsible caretakers of the world that belongs to God.

The Bible says God made both men and women "in the image of God" and that men and women need each other. They are to work together to manage the universe.

God did not make the world and everything in it, and then leave. God is still active in the world and is concerned with everything He has made.

See Genesis 1—2; Hebrews 11:3.

on a cross shaped like the one on the left.

2. The word *cross* also stands for the Gospel of salvation through Christ.

3. Jesus used *cross* as a word picture of obedience to Him that could include trials, suffering, and death. Jesus told His disciples they must take up their cross and follow Him. See Matthew 10:38; Luke 14:27; I Corinthians 1:18.

CROWN

is a band that goes around the head.

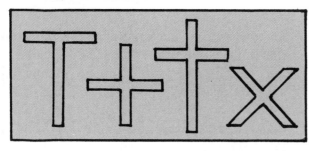

There are four kinds of crowns mentioned in the Bible.

1. The high priest's crown was a turban. Fastened to it was a gold piece across the forehead with the words *Holy unto the Lord*. The crown was a symbol of the priest's consecration to God.

2. Kings wore crowns, usually made of gold, as a mark of their royal position.

3. In the New Testament, *crown* sometimes refers to a head wreath worn by athletes as a sign of victory. Christ's crown of thorns was made like an athlete's crown of victory, but it was to mock Him.

4. *Crown* sometimes stands for the future reward and blessings that Christians will receive from Christ. This is the meaning in I Peter 5:4 and James 1:12.

CROWN OF THORNS

was the circle made of briars that the soldiers pushed down on Jesus' head after Pilate had sentenced Him to death. It was done to make fun of Him while they spit on Him and knelt before Him saying, "Hail, King of the Jews." See Matthew 27:29; Mark 15:17-20; John 19:2, 3.

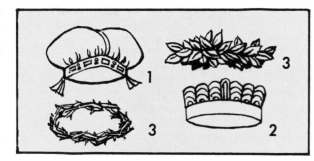

CRUCIFIXION *(kroo-suh-FIK-shun)*

was the kind of death Jesus suffered to make salvation possible for us. It was a terribly painful way to die.

Romans used crucifixion to execute criminals who were not citizens of Rome. Hands and feet were nailed to the wood, and the person was left to hang until he died of fever and infection. Death usually took two to eight days, but Jesus died in a few hours—perhaps because He had been badly beaten before the crucifixion.

CUBIT (see *Measures*)

CUPBEARER

was a palace official who served wine to the king. Only a man of proven loyalty and trust was chosen as a cupbearer. Nehemiah was a cupbearer to the king of Persia (Neh. 1:11; 2:1).

CURSE, CURSING

in the Bible does *not* mean profanity or swearing. When God curses something or someone, it means He pronounces judgment. When a person curses something, he wishes harm upon it. Christ said His followers should "bless those who curse you," (Luke 6:27).

CUSTOM

has two meanings in the Bible:

1. Habit, tradition, or the expected way of doing things (Luke 1:9).

2. Tax. Matthew, who became one of the disciples of Jesus, was a tax collector; he "sat at the receipt of custom" (Matt. 9:9,).

CYPRESS (see *Plants*)

CYPRUS *(SY-prus)*

is an island in the eastern Mediterranean

Jesus was crucified on a cross for our sins. He suffered to make salvation possible for us today.

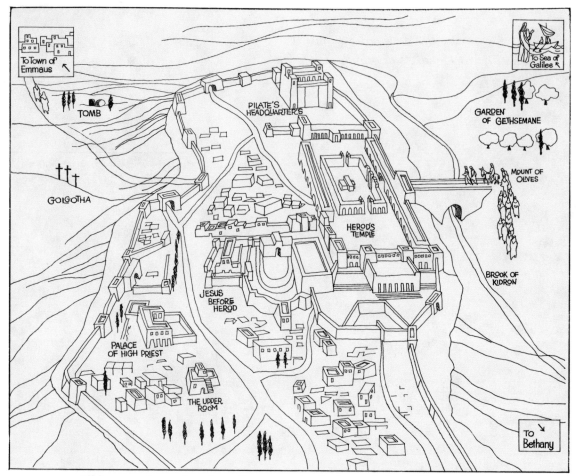

This map shows the places Jesus was in the hours before His crucifixion.

Sea. It is 148 miles long and about forty miles across.

Paul and Barnabas visited Cyprus on their first missionary journey. On the island, a government official named Sergius Paulus heard the message of Christ and believed (Acts 13:4-12).

Barnabas and John Mark later came back to Cyprus to preach (Acts 15:36-39).

CYRENE (sy-REE-nee)

was a city in North Africa. A man named Simon from this city was in Jerusalem when Jesus was crucified. The soldiers made him carry Jesus' cross (Luke 23:26).

There were many Jews in Cyrene, and some of them were in Jerusalem at Pentecost (Acts 2:10). Some of them became Christians and later went to Antioch to tell about Christ (Acts 11:20).

CYRUS (SY-rus)

was the founder of the Persian Empire. When Cyrus came to power, most of the Jews had been forced out of their own land and sent to Babylonia. Cyrus allowed the Jews to return to their land and to rebuild the temple that had been destroyed. See Ezra 1:1-11; 5:1—6:15; Isaiah 45:1.

DAGON *(DAY-gun)*

was the chief god of the Philistines. Scholars are not sure whether Dagon was a fish-god or a god of agriculture, but the people built many temples to honor this god.

When Samson was blinded by the Philistines, they brought him to a temple of Dagon to make fun of him. Samson prayed for strength, put his arm around

David was thirty years old when he became king.

85

two pillars, and pulled down the whole temple (Judg. 16:23-30).

Another time when the Philistines were fighting the Israelites, they captured the ark of God in a battle and took it to a temple of Dagon. The next day they found the image of Dagon face down in front of the ark. The Philistines put it back, but the next day it had fallen again and its head and hands had broken off (I Sam. 5:1-5).

Many years later, the Philistines took the head of King Saul after he had been killed in battle and placed it in one of their temples of Dagon (I Chron. 10:10).

DAMASCUS (duh-MAS-kus)

is still an important city today; it is the capital of modern Syria. On our maps it is sometimes called Dimashq. It is at least 4,000 years old—probably the oldest continually inhabited city in the world.

It is mentioned in Genesis 15:2 as the city from which Abraham's servant came.

David once captured Damascus, but usually it belonged to Israel's or Judah's enemies (II Sam. 8:5, 6).

In the New Testament, Saul was going to Damascus when Christ appeared to him in a vision. Saul lost his sight and was taken to Damascus, where it was restored. Disciples in Damascus taught Saul about Christ, and he began preaching in the synagogue there. Eventually, he had to escape by being let down over the walls in a basket (Acts 9:1-22).

DAN

was the name of one of the tribes of Israel and also the name of a city.

The tribe was named for the fifth son of Jacob. They settled in the northern area and called their main city Dan. The city was in the extreme northern part of Israel. Jeroboam, king of Israel, once made a golden calf and set it in Dan as a place for the Israelites to worship (I Kings 12:28-30).

DANIEL (DAN-yull)

is best known for being thrown into a den of lions when he refused to stop worshiping God. But Daniel was more than a brave man—he was a prophet and a high government official.

In 605 B.C., Daniel was a young man when Babylon defeated his nation, Judah. Daniel and many other Hebrews were taken from Judah to Babylon. It was the custom for the winners in war to take the leaders and the most promising young people away from the defeated country so they could not begin a rebellion against the new rulers.

In Babylon, Daniel and three of his friends were trained to serve in the court of King Nebuchadnezzar. They were

Daniel was thrown into the den of lions, but he was not harmed. God shut the lions' mouths.

treated well and given the same food as the king. However, some of the food was "unclean" (see *Unclean*) to the Hebrews. So Daniel asked that, as an experiment, they be fed simple food—vegetables and water (Dan. 1). They became so healthy and strong on this diet that they were allowed to continue eating that food.

During Daniel's second year in the court, Nebuchadnezzar had a troubling dream, but he could not remember what it was. Daniel was the only wise man in the court who could tell Nebuchadnezzar what his dream was and also what it meant. The king rewarded him by making him chief of his wise men and ruler over the province of Babylon. However, Daniel did not want to be ruler. He asked the king to appoint his three friends to that work instead (Dan. 2).

Later, Daniel had to interpret another dream, which showed that Nebuchadnezzar would become mentally ill for a while. He would recover later (Dan. 4). The prophecy came true.

A few years after Nebuchadnezzar's reign, Belshazzar became king. During a fancy banquet, handwriting mysteriously appeared on the wall (Dan. 5). Daniel was the only person who could read it. He told the king that it said his kingdom would be destroyed. Belshazzar died that same night as Persia conquered Babylon.

The new ruler was Darius. He recognized Daniel's abilities and made him one of the three top officials of the country. Other officials were jealous and plotted to get rid of Daniel. They persuaded Darius to make a law that no one could make any requests to any god or man, except to Darius. If any person broke the law during the next thirty days, he would be thrown into a den of lions.

Daniel kept on praying to God three times a day. He was thrown to the lions, but God protected him and the lions did not hurt him (Dan. 6). The next day he was taken out and returned to power.

Although Daniel was an important government leader, he was also a great prophet. His prophetic visions are recorded in Daniel 7—12.

DANIEL, BOOK OF

tells in the first six chapters about the life of Daniel and the dreams he interpreted. The second half of the book, chapters 7—12, tells about the visions Daniel had. Bible scholars do not agree about what the visions mean, but they do agree that the writings helped bring confidence in God to the Jewish people who had been forced away from their land.

DARIUS *(duh-RYE-us)*

was the name of several rulers of the Medo-Persian Empire. One Darius is mentioned in the story of Daniel. He was the king who made Daniel a ruler. Some officials were jealous and planned to get rid of Daniel. They had Darius sign an unchangeable law that no one could pray to any god except Darius for thirty days.

Daniel kept on praying to his God, was caught and thrown to the lions (Dan. 6). When the king found out that Daniel remained unharmed by the lions, he ordered the men who had accused Daniel to be thrown to the lions. Darius then wrote a law that his people were to fear the God of Daniel.

Another King Darius appears later in the Book of Ezra. During his reign, some people tried to stop the rebuilding of the temple in Jerusalem. Darius looked through old records and found a decree from Cyrus, king of Persia, saying that the Jews were free to rebuild the temple. Darius ordered that the rebuilding could continue (Ezra 6:1-15).

DAVID

king during Israel's time of greatest glory, had many talents. He was a great ruler, a poet, a fine musician, a skillful military commander, and intensely loyal to his friends.

He had deep feelings that showed in his poetry. He was often discouraged; he often wept. He was tempted and did some wicked things. But he was not afraid to repent and show sorrow for his sin.

David was born in 1040 B.C., the youngest son in a family of shepherds. He was anointed by Samuel to be the next king of Israel (I Sam. 16:1-13).

Saul, who was king before him, often had times of nervousness that could be calmed with music. David became his musician. In the palace, David also became a close friend to Saul's son Jonathan.

David first became known for using his sling and a stone to kill Goliath, a Philistine giant (I Sam. 17). Because of his bravery, David became popular, and Saul grew jealous of him.

Even after David married Michal, one of Saul's daughters, Saul was so jealous of David he tried to kill him. Finally David had to flee to the hills, where he could hide in the caves. Others joined him. They included many men who, like David, were hiding from enemies. This group grew into a small army.

Saul tried to find David and kill him, but he could not. Twice David could easily have killed Saul, but he refused to do so. David stayed away from Israel until he learned that Jonathan and Saul had died during battle with the Philistines. When David returned to Judah, the people quickly proclaimed him king.

At first, David was king only of Judah (the southern portion of Canaan). After seven years, the northern tribes also accepted him as their king.

The Israelites gradually defeated the Philistines and forced them out of the country. At that time, the city of Jerusalem belonged to a group called the Jebusites. David captured the city and made it the capital of Israel (II Sam. 5:6-10). He built a simple tabernacle there and brought the ark of the covenant to the tabernacle.

David and his army then conquered neighboring kingdoms to the east and the north until Israel became the strongest nation in the area.

With all these people to govern, David set up a large central government and appointed officials over the conquered lands. He also carefully organized his army.

Even though David was a skillful leader, his own family life was sad. He had many wives, among them Bathsheba, whom he took from another man (II Sam. 11—12). Some of his own children killed each other, and two sons led rebellions against him (II Sam. 15:1—18:15; I Kings 1:5-53).

*The story of David and his sling
is one of the Bible's highlights.*

Near the end of his life, David ordered that the people be counted (II Sam. 24:10-25). This was against the will of God, and God sent a plague that killed 70,000 people. It was miraculously stopped at a place just north of Jerusalem. David purchased that land and built an altar to God there. Later Solomon built the Temple there.

David's name is in the title of seventy-three of the Psalms—the most famous being the 23rd, which begins, "The Lord is my shepherd, shall not want."

DAY OF ATONEMENT
(uh-TONE-ment)

is the most solemn and important day of the Jewish religious calendar. It is in September, ten days after the Jewish New Year. Jews today observe it by not eating and not working.

In Bible times, the Day of Atonement included a series of ceremonies and sacrifices by the priests (Lev. 16). It was the only time of the year the high priest entered the holy of holies—the most sacred part of the tabernacle or temple.

As part of the ceremony for the Day of Atonement, the high priest purified himself by a ceremonial bath and put on white garments. Then he sacrificed a bull as a sin offering for himself and the other priests. He took some of the blood of the bull into the holy of holies and sprinkled it on the ark of the covenant.

Then two goats were brought to the tabernacle or temple. One was sacrificed as a sin offering for the people, and some of its blood was sprinkled in the holy of holies. The high priest confessed the sins of the people over the head of the other goat and then sent it into the wilderness as a symbol of sin being removed.

Toward the end of the day, other sacrifices were made.

After the Jerusalem temple was destroyed in A.D. 70, the sacrifices described in the Old Testament stopped.

Christians see the Day of Atonement as a symbol of the sacrifice of Christ for the sins of the world.

DAY'S JOURNEY

was usually the distance a person could walk in seven or eight hours—about twenty to thirty miles.

DEACON *(DEE-kun)*

comes from a Greek word that means "servant" or "minister." Household servants and those who waited on tables were called deacons. Paul called himself a deacon or servant in I Corinthians 3:5.

In I Timothy 3:8-12, *deacon* seems to apply to certain persons in the church who had particular responsibilities. We are not sure exactly what those responsibilities were, but they seemed to be important to the church.

DEAD SEA

in southern Israel, has four times as much salt as the ocean. It is called "dead" because nothing lives in it. Even a non-swimmer can float on the Dead Sea because it is so salty. Its surface is 1,300 feet below sea level, and in some places the water is more than 1,000 feet deep. The Dead Sea is forty-seven miles long and about seven miles across—the largest body of water in Israel. Sodom and Gomorrah were somewhere near the Dead Sea.

DEAD SEA SCROLLS (see box on page 92)

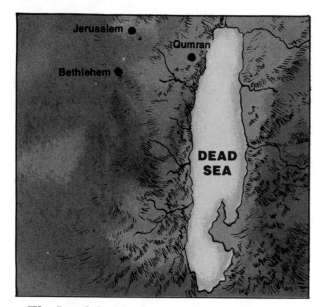

The Dead Sea is forty-seven miles long and about seven miles across.

DEATH

has two meanings in the Bible. Death is the end of physical life. For example, in Deuteronomy 34:5 the Bible says flatly, "So Moses the servant of the Lord died." In other places the Bible speaks of death as "sleeping with his fathers," as in II Kings 13:9, "So Jehoahaz slept with his fathers, and they buried him in Samaria."

But the Bible also speaks of death as a spiritual separation from God. Romans 6:23 says, "The wages of sin is death, but the gift of God is eternal life." This "new life" of fellowship with God shows itself in the way we live. "We know that we have passed out of death into life, because we love the brethren," according to I John 3:14.

DEAD SEA SCROLLS

are a group of ancient writings discovered in 1947 by Arab shepherds who were exploring some caves near the Dead Sea.

Archaeologists recognized the value of

Our oldest copies of parts of the Bible were found in these caves near the Dead Sea.

the scrolls and began to search other caves in the area near the ruins of a small village called Qumran (*KOOM-ron*). Many other scrolls were found. They included parts of every book in the Old Testament except Esther. Written in ancient Hebrew and Aramaic, these are the oldest Old Testament scrolls ever found. They help translators of the Bible know more accurately what the original writings said.

Many other scrolls at Qumran were writings about the history of the Qumran people, their religious beliefs, and how they lived. The Dead Sea Scrolls reveal that about 100 B.C. or earlier, a few hundred Jews from Jerusalem built this small village, far from other cities, as a place to study the Old Testament Law and wait for God to send a strong new leader. The community apparently died out about A.D. 70.

Those who are forever separated from God are said to experience the "second death" (Rev. 20:6, 14).

DEATH OF CHRIST

is one of the central events in the Christian faith. The Bible says that Christ died to show God's love for people. He did not die for us because we are good, but because we are sinful. We deserved to die, but His death became a *substitute* for our death (Rom. 5:8; I Pet. 3:8; 2:21, 25).

Christ was put to death by the cruel method of crucifixion. He had been accused of blasphemy because He said He was the Son of God (John 19:7).

Even as Jesus was dying in great pain, He thought of others (John 19:25-27; Luke 23:34 ,43). He saw His mother, Mary, and asked one of His followers to care for her. He talked kindly to the two robbers being crucified with Him. To one He said, "This day you will be with me in Paradise." He thought about the Roman soldiers and those who wanted Him to die, and He said, "Father, forgive them, for they know not what they do."

Although Jesus' death was a terrible event in history, it was the only way we could know God as a friend. John 3:16 says that God gave His Son to die for us because He loved us so much.

DEBORAH *(DEB-er-uh)*

was one of the greatest judges of Israel. (During the 400 years before the Israelites asked for a king, they were ruled by judges, through whom God spoke and led His people.)

Together, the tribes of Israel had not won a war for 175 years before Deborah became ruler. She led them to victory over Jabin, king of Canaan, who had been threatening Israel for twenty years.

Deborah was also a prophetess, and God gave her instructions on how to defeat Jabin even though he had 900 iron chariots. Deborah went with her soldiers into battle as they defeated the enemy on Mount Tabor. After the victory, Deborah and Barak composed and sang a song of praise to God.

See Judges 4—5.

DEBT, DEBTOR *(det, DET-er)*

A debt means something owed to someone else—usually money. A debtor is the one who must pay it.

The Law of Moses said that Hebrews could not charge interest on debts to another Hebrew, especially if he was poor (Exod. 22:25; Deut. 23:19). This law, however, was largely ignored in New Testament times (Matt. 25:27).

People sometimes had to sell their children and wives as slaves to pay their debts (Matt. 18:23-30). Jesus always showed sympathy and care for people in debt, and He often used stories about them in His parables.

The word *debt* in the Lord's Prayer, however, refers to sins that we do. *Debtors* are people who sin against us.

DELILAH *(dee-LYE-luh)*

was a wicked Philistine woman who pretended to be in love with Samson (the strong man and judge of Israel). She wanted to find out the secret of his great strength. Three times he misled her when she asked where he got his strength. She tried each of his suggestions, but they did not take his strength away. Finally he admitted that he was strong because of his vow to God that he would never cut his hair. While he slept, she called in his enemies to cut his hair. His strength was gone, and he was captured (Judges 16:4-22).

DEMONS *(DEE-muns)*

are evil spirits. They are often mentioned in the Bible. Sometimes they are called the devil's angels. They do not have bodies. They are servants of Satan (the devil). They are intelligent and do all they can to oppose God and those who serve God. The New Testament tells about demons who made people mentally ill, or blind, or unable to speak. (See also Luke 8:26-39; Matt. 12:22.) The KJV says that Mary Magdalene had seven devils, but the newer translations have the more correct term, *demons* (Luke 8:2).

The New Testament teaches that Jesus has power over demons and protects His followers from them. At the end of the world, all demons will be destroyed with Satan, their master (Matt. 25:41).

DERBE *(DUR-bee)*

was a city in what is now the country of Turkey. Paul visited there on his first and second missionary journeys and perhaps on his third. See Acts 14:20; 16:1.

DESERT *(DEZ-ert)*

in the Bible does not mean a sandy wasteland like the Sahara. It usually refers to an area where grass grew but that needed more rain to make it good farmland. An Israeli desert (or wilderness) was often a place where sheep grazed.

DEUTERONOMY

(DOO-ter-ON-uh-mee)
is the fifth book in the Old Testament. It

begins by telling how the Israelites arrived at the Jordan River after forty years of wandering in the wilderness. They were now ready to enter the promised land.

As the thousands of Hebrews gathered at the edge of the Jordan, Moses reminded them of God's Covenant (or agreement) with them. He told them why they had not been able to enter Canaan forty years before—their unbelief had kept them out until all of the older people from Egypt were dead. He repeated many of the stories of their years in the wilderness.

Then, Moses declared again all of the laws of God that they were to obey. The Ten Commandments were repeated, and Moses included the laws about feast days and offerings to God (Deut. 12:5—16:17).

Chapters 22 to 26 review the laws about taking care of property and each other. They tell how disagreements were to be settled. Then Moses reminded the people what would happen if they disobeyed God.

The closing chapters tell how Moses chose Joshua to lead the Israelites in their conquest of Canaan. Then Moses went to the top of Mount Nebo, where he looked across the Jordan River to the promised land. There Moses died.

Deuteronomy is the last of the five books of Moses known among the Jews as "the Law."

DEVIL

is one of the common names for Satan (see *Satan*). Other names are Beelzebub (Matt. 12:24), Abaddon (Rev. 9:11), the great dragon (Rev. 12:9), the ancient serpent (Rev. 12:9), and the deceiver (Rev. 20:2, 3).

DIANA *(die-ANN-uh)*

is the Latin name of the Greek goddess called Artemis (see *Artemis*).

DISCIPLE *(dih-SY-pul)*

means "learner" and refers to someone who accepts and follows the ideas and practices of a certain teacher. John the Baptist had disciples (Matthew 9:14), and so did the Pharisees (Matthew 22:16).

In the New Testament, *disciples* usually refers to those who were followers of Jesus. Sometimes it means the twelve apostles (Matt. 10:1). Other times it refers to all those who believe in Christ (Matt. 28:19, 20; Luke 6:17; John 8:31). In the Book of Acts, it always means believers in Christ who live according to His teachings (Acts 6:1).

DISEASES

or sickness were common in Bible times. They are usually described rather than named. For example, Matthew 8:14 says Peter's mother-in-law was sick with a fever. We don't know what disease caused the fever. It may have been due to malaria (quite likely) or to typhus, typhoid, or some other infection.

People and animals are described as having "boils" or "sores." There are many reasons for boils and sores, but the Bible writers did not name the diseases causing them. The writers recognized that how people think affects their health

Jesus heals a blind man.

and feelings. Proverbs 16:24 says, "Pleasant words are like a honeycomb, sweetness to the soul and health to the body."

Sometimes a general term is used to describe a whole family of diseases. *Pestilence* could mean cholera, dysentery, or other diseases that spread easily and are caused by poor diet, crowding, and unsanitary habits.

When names of diseases are used, the Bible names are sometimes not the same ones we use today. For example, the Bible mentions "scurvy." We know scurvy today as a disease caused by lack of Vitamin C. Fresh fruits and vegetables were the main diet of the people in Bible times, so they would not have had our kind of scurvy. Their "scurvy" was some kind of fungus disease.

Here are some of the diseases the Bible mentions.

Blindness is not being able to see. Some blindness was caused by eye infections; others were the result of gonorrhea, cataracts, or glaucoma. Moses gave special instructions to provide for the blind and the deaf. Jesus healed several blind people. These are mentioned in John 9:1-7; Matthew 20:30-34; Mark 8:22-25.

Sometimes blindness is used as a word picture of a person who refuses to see what God wants him to do. Jesus spoke of the Pharisees as "blind guides" (Matt. 15:14).

Boils were red, inflamed swellings of the skin that could be caused by several different diseases. Some scholars think that Job's boils may have been smallpox. The "boils" of the cattle in Exodus 9:9 may have been anthrax.

The boil of Hezekiah in II Kings 20:7 was probably a carbuncle—large, aggra-vated boil. The prophet Isaiah prescribed a fig poultice for his boil.

Dropsy (*DROP-see*) is involved in several diseases. It means that too much watery fluid collects in the body, the feet, or the legs (Luke 14:2). It is often present in diseases of the heart or kidneys.

Dysentery (*DIS-in-tare-ee*) is a serious, painful infection and inflammation of the colon. It can cause death if not properly treated (Acts 28:8).

Epilepsy (*EP-uh-lep-see*) is a disorder of the central nervous system that brings occasional seizures or convulsions. Jesus healed epilepsy (Matt. 4:24). In Matthew 17:14-18, Jesus healed a boy who was demon possessed and who also had epilepsy.

Fever is a symptom of many diseases, including typhus, malaria, dysentery, and cholera. Peter's mother-in-law, who was healed by Jesus in Matthew 8:14-16, may have had malaria. In Acts 28:8, Publius's father had both fever and dysentery—the fever probably caused by the dysentery.

Itch in Deuteronomy 28:27 was probably either ringworm or scabies, a disease caused by a tiny insect that burrows under the skin and causes intense itching. It easily spreads to other people.

Leprosy is caused by a microorganism that attacks the skin. Today it's called Hansen's disease. In the Bible, *leprosy* may also have meant some other skin diseases. Leviticus 13 tells what people were to do about skin diseases and leprosy. A person with these kinds of disease was to stay away from other people for certain periods of time until the disease showed signs of healing.

Madness is mental illness. It was common in Bible times. King Saul apparently became more and more unbalanced. He

When Naaman asked to be healed of his leprosy, he was told to go bathe in the Jordan River.

was moody and suspicious. He became more and more unable to perform his duties as king.

Nebuchadnezzar suffered from a mental illness that made him think he was an animal. It is called boanthropy. Other times madness was caused by demon possession (Luke 8:26-33).

Palsy (*PALL-zee*) is a general term used in the King James Version to mean paralyzed in some way).

Paralysis (*puh-RAL-uh-sis*) means some part of the body is crippled or won't work. The paralysis may have been due to polio, birth injuries, or other illnesses.

Pestilence (*PEST-uh-lunss*) usually refers to a disease that spreads rapidly. Pestilences probably included cholera, undulant fever, typhoid, dysentery, and other diseases that often go with poor diet, crowding, and unsanitary habits (Deut. 28:21). The difference between pestilence and plague is not always clear.

Plague can include any serious epidemic, but in I Samuel 5—6 it probably referred to the dreaded bubonic plague. Bubonic plague brings high fever, a swelling of the glands in the groin ("tumors"), and swift death. It is usually spread by rats. When the plague broke out among the Philistines, they thought it was because they had captured the ark of God from the Israelites. When they sent the ark back, they included a "guilt offering" of "five golden tumors and five golden mice." They recognized some connection between the tumors and the mice.

Scab and **scurvy** are skin diseases probably related to eczema, psoriasis, or impetigo. Scurvy in the Bible is not the scurvy of our day caused by a lack of Vitamin C. The year-round diet of fresh fruit and vegetables would make that unlikely. The diseases are mentioned in

Leviticus 21:20; 22:22.

Scabies (*SKAY-beez*) (see *Itch*, above).

Sores or skin ulcers are infections on the skin, often developing around wounds, bruises, or skin eruptions that become infected. Lazarus had sores (Luke 16:20, 21).

Tumors (*TOO-murs*) are mentioned in I Samuel 5—6 in connection with the plague sent on the Philistines after they captured the ark of God. They were probably swollen glands in the groin that came with bubonic plague.

Ulcers (*UL-sers*) or sores were wounds or skin openings that would not heal. They often appeared with bubonic plague or with leprosy.

Withered hand was some form of paralysis that affected the hand only. It may have been caused by polio. Withered hand is mentioned in Matthew 12:9-14; Mark 3:1-6; and Luke 6:6-11.

Worms caused the death of Herod Agrippa in Acts 12:21-23. They were probably intestinal roundworms. They are common in lands where sanitation is poor. These worms form a tight ball and block the intestine, causing death.

DIVORCE *(dih-VORSE)*

is the dissolving of a legal marriage. In Deuteronomy 24:1-4 Moses discussed a bill of divorce, so we know divorce was permitted among the Israelites. Jesus said, "For your hardness of heart, he [Moses] wrote you this commandment." Jesus' teachings showed that marriage was intended to be permanent (see *Marriage*). See Mark 10:2-12; Luke 16:18; Matthew 19:3-12.

DORCAS *(DOR-kus)*

was a woman disciple who lived at Joppa (on the Mediterranean coast). She showed her love for Christ by making clothing for those in need and helping in

Dorcas was a Christian woman who often made clothes for needy people. She died—and was raised to life again through Peter's prayers.

other ways. When she became ill and died, other Christians learned that Peter was in a nearby town and sent for him.

When Peter arrived, he was surrounded by weeping women who showed him the clothing Dorcas had made for them. He sent everyone out of the room, then knelt and prayed beside Dorcas's body. Finally he said, "Tabitha [the Aramaic word for Dorcas], arise." Dorcas opened her eyes, sat up, and was well (Acts 9:36-42).

DOVE (see *Birds*)

DREAMS

were used by God to communicate with people. Ecclesiastes 5:3 says, "A dream comes with much business," showing that people in Bible times realized that dreams were usually related to their activities.

The Bible has many examples of God speaking to people through dreams—both to people who worshiped Him and to those who did not. Pharaoh had a dream of seven fat cows and seven thin ones. Joseph interpreted the dream as showing there would be seven years of very good crops followed by seven years of famine. Joseph also interpreted the dreams of a butler and a baker in prison (Gen. 40:1-20; 41:14-36).

In Deuteronomy 13:1-5, the Israelites were told that any prophet or dreamer who told them to serve other gods should be put to death.

The New Testament also has examples of God speaking to people through dreams or visions. God spoke to Joseph twice through dreams; once before the birth of Jesus, and again before he fled with Mary and Jesus to Egypt (Matt. 1:20-24; 2:13-14).

Dreams and visions are not the same. In a dream, the person is in a natural sleep. In a vision, such as Paul's vision (to Damascus), the person is clearly awake.

DRUNKENNESS

is condemned in the Bible. Wine was common among the Israelites and their neighbors, and too much drinking was often a problem. Proverbs 23:29-34 shows the foolishness of drinking too much. Amos 4:1 shows that women also had problems with drink in Bible times. Ephesians 5:18 says, "Do not get drunk with wine, for that is debauchery, but be filled with the Spirit."

Jacob set up a stone to mark the place where God spoke to him in a dream.

Queen Esther waited until the perfect moment to expose Haman, the enemy of the Jewish people.

EAR

played a significant part in some Old Testament Jewish ceremonies. To be made holy for the priesthood, Aaron and his sons had their right ears touched with blood (Exod. 19:19-21). This action symbolized forgiveness or cleansing. The right ear of a healed leper was also touched by blood (Lev. 14:14). A slave's

Soft clay can be shaped while spinning on a disc.

ear was pierced to show he belonged to someone else (Exod. 21:6).

Ear is often used as a word picture of understanding and obeying God. Jesus said, "He who has ears to hear, let him hear." In this verse, *hearing* means "obeying." When Jesus said, "Let those words sink into your ears, meant, "Understand what I am saying to you." See Matthew 11:15; Luke 9:44.

EARTHENWARE *(ER-thun-ware)*

is clay dishes, bowls, and containers. To make earthenware, a potter shaped the clay on a potter's wheel with his hands. He then glazed the clay dish and baked it in a furnace. In the Bible the potter and his earthenware sometimes stand for God and His people. See Isaiah 45:9; Jeremiah 18:4; II Corinthians 4:7.

EARTHQUAKE

is a movement of the earth that often causes great destruction (Num. 16:31-33; Jer. 4:24; Zech. 14:4, 5). The Bible mentions several earthquakes and describes what they did. Elijah experienced one (I Kings 19:11-12). Another one occurred during the reign of Uzziah (786-735 B.C.).

See Amos 1:1; Zechariah 14:5. Earthquakes happened at the time of Jesus' death and resurrection (Matt. 27:51; 28:2). Paul and Silas were freed from prison by an earthquake (Acts 16:26).

The Book of Revelation says earthquakes will be part of God's judgment in the future (Rev. 8:5; 11:13, 19; 16:18).

EASTER

is the day when Christians celebrate Christ's resurrection. The New Testament doesn't mention an Easter celebration. Soon after Christ's death, Jewish Christians celebrated Christ's resurrection on Passover, while Gentile Christians celebrated it on a certain Sunday. In A.D. 325 the Council of Nicea ruled that Easter should be celebrated on the first Sunday after the full moon in the spring (a Sunday between March 22 and April 25).

Easter eggs and the Easter bunny have nothing to do with the real meaning of Easter.

ECCLESIASTES

(ee-klee-zee-AS-teez)

is an Old Testament book. Some scholars believe the author was Solomon, writing in his old age. Ecclesiastes 1:1 and 1:12 say the writer was the son of David and king over Israel.

The word *ecclesiastes* means "preacher." The writer called himself "the Preacher"

No one knows exactly where Jesus was buried and rose again, but this garden tomb is a likely possibility.

and said he had tested out many things. He tried pleasure and found it to be vanity, or emptiness. He saw that wisdom was better than foolishness; but since both wise and foolish men die, he decided wisdom was worthless, too.

The writer ended almost every section of the book with "This also is vanity and a striving after wind." He also repeated, "Vanity of vanities." He meant he had decided everything was useless.

This man seemed to know very little about life after death, and that may be part of the reason life looked so dark to him.

But the Preacher also gave some wise advice. He said people should enjoy their work, go to God's house, keep their promises to God, and be trustworthy.

Chapter 12:1-8 is a word picture of growing old and the changes that come to the body with age.

Some scholars think the Book of Ecclesiastes shows that even the wisest person can't find out what God has planned for his life unless God tells him.

EDEN *(EE-den),* GARDEN OF

was the beautiful place God created for the first man and woman, Adam and Eve (Gen. 2—3). In it grew many fruit trees and two special trees: the tree of life and the tree of the knowledge of good and evil. Adam and Eve lived in the garden until they sinned against God by eating the fruit of the tree of the knowledge of good and evil that God had told them not to eat.

The story of the garden of Eden shows what life would have been like if people had not sinned. In Eden there was peace between people and God, between people and nature, and between Adam and Eve. When sin came, all this peace was destroyed.

People have always wondered where the garden of Eden was located. The only clue is Genesis 2:10-14, which says a river in the garden divided into four rivers: Pishon, Gihon, Tigris, and Euphrates. We know where the Tigris and Euphrates rivers are. We do not know where the Pishon or Gihon rivers were. The Bible says Pishon flowed through a place called Havilah, where gold was found. This may have been India. The Gihon flowed through Cush, perhaps Ethiopia. So no one knows for sure where the garden of Eden really was.

The Old Testament sometimes speaks of Eden as the garden of God (Ezek. 28:13). A description of a garden somewhat like Eden (although part of a city) is used in Revelation 22:1, 2 as a word picture of heaven.

In the garden of Eden, animals lived together with Adam and Eve without hurting one another.

EDICT *(EE-dikt)*

was the written law or decree of a king. After his seal was put on it, it was read in public. To disobey a king's edict meant death. Pharaoh made an edict that all Hebrew boy babies were to be killed (Exod. 1:22; Heb. 11:23). In the time of Esther, the king made an edict that all Jews were to be killed (Esth. 3:12; 8:8, 9, 17; 9:1, 13).

EGYPT (see box on page 104)

ELDER *(ELL-dur),*

in the Old Testament, was an older man of a village. Elders governed the community and made major decisions. Each town had its group of elders (Ruth 4:1-4; I Sam. 16:4; Ezra 10:14).

The Sanhedrin at the time of Christ was a ruling body made up of elders, priests, and scribes (Matt. 27:12). This group helped bring about the crucifixion of Jesus.

In the New Testament church, the idea of ruling elders was probably carried over from Jewish life. Paul appointed elders in every church (Acts 14:23). (*Elder* and *bishop* mean the same thing in the New Testament.) Elders taught the people and encouraged spiritual growth among the Christians. Because an elder's job was very important, Paul wrote about what kind of person should be appointed as an elder (I Tim. 3:1-7; Titus 1:5-9).

ELI *(EE-lie)*

was both judge and high priest of Israel for forty years. He lived at Shiloh, near the tabernacle.

While Eli was priest, Hannah came to the tabernacle to pray for a son. Eli thought Hannah was drunk because she cried so loud as she prayed. Hannah had a son and named him Samuel. When Samuel was very young, she left him in Eli's care.

EGYPT

of the Old Testament covered about the same territory as Egypt does today. It is about the size of Texas and Colorado combined. The only thing that keeps the land from being all desert is that the Nile River floods every year. The floods water the fields and deposit rich black soil.

The Pyramids and Sphinx tell us the Egyptians were an ancient, highly civilized people.

The Israelites called Egypt "Mizraim." They asked Egypt for help during times of famine. The seven years of famine during the time of Joseph were probably caused by the Nile not flooding to its usual level. Interesting details of ancient Egyptian life are told in the stories of Joseph's life and the slavery of the Hebrews up to the Exodus. Egypt was at war with Israel several times in the Old Testament period.

Egyptian pharaohs were buried inside the pyramids.

See Genesis 12:10; 37; 39—50; Exodus 1—15; II Chronicles 12:1-9; 35: 20-27.

Eli had two grown sons, Phinehas and Hophni. They were irresponsible and worthless, and they did evil things. But Eli did not correct them. A prophet warned Eli that his two sons would die on the same day.

When Eli was ninety-eight years old, his two evil sons carried the ark of the covenant out of the tabernacle and into battle for the Israelites. They thought that would help Israel win. But Israel was badly defeated, Eli's two sons were killed, and the ark was captured by the Philistines.

When the sad news was brought to Eli, he fell off his seat and died of a broken neck.

See I Samuel 1:1—4:18.

ELI, ELI, LAMA SABACHTHANI (AA-lee, AA-lee, LAH-muh, suh-BACH-thuh-nee)

are Hebrew or Aramaic words that Jesus cried from the cross. They mean, "My God, my God, why have you forsaken me?" Jesus was quoting from Psalm 22:1. The people standing near the cross thought Jesus was calling for Elijah and waited to see if Elijah would come. But immediately after Jesus said these words, He died (Matt. 27:45-50; Mark 15:33-37).

ELIJAH (ee-LIE-juh)

was an Old Testament prophet famous for his fiery words and for courageously opposing Queen Jezebel.

Elijah would appear without warning, wearing his leather loincloth and cloak made of woven goat hair. He would deliver a message from God to Israel's rulers—and then he would disappear again. Kings listened to his words, because they recognized that he was a prophet of God. Elijah lived during the reigns of King Ahab, his son Ahaziah, and his grandson Jehoram.

Elijah's story begins in I Kings 17, where he told King Ahab there would be no rain. The Lord cared for Elijah during the drought. First He sent him to the brook Cherith (*KEE-rith*), where ravens brought food to him (I Kings 17:3-7). After the brook dried up, God told Elijah to go to the town of Zarephath (I Kings 17:8-16). A widow and her only son were preparing a meal with their last grain and oil when Elijah met them. He asked them to share the last of their food. During the time Elijah stayed with them, their supplies of grain and oil never ran out. The woman's son became deathly sick, but after Elijah prayed, the boy was healed (I Kings 17:17-24).

Meanwhile, King Ahab and his wicked wife, Queen Jezebel, kept on worshiping Baal. After three years of drought, Elijah put the prophets of Ahab's pagan gods to a test.

On Mount Carmel, the 450 prophets of Baal built an altar and placed a sacrifice on it (I Kings 18:18-40). Elijah did the same thing. They all agreed that the true God would send down fire to burn up the sacrifice offered to God. The priests and prophets of Baal prayed, chanted, cut themselves, and cried out for many hours, but no fire came.

The widow's son borrowed many jars.

ELIJAH

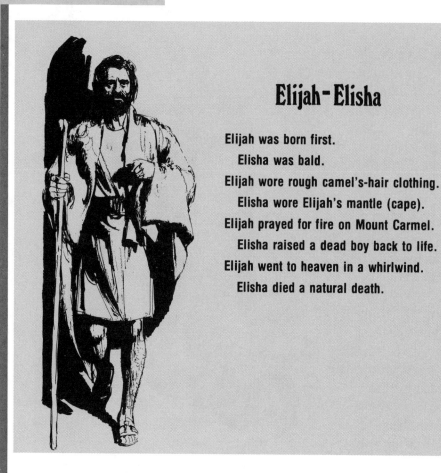

Elijah-Elisha

Elijah was born first.
Elisha was bald.
Elijah wore rough camel's-hair clothing.
Elisha wore Elijah's mantle (cape).
Elijah prayed for fire on Mount Carmel.
Elisha raised a dead boy back to life.
Elijah went to heaven in a whirlwind.
Elisha died a natural death.

Then Elijah's turn came. He shocked the crowd by pouring water over his sacrifice and filling up a trench that was dug around the altar. Then he prayed. The Lord sent a fire so hot it burned up not only the sacrifice but the altar and water as well.

Elijah then prayed for rain to end the three-year drought, and God sent rain.

Then Elijah went to Mount Horeb (I Kings 19:9-13). This is probably the same as Mount Sinai, where God had given Moses the Ten Commandments. When Elijah came to the mountain, he experienced a great wind, an earthquake, and fire. But after all that, God chose to speak to him in a still, small voice.

Elijah then returned to Israel and anointed Elisha to be a prophet after him (I Kings 19:16-21).

When King Ahab and Queen Jezebel murdered a man named Naboth so they could steal his vineyard, Elijah told Ahab and his family that God would punish them (I Kings 21).

King Ahaziah once sent three captains with 50 men each to capture Elijah (II Kings 1:9-16). But Elijah prayed, and fire from heaven burned up the first two captains and their men. The third captain begged for his life, and Elijah agreed to go with him.

Elijah never did die. Instead, God took him to heaven in a whirlwind with fiery horses and a chariot (II Kings 2:1-12).

In the New Testament, Jesus called

Elijah was taken to heaven in a fiery chariot and a whirlwind.

ELISHA

Elisha was hardly afraid of the Syrians at Dothan—not with God's fiery army nearby.

John the Baptist "Elijah" (Matt. 11:14). The prophet Malachi had said God would send Elijah before the Day of the Lord would come (Mal. 4:5-6). Jesus said that John fulfilled Malachi's prediction because John came "in the Spirit and power of Elijah."

Elijah and Moses met with Jesus on the Mount of Transfiguration (Matt. 17:1-3).

ELISHA *(ee-LlE-shuh)*

was an Old Testament prophet to whom God gave power to do many miracles. He was a counselor and adviser to several kings, always delivering the message God had given him.

He was anointed by Elijah. to take his place when Elijah went to be with God. Elijah showed this choice by throwing his prophet's mantle over Elisha's shoulders. Elisha became a companion to Elijah until Elijah was taken to heaven in a fiery chariot and a whirlwind. Elisha had asked Elijah for a "double share of your spirit," and Elijah said it would be his if he saw God take him to heaven.

Elisha was a prophet during the reign of four kings of Israel—Jehoram, Jehu, Jehoahaz, and Jehoash. These were some of the miracles that God worked through Elisha:

1. Made a dry path through the Jordan River by striking the water with his mantle (II Kings 2:13, 14).

2. Made the bad waters of a spring turn good (II Kings 2:19, 22).

3. Saved a widow from losing her sons to slavery by making her oil supply keep going until she had enough to pay her debts (II Kings 4:1-7).

4. Told the Shunammite woman she would have a son even though her husband seemed too old to have children (II Kings 4:11-17).

5. Restored to life the son of the Shunammite woman (II Kings 4:18-37).

6. Saved prophets from dying after eating poisonous food (II Kings 4:38-41).

7. Healed Naaman from leprosy (II Kings 5:1-27).

8. Made a borrowed iron axhead float (II Kings 6: 1-7).

9. Led the Syrian army, blinded, to Samaria (II Kings 6:11-23).

He also prophesied some miraculous military victories, such as the defeat of Benhadad's army that had been besieging Samaria. He ordered Jehu to be anointed the next king of Israel, in place of Ahab's descendants.

When Elisha was old and sick, King Jehoash came to visit him. The dying prophet used the little strength he had left to do one final prophetic act. He told Jehoash to shoot an arrow through a window. The king did so, and Elisha assured him it was "the Lord's arrow" that would conquer the Syrians. The prophecy came true, but Elisha did not live to see it.

Elisha was a true spiritual leader. He trained and taught many younger prophets and destroyed the last remains of Baal worship in Israel(I Kings 19:15-21; II Kings 2—13).

ELIZABETH *(ee-LIZ-uh-beth)*

was the mother of John the Baptist. She was the wife of a priest named Zechariah, and she was a descendant of Aaron. Both she and her husband were faithful, godly people. But Elizabeth could not have any children.

When Zechariah and Elizabeth were too old to have children, an angel of the Lord told Zechariah that Elizabeth would have a son. When Elizabeth was six months pregnant, her cousin Mary, the virgin mother of Jesus, came to visit her. Elizabeth greeted Mary with Spirit-filled words, and Mary rejoiced by singing a song of praise to God.

Elizabeth's son was John the Baptist, who prepared the people of Israel for the coming of the Lord.

See Luke 1:5-57.

ELKANAH *(el-KAY-nuh)*

was the father of the prophet Samuel. Elkanah had two wives, Peninnah and Hannah. Peninnah had children, but Hannah did not. This made Hannah very sad. She asked God to give her a son. She promised that she would dedicate the son to serve God all His life.

God answered her prayer, and Samuel was born. Elkanah loved Hannah and their son, Samuel, but he agreed with Hannah that the child should be taken to the house of God to serve Eli the priest. Samuel was Eli's helper from the time he was very young.

See I Samuel 1:1-28; 2:11.

ELYMAS *(EL-uh-mus)*

was a Jewish magician and a false prophet. His real name was Bar-Jesus, which means "son of Jesus (or Joshua)." But he was called Elymas because that name is connected with magic.

Paul and Barnabas met Elymas when they came to the town of Paphos on the island of Cyprus. Elymas was with Sergius Paulus, an intelligent Roman officer. Sergius Paulus wanted to hear Paul's message about Jesus, but Elymas tried to prevent it. Paul rebuked Elymas and told him he would be blinded for a time. When Elymas stumbled away, looking for someone to lead him, Sergius Paulus believed Paul's message (Acts 13:4-12).

EMMAUS *(ee-MAY-us)*

was a village about seven miles from Jerusalem. Two of Jesus' disciples walked to Emmaus with Christ after His resurrection. They finally recognized Him when He broke bread at dinner. See Luke 24:13-35.

EMPEROR *(EM-purr-er)*

was the highest Roman ruler. Julius Caesar was the first Roman to call himself emperor. Rulers after him were also called emperors or caesars.

EMPEROR *(EM-purr-er)* WORSHIP

was the reverence and worship of both the dead and living emperors throughout the Roman Empire. Julius Caesar was praised as "a god . . . and the savior of the whole human race." Usually, the living emperor did not claim to be a god. But after his death, the people often called him divine and built temples to him.

Emperor worship was not intended to

ENDOR

While walking on the road to Emmaus, Cleopas and his friend didn't recognize Jesus until they had gone several miles.

replace the worship of other gods. On Roman coins both the emperor and a Roman god or goddess were pictured. To burn incense before the statue of an emperor was patriotic as well as religious.

But Christians could not worship the emperor because the names commonly given to emperors—savior, son of god, god, lord—belonged to Jesus Christ alone. Because Christians would not say "Caesar is Lord," they sometimes suffered terrible persecution, and many died.

ENDOR *(EN-door)*, WITCH OF

lived in the town of Endor during the reign of King Saul. She was a sorceress or medium who said she could call up dead men's spirits to tell future events.

God had told the Israelites in Deuteronomy 18:10-14 and Exodus 22:18 that they should not go to mediums. Isaiah 8:19 says, "When they say to you, 'Consult the mediums . . .' should not a people consult their God? Should they consult the dead on behalf of the living?" Mediums got their information from Satan.

But when the Philistines started a war against the Israelites, King Saul went to the medium of Endor and asked her to bring Samuel's spirit back from the dead, even though Saul had once ordered all mediums to leave the country. The medium of Endor said she saw an old man in a robe. This old man, actually a spirit, told Saul he and his sons would die the next day, and they did.

First Chronicles 10:13, 14 says Saul died for his unfaithfulness, because he asked for guidance from a medium and not from the Lord.

See I Samuel 28:3-25.

ENEMY *(EN-uh-me)*

is one who hates somebody else and tries to hurt him. An enemy can be a person or a nation. Jesus said that people who belonged to Him were to love their enemies. See Matthew 5:43-46; Romans 12:14-21.

ENOCH *(EE-nuk)*

was one of the two persons in the Bible who never died. Instead, the Bible says, "God took him." (The other person who did not die was Elijah the prophet, who was taken to heaven in a whirlwind and chariot.)

Enoch was born seven generations after Adam. When he was 65 years old, his son Methusaleh was born. Methusaleh lived to be the oldest man in the Bible.

The Bible says that Enoch "walked with God" and that his faith pleased God. Enoch lived to be 365 years old, and then God took him to heaven.

See Genesis 5:18-24; Hebrews 11:5.

EPAPHRODITUS

(ee-PAF-ro-DIE-tus)

was a messenger between the church at Philippi and the apostle Paul. The church at Philippi sent Epaphroditus with gifts for Paul, who was in prison in Rome. Paul appreciated the gifts and was cheered up by Epaphroditus.

Epaphroditus got sick and almost died while he was with Paul. When he got well, Paul sent him back to the church with the letter to the Philippians that is now a part of our New Testament.

Paul thanked the believers in Philippi for the gifts they had sent and told them to welcome Epaphroditus back with honor because he had risked his life while serving Christ. Paul called him "my brother and fellow worker and fellow soldier." See Philippians 2:25-30; 4:18.

EPHAH (see *Measure*)

EPHESIANS *(ee-FEE-shunz)*

is a New Testament letter that Paul wrote, probably when he was a prisoner in Rome around A.D. 59-61. Biblical scholars believe the letter was sent to more churches than just the one at Ephesus. It probably went to many small churches in the province of Asia, an area in what is now known as Turkey.

Paul's friend Tychicus took the letter and personal news about Paul to the churches. Tychicus delivered the letters we call Colossians and Philemon at the same time.

The letter to the Ephesians has two sections. In the first part, Paul talks about God's plan to bring all creation together in Christ. Paul tells how God chose His people, forgave their sins, and gave them the Holy Spirit (Eph. 4:1—6:20). Paul also points out how Christ and His church are a part of each other.

In the second part, Paul urges Christians to show that they love each other in their daily lives. In this way, the church would help bring about God's plan of unity.

Paul uses many pictures to show how the church is related to Christ (Eph. 1:3—3:21). All Christians are like a body and

111

EPHESUS *(EF-uh-sus)*

was the capital city of the Roman province called Asia (now a part of Turkey). It was an important, old, beautiful city during the time of the New Testament.

In Ephesus was an enormous white temple dedicated to the goddess Diana (whose Greek name was Artemis). It was known as one of the seven wonders of the ancient world. In the center of the temple was a sacred stone, perhaps a meteorite, that had fallen from the sky. People said it looked like the goddess. Diana was the goddess of fertility. The myths said she was the mother who nursed the gods, people, animals, and plants. Her images were ugly statues of a creature with many breasts. Worship in her temple included immoral sexual acts. Many merchants in Ephesus made their living by selling silver statues of the ugly goddess.

Paul stayed in Ephesus for nearly three years on his second missionary journey and helped many people become Christians. The merchants were afraid people would stop buying the idols they made, and so they started a riot. In spite of this, a strong church was established at Ephesus. See Acts 18:19, 24—19:40.

When the Christians at Ephesus understood God's truth, they burned their occult books and scrolls.

Jesus is the head. Or Christians together are like a building and Jesus is the important cornerstone. Or again, Christians are like a wife and Jesus is the husband.

EPHOD *(EE-fod)*

was sacred clothing worn by the Jewish high priest. It was beautifully made with many colors of materials, woven gold, and precious stones. Others who served in the temple wore simple linen ephods.

Gideon and Micah turned the beautiful ephods into idols (Exod. 28:5-35; I Sam. 2:18; II Sam. 6:14; Judg. 8:27; 17:5).

EPHRAIM *(EE-free-rnm)*

was the younger son of Joseph (Gen. 41:50-52). His mother, Asenath, was an Egyptian. When Ephraim's grandfather, Jacob, was old, he adopted both boys as his own sons. Jacob blessed them, but gave Ephraim the firstborn's rights, even though Joseph disapproved (Gen. 48:8-20). Ephraim's descendants became one of the twelve tribes of Israel.

After the country was divided into the northern kingdom and the southern kingdom, the northern part was sometimes called Ephraim because it was the strongest tribe (Isa. 7:2,5, 9; Hos. 9:3-16). (The southern part was known as Judah because it was the strongest southern tribe.)

EPISTLE *(ee-PIS-ul)*

is a letter. Examples of epistles in the Old Testament include: David's letter to Joab in II Samuel 11:14, 15; Queen Jezebel's letter in I Kings 21:8,9; and Sennacherib's letter to Hezekiah in II Kings 19: 14.

However, the word *epistle* usually refers to the twenty-one1 letters in the New Testament. These epistles were written by Peter, Paul, James, John, Jude, and the author of Hebrews. Paul wrote thirteen letters.

Some letters were written to one church, others to several churches, still others to individuals or to all Christians. Many of the letters were written to help deal with specific problems, encourage the Christians, teach them, or correct false ideas.

An epistle usually began with the name or title of the author and the name of the people who were going to get the letter. Words of greeting came next, then the main message. The letter usually closed with the author's name.

The apostles probably wrote other letters that were lost or destroyed. I Corinthians 5:9 refers to a letter written to Corinth before I Corinthians. In Colossians 4:16, Paul mentioned an epistle written to the Laodicean church. Neither of these is in our New Testament.

ESAU *(EE-saw)*

was the firstborn son of Isaac and Rebekah. His brother, Jacob, was his twin. Before their birth, God told Rebekah that the elder would serve the younger (Gen. 25:21-25). This was the opposite of the custom of that time—usually the older person had more authority. The elder son always received a birthright, which was a special blessing and double inheritance from his father.

Esau loved hunting in the fields, but he seemed to care nothing for God or His blessings. Once when he was hungry, he sold his birthright to Jacob for a bowl of bean soup (Gen. 25:27-34).
When he was forty years old, Esau married two Hittite women (Gen. 26:34-35). These women made life bitter for Isaac and Rebekah .

When the time came for Isaac to bless his sons, Jacob tricked his father into giving him the blessing that belonged to the oldest son (Gen. 27:1-45). Esau was angry and begged his father to bless him too. But Isaac's blessing had already said Esau would serve his brother. Esau planned to murder Jacob for this, but Jacob escaped.

Years later, when Esau was living at Mount Seir, he heard that Jacob was returning. Jacob sent a large gift of cattle and sheep to Esau because he was afraid. Esau took 400 men with him when he

Esau had been hunting all day and was starving when Jacob talked him into trading his birthright for some soup.

went to meet Jacob. But when he saw him, Esau ran to his brother and kissed him (Gen. 33:1-9).

Hebrews 12:16, 17 warns against being careless about God as Esau was.

Paul used the story of Esau and Jacob to show how God carries out His plans (Rom. 9:10-13).

ESTHER *(ES-ter)*

was a Jewish orphan girl who became the queen of Persia about 475 B.C. Her story is told in the Old Testament Book of Esther.

Ahasuerus, who was then king of Persia, became very angry with his queen,

Vashti, because she would not appear with him at a drunken feast. He divorced her and looked for a beautiful new queen. He chose young Esther out of many candidates.

Esther had been brought up by her cousin Mordecai, who told her not to tell anyone that she was Jewish. Mordecai kept in touch with Esther after she became queen. One day Mordecai heard of a plot against the king's life. He told Esther, and she told the king, so she saved his life.

Ahasuerus's chief assistant was Haman, who was very proud. He wanted everyone to bow before him. When Mordecai refused, Haman became very angry and looked for a way to get revenge. He got the king to sign a decree that all the Jews were to be killed. The king signed, not knowing that Esther was Jewish. But Haman was so angry at Mordecai that he couldn't wait for the general killing. He had a gallows built just to hang Mordecai.

Mordecai sent word to Esther about the new law that Jews were to be killed. At the risk of her life, Esther told the king that she was among those who would die because of his new law. He was so angry at Haman that he ordered him hanged on the gallows that had been built for Mordecai. He then made Mordecai his chief assistant in place of Haman. He could not change the law he had made, but he gave permission for the Jews to protect themselves.

Jews today still celebrate the Feast of Purim to remember how God delivered Esther and the Jews at this time.

ETERNAL (ee-TUR-nul) LIFE

means more than life that does not end. It means life under God's saving rule. It comes from God through Jesus Christ. It

The tomb of Queen Esther as it appears today.

begins when we accept Jesus Christ as Savior and seek to do the things that please Him instead of the things that please ourselves. The eternal life of the Christian keeps on growing through all of life on earth and into future life with God in His eternal kingdom. We share in the eternal life of Jesus Christ, God's Son, who died and rose again for us (John 3:36; 10:28; 17:2-3).

ETERNITY (ee-TUR-ni-tee)

means all that is past and all that is yet to come. It means time that didn't have a beginning and will not end. Psalm 90 is a beautiful poem showing God is eternal—He has neither beginning nor end.

ETHIOPIA (ee-thee-OH-pea-uh)

is a country whose history stretches back to before Moses' time. It was south of Egypt along the Red Sea. In Old Testament times it included much of today's Sudan as well as modern Ethiopia. The Hebrews called Ethiopia "Cush" and its peoples "Cushites." Cush was the grandson of Noah, and his descendants formed Ethiopia (Gen. 10:6-10). Moses married an Ethiopian woman (Num. 12:1).

In the days of King Hezekiah, the Ethiopian king, Tirhakah, attempted to conquer Judah, but failed (II Kings 19:9). In New Testament times, Ethiopia was ruled by Queen Candace (Acts 8:27).

ETHIOPIAN EUNUCH

(see box on page 116)

EUNUCHS (YOU-nuks)

were men who could not have sexual relations because their sexual organs were damaged or defective. These men were often put in charge of a king's harem, as

ETHIOPIAN EUNUCH
(ee-thee-OH-pea-un YOU-nuk)
was a treasurer for Candace, queen of Ethiopia. He was a Gentile who had become interested in the Jewish religion. One time, after he had gone to Jerusalem to worship, he was riding back to Ethiopia in his chariot, reading aloud in Isaiah 53. Philip, who was sent by the Holy Spirit, came alongside the chariot and asked if he understood what he was reading. Philip explained that Isaiah 53:7, 8 was a prophecy about Jesus the Messiah. The

eunuch believed in Christ, was baptized in water near the road, and went home rejoicing (Acts 8:26-40).

in Esther 2:14. Sometimes the title *eunuch* meant a royal officer. These officers were not necessarily physically handicapped.

In Deuteronomy 23:1 the Law says that a physically handicapped eunuch could not enter the religious congregation. Isaiah 56:3-5 promises that the eunuch who loves and honors God will receive a blessing better than sons and daughters.

Jesus spoke of men making themselves eunuchs in Matthew 19:12. These men remained unmarried so they could give more time and energy to God's work. It did not mean their sexual organs were damaged or defective.

EUPHRATES *(you-FRAY-teez)* RIVER
is an important river that runs 1,780 miles from Turkey through Syria and Iraq to the Persian Gulf. The garden of Eden was near the Euphrates and Tigris rivers.

It was the largest river known to the Hebrews and is often mentioned in the Old Testament simply as "the river" or "the great river." See Genesis 2:10-12;

Deuteronomy 1:7; Isaiah 8:7.

EVANGELIST *(ee-VAN-juh-list)*
is a person who announces the good news about Jesus, often to people who have never heard or understood it before. An evangelist may go from city to city, spreading God's message. Ephesians 4:11 says that an evangelist's work is a gift from the Holy Spirit. Acts 21:8 and II Timothy 4:5 show that Philip and Timothy were evangelists.

EVE
was the first woman. Her name means "life," and Adam called her Eve because she was the mother of all people.

God made Eve from one of Adam's ribs. She was to be his closest companion. When Adam first saw her, he said with wonder, "This at last is bone of my bones and flesh of my flesh." The Bible says that the relationship between a husband and wife is meant to be even closer than the relationship between parents and children.

Adam and Eve lived in the garden of Eden. They could walk and talk with God face to face. But Satan, appearing as a serpent, talked Eve into thinking God was keeping something good from them. She ate the one fruit God had told them never to eat, and she gave some to Adam. Their disobedience to God was the Fall of mankind. From that day on, their relationship with God, with each other, and with nature were all spoiled by sin.

Yet God promised that one day someone would be born from a woman who would have victory over Satan. He would bridge the gap between God and people. Christians know this person is Jesus Christ.

Eve was the mother of Cain, Abel, Seth, and many other children.

In II Corinthians 11:3, Paul warned Christians about being deceived by Satan, as Eve was.

See Genesis 2:15—4:2; 4:25—5:4.

EVIL

is anything that is against the will of God. Evil causes moral or physical damage to ourselves or to other people. It also hurts our relationships with other people and with God. Evil damages everything God created.

Evil began in the world when Adam and Eve disobeyed God. Sometimes in the Bible, evil is called "the works of the flesh." These include bad thoughts, immoral actions, hatred, fighting, loving something more than God, trying to have supernatural power or knowledge, wanting everything, complaining, dividing up into little groups, and getting drunk or taking drugs.

God did not create evil, but He permits it to exist in a world that is rebelling against God and going its own way. He created people so that they could choose for themselves whether to do evil or good. One day God will create a new

The Jews never thought they would be forced to leave their country—but they were.

117

heaven and a new earth, and evil will not exist.

See Romans 1:18-32; Galatians 5:19-21; Revelation 21:1-5.

EXILE

means someone makes people leave their own country and live somewhere else. A country that had defeated another country in war would often make the leaders and most of the young people who could become leaders move to the country of the conqueror. The poor, the old, and those who were sick could stay in their own land, because they would not be able to stir up a revolution against the conqueror. Then the victorious nation would send some of its own loyal people to settle in the defeated land.

This is what happened to both the northern kingdom (Israel) and the southern kingdom (Judah). The northern kingdom was defeated by Assyria in 722 B.C. Many of its people were forced to move to Assyria. Only a few came back. The southern kingdom (Judah) was defeated by Babylon. Its leaders were exiled to Babylon. Their capital city and beautiful temple were finally destroyed by the army of Nebuchadnezzar in 586 B.C.

The term *The Exile* usually refers to the seventy-year period when many of the people of Judah were forced to live in Babylon.

The people were not prisoners. They were free to build homes, start businesses, or work at their trade. But they could not go back to their own land. And that made them very sad, because God had told the Hebrew people that Israel was the promised land that He had given them. The Book of Lamentations is a group of five poems Jeremiah wrote to show how he felt about the terrible destruction that had come to the land and why God had permitted this to happen.

While in Babylon, the Jews gathered in small groups to pray and study the Law of Moses. Many scholars believe these small groups were the beginning of Jewish synagogues.

After King Nebuchadnezzar of Babylon died, his country was conquered by the Persians in 539 B.C The king of the Persians, Cyrus, allowed the Jewish people to go back to their own land if they wanted to. Many of them did, and they rebuilt the temple and the city of Jerusalem. The Books of Ezra and Nehemiah tell about the rebuilding.

EXODUS, BOOK OF

is an Old Testament book written by Moses. It tells about the Hebrews going out of Egypt toward their promised land.

The first twelve chapters of Exodus tell how the Hebrews had to live as slaves. Many years after Joseph died, the Egyptian rulers became afraid of the Hebrews because there were so many of them in Egypt. They made all the Hebrews slaves. Later, God chose Moses to lead His people out of Egypt. God had to send ten plagues on Pharaoh and the Egyptians before they were willing to let the Hebrews leave Egypt.

A large number of people took their flocks and household equipment and left Egypt with Moses and Aaron. Chapters

13 to 19 tell how God worked many miracles to keep them alive as they traveled across the wilderness. God destroyed Pharaoh's army in the sea; God fed the Israelites with manna and quail as they traveled southeast from Egypt to Mount Sinai. The rest of the Bible often talks about this deliverance out of Egypt.

Chapters 19 to 40 tell how God gave the Ten Commandments and other instructions to Moses on Mount Sinai. These instructions helped the Israelites live in the wilderness for forty years. Even more important, God's words helped them realize what it meant to be His people.

Exodus includes God's instructions for building the tabernacle and His instructions to the priests who would help the people worship God. God told Moses to tell the people why there has to be sacrifice for sin and why they should obey all His commands.

This book tells how God worked through His servant Moses to change a group of fearful, depressed slaves into a great, powerful nation.

EXODUS ROUTE

is unclear because although many places where the Israelites went are named, most of these places are unknown.

Exodus 12:37 says the Israelites left from Rameses in Egypt and went to Succoth. Archaeologists believe that Succoth was about thirty-two miles southwest of Rameses. Exodus 13:17 says, "God did not lead them by way of the land of the Philistines, although that was near," because the people would be so frightened they would turn around and go back to Egypt. The land of the Philistines was along the coast of the Mediterranean Sea and would have been the

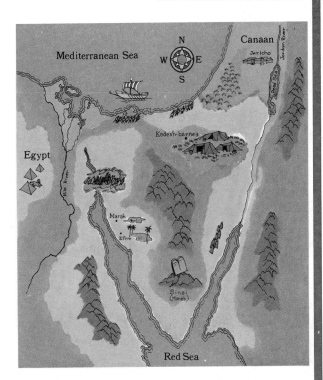

closest route to Canaan.

Exodus 13:20 says, "And they moved on from Succoth, and encamped at Etham, on the edge of the wilderness." The location of Etham is not certain.

Most scholars believe that the sea through which God miraculously brought the Israelites was the Reed Sea rather than the Red Sea. The Hebrew word actually means "reed." All we know about the location of the Reed Sea is that it was a boundary between Egypt and the Sinai wilderness. When the Suez Canal was built in the 1860s, the lakes in the area were changed, so the exact location can never be known.

After they crossed the sea, the Hebrews went into the wilderness of Shur and came to a place called Marah. Many scholars think this was an oasis in the Sinai desert about halfway down the coast. Then they camped at Mount Sinai, in the southern part of the peninsula, for about a year. God gave Moses the Ten Commandments and the rest of the Law on Mount Sinai. The places listed between Mount Sinai and Kadesh-barnea (where the Israelites wandered for nearly forty years) are not known, although we do know where Kadesh-barnea was.

When the Israelites were ready to begin their war against Canaan, Moses led them by a long route to Ezion-Geber and then north toward the Dead Sea. Maps of the route are only approximate, since most of the places cannot be identified.

EYE

was highly valued in Bible times as it is in our day. Exodus 21:26 says a slave had to be set free if his owner blinded him. II Kings 25:7 tells how prisoners were blinded by cruel heathen nations.

Eye is also a word picture of spiritual understanding. Psalm 19:8 says the Word of God enlightens the eye.

EZEKIEL *(ee-ZEE-kee-ul)*

was a Jewish prophet who lived in Babylon when many of the people of Judah were in exile there. He wrote one of the important prophetic books of the Old Testament. He foretold that the Jews would return to Jerusalem and rebuild the temple. His prophecies emphasized that people are free to choose their own way and that they are responsible to God for what they choose.

Ezekiel was a priest as well as a prophet (Ezek. 1:1-3). He was forced to move from Jerusalem to Babylon in 597 B.C The army of King Nebuchadnezzar captured the city and took many of the furnishings of the temple. Nebuchadnezzar forced thousands of priests, scribes, and skilled workers to move to Babylon,

about 900 miles away. This was the usual way conquerors in ancient times treated defeated countries. In 586 B.C, when the city of Jerusalem was destroyed, more people were forced to move to Babylon.

Ezekiel built a house for himself and his wife in Babylon. He also continued to be a spiritual leader. He taught the people how to practice their Jewish religion even though they had no temple in which to worship. He encouraged them to gather together to pray and study the Scriptures. Many scholars believe this was how Jewish synagogues became the place of worship instead of the temple. Jews today still worship in synagogues.

When Ezekiel had been living in Babylon five years, God called him to be a prophet. He was walking in the country when a violent thunderstorm came. He had a vision of four strange living creatures, wheels of a heavenly chariot, and a vision of God on a throne. In that vision God commanded him to give a message to His people. It was the first of many visions that Ezekiel received. They are recorded in the Old Testament Book of Ezekiel (Ezek. 1:4—3:15).

Ezekiel was often told to help people remember his prophecies by acting out the message (Ezek. 4). Before Jerusalem was finally destroyed in 586 B.C, he foretold its fate by making a brick model of Jerusalem with armed soldiers around it. He lay down beside it and did not eat or drink much so that he could show the misery and hard times that were coming to Jerusalem.

He taught the people that God was with them in Babylonia just as much as He had been with them in Judah. Ezekiel said they must obey God wherever they were.

When Ezra read God's Law to the people, it was news to many of them.

After the final destruction of Jerusalem, Ezekiel was able to encourage his people by prophesying that Jerusalem and the temple would be restored (Ezek. 37:24-28). These prophecies began to be fulfilled about 50 years later, in 538 B.C., during the time of Ezra and Nehemiah. Ezekiel had no more prophetic visions for about thirteen years. Later in his life, God showed him in visions that Israel and Judah would again be united and governed by a Messiah who would be a descendant of King David.

Ezekiel died in Babylonia without ever returning to his own land or seeing Jerusalem restored. He gave encouragement and spiritual help to his people in exile. He helped them keep on believing in God and looking forward to the day when they could return to their own land (Ezek. 18:30-32).

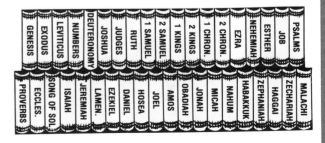

EZRA *(EZ-ruh)*

was a priest, scribe, and scholar who helped his people start worshiping God again. He probably wrote the Old Testament book called Ezra and might have also written Nehemiah and I and II Chronicles.

Ezra himself had been in exile in Babylonia. Many Jews like him had been forced to move to Babylonia after Nebuchadnezzar conquered Judah in 586 B.C. However, Babylonia was conquered by Persia in 539 B.C. The new Persian rulers told the Jews they were free to return to their own land. However, many people did not want to go back. They had homes and businesses in their new land, and they were free to practice their own religion.

They studied the Old Testament in small groups in their own villages. The scribes among the exiles were men like Ezra who knew how to read and write Hebrew. They were kept busy making copies of the Old Testament by hand so these groups could use them.

But Ezra was also an adviser to the king about the Jews and their religion. He asked the king for permission to return to Judah so he could teach the Law of God there. The king approved and also gave him authority to appoint judges to enforce the Jewish laws (Ezra 1).

Ezra took with him about 5,000 other Jews who decided to go back to their homeland (Ezra 7—8). He found that many of the people who lived in Judah had wandered away from God and were not keeping God's commands. He wept in sorrow.

Ezra began offering sacrifices to the Lord at the temple. He gathered the people of the land together and read the Law of Moses to them. The people listened. When they heard God's Word and realized how they were sinning against God, they cried.

Ezra also taught the people to celebrate the festivals of the Old Testament. On the eighth day of the feast of booths, Ezra led the people in a prayer of confession of sin (Ezra 9:7-15). The people all agreed to renew their covenant with God to keep His laws.

Ezra found that many of the men in Judah had married women who were not Jewish and who practiced pagan religions. The people agreed to obey the Law of Moses and no longer live with their foreign wives (Ezra 10:9-17).

Ezra tried to arrange for each group of ten families to have their own copy of the Old Testament teachings to study. As they read God's Word for themselves, their faith was strengthened, and the Jewish people never again worshiped idols like the people in surrounding countries (see also *Exile* and *Nehemiah*).

FAITH

has two meanings in the Bible: one meaning is trusting or believing; in other cases, when the Bible speaks of "*the* faith," it means the Gospel of Christ—the message of Christianity.

1. Faith is the act of trusting or believing. Often a child has faith in his parents because he knows they love him and care for him. The Bible says people should place their trust—their faith—in God because He loves them very much.

In the Old Testament, the word *faith* does not appear often (Ps. 119:66; Jer. 17:7). But the Old Testament has many examples of faith.

Abraham is the most famous. Abraham obeyed God because he had faith. Abra-

Feasts in ancient times were major events that sometimes went on for hours.

123

ham had a close relationship with God because of his faith.

Hebrews 11 in the New Testament lists many other Old Testament examples of faith: Abel, Enoch, Noah, Joseph, Moses, and others. All of these people believed God. They had faith that God would care for them in every situation. They had experienced God's care.

In the New Testament the words *faith* and *believe* (a word that means almost the same thing) are found more than 500 times. Jesus said that faith is powerful and valuable. Only through faith in Jesus can we know God.

The writings of Paul in the New Testament explain what faith is and why we need it (Eph. 2:8-10; Heb. 11). Paul said God had fulfilled His promises by sending Jesus to die for our sins. "You have been saved through faith," Paul wrote to the Ephesians. We cannot earn our relationship with God. It comes only through trusting who Jesus is and what He did. But faith is not just believing certain facts about God. Paul also said that

FALL

refers to Adam and Eve's first sin in the garden of Eden (Gen. 3). God had told Adam and Eve—the first people—that they could eat from any tree in the garden except from "the tree of the knowledge of good and evil." But the serpent (Satan) tempted Eve, and she ate fruit from that tree. She gave some fruit to Adam and he also ate. Their disobedience caused the Fall.

The Fall describes what happened to Adam and Eve when they sinned. They "fell" out of their good relationship with God. Before they disobeyed God, Adam and Eve had been very close friends with God. After they sinned they felt guilty and hid from God. Their relationship with Him was spoiled by sin. They even had to leave the garden of Eden.

The Bible teaches that just as Adam and Eve "fell," so all people have "fallen." "All have sinned and fall short of the glory of God," says Romans 3:23. Sin came into the world when Adam and Eve sinned, and ever since then sin has affected all people.

The Bible teaches that the remedy for our spoiled relationship with God is in Jesus Christ. He died for our sins so we can have a new relationship with God (Rom. 5).

faith is obeying God's commands.

The Letter of James in the New Testament explains that faith is seen in what we do. When we trust God, we show our faith by obeying God. True faith is seen in how we act. If a person has faith in God but doesn't help others, his faith is dead, said James.

Hebrews 11:6 says that without faith it is impossible to please God. And in Galatians 2:20 Paul writes that Christians live by faith.

2. *The faith* sometimes means the whole message of the Christian Gospel—the truth of Christ's coming to live and die for our sins so we can have a new relationship with God (Col. 1:23; II Tim. 4:7).

FAMILY

today, usually means a father, mother, and children. But in the Bible, *family* had broader meanings.

In the early Old Testament, a family included not only father, mother, and children, but also grandparents, uncles, aunts, cousins, servants, friends, and visiting strangers. Jacob's family included at least sixty-six people.

Hebrew families were the beginning of the Israelite nation. God promised Abraham that his descendants would fill the earth. As the family of Isaac became the twelve tribes of Israel, the people saw their whole nation as a family. Genealogies became important family records, and they were preserved carefully.

There were many reasons for the large Hebrew families in the days when they lived as shepherds. A large group was safer than a smaller group; they could protect each other against invaders. It was also easier for large families to take care of each other, since the governments did not help poor people or sick people. Each family group was like a small village.

Another reason Old Testament families were large was the custom of fathers to have more than one wife. This is called polygamy (*puh-LIG-uh-mee*). The Hebrews probably copied this custom from other countries around them. Having many children was very important to the Hebrew people, and extra wives meant more children. The Hebrew people thought having a large family meant God was pleased with them. A woman who had no children was thought to be cursed.

Since children in the Hebrew family were so important, there was much joy at the birth of a baby—especially of a son, since sons were necessary to inherit land. Firstborn sons had special family privilege—they got a double portion of the inheritance.

Like the pagan people around them, many Hebrews considered wives to be like property—something men owned. Men could divorce their wives, but wives could not divorce their husbands. The Old Testament commandments, however, teach that equal honor was to be given to fathers and mothers. Children are told to obey their parents and listen to the teachings of both father and mother (Exod. 20:12; 21:15, 17; Prov. 1:8; 6:20-21; 20:20; Eph. 6:1-3; Col. 3:20).

Marriage customs were different in Bible times from our day. Almost all marriages were arranged by parents. The man paid a price, either in money or work, for his bride. This did not mean that the husbands and wives did not love each other. There are many beautiful pictures in the Old Testament of love and respect in marriage. The Song of Solomon is a series of beautiful love poems.

In the New Testament times, families were smaller. By then most men had only one wife, and families in cities lived in small houses.

The New Testament gives clear teachings about family relationships. In Ephesians 5 Paul tells Christians that family members should treat each other with love and respect. He says in a letter to Timothy that families should also take care of each other.

Jesus had a family with brothers and sisters. He apparently stayed with them until His baptism. One of the last things He did before He died was to make sure someone would take care of His mother (Matt. 13:55, 56; Mark 6:3).

The New Testament uses family relationships to describe our relationship with God and with other Christians. God is our Father, and we are members of His family (Eph. 2:19). Christians sometimes call themselves brothers and sisters.

The first churches were formed in the New Testament when families of Christians met together in houses to study God's Word, pray, worship, and break bread (share a meal).

FAMINE

means there is not enough food in a country to keep people alive. Famines can be caused by war, lack of rain, bad storms, or by attacking insects (such as locusts) that eat crops. The Bible tells about many famines, including the one in Genesis 41 that brought Joseph's brothers to Egypt to look for food.

In Matthew 24:7, Jesus said that famines will be a sign that His Second Coming is near.

See Genesis 12:10; Isaiah 14:30; Acts 11:28.

FASTING

means going without food or water for a period of time. The Bible mentions several reasons for fasting. Some people fast during times of grief or repentance. Others fast to gain God's answer to prayer or to draw closer to God. Isaiah warned the Israelites that fasting was useless unless their attitudes and actions were right.

Fasting was also practiced in the New Testament. Some religious Jews, including Pharisees, fasted every Monday and Thursday. Jesus fasted when He was in the wilderness for forty days after His baptism (Matt. 4:2). He also warned His followers that fasting should be private, not to show how religious they were (Matt. 6:16-18). Christians in the early church often fasted when faced with a big decision or special need (Acts 13:2-3).

See also Exodus 34:28.

FATHER

has different meanings in the Bible. The most common meaning is the male parent. Fathers in the Bible were important and respected leaders in their families.

Father is also used in the Bible to refer to ancestors. The fathers of Israel were men like Abraham, Isaac, Jacob, and David. When David died, I Kings 2:10 says that ". . . he slept with his fathers."

Sometimes people used *father* as a title of respect for older men outside their own family. In I Samuel 24:11 David called Saul "my father" even though he wasn't his son. In the early Christian church, some of the older, respected leaders were called fathers.

Father can also refer to a person who is the first one to do something. Jubal was the "father of musicians (Gen. 4:21)."

Abraham is said to be "the father of all who believe" (Rom. 4:11). And, Satan, says John 8:44, "is the father of lies."

In a very special sense the Bible uses Father to describe God. "Have we not all one father?" asks Malachi 2: 10. "Has not one God created us?"

In the New Testament, God is the Father of Jesus. All who believe in Jesus become "children of God." We follow Jesus' example and pray to God as "our Father who art in heaven" (Matt. 6:9).

FATHERLESS

describes boys or girls whose parents had died. They were also called orphans. The Israelites took special care of these children, giving them gifts of money and food. Both the prophets in the Old Testament, and James in the New Testament, said that God wants us to take care of the fatherless. See Deuteronomy 14:29; 24:19-21; Jeremiah 22:3; James 1:27.

FEASTS

were holidays when the Jewish people celebrated God's goodness to them. Some feasts were like huge parties; the people ate, drank, sang, had parades, danced, and praised God. There were three main feasts each year: the feast of Passover, the feast of Weeks, and the feast of tabernacles. During these three feasts all Jewish men thirteen years and older traveled to Jerusalem for the celebration if possible.

The Feast of Passover was the most important feast for the Hebrew people. It was held during the middle of April to celebrate God's rescue of the Hebrews out of slavery in Egypt. The name *Passover* comes from the way the death angel in Exodus 12 "passed over" the Hebrew homes on that terrible night in

God's death angel will pass over homes with lamb's blood on the door frame.

Egypt when all of the firstborn sons were killed. That plague—the tenth and final one God sent—convinced Pharaoh to let the Israelites go.

The Passover has been celebrated by the Jews for thousands of years. It is a very holy day. It begins at sundown on the fourteenth day of the Jewish month Nisan and lasts for twenty-four hours. During Bible times, special meals were prepared using unleavened bread (to remind them of the bitter slavery they had endured in Egypt). Wine was served, and a lamb was cooked. The story of Israel's deliverance was told, songs of thanksgiving were sung, and prayers of praise were spoken to God.

In New Testament times, the feast of the unleavened bread, which lasts seven days, was celebrated with Passover, making it an eight-day feast.

Passover also has a special meaning for Christians. Jesus' last supper with His disciples was the Passover meal. Jesus washed His disciples' feet and told them to "eat my body and drink my blood." That part of the meal became the Christian Communion, (Lord's Supper). "Christ is our Passover [lamb] who is sacrificed for us," Paul wrote to the Corinthians.

Today many Jewish people still faithfully celebrate the Passover with special meals in their homes. It is a time when Jews remember that God took them out of slavery in Egypt to give them freedom in the promised land.

See Exodus 12; I Corinthians 5:7.

The Feast of Weeks or **Pentecost** was also called the feast of the harvest, because it was a one-day celebration at the end of the wheat harvest. The feast was held fifty days after Passover. The Jewish people sang and danced and gave sacrifices to thank God for watching over their crops. Later they also used this occasion to thank God for giving them His Law.

The feast of weeks or Pentecost received a new meaning for Christians when the Holy Spirit came to the church on that day. Many churches celebrate Pentecost to thank God for sending His Holy Spirit.

See Exodus 23:16; 34: 22; Numbers 28: 26-31; Acts 2.

The Feast of Tabernacle or **Booths** was an important eight-day celebration in autumn. It began five days after the Day of Atonement.

Because this feast was held at the end of the final harvest of olives and fruits, and because it was near the beginning of the Jewish year, the people celebrated it like Thanksgiving and New Year's Day rolled into one. They thanked God for giving them good crops, and they asked Him to watch over them in the year ahead.

During the feast of booths the people camped out in little shelters (called "booths"). They did this to remember how their ancestors had lived while they wandered in the desert for forty years.

Jesus secretly traveled to Jerusalem one year to go to the feast of booths. This feast has always been a very happy occasion for Hebrew people.

See Exodus 23: 16; Leviticus 23: 33-36; Numbers 29:12-32; John 7.

Besides these three main feasts, the Jewish people also have other feasts during the year.

The Feast of Dedication or **Lights** is a happy, exciting holiday that lasts for eight days in December. It is also called Hanukkah (or Chanukah), which is the

Hebrew word for "dedication." This celebration is to remember how Judas Maccabeus rescued, cleansed, and rededicated the temple in Jerusalem in 165 B.C.

During the feast of dedication the Israelites marched to the synagogues carrying lighted torches. Singing and dancing filled the air with music. At the synagogues the children were told about the brave deeds of Judas Maccabeus.

Jesus was in Jerusalem for one feast of dedication, according to John 10:22.

Jews today still celebrate this feast.

The Feast of the New Moon was a one-day festival held in October to celebrate the first day of the Hebrew New Year. (It was on the first new moon of the Hebrew month Tishri.) On this day silver trumpets were blown all during the day. All work was stopped, special sacrifices were offered to God, and families gathered together for a special meal. It became a Jewish custom to have a public reading of God's Law. The people celebrated after the Law was read, remembering that God has always kept His promises to His people. See Numbers 28:11-15; 2 Kings 4:23; Amos 8:5.

The Feast of Purim (*POOR-im*) celebrates the victory of Queen Esther and Mordecai over Haman, the wicked Persian who wanted to kill all the Jews. This two-day festival is held in the middle of March. It begins with all the people gathering in the synagogue to hear a reading of the Book of Esther. (Whenever Haman's name is mentioned, the people boo and hiss!) Afterward large parties are held with much singing, dancing, eating, and excitement. Prayers of thanksgiving are also given to God for rescuing the Jewish people. See Esther 9:1-10, 20-32.

The Hebrews built outdoor "booths" once a year.

FELIX *(FEE-licks)*

was the governor of Judea during Paul's missionary travels. His full name was Antonius Felix. He was a friend of the Roman emperors Claudius and Nero. He was known as a cruel and treacherous tyrant who had "the power of a king with the mind of a slave." He seduced Drusilla, the wife of the king of Emessa, and later married her.

When Felix and Drusilla were in Caesarea, Paul was brought before them after being arrested in Jerusalem. Paul pleaded for freedom, but Felix kept him in prison, hoping that Paul would give him money. Paul didn't, and he was still in prison when Felix was replaced as governor in A.D. 59. See Acts 23:24—25:14.

FESTUS *(FESS-tuss)*

was a governor of Judea. After hearing Paul's defense, Festus wanted to send Paul back to Jerusalem for trial. Paul preferred to go to Rome to be judged by the emperor, so Festus allowed him to go. Festus died in Judea in A.D. 62. See Acts 24:27—26:32.

FIG TREE (see *Plants*)

FIRKIN (see *Measure*)

FIRSTBORN

was the oldest child in a family. A firstborn son had special privileges in a Hebrew family (Gen. 43:33). He became the leader of the family after the father died, and he received twice as much inheritance as his brothers. This birthright Esau sold to Jacob (Gen. 25:21-34).

Israel was called the Lord's firstborn among the other nations, meaning the Israelites had a special relationship with God (Exod. 4: 22).

FIRSTLING *(FIRST-ling)*

was the first lamb or calf born to a mother. The firstlings were brought as sacrifices to God. Abel gave God the firstlings of his flock, and God was pleased with this sacrifice. See Genesis 4:4; Exodus 13:2; Leviticus 27:26.

FLOOD

refers to the time when God sent water to destroy wicked people. Only Noah and his family and the animals that were with them on the boat (or ark) were saved from the Flood.

When God saw how wicked people had become, He was sorry He had made them. He decided to destroy them all in a flood. But Noah was a good man who trusted God, so God warned Noah about the coming destruction. God told Noah how to build a huge boat (Gen. 6:11-22). Noah spent many years building the boat. When it was finished, Noah and his family and pairs of every kind of bird and animal entered the ark.

FISH

of many kinds were found in Palestine during Bible times. Fish were an important food for the Jewish people. Hooks, nets, and spears were used to catch fish.

Fish are mentioned in many parts of the Bible. One of the plagues against Egypt was the killing of all fish in the Nile River (Exod. 7:20, 21). Jonah was swallowed by a great fish (Jonah 1—2). And at least seven of Jesus' disciples were fishermen (Matt. 4:18-22; Luke 21:1-3). After He was resurrected, Jesus appeared to His disciples while they were fishing (John 21:1-8).

The fish is also used as a symbol. When it was illegal to worship Jesus, Christians in the Roman Empire used secret codes to announce meeting places. One of those secret codes was the Greek word for *fish*: *ICHTHUS*. The letters of that word in Greek were also the first letters of the words "Jesus, Messiah, God, Son, Savior."

Noah, his family, and the animals spent more than a year on the ark.

Then the water came (Gen. 7:1—8:12). It rained for almost six weeks without stopping! Water also rushed up from below the ground. Soon everything was under water. It stayed that way for more than a year. The people and animals outside the ark drowned.

Noah's ark finally landed on the mountains of Ararat. (There are mountains in Turkey today with this name.) Noah sent out birds to see if the land was drying up, and when a dove came back with a freshly picked olive leaf, Noah knew the Flood was over.

Noah thanked God by building an altar and offering sacrifices. God made a covenant—an agreement—with Noah that He would never again send a flood to destroy the earth (Gen. 9 8-17). The sign of the covenant was the rainbow. It still reminds us of God's promise.

The Flood is an important Bible event. Stories about a huge flood are also found in other ancient writings.

See also Matthew 24:37-39; Hebrews 11:7; I Peter 3:20; II Peter 2:5; 3:3-7.

FLOUR

was crushed grain something like we use today, except that flour in Bible times was brown. The Israelites used flour in baking, even though it was very expensive. Sarah used flour to make cakes for three special visitors in Genesis 18: 6.

FLUTE (see *Musical Instruments*)

FOOD

in Bible times did not have much variety. Only rich people ate meat regularly. Poor people served meat when they had important guests, or at special celebrations, or when they made a sacrifice to God.

Then a certain portion was given as a sacrifice, another portion to the priest, and the rest was eaten by the family. Since there was no refrigeration, meat had to be eaten within a few hours after the animal was killed, or else it would spoil.

People did not usually drink milk, but made it into cheese and yogurt. Cows and goats were raised for their milk rather than meat. Sheep were raised primarily for their wool rather than to be eaten.

The most common food in the Bible was bread. It was the main part of every meal. Poor people usually had bread made from barley. People with more money ate bread made of wheat.

Vegetables were not common, except for onions, cucumbers, leeks, garlic, beans, and lentils. Beans and lentils were used in soups and sometimes mixed with flour to make bread.

Grapes were the most common fruit, and they were usually made into wine. Olives were made into oil. The only fruits that were normally eaten raw were figs, pomegranates, and perhaps apples.

The Hebrews knew that all food was a gift of God, because unless God sent rain, there would be nothing to eat.

Food was important not only for staying alive, but also as a sign of friendship. People who were not friends never ate together. People who ate together were expected to be loyal to each other. All kinds of agreements were completed or sealed by eating together.

FOOT

is the lowest part of a person's body, and so it is often used in word pictures to teach us to be humble. Mary sat at Jesus' feet to show she was a learner (Luke 8:35; 10:39). The sinful woman who kissed

Jesus' feet and washed them with her tears was showing her humility (Luke 7:38). God told Moses to stand barefoot near the burning bush because he was standing on holy ground (Exod. 3:5).

Feet are also what we use to get us from place to place. The Bible uses *feet* in word pictures about going in the direction God wants us to go, or standing on something we know won't fall apart, like God's Word (Ps. 18:36; 40:2; 101, 105, 119:59).

FOOT WASHING

was a special way to greet guests after they traveled. People traveled mainly by walking on the hot, dusty roads of Israel. After a long journey, their feet would be tired and dirty. Servants would use a bowl of cool water and fresh towels to bathe the feet of the travelers.

Jesus washed the feet of His twelve disciples at the Last Supper. He was teaching them that we must be each other's servants. Some churches today have foot washing services to remember Jesus' example.

See Genesis 18:4; I Samuel 25:41; John 13:1-17; I Timothy 5:10.

FORERUNNER

was a scout or messenger in the army who ran ahead of the chariots to clear the path and to announce that the troops (or the king) were coming. John the Baptist was a forerunner for Jesus; he prepared the way for Him. Jesus is a forerunner for us; He has gone ahead into the presence of God to prepare the way for us. See Malachi 3:1; Matthew 3:11; 11:10; Hebrews 6:20.

Jesus washed the disciples' feet.

FORGIVENESS

refers to blotting out sin and guilt. After this happens, the person who did wrong can again be friends with the one to whom he did the wrong.

All people sin against God. If they are to be friends with God and enjoy His love and kindness, they must be forgiven by God.

When people do wrong things to each other, forgiveness cannot really come until the person who did wrong is willing to pay his debt or make up in any way he can for what he did. However, there is no way we can make up to God for our sins. Instead, Jesus came to pay our debt. He gave His life in our place so we could be friends with God. Our sins and guilt have been blotted out if we let Jesus take our place.

However, Jesus said that God does not forgive our sins unless we are willing to forgive one another.

See Matthew 18:23-35; 6:12; Colossians 1:13, 14.

FORNICATION *(FOR-nih-KAY-shun)*

means sexual intercourse between people who are not married to each other. The Bible says fornication is sin. In the Bible, the words *fornication, adultery, immorality* and *harlotry* mean almost the same thing.

In the Old Testament, *fornication* or *harlotry* was sometimes a word picture of how Israel was disloyal to God and went after other gods .

See Ezekiel 16:15-43; Matthew 15:19; I Corinthians 5:9-13; Hebrews 13:4.

FOUNTAIN

is a spring of water flowing out of an opening in a hillside. Because Israel was such a dry land, fountains were very important. Towns and cities often grew up around fountains, springs, or wells.

Because water is so important for life, the words *fountain, spring,* and *well* are often used as word pictures of spiritual truths. For example, Jesus said, "The water that I shall give him will become in him a spring of water welling up to eternal life."

See Deuteronomy 8:7; Psalm 36:9; John 4:14; Revelation 21:6.

FOX (see *Animals*)

FRANKINCENSE *(FRANK-in-sense)*

was a sweet-smelling perfume made from the sap that comes from a terebinth tree. These trees grew in warm, dry places. The Israelites used frankincense in religious ceremonies, and it was one of the special gifts that the wise men gave to Jesus in Bethlehem. See Exodus 30:34; Isaiah 60:6; Matthew 2:11.

FRIENDSHIP

was very important in the Bible. David and Jonathan were such close friends that the Bible says their souls were "knit together" (II Chron. 20:7). The Book of Ruth tells of the beautiful friendship between Ruth and her mother-in-law, Naomi. Jesus called Lazarus His friend (John 11:11).

One of the deepest and highest friendships in the Bible was between Abraham and God (Isa. 41:8; Jas. 2:23).

Jesus told the people who followed Him, "You are my friends if you do what I command you" (John 15:14).

"A friend loves at all times," says Proverbs 17:17. The writer of Ecclesiastes says that it is good to have a friend, because if either of them fell, the one

FRONTLETS *(FRONT-lets)*

were tiny pouches of leather that Hebrew men wore on their foreheads during prayer. Frontlets were also called phylacteries *(fil-LAK-tur-eez)*. In the pouch were pieces of parchment with the words of Exodus 13:1-16, Deuteronomy 6:4, and Deuteronomy 11:13-21 on them. Jesus criticized some Jews for using the frontlets to show other people how religious they were. Orthodox Jews still wear frontlets when they pray (Matt. 23: 5).

Some Jews in Israel thy still wear phylacteries.

could lift up his friend (Eccl. 4:4-12).

FRUIT

in Bible times was mostly grapes, olives, figs, and pomegranates.

Fruit is often used as a word picture referring to the outcome or results of actions. The Bible speaks of the "fruit of righteousness" or the "fruit of lies."

Jesus said that people would be known by their fruits. If we let the Holy Spirit rule our lives, our fruit will be such things as love, joy, and peace.

See Isaiah 3:10; Matthew 7:16-20; Luke 1:42; Galatians 5:22-23.

FURLONG (see *Measure*)

FURNACES

in Bible times were not used in houses. They were used for baking pottery and bricks; for melting silver, gold, copper, brass, and bronze; and for smelting iron and other ores. They were of many sizes and were usually made of stone and brick.

Solomon built huge smelting furnaces. Daniel's three friends, Shadrach, Meshach, and Abednego, were thrown into a furnace for not obeying Nebuchadnezzar; but God rescued them. Jesus compared the agony of hell with the "furnace of fire."

See Proverbs 17:3; Daniel 3:13-30; Matthew 13:42.

Gideon's raid on the Midianites was one of the most unusual attacks in the history of warfare.

GABRIEL *(GAY-bree-ul)*
is an angel mentioned four times in the Bible. Each time, he came with an important message from God.

He appeared twice to Daniel to explain visions that Daniel had (Dan. 8:16-26; 9:21-27). He also appeared to Zechariah, the priest, in 6 B.C. to say that he and his wife would have a son who should be called John (Luke 1:8-20). The son became John the Baptist.

Gabriel's most important appearance was to Mary (Luke 1:26-38). He told her she would have a child who would be the Son of God; His name was to be Jesus.

Gabriel once called himself "Gabriel, who stands in the presence of God."

GAD

was the name of two different men: the seventh son of Jacob, and one of David's prophets.

1. Jacob's son founded one of the twelve tribes of Israel (Gen. 30:9-11). The tribe of Gad was made up mostly of shepherds. They asked Moses to let them stay on the east side of the Jordan River when most of the Israelites went into Canaan (Num. 32:1-36). Moses said they could if their men would promise to fight in the battles to conquer Canaan. They did as Moses said.

2. The prophet Gad was a court prophet who helped David during most of his life. Usually court prophets only prophesied good things to their king. But Gad delivered God's message to David whether it was good news or bad.

Gad once gave David advice on how to escape when Saul was trying to kill him (I Sam. 22:5).

After David became king, he sinned against God by counting his fighting men. Then Gad brought God's message about his punishment (II Sam. 24:11-17; I Chron. 21:9-17). Gad also told David to build an altar to God, and God stopped the terrible disease that was killing thousands of people (II Sam. 24:18).

Gad was also a musician and a writer. He helped David arrange musical services for the temple and wrote a history of David's reign in Israel (II Chron. 29:25; I Chron. 29:29).

GAIUS (GAY-us)

is the name of three or four people in the New Testament:

1. A Corinthian man whom Paul baptized—probably the man in whose house the church met (Rom. 16:23; I Cor. 1:14).

2. A man from Macedonia who went with Paul on his third missionary journey (Acts 19:29). Some people think that the Gaius who is mentioned in Acts 20:4 is the same man. However, this Gaius is from Derbe, in Asia Minor, not Macedonia (a part of Greece).

3. The man to whom the apostle John wrote III John. John praised him for his kindness to traveling preachers of the Gospel (III John 3-8).

GALATIA (guh-LAY-shuh)

was a large province in Asia Minor (now Turkey). Paul visited Galatia on his missionary journeys and wrote one of his letters (Galatians) to the churches in that province.

GALATIANS (guh-LAY-shuns)

is a letter the apostle Paul wrote to the churches in the province of Galatia in Asia Minor. Some of these churches were at Antioch of Pisidia, Iconium, Lystra, and Derbe. They had all been started by Paul during his first missionary journey.

The Christians there had been growing well in their knowledge of the Christian message when Paul left them.

Some of the Jewish teachers came who claimed to be Christians. Their teachings were not like Paul's. They said that Gentile Christians must be circumcised and must keep all the rituals of the Old Testament if they were to be Christians.

The new Christians in Galatia were very confused, so Paul wrote this letter to try to help them (Gal. 1:11, 12; 2:18). He reminded them that Abraham was made right with God through faith (Gal. 3)—before the Old Testament Law of Moses was ever announced. Gentile Christians, he said, are the true "sons of Abraham." He also said that believers are now part of Christ. There is no place for race prejudice, sex prejudice, or class prejudice, because all believers are "one" (equal) in Christ.

The Letter to the Galatians says that the Old Testament Law was given so people would know that they are sinners. But sins are forgiven through faith in Christ. Christians are free to follow Christ.

But Paul also told the Galatians that they were not free to sin or live in ways that did not please God. The Spirit of God does not lead people to sin, but to be gentle and loving (Gal. 5:16-26). Galatians 5:22 says, "The fruit of the Spirit is love, joy, peace, patience, kindness, goodness, faithfulness, gentleness, self-control."

GALILEE *(GAL-uh-lee)*

was the northern province of Israel in Jesus' day. Jesus grew up in Nazareth, a city of Galilee, and preached His first sermon in the synagogue there. Almost all His disciples were from Galilee.

The southern part of Galilee, where Jesus grew up, had more cities and people than the northern part. Southern Galilee had fertile valleys and a mild climate that were good for farming. The

GALILEE, SEA OF *(GAL-uh-lee)*

is sometimes called the Sea of Gennesaret, the Sea of Tiberias, and the Sea of Chinnereth. It is a freshwater lake about thirteen miles long and eight miles wide

The Sea of Galilee still has its fishing boats.

in northern Israel near where Jesus grew up.

During the time of Jesus, the Sea of Galilee had rich fishing industries. Four of Jesus' disciples were men who fished in the Sea of Galilee (Matt. 4:18-22; Luke 5:1-11).

Many of Jesus' sermons and miracles took place along the shore. The sea was known for its sudden and violent storms. Jesus rescued His disciples in two such storms (Matt. 14:22-33; Mark 4:35-41; John 6:16-21). Jesus sometimes taught large crowds from a boat anchored near the shore (Mark 4:1).

During Jesus' time there were nine large, thriving cities around the lake. Only Tiberias still exists, plus one tiny village, Magdala.

WHAT DID JESUS PLAY?

northern part was not as good for farming because it was more hilly. Olive trees, however, grew well there.

GALLIO *(GAL-ee-oh)*

was a Roman official known for his fairness. Some Jews in Corinth brought the apostle Paul before Gallio, saying that he persuaded people to worship "contrary to the law." But Gallio refused to listen to their charges, since they had to do with the Jewish religion, and Paul was freed
See Acts 18:12-17.

GAMALIEL *(guh-MAY-lee-ul)*

was a famous Jewish Pharisee and teacher who lived in Jerusalem. The apostle Paul was one of his students before Paul became a Christian.

When the church was just beginning in Jerusalem, the Pharisees and priests ordered the apostles not to preach about Christ. The apostles said they must obey God rather than men. The Pharisees and priests were so angry they wanted to kill them. The highly respected Gamaliel advised against it, saying that if this new teaching were just the idea of the apostles, it would die by itself. If it were of God, no one could stop it anyway. The council took his advice.
See Acts 5:27-40; 22:3.

GAMES

were part of life in Bible times, even though only a few kinds are mentioned. Music and dancing were common, both as part of celebrations and as part of worship (Jer. 31:4, 13, 14; Luke 15:25).

The Old Testament frequently refers to riddles so we can guess that they were popular (Judg. 14:12-18; Prov. 1:5, 6;

139

GAZA *(GAY-zuh)*

was a Philistine city on the coast of the Mediterranean Sea. It still exists, but is now called Chazzah. It is the most important city on the Gaza Strip in the southwest corner of Israel.

Gaza is best known in the Bible as the city where Samson died. He pulled down the pillars of the temple of Dagon and killed the crowd inside—including himself (Judg. 16:21-30).

The city was not fully defeated by the Israelites until the time of Hezekiah, about 713 B.C. (II Kings 18:8).

Gaza is mentioned in the New Testament only once. Philip, the evangelist, was told to go to the road that ran from Jerusalem to Gaza (Acts 8:26). There he met an Ethiopian who wanted to know about Christ.

Samson's last act was to collapse Gaza's temple.

Ezek. 17:2). Archaeologists have dug up many game boards from Old Testament times. Some were quite difficult. Chess is a very old game and may have been played in Israel. Some old carvings from Egypt suggest that boys played tug-of-war and girls juggled balls.

In the New Testament, Jesus speaks of children playing make-believe weddings and funerals with music (Matt. 11:1-19; Luke 7:31-35).

The New Testament also refers to the Greek footraces and other contests that were well known in that time (I Cor. 9: 24-27; II Tim. 2: 5). These included chariot races, throwing the discus and javelin, wrestling, boxing, and horse racing.

GARDEN OF EDEN (see *Eden*)

GARDEN OF GETHSEMANE
(see *Gethsemane*)

GATE (see *City Gate*)

GENESIS *(JEN-uh-sis)*

is the first book of the Bible. It is a book about beginnings. It tells how God created the world and people. It tells about the beginning of sin, the beginning of God's judgment on sin, and His mercy to sinners. It also tells about the beginning of the nation of Israel, from which the Redeemer of the world—Jesus Christ—would be born many years later.

Genesis 1 and 2 tell about the creation of the world. The words do not tell exactly *how* God created, but they state clearly that God did it and that He cared deeply about what He had made. He called everything He made "very good."

God had close fellowship with Adam and Eve, who were made "in the image of God." That fellowship was destroyed when Adam and Eve sinned. But God began His work of redemption with them. He did not destroy them, but He sent them away from the garden of Eden. God said the seed of the woman (Jesus) would crush the head of the serpent (Satan). This was the first promise that Satan and sin would finally be conquered.

Genesis also tells about God sending the Flood because people became so sinful. But God was merciful again and saved Noah and his family and some of each kind of animal so life on earth could go on.

Genesis also tells about the beginning of the Hebrew people. They came from Abraham, "the man of faith," his son Isaac, and his grandson Jacob. Jacob's son Joseph helped all the people come to Egypt. He got food for them during the years when the farmers couldn't raise enough.

GENTILES *(JEN-tiles)*

means all people who are not Jewish by nationality or religion. In Bible times, Jews and Gentiles did not have much to do with each other. The Gentiles often persecuted the Jews for their religion, and the Jews hated the Gentiles and looked down on them.

Jesus did most of His teaching and miracle working among Jews. He rarely taught Gentiles, but He healed them when they came to Him (Luke 7:2-10; John 12:20-36). He healed the servant of a Gentile

The Garden of Gethsemanne is beside the church along the road (right center).

soldier. He taught Greeks who came to see Him.

After Jesus' death and resurrection, the church began to include both Jews and Gentiles who believed in Christ. The apostle Paul said that the gospel of Christ has broken down the wall between the two groups (Eph. 2:11-22).

The church today is made up mostly of Gentiles. But the people of God in Old Testament times were mostly Jews. It was through the Jews that God brought salvation to all people.

GETHSEMANE *(geth-SEM-uh-nee)*

was the garden where Jesus prayed just before He was arrested and then crucified. It was on the Mount of Olives, just outside Jerusalem. See Matthew 26:36-56; Mark 14:32-50; Luke 22:39-54.

GIANT

in the Bible refers to actual human beings (not make-believe creatures) who are large, tall, and powerful. Tribes of these very large people lived in Canaan

The Gibeonites tricked Joshua and his army by pretending to have come from a long distance.

before the Israelites conquered it (Num. 12:32-33). Perhaps Goliath, who fought David, was one of these (I Sam. 17:1-51). He was more than nine feet tall. Very large people are often called *Rephaim* or *Nephilim* in the Old Testament. There is no reference to these people in the New Testament.

Og, the king of Bashan, slept in a bed 9 cubits long and 4 cubits wide (13-1/2 feet by 6 feet). He was the last of the Rephaim. See Deuteronomy 3:11.

GIBEON *(GIB-ee-un)*

was a city in Canaan about fifteen miles west of Jerusalem. When the Gibeonites heard that the Israelites had defeated Jericho and other cities, they tricked Joshua into making a treaty with them (Josh. 9:3-27).

They said they had walked many days to come see Joshua. They showed him moldy bread and worn-out shoes as proof. So Joshua made a treaty not to destroy them. When Joshua discovered they lived in the area, he said they would have to become servants of the Israelites, but he would keep his word and see that they were not destroyed.

Later, others attacked the Gibeonites because they had made peace with Joshua. The Gibeonites called for help, and Joshua came with his army. God sent giant hailstones on the enemies and miraculously lengthened the day to give the Israelites time to defeat them (Josh. 10:1-14).

Saul once tried to kill the Gibeonites in spite of the treaty, but God sent punishment on his family as a result (II Sam. 21:1-14).

GIDEON *(GID-ee-un)*

was one of Israel's great ruler-judges. During his time the Midianites made life miserable for the people of Israel, stealing their cattle and destroying all their crops.

One day as Gideon was working, God's angel appeared to him and told him that the Lord would help him defeat the Midianites. God told Gideon to tear down the altars to false gods and build an altar to the true God. Gideon did this, but the people in Ophrah, his city, were so angry they wanted to kill him.

Gideon was afraid to fight the Midianites. He asked God to let him know for sure that God would lead him. Gideon put a sheep fleece on the ground. In the morning the fleece was soaking wet, but the ground was dry. The next night, the fleece was dry, but the ground was wet. Gideon was satisfied that God would be with him.

Gideon called for men to help him defeat the Midianites, and 22,000 responded. God said it was too many. By a series of tests, Gideon cut the number to 300.

Gideon gave each of the 300 men a trumpet and a jar with a torch inside. One hundred men went to each of three sides of the Midianites' army camp. They all broke their pitchers and blew trumpets at the same time. The Midianites were so frightened and confused they began killing each other. Gideon's men won a

Gideon and his servants tore down an altar to a false god one night.

Ruth first met Boaz by gleaning in his fields during harvest.

great victory.

Later, the Israelites wanted to make Gideon king, but he refused. He said God should rule over them. The Israelites had peace for forty years. But after Gideon died, the Israelites again began to worship false gods.

See Judges 6:1—8:33.

GLEANING *(GLEEN-ing)*

means going into the fields after the main harvesting to find whatever has been missed. In Old Testament Law, farmers were told they should let the poor come into their fields and glean the remaining grain (Lev. 19:9; 23:22; Deut. 24:19-21).

GOD

lives, the Bible says. It never tries to prove God exists; it assumes that everyone knows He does.

The Bible shows us what God is like by letting us see what He does and how He responds to people and the things they do. But the most important way we know who God is and what He is like is to see Jesus Christ. Jesus Christ was God in a human body. He said, "He who has seen me has seen the Father; I am in the Father and the Father [is] in me."

Many names are used for God in the Bible. These names show certain qualities about God. Psalm 23:1 says "The Lord is my shepherd," showing that He cares for His people. "The Lord, your healer" is a name God gave Himself in Exodus 15:26.

The Bible tells us many things about God:

1. *God loves us* (John 3:16).

2. *God is everywhere.* He is not confined to one place.(Ps. 139:7-12).

3. *God knows everything.* He is truth itself (Job 28:20-28; Titus 1:2).

4. *God has always been and always will be.* He neither began (like a baby is born) nor will He end (He will not die) (Isa. 44: 6).

5. *God is holy.* Unlike people, He has never sinned, and could never sin (Lev. 11:44).

6. *God is angry with sin* because it has spoiled the perfect world He created. It

also hurt the friendship He could have had with people. Someday God will destroy Satan, the author of sin.

7. *God is Spirit.* He does not have a physical body as people have, although Christ had a physical body when He was on earth (John 4:24).

The Bible does not tell us everything about God. God is so big, so great, so wonderful that our minds can never understand all about him. But we can understand enough to know that God wants us to believe Him, to trust Him, to love Him, to obey Him. We can start by learning about Jesus, who came to earth to be our Savior and to reveal God to us.

GODLINESS, GODLY
(GOD-lee-ness, GOD-lee)
means having an attitude of respect and reverence toward God and obeying Him. See I Timothy 2:2; 4:7-8; 6:3, 5, 6, 11.

GOLD
is mentioned hundreds of times in the Bible—from Genesis to Revelation.

Gold was valuable in early times for the same reason it is valuable now—it is beautiful, it is almost indestructible, and it is scarce.

In Bible times it was used for jewelry, for money, and to decorate fine furniture, pottery, spoons, and other household things. But its main use was in decorating palaces and temples and the things used inside them.

The word *gold* is also sometimes a word picture to describe heaven.

See Genesis 2:11, 12; Exodus 25:3, 11; Matthew 2:11; Revelation 21:15, 18, 21.

GOLDEN CALF
was an image Aaron made while Moses was on the mountain receiving the Ten Commandments from God. The people

GOLIATH *(guh-LIE-uth)*
was a huge Philistine soldier, more than nine feet tall. In a battle, Goliath challenged the Israelites to send one man to fight him instead of having the armies fight. When no one from the Israelite army dared to go, David, the young shepherd boy, volunteered. He believed God would save him from Goliath.

With his sling and a smooth stone, David hit Goliath in the forehead. Goliath fell to the ground. David then ran to him and killed him with Goliath's own sword.

David became more and more popular after this, and Saul began to get jealous of him.

See I Samuel 17:1-58.

had become impatient because Moses had been gone so long. The statue was probably similar to the Egyptian bull-calf images that the people had known. Moses said Aaron's act was a terrible sin (Exod. 32:1-35).

Much later, King Jeroboam made two golden calves (I Kings 12:25-33; Hos. 8:5, 6; 13:2). After the Hebrew people were divided into two countries, he did not want his people to go to the temple in Jerusalem to worship because it was in Judah. So he made new places of worship in Dan and Bethel and created golden calves for the people to worship. This was sinful and is mentioned several times in the Old Testament as an example of Israel's going away from God.

GOLDEN RULE

is what we call Jesus' command, "As you wish that men would do to you, do so to them" (Luke 6:31; Matt. 7:12).

GOLGOTHA (GOL-gah-thuh)

is an Aramaic word that means "place of the skull." It is the name of the place where Jesus was crucified. See Matthew 27:33; Mark 15:22; John 19:17.

GOMORRAH (guh-MOR-uh)

was one of two cities destroyed by God for its wickedness. It was located along the shores of the Dead Sea. God sent "fire and brimstone from heaven," probably in the form of an earthquake and volcanic explosion that destroyed the cities and caused the Dead Sea to spread over the remains. Lot's family, except for his wife, escaped. See Genesis 18:20. 21;19: 24-29.

GOPHER WOOD (GO-fur)

was the material from which Noah built the ark. Scholars do not know exactly what kind of wood it was. See Genesis 6:14.

GOSPEL (GOS-pul)

means "good news." The good news is that God has provided a way for any person to become His child, part of His family. This way is through faith in Jesus Christ, who gave His life so believers could live forever in fellowship with God. The story of the life, death, and resurrection of Jesus Christ is given in the four Gospels—the first four books of the New Testament.

GOSPELS

are the first four books of the New Testament—Matthew, Mark, Luke, and John. Each one tells about the life, death, and resurrection of Jesus Christ.

Information about the life of Christ was spread by word of mouth for about thirty years after the resurrection and ascension of Jesus. But the young church needed a more permanent record of the things Jesus said and did. The four Gospel writers each collected information from his own experiences and from other sources and each wrote his history.

We are not sure which Gospel was written first. Many believe the Gospel of Mark was first. It is the shortest and it emphasizes the things Jesus did.

The Gospel of Matthew seems to have been written especially for Jewish Christians. It tells more about Jesus' teachings than Mark's Gospel.

The Gospel of Luke tells more about Jesus' last visit to Jerusalem than do Matthew or Mark. It also tells more about some of the important women in the life of Jesus. It tells about Mary, the mother of Jesus, and Elizabeth, the mother of John the Baptist.

Moses was so furious about the golden calf that he smashed the stone tablets God had given him.

Matthew, Mark, and Luke are called the "synoptic" Gospels. Synoptic *(sin-OP-tik)* means "seen together." These three accounts tell many of the same things, sometimes in ways that are very much alike.

The Gospel of John is different from the Synoptics. Most writers think John wrote his Gospel last. He tells many things that the other writers did not tell—especially about the last week of Jesus' life.

GOVERNMENT

in Old Testament times had several forms. After the Israelites escaped from slavery in Egypt, they were supposed to

147

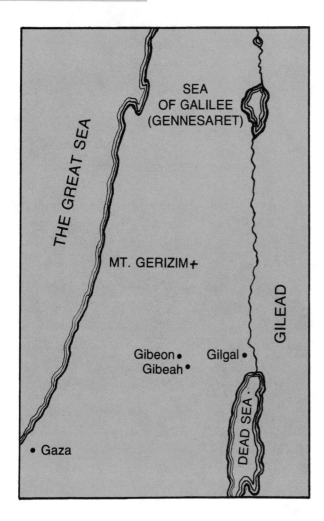

the nations around them. From that time until Israel was conquered by its enemies, there were kings. Some were good; some were evil. In 722 B.C. the northern kingdom of Israel was conquered by Assyria and most of its people forced to move to Assyria. In 586 B.C. the southern kingdom of Judah was conquered by Babylonia.

When some of the Israelites came back to Israel after their exile in Babylon, Persia was ruling Israel. However, the people had local officials who were called princes. The Jewish priests also had strong powers. Later, when the Syrians gained control of Israel, the high priest became the ruler with the most authority, even though he was always subject to Syria.

In New Testament times, Israel was ruled by the Romans. The Roman government, however, gave a great deal of self-rule to its various areas. Israel was divided into three parts—each part had a king appointed by Rome. In New Testament times, these local kings were part of the Herod family and were themselves Jewish.

The city of Jerusalem was ruled by the Sanhedrin—council of seventy Jewish religious leaders. They had power over most local matters, but they could not put anyone to death. That is why Jesus had to be brought before Pilate, the Roman procurator of the area.

The Jewish people hated the Roman rule—they wanted a kingdom of their own as they had under David. Some Jewish people became terrorists, called Zealots. Simon the Zealot was one of Jesus' disciples. Other people withdrew from all contact with the Romans and lived in small colonies or communes far

live under a theocracy. This means "rule of God." Moses received instructions from God, and the people were to carry out those instructions. Sadly, the people did not always obey what God said through Moses. During the forty years in the wilderness, Moses appointed people to help him judge or settle disputes.

After the Israelites settled in Canaan, they had "judges" as chief rulers. These judges were leaders in battle and rulers in peace. The Bible is not clear whether each judge was responsible for all the tribes or only a few. This period lasted for several hundred years.

Later the Israelites wanted a king, like

away from cities. The Sadducees worked right with the Romans.

In A.D. 68, about thirty-eight years after the crucifixion of Christ, the Jews rebelled against the Romans. The Romans crushed the rebellion and destroyed the city of Jerusalem.

GOVERNOR *(GUV-uh-ner)*

in the Bible means someone who is in charge of a country but who works for a higher ruler. Joseph was governor in Egypt, second only to Pharaoh. Pilate was a governor of Judea; he was appointed by the emperor of Rome. Governors could always be removed from office by whoever appointed them. See Genesis 42:6; Matthew 27:2; Acts 23:26.

GRASSHOPPER (see *Locust*)

GRAVE

is a place of burial. Since most of Israel is very rocky with only a small layer of topsoil, graves were usually holes in the limestone hills. Sometimes they were natural caves; other times they were holes dug into the hillsides. These places often became family graves. Abraham, Sarah, their son Isaac and his wife Rebekah, and their son Jacob and his wife Leah were all buried in the family cave at Machpelah (Gen. 23:19, 20; 49:29; 50:13).

If a person died a distance away from the family grave, he or she might be buried under the ground, as Rachel was buried beside an oak tree (Gen. 35:19, 20).

The grave of Jesus was cut into the side of a rocky hill. It was apparently the family grave of Joseph of Arimathea, but it had not been used at the time of the crucifixion (Matt. 27:59, 60).

GRAVE CLOTHES

were the strips of linen cloth that were wrapped around a body before burial. Hands and feet were tied with more pieces of linen, and another piece was placed over the face. This is the way Lazarus appeared when Jesus raised him from the dead (John 11:38-44).

GRAVEN IMAGE *(GRAY-vun IM-aj)*

was an idol shaped of wood, metal, or stone. Such idols were worshiped by the Canaanites, Babylonians, and Chaldeans. God told the Israelites in the Second Commandment that they were not to make such things, but they often disobeyed Him (Exod. 20:4; Isa. 45:20).

GREAT SEA

refers to the Mediterranean Sea—the largest body of water the Israelites knew. It is also called the Western Sea and the Sea of the Philistines, because the Philistines lived along its coast.

GREECE

is the peninsula and surrounding islands in the Mediterranean Sea east of Italy. People have lived in Greece since about 4000 B.C. From about 400 to 300 B.C., it was the most advanced civilization of its time. Ancient Greek culture, ideas, and form of government still influence our world.

By 300 B.C. Greek language and culture had spread over all the countries around the Mediterranean Sea. Greek language and culture were most important during New Testament times, although the ruling power was then the Roman Empire. Jesus and the disciples spoke mainly Aramaic, the native language of Israel, but the New Testament was written in Greek, and the Christian message spread around the world of that day in the Greek language.

During New Testament times, the area we now know as Greece was divided into two Roman provinces—Macedonia in the north, and Achaia in the south. The apostle Paul visited both parts on his missionary journeys.

People who lived in Greece or spoke the Greek language were called Grecians.

GREEK LANGUAGE

is the language in which most of the New Testament was originally written. It was the language of business all through the Roman Empire in New Testament times.

It was originally the language of just Greece. But when Alexander the Great was conquering the world (about 336-323 B.C.), the Greek language spread to all the countries around the Mediterranean. Even after Greece became part of the Roman Empire in 146 B.C., Greek remained the most important language of its time.

The gospel of Christ was able to spread much more rapidly because so many people in different countries understood the Greek language.

GREEKS

was a term used in New Testament times to mean people who were not Jews—it meant the same as "Gentiles." Paul uses it this way in Romans 1:16: "For I am not ashamed of the gospel; it is the power of God for salvation to every one who has faith, to the Jew first and also to the Greek."

HABAKKUK *(huh-BACK-uk)*

was a little-known prophet who wrote an Old Testament book sometime between 605 and 586 B.C. In this book, he asked why the Jewish people had become so wicked (Hab. 1—2). He told them to be sorry for their sins and to repent. If they didn't repent, he said, God would allow their enemies to the north, the Chaldeans, to destroy Judah. And then God would let the Chaldeans—who were even more wicked—be destroyed also.

But even after bad times come to God's people, Habakkuk said, they must remember God's faithfulness and trust Him. In his book, Habakkuk asked questions and then quietly listened to God's answers.

The last chapter of Habakkuk is a lovely poem that was meant to be sung (Hab. 3). The poem expressed Habakkuk's faith in God's power and control of the world. He is sure that God will do what is right, and that he can always rejoice in God.

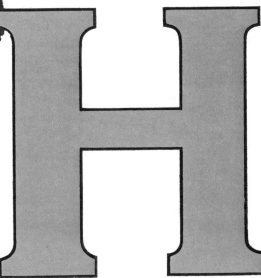

Hannah prayed to the Lord with such emotion that Eli the priest thought she was drunk. But she was simply pleading with the Lord for a son. God answered by giving her Samuel.

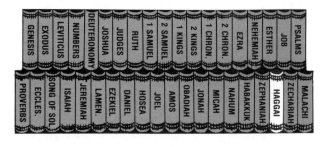

HAGAR (see box below)

HAGGAI *(HAG-ee-eye)*

was a prophet who wrote an Old Testament book about 520 B.C. The Jews had returned from captivity in Babylon and had started to rebuild the temple at Jerusalem. But they stopped work because the lack of rain had ruined their crops, and poverty had discouraged them. Haggai encouraged the Jews to go back to the rebuilding. He said they should work hard to complete the temple so the Jews could have a place to worship God.

The prophet told the people that the Lord promised to fill the building with His glory when it was finished (Hag. 2:7). Haggai reminded them of the glory given to the Lord by Solomon's temple long ago. He wrote about the power of the Lord over the whole universe, using a word picture of the Lord shaking the world (Hag. 2:21-23). Such a Lord deserves to be given glory, Haggai said.

HAIR

to some Jews in Old Testament times, was a picture of life itself because it keeps on growing. Some people, known as Nazirites, made vows never to cut their hair. Their long hair was presented to God as a picture of their lives being given to Him. Samson's strength was in this

HAGAR *(HAY-gar)*

was Sarah's Egyptian maid. She was also the mother of Abraham's son Ishmael. Sarah became jealous of Hagar and her son, even though it had been Sarah's idea for Hagar and Abraham to have the child. Sarah treated Hagar badly because Sarah wished she could have a son. Abraham did not stop Sarah from being mean to Hagar, and eventually Hagar took her son and ran away. But God promised Hagar that the descendants of her son Ishmael would become a large nation. When God heard Hagar crying in the wilderness, He said, "What troubles you, Hagar? Fear not. Arise, lift up the lad. I will make him a great nation."

When Hagar and young Ishmael had to leave Abraham's home, they almost died of thirst.

God was with Ishmael, and he grew to be a strong man and a good hunter. His descendants became a part of the Arab people, who still live in the Middle East.

See Genesis 16; 21:1-21.

dedication to God, so when his hair was cut, he lost his strength.

In both the Old Testament and the New Testament, hair was a mark of beauty (II Sam. 14:25, 26). In Old Testament times long hair on men was greatly admired, but in New Testament times men's hair was shorter and long hair on women was considered beautiful (I Cor. 11:14, 15).

HALLELUJAH (HAL-uh-LOO-yuh)

means "you, praise the Lord" in Hebrew.

HAM

is the name for three people or groups of people in the Bible:

1. Ham was the youngest son of Noah (Gen. 9:20—10:20). He lived through the Flood on the ark with his family. Because Ham looked at Noah when Noah was naked and drunk, his father later cursed him and his son. However, Ham still became the father of many nations.

2. The group of descendants from the original man named Ham is also called by his name. In the Psalms the word refers especially to those descendants of Ham who became Egyptians. See Psalms 78:51; 105:23; 106:22.

3. Ham was a city east of the Jordan River in Abraham's time (Gen. 14:5).

HAMAN (HAY-mun)

was a selfish man who tried to destroy the Jewish people during the days of Queen Esther. He was a prime minister of Persia about 480 B.C., but he wanted to be treated like a king. He wanted all the people to bow down to him when he passed by. Because Mordecai, a Jew, would bow only to God, Haman tried to trick the king into hanging Mordecai. But Queen Esther showed the king what Haman was up to,

and Haman himself was hanged on the gallows he had built for Mordecai. See Esther 7.

HANNAH (see box on page 154)

HANUKKAH (HANH-uh-kuh)

is a Jewish festival of dedication in early December. It reminds the Jewish people of one of their brave heroes, Judas Maccabeus. In 165 B.C. he removed the signs of pagan worship that had been placed in the temple by the Romans. Then he rededicated it for the worship of God. Jewish people each year light candles to remember God's miraculous help at that time.

HARAN (HAY-run)

was a city in northern Mesopotamia. Here Abraham buried his father, Terah, after they had both left the city of Ur (Gen. 11:31; 12:4). In this city Abraham's brother, Nahor, decided to stay while Abraham set off for Canaan. Later Abraham sent his servant to find a wife for his son Isaac among his relatives there (Gen. 24:4). Still later, Isaac's son Jacob fled to Haran and met his wives there (Gen. 29:4, 5).

HARP (see Musical Instruments)

HART (see Animals)

HATE

is a word used in two different ways in the Bible. God hates evil, idolatry, unfairness, and religious pretending (Deut. 12:31; Prov. 6:16-19). Believers also should hate these things. Even though God hates these sins, He still loves the persons who do them, and Christians are to do the

HANNAH *(HAN-uh)*

was a godly woman who dedicated her firstborn son Samuel to serve God. When Hannah had no children, she prayed for a long time that she would have a child. One feast day in the tabernacle she promised God that if He gave her a son she would bring him to serve in God's house.

Later, when Hannah and her husband Elkanah had a baby boy, Hannah dedicated him to the Lord. She was so happy she sang a beautiful song of praise. After her son Samuel moved into the tabernacle to serve the priest Eli there, the Lord gave Hannah three more sons and two daughters to love.

See I Samuel 1—2.

same. Christ said we are to love our enemies (Matt. 5:44). John says that anyone who hates his brother is a murderer and is in darkness of sin (I John 3:15).

Hate in the Bible is sometimes a word picture of turning away from something or someone. When God said He "hated" Esau (Mal. 1:2, 3), it meant that Esau and his descendants were not chosen by God as His special people.

Jesus used *hate* as an exaggerated word to show us that we should not love someone more than God. Jesus said in Luke 14:26, "If anyone comes to me and does not hate his own father and mother and wife and children and brothers and sisters, yes, and even his own life, he cannot be my disciple." However, He did not mean an active dislike or that we should not like our family members. He meant,

"Whoever does not put Me first—before even his family or himself—cannot be My disciple."

HEAD

in the Bible usually means the top part of a person's body. However, it is sometimes used in other ways.

1. The top of some object, such as a mountain, tower, ladder, lampstand, or pillar.

2. The leader or chief of a group.

3. The first in line, or the beginning. It is used this way when speaking of the "head of a tribe," the "head of a river," or the "head of a line of march."

When the Bible uses *head* as a word picture, it is important to try to decide which of these meanings it has. In Colossians 1:18, Christ is called the "head" of the church. We know that Christ is the leader of the church, but in this verse *head* does not mean "leader." It says He is the "beginning, the first-born from the dead," showing that the meaning here is "first in line, or the beginning or source of the church."

Our modern understanding of the body says that the head or brain is the place of thinking and decision making. However, people in the Bible used the word *heart* for this.

HEALING

was an important part of Jesus' ministry (Luke 4:33-39). When He sent His disciples out to tell about salvation, He gave them a special gift—the ability to heal as He did (Luke 9:1).

After Jesus left this earth, the leaders of the early church received gifts of healing (Acts 3:6, 16). "In the name of Jesus,"

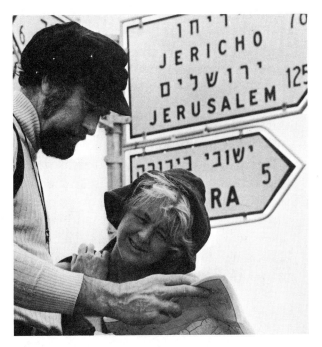

Road signs in Israel today are printed both in Hebrew and English.

sick people were restored to health by Jesus' followers.

HEART

in the Bible seldom means just the organ that pumps blood through a body. To people in Bible times, all the emotion or feelings of a person came from his heart. People talked about their hearts being glad (Prov. 27:11), sad (Neh. 2:2), fearful (Isa. 35:4), full of hatred (Lev. 19:17), full of love (Deut. 13:3), or having secrets (Ps. 44:21).

The heart was also considered the place of intelligence (I Chron. 29:18; Ps. 4:4; 10:6; Mark 2:6). The heart was the innermost part of a person, where all his thinking and deciding was done. So the heart was also the center of the will.

The heart, because it involved the emotions, mind, and will, was also the place of meeting with God. The Bible says God looks on the heart and knows its secrets (I Sam. 16:7; Ps. 44:21). A person speaks to God from his heart and can keep God's Word there (Deut. 30:14; Ps. 27: 8).

Sometimes heart also means a person's whole nature (Jer. 17:9).

HEAVEN *(HEV-un)*

in the Bible may mean either the part of the world that seems to arch over the earth, or it may mean the place where God lives.

1. Ancient peoples saw the universe as being in two parts: the earth and the heavens. They saw the heavens as a kind of dome over the earth. From the heavens—sometimes called the firmament—came the rain and the sunlight needed for life. The beauty of the heavens reminded the people of God (Ps. 8).

155

2. Heaven is also the place where God lives and where His children will live with Him after the resurrection (Gen. 28:17; Matt. 5:12). Right now, Jesus is in heaven praying for His followers and helping to run the universe (Heb. 9:24). We don't know where heaven is or what it looks like, but the word pictures in the Book of Revelation tell us it is a happy place where everyone enjoys God.

HEBREW *(HEE-bru)*

is a name for the nation that descended from Abraham and Sarah. It is also the name for any member of that nation as well as the language they speak. In our day, Hebrew people are often called Jews.

HEBREW LANGUAGE

is the major language of the Old Testament. Most of the Old Testament books were written in Hebrew; only half of Daniel and a few parts of Ezra were in Aramaic, a kind of "cousin" language of Hebrew.

Hebrew was the language the Israelites spoke in Old Testament times. However, after the northern kingdom and the southern kingdom of Israel were carried into exile in 722 and 586 B.C., the Hebrew language slowly began to die. The people began to speak Aramaic like the nations around them did. By the time

of Christ, Hebrew was a "dead" language—it was not spoken by anyone in normal conversation. It was used primarily by rabbis and teachers to study the Old Testament and to write about Judaism.

But in the new nation of Israel that began in 1948, Hebrew is the official language, although it has changed some since Bible times.

Hebrew is read from right to left instead of left to right as we read English. Also, all the letters in Hebrew are consonants. Although some consonants can be used as vowels, there are no letters for vowels—*a, e, i, o, u*—only dashes and dots. These dashes and dots are placed between the consonant letters or above and below the line of print to tell what vowel sounds should be used.

HEBREWS *(HEE-brooz),* LETTER TO

is a New Testament book written to Christians, many of them Jewish, to remind them that Jesus' way to know God was better than the old way described in the Law. We do not know who wrote the Book of Hebrews. The book itself does not say, and no other New Testament books tell us for sure.

Whoever the author was, he was a good writer who knew the Old Testa-ment. The letter shows that he also expected his readers to know the Old Testament. His purpose was to show his readers that Christ was greater than angels (Heb. 1:4-14), greater than Moses (Heb. 3:1-6), and greater than any high priests (Heb. 4:14-16; 5:1-10; 7:1-26; 9:11-28). Christ was the highest revelation of God.

The author wanted his readers to renew their commitment to Christ. He reminded them of people in the past whose faith

remained true even when they were tested (Heb 11). Hard times were coming for the Christians who would read that letter, just as they may be for Christians at any time. The writer said that Christians are on a pilgrimage—a kind of camping trip—on their way to a heavenly city to which Christ has already gone. Through Christ we already have citizenship in this heavenly city. Christians will find eternal rest and joy at the end. So we shouldn't be weary or lose hope. We must keep on following Jesus (Heb. 10:19—12:29).

HEIR *(air)*

is a person who receives or has the right to receive someone's property or position after that person dies. In Bible times, the heir was always the son of the property owner. He was a very important person in a household. Everyone who has Jesus as Savior is an heir of God. Each one of us is important to Him (Rom. 8:17; Gal. 4:4-7).

HELL

is both separation from God and the eternal place of those who choose to be separated from God. It is a place of punishment for those who have chosen to turn away from God. It is the place of the devil and his angels. The Bible has many word pictures to show how terrible it is to be forever separated from God. See Matthew 5:22, 29, 30; 18:9; 23:15, 33; Mark 9:47; James 3:6; II Peter 2:4.

HELMET (see box at right)

HERDSMAN (see *Occupations*)

HERMON *(HER-mun),* MOUNT

is the tallest mountain in northern Israel.

HELMET

is a covering to protect the head, often worn during battle. In the Bible it is also

a word picture of salvation. The helmet of salvation is protection against anyone who wants to keep the believer from serving the Lord (Eph. 6:17).

A Roman helmet.

It is the source of the streams that become the Jordan River. It is snow-capped most of the year and is one of the most beautiful sights in the area.

HEROD *(HAIR-ud)*

called "the Great," was king over Israel and some surrounding areas about 37 to 4 B.C. At that time, the area was part of the Roman Empire, but Herod was the local Jewish ruler. Jesus was born during Herod's reign. Herod ordered the killing of all baby boys in Bethlehem when he heard a new king had been born (Matt. 2:1-18).

Herod was also the family name for several rulers after Herod the Great.

One was **Herod Archelaus,** the son of Herod the Great, who became ruler of Judea and Samaria after his father died (Matt. 2:19-23). God warned Joseph in a dream of the danger from this king. So he took his family and settled in Nazareth when they returned from Egypt. Arch-

*When King Hezekiah was sick,
he prayed to the Lord to make him well again.*

elaus's rule was short. He was banished to what is now France in A.D. 6.

Another son of Herod the Great was Herod Antipas, who became ruler of Galilee after the death of his father. Jesus called him "that fox." Herod Antipas was the ruler who had John the Baptist killed (Matt. 14:1-12; Mark 6:14-29; Luke 3:19, 20).

Herod Agrippa I was the grandson of Herod the Great. He ruled most of Israel from A.D. 40 to 44. He is the ruler who had the apostle James killed and Peter imprisoned (Acts 12:2-23). He died suddenly in A.D. 44.

Herod Agrippa II is known in the Bible as "King Agrippa." He was the son of Herod Agrippa I. He ruled Galilee and some areas east of the Sea of Galilee from A.D. 53 to 70. He is the ruler who heard Paul defend himself against Jewish charges (Acts 25:13—26:32).

Although all the Herods were under the Roman emperor, they could rule their own country as long as they did not go against the Roman rulers. Many Jews resented them.

HEZEKIAH *(hez-uh-KY-uh)*

was the thirteenth king of Judah. He came to the throne when he was twenty-five and ruled for twenty-nine years, from 724 to 695 B.C. Hezekiah was a good ruler who tried to restore proper worship of God (II Kings 18—20; II Chron. 29—32). Later in his life, pride was his downfall.

When Hezekiah came to power, many of the people in Judah had stopped worshiping God. There were also political problems, with both Egypt and Assyria wanting to conquer Judah. Hezekiah started out right as a young king. He reopened the temple, destroyed pagan altars, and led a Passover celebration.

Caiaphas was the high priest who accused Jesus.

HIGH PRIEST

was the most important priest for the Old Testament worshipers. Toward the end of Old Testament times, when Israel had no king, the priest had power like that of a king, because religion and government were tied closely together. The priest was the spiritual leader of the Israelites.

High priests were descendants of Aaron, Moses' brother. After a high priest was consecrated, he held his job for life. The high priest wore elaborate and beautiful clothing. Because he was the go-between for the people and God, his clothes were to reflect the beauty and glory of God (Exod. 28:1-39).

On the Day of Atonement, the most important day of the year, the high priest put aside his colorful robes. Instead he put on plain linen clothes to enter the holy of holies.

Only on this yearly Day of Atonement would the high priest enter the holy of holies. He sprinkled the mercy seat with blood to make atonement for his own sins and for the sins of all the people (Lev. 16:1-28).

Although the high priest was meant to be the spiritual leader of Israel, the high priests Annas and Caiaphas opposed Jesus and worked to bring His death (John 11:47-57; 18:12-32).

But he had a hard time. The Assyrians captured many of the cities of Judah and threatened to take Jerusalem. Hezekiah offered to pay them not to attack Jerusalem. He even took gold from the temple to pay them.

The Assyrians, under King Sennacherib, decided to attack anyway. Sennacherib gathered a huge army outside Jerusalem. But one night, God sent an angel, who killed 185,000 of his soldiers (II Kings 18:13—19:36). This saved the city, and Sennacherib and the few left went back to Nineveh.

Later, Hezekiah became sick. He prayed, and God gave him another fifteen years of life (II Kings 20:1-11). But as Hezekiah got older, he became proud. When ambassadors came from Babylon to see him, he showed off his great wealth (II Kings 20:12-19). Isaiah the prophet scolded him for his foolish pride. He said, "The days are coming when all that is in your house . . . shall be carried off to Babylon." And that is exactly what happened—not during Hezekiah's lifetime but later to his children and grandchildren.

HIND (see *Animals—Hart*)

HIRAM *(HI-rum)*

was a friend of David and Solomon. He was king of Tyre, which today is in Lebanon. When David and Solomon were building the city of Jerusalem and the temple, Hiram supplied materials and builders. He sold some of the cedar and fir trees of Lebanon to Solomon and floated them down to Joppa on rafts. See II Samuel 5:11; I Kings 5:1-10.

HIRELING *(HIRE-ling)*

was a laborer who worked for money. Some hirelings were hired for a day, while others worked for longer periods. See Mal.3:5; John 10:12, 13

HOLINESS *(HOLE-ee-nus)*

comes from a Hebrew word that means set apart as sacred, consecrated, or dedicated. It is a word that describes God. God is different from us (Exod. 15:11; Ps. 30:4; Isa. 6:3)). He is pure and loving, without sin. Jesus Christ is holy also (Luke 1:35). He is without sin, dedicated to doing what God wants. His nature is the same as that of God the Father. Even the evil spirits knew Jesus as the holy one of God (Mark 1:24; Luke 4:34).

Jesus' death and resurrection give those who believe in Him the power to be holy (Lev. 20:7; Rom. 12:1; Heb. 12:14). They can become pure and loving like Christ. A faithful believer separates Himself from sin.

All true holiness comes from God. Things, places, times, and persons can become holy as they are used for God's purposes. This holiness always means to become more and more like the nature of God.

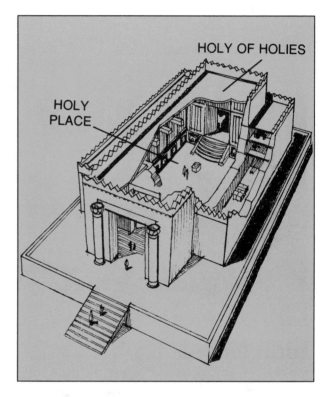

HOLY GHOST (see *Holy Spirit*)

HOLY OF HOLIES

was an inner section in the tabernacle or temple. To the Jewish people it was the most sacred place. Only the high priest could enter the holy of holies, and he could go in only on the Day of Atonement. He entered to ask forgiveness for his own sin and the people's sins. The ark of the covenant was kept in the holy of holies (see also *temple, tabernacle*).

HOLY PLACE

was a part of the Jewish people's temple or tabernacle. As part of the daily worship service, the priests lit candles and burned incense. In the holy place were a table on which fresh bread was placed each week and a seven-branched candlestick to remind God's people of His care during the escape from Egypt.

HOLY SPIRIT

is God's presence in the world. Jesus Christ was God who became a man in the world. When God is called Father, we speak of His care and love for all of His creation.

Genesis 1:2 tells us that the Holy Spirit helped bring the world into being. In John 16:13, Christ said the Holy Spirit would guide the disciples into all truth. The Holy Spirit explains God's purposes and draws attention to Jesus Christ.

Jesus called the Holy Spirit the helper, comforter, advocate, or counselor. Jesus told His disciples that the Holy Spirit would lead them into truth and would teach them how to share truth with others (John 14:15-17; 15:26, 27; 16:7-15). The Holy Spirit would convince non-Christians of their sin in not believing in Christ and would show them the goodness in how Jesus lived. He would show them how Jesus' death defeats Satan.

Many word pictures in the Bible help us understand the Holy Spirit. Wind and breath are the most common (Gen. 1:2; Job 32:8; 33:4; Ezek. 37:9. 10; John 20:22). *Wind* shows the power of the Holy Spirit; *breath* in the Bible stands for life itself. Other word pictures include a dove, oil, and fire for purification. The dove is a picture of the peace of God (Matt. 3:16; Mark 1:10; John 1:32); the oil (for a lamp) shows the Holy Spirit as light that shines in darkness (I John 2:20, 27). The fire pictures judgment (Acts 2:3).

In the Bible we read of the Holy Spirit coming upon certain persons to give them power for certain work. This happened to John the Baptist and to his parents (Luke 1:15, 47, 67).

At the Day of Pentecost, after Jesus had gone back to heaven, the Holy Spirit came in a new way(Acts 2). He gave power to all believers to help them proclaim Christ. He came with a rush of mighty wind and flames like fire to show His power and His desire for holiness.

This power of the Holy Spirit helps us tell other people about Jesus Christ and helps those people believe in Jesus. The Holy Spirit also gives many different gifts to believers so they can serve God and help others (Rom. 12:6-8; I Cor. 12—14).

See also Galatians 5:22, 23.

HOPHNI and PHINEHAS
(HOP-nee, FIN-ee-us)

were sons of Eli, an Old Testament priest and judge. When Hophni and Phinehas became priests, they embarrassed both their father and the Lord by their evil practices. They were immoral and greedy, taking more than their share of the sacrifices given by the people during worship (I Sam. 1:3—3:13). Their father, Eli, had once been a godly priest, but he did not punish his sons for their wicked ways. As a result, Hophni and Phinehas were killed in battle, their father soon died, and their family was no longer allowed to serve as priests (I Sam. 4:4-18).

HOR, MOUNT

is the name of two mountains:

1. The mountain where Aaron was buried. This mountain is probably a sandstone mountain in what is now the Sinai Peninsula about 100 miles south of Jerusalem. It has twin peaks (Num. 20:22, 23; 21:4; Deut. 32:50).

2. The mountain that marked the northern boundary of Israel's land. It is probably one of the peaks in what we know as the Lebanon mountain range (Num. 34:7, 8).

HORSES (see *Animals*)

HOSANNA *(hoe-ZAN-uh)*

was a shout used in Hebrew worship to show praise. It means "Save now!" A few days before Jesus was crucified, children and grown-ups shouted "Hosanna" to Him as He rode into Jerusalem on a donkey. That day is what we call Palm Sunday. See Matthew 21:9.

HOSEA *(hoe-ZAY-uh)*

was an Old Testament prophet who called his people back to God. Hosea's own life became a picture of God's love for His sinful people.

God told Hosea to use marriage as a picture of God's relationship to His people Israel (Hos. 1—3). God was the bridegroom, Israel was the bride. God told Hosea to marry a woman who would be unfaithful to him. Her name was Gomer. They had three children. But Gomer found other men to love, and she left Hosea, just as Israel found other gods to worship.

But Hosea, like God, brought Gomer back to his house and loved her even after what she had done. This pictured God's love and His desire to have His people back with Him (Hos. 4—14).

Hosea then begged Israel to repent and return to the ways of the Lord.

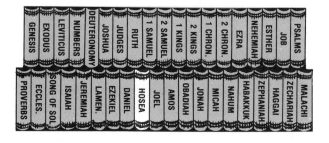

HOUSE

can mean (1) a building where people live; (2) a group of people who live in a certain building; (3) a building where God is worshiped, or (4) a group of people who believe in God.

1. In Bible times, as in our time, the houses where people lived were not all alike. Most of them looked more like boxes than our houses because they usually had flat roofs. There was no need for a slanting roof in a land with so little rain. Walls were usually thick, made from stone or brick. From the street, you first entered a small courtyard that often served as the kitchen. Beyond the courtyard, doors opened into a living room. Small bedrooms were beyond the living room.

The floor of the house would be clay or stone, depending on what the owner could afford. Doors were made of wood, cloth, skins, or woven rushes. The windows were small and high. Since there were no chimneys, smoke from the indoor stoves—used for cooking and heating—escaped through windows or doors.

The flat roofs were important to people of Bible times. They could be used for extra sleeping space, for drying flax, and for other activities. Stone steps often led from the courtyard to the roof.

Houses of richer people sometimes had an upper room built on the roof. Stairs to the upper room were usually outdoors.

Often houses were part of the city wall or had a wall in common with a neighboring house. The owner and his family often shared the house with farm animals.

2. *House* also meant a group of people who lived together within a certain home. This could include grandparents, aunts, uncles, parents, children, servants, and slaves. The word *household* is also used this way.

3. *House* sometimes meant a building where God was worshiped. The Bible speaks of the temple as the "house of God."

4. *House of God* also means a group of people who believe in God. It means the same as the "family of God." Hebrews 10:21 says Christ is a "great priest over the house of God." Hebrews 3:6 says that He was also a faithful Son over God's house; Moses was a servant in this same household. Both of these Scripture passages refer to the "house" as the family of believers everywhere. First Peter 2:5 says that Christians are to be built into a "spiritual house."

HULDAH (HUL-duh)

was a woman prophet in the days of King Josiah. When Josiah first found the Books of the Law while cleaning the temple, he sent the high priest to ask Huldah what it all meant. She prophesied God's judg-ment on the nation (II Kings 22:16-20).

She encouraged Josiah and all the people to follow the Law in the books they had found. Josiah wanted to lead the people back to God. He tore down the altars to the false gods (II Kings 23:1-25).

But Josiah was too late. The people had been too wicked. God had to send His judgment anyway. Huldah comforted the king by telling him that he would not see what would happen. Huldah's prophecies of judgment and of Josiah's death came true.

HUNTER (see *Occupations*)

HUSHAI (HUSH-eye)

was a spy for King David when David's son Absalom was leading a rebellion against his father. Hushai pretended to have changed from David's side to Absalom's. When Absalom asked him about attacking King David, Hushai gave advice that delayed the attack. Then David had time to escape across the Jordan River

See II Samuel 16:15-19; 17:5-15.

HYMNS (hims)

are songs for praising God. Singing was a part of worship in both the Old Testament and the New Testament. Earliest Christian hymns were psalms from the Old Testament. The hymn Jesus sang with the disciples at the end of the Last Supper was probably Psalms 113—118 (Matt. 26:30; Mark 14:26). Paul and Silas sang hymns when they were in jail (Acts 16:25). Christians are told to sing hymns to encourage each other as well as to praise God

See Ephesians 5:19; Colosians 3:16.

ICONIUM *(eye-KON-nee-um)*

is a city in what is now Turkey. It still exists but is now known as Konya. In New Testament times Paul visited there on his first and second missionary journeys.

On his first visit, Paul and Barnabas preached to both Jews and Gentiles. Many believed, and a church was formed. However, the two men were forced to leave when some unbelieving Jews threatened to stone them. Some of these unbelievers from Iconium followed Paul to Lystra, where they stoned him and dragged him out of the city. But Paul and Barnabas went back to Iconium after a while, continued to preach, and encouraged the church.

Paul and Timothy visited Iconium later. See Acts 14:1-7, 19-23; 16:1-5.

When Isaac was born, his parents were overjoyed; God had kept His promise after all!

Perhaps the most famous idol in the Bible was Aaron's golden calf.

IDOL *(EYE-dul)*

usually means an image that is worshiped. Such images were usually made of wood, stone, metal, or some other material.

In the Old Testament, the nations around Israel had idols of many kinds. Some were images, others were groves of trees or pillars. The Second Commandment given to Moses was "You shall not make for yourself a graven image or likeness of anything that is in heaven above or that is in the earth beneath, or that is in the water under the earth; you shall not bow down to them or serve them" (Exod. 20:4). This was a warning to the Israelites not to worship idols as the nations around them did. However, the Israelites often disobeyed, and God sent many prophets to warn them against this.

In the New Testament, Christians were told not to deliberately eat meat that had been offered to idols, because it might confuse people who did not understand that "an idol has no real existence" (I Cor. 8:4-11).

IDOLATRY *(eye-DOLL-uh-tree)*

is the worship of false gods or idols. It includes not only worship of objects made by people, but also the worship of the sun, moon, or stars.

Although the Israelites were told many times not to practice idolatry, they often did. In Judges 17—18 is a story of a Levite who was supposed to be a priest of God but worked as a priest for an idol.

During the time of the prophet Elijah and during other periods as well, many Israelites worshiped the god Baal. Baal worship was common in Israel for hundreds of years.

Sometimes the Israelites worshiped false gods in the ways they were supposed to worship the true God. They offered burnt sacrifices (II Kings 5:17), burned incense (I Kings 11:8), and brought money, grain, and oil as offerings (Hos. 2:8).

In the New Testament, the apostle Paul wrote about idolatry as putting other things before God. He said that covetousness (a strong desire to have something that belongs to someone else) is one form of idolatry (Eph. 5:5; Col. 3:5).

IMMANUEL *(im-MAN-you-el)*

is a name that means "God with us." The prophet Isaiah foretold the birth of a child whose name would be called Immanuel. In the New Testament, this prophecy was applied to the birth of Jesus Christ (Isa. 7:14; Matt. 1:23).

IMMORALITY *(IM-more-AL-it-ee)*

in the Bible refers primarily to sexual sins of all kinds—fornication, adultery, homosexuality, incest. Immorality is always condemned in the Bible.

In our modern usage, immorality includes many kinds of wrongdoing, such as lying, stealing, and murder. These are also condemned in the Bible, but the term *immorality* in the Bible refers to sexual sins. See I Cor. 6:18; II Cor. 12:21; Gal. 5:19.

INCENSE *(IN-sens)*

is material made of spices and gum that is burned to make a sweet smell. In the Old Testament tabernacle and temple, there was a special altar where incense was burned as a part of worship.

INHERITANCE *(in-HAIR-ih-tunce)*

refers to property or money that parents give to children or grandchildren.

INCENSE *(IN-sens)*, ALTAR OF

was a special altar used only for burning incense in the tabernacle and later in thetemple. It was about eighteen inches square and stood about thirty-six inches high. It had a thin covering of gold. Its upraised sections on each corner were called horns.

Incense burning was an act of worship, but it also improved the smell in the place where many animals were killed and burned as sacrifices.

At first, only the high priest burned incense at the altar each morning. By the time of Christ, ordinary priests were chosen to burn incense at a specified time each day (Exod. 30:1-9). The priest took fire from the altar of burnt offering and brought it into the holy place to the altar of incense.

Zechariah was bringing incense to the

Priests burned incense on a special altar each day.

altar of incense in the temple when an angel appeared to him (Luke 1:5-23). He told Zechariah that he would have a son whose name would be John.

The main caravan routes had inns with open courtyards and stables for travelers' animals.

In Old Testament times, there were strict laws of inheritance, especially regarding land. When the Hebrews went into the land of Israel, they believed God had given them the land as their inheritance. The land was divided among the twelve tribes. Each tribe and each family within that tribe received certain land. This land was passed on from family to family, one generation after another.

The oldest son always received twice as much of his father's goods as the other sons. Daughters did not receive anything, unless there were no sons. In that case, they inherited the land, but they were required to marry someone within their own tribe so that their land would stay within that tribe. There were many other customs and rules about inheritances.

In the New Testament, some of the same customs were followed. However, Jesus talked about the "eternal inheritance" that belongs to those who believe in Him. As God's Son, He is the heir (the one who inherits) of God, and believers in Him become "fellow-heirs."

See Deuteronomy 21:15-17; Romans 8:17.

INIQUITY (see *Sin*)

INN

was not like a modern hotel or motel. There were three main types of inns or lodging places for travelers:

1. A resting place (something like a camp) for individuals or caravans as they traveled. Such inns would be near a well and might have some protection with rocks and trees.

2. A large courtyard with a gate that could be locked. Around the sides were rooms or stalls for animals and travelers. A well would be in the courtyard. Travelers carried their own food for themselves and their animals.

3. Guest rooms in private homes.

We do not know which kind of "inn"

The most frightening day of Isaac's life was when his father offered him as a sacrifice.

Mary and Joseph were turned away from for lack of space at the birth of Jesus (Luke 2: 7).

Innkeepers of ancient times had bad reputations, especially those who had large inns with a courtyard and a gate. This is one of the reasons Christians were urged to welcome traveling Christians into their homes (Rom. 12:13; I Pet. 4:9).

INSCRIPTION *(in-SKRIP-shun)* ON THE CROSS

were the words written on the sign fastened to Christ's cross. (Such inscriptions usually told the crimes for which the person was being put to death.) For Jesus, the sign said, "This is Jesus of Nazareth, the King of the Jews."

As far as the Romans were concerned, Jesus was charged with plotting to overthrow the government and become king.

See Matthew 27:37; Mark 15:26; Luke 23:38; John 19:19-21.

IRON

in Bible times is much like the iron of today. It was used to make axes and other tools. When the Israelites first came into Israel, they had very little iron. This kept them poor, because they did not have good farming tools, or swords and spears for their armies. Later, when they defeated the Philistines and took over the land, they were able to learn how to smelt iron.

ISAAC *(EYE-zek)*

was the only son of Abraham and Sarah, born by a miracle of God when Abraham was 100 years old and Sarah was 90 (Gen. 17:17-19; 18:9-15; 21:1-8). God promised that the nation of Israel would descend from Isaac.

When Isaac was a young boy, God told Abraham to sacrifice Isaac to Him on a mountain in the land of Moriah (Gen. 22:1-14). With great sorrow, Abraham

MAIN EVENTS IN THE HISTORY OF ISRAEL

APPROXIMATE TIME	EVENT
2000 B.C.	Abraham leaves his home to go toward Canaan.
1876 B.C..	Joseph invites his family to live in Egypt because of the famine in Canaan.
1876—1450 B.C.*	Israelites become slaves in Egypt.
1450—1406 B.C.*	Israelites are led out of Egypt by Moses and wander in the wilderness, waiting for God to give them permission to enter the promised land— Canaan.
1406—1400 B.C.*	Israelites fight for control of the land of Canaan under the leadership of Joshua. They conquer enough to divide the land among the various tribes.
1400—1050 B.C.*	Various judges rule the tribes. Frequent war with surrounding enemies and sometimes between tribes. Prominent judges are Deborah, Gideon, Samson, and finally Samuel.
1050—1010 B.C.	Israelites request a king. Samuel anoints Saul. The tribes are drawn together into a unified country.
1010—-970 B.C.	David rules all of Israel. He captures the city of Jerusalem, which had never before been a part of Israel. Although there are periods of war, it is considered the "golden age" of Israel.
970—930 B.C.	Solomon runs a prosperous, united Israel. He builds a beautiful temple. But he also begins to worship other gods.
930 B.C.	Solomon dies, and civil war divides the northern tribes, called Israel, from the southern tribes, called Judah.
722 B.C.	Northern kingdom (Israel, or Ephraim) is conquered by the Assyrians. Many people are taken away into Assyria. Most of them never return.
586 B.C.	The southern kingdom (Judah, or now called Israel) is conquered by Babylon. Many of the people are taken away to Babylon. Jerusalem and the Temple are destroyed.
538 B.C.	Some of the people return to rebuild Jerusalem's temple and walls.
167 B.C.	Antiochus IV, then ruler of Judea, sacrifices a pig on a pagan altar in the holy place of the temple in Jerusalem. This causes a revolt among the Jews living there that continues until 164 B.C., when the temple is again consecrated to God. The Jews become largely self-ruling.
67 B.C.	Civil war breaks out in Palestine between followers of two Jewish men who want to rule Judea. The Roman government conquers Jerusalem in 63 B.C.
40 B.C.	Herod the Great becomes ruler of most of Israel. He rebuilds the temple in Jerusalem. This is the temple in which Jesus taught.
5 B.C.	Birth of Jesus Christ.
4 B.C.	Herod the Great dies. He arranges to have his kingdom divided into three parts—one part for each of his sons.
A.D. 30	Crucifixion of Jesus Christ.
A.D. 68-70	Jewish war with Rome. Jerusalem is destroyed. Six hundred thousand Jews are killed.
A.D. 73	Destruction of Masada, the last Jewish fortress in Israel.
A.D. 70—1920	Jewish people are scattered over the world. During the centuries, many different groups conquer the land: Persians, Muslims, Crusaders, Tartars, Egyptians, Turks.
A.D. 1920	Mandate (rule) of Palestine is assigned to Great Britain.
A.D. 1948	New state of Israel is proclaimed, followed by bitter war with the Palestinian Arabs.

*Scholars do not agree about these dates.

went to Moriah and got ready to sacrifice Isaac. When everything was set, God appeared to Abraham and said, "Do not lay your hand on the lad or do anything to him; for now I know that you fear God, seeing you have not withheld your son, your only son, from me."

At age forty, Isaac married Rebekah, a relative from Mesopotamia (Gen. 24). He and Rebekah had twin sons, Esau and Jacob.

When Isaac was about 100 years old and his eyesight was poor, he intended to give the usual blessing to his sons. According to custom, the oldest son (Esau) was to receive the birthright, which included a double amount of the inheritance. However, Rebekah wanted Jacob to get that blessing, and she helped Jacob dress up like Esau and pretend to be Esau. Her plan fooled Isaac, and he gave the birthright blessing to Jacob instead of Esau (Gen. 27).

Esau became so angry that he threatened to kill Jacob. At Rebekah's suggestion, Isaac sent Jacob to the country his mother had come from.

Isaac died at age 180 (Gen. 35:27-29). Isaac is always mentioned as one of the three ancestors of the Hebrew nation—Abraham, Isaac, and Jacob.

ISAIAH *(eye-ZAY-ah)*
is an Old Testament prophet who is quoted more in the New Testament than all other prophets combined (Luke 4:16-21). More than any other prophet, Isaiah seemed to be looking for the coming of the Messiah.

Most of the Old Testament prophecies that are applied to Jesus Christ come from the writings of Isaiah. Many of the words in Handel's famous oratorio *The Messiah* are found in the Book of Isaiah.

We do not know much about the prophet Isaiah except that he prophesied from 740 to 680 B.C. during the reign of four kings of Judah—Uzziah, Jotham, Ahaz, and Hezekiah.

He was married to a prophetess (Isa. 8:3), whose name we don't know. They had two sons.

Isaiah must have been well known and welcomed in the courts of the kings, for his book mentions talking with them often.

Besides his remarkable prophetic poems, the Book of Isaiah also has sections that tell about the history of Judah and surrounding nations. Chapters 36-37 tell bow King Sennacherib of Assyria threatened to overrun Jerusalem. When Hezekiah received Sennacherib's threatening letter, he took it to the temple, spread it before the Lord, and prayed for deliverance. God answered and destroyed the Assyrian army.

Isaiah was a prophet of great imagination and skill as a writer. He used colorful word pictures to describe the sins of his people: "The ox knows its owner, and the ass its master's crib; but Israel does not know, my people does not understand."

He showed God as the great holy Creator of the universe—one who has great power and knowledge but also loves His people deeply.

Isaiah warned the people that God was more interested in right living than in animal sacrifices. God hates sin and idol worship.

Probably the most well-known chapter is Isaiah 53, where the picture of a suffering Savior seems to describe the life and ministry of Christ with stunning accuracy.

The importance of the Book of Isaiah is shown in the fact that Jesus began His public ministry in Nazareth by reading from Isaiah 61. Then He said, "Today this scripture has been fulfilled in your hearing."

ISHBOSHETH *(ish-BOW-sheth)*

was the fourth son of Saul. He was king over Israel for two years after Saul and his three older sons died in battle. He was proclaimed king by Abner, the captain of Saul's army.

But the tribe of Judah had made David king. Ishbosheth fought against David for two years, until Abner turned his loyalty to David. Later, Ishbosheth was murdered by his own captains.

See II Samuel 2:8—4:11.

ISHMAEL *(ISH-may-el)*

was the son of Abraham and Hagar (Gen. 16:1-7). Hagar was an Egyptian maid of Sarah, Abraham's wife.

Ishmael was fourteen years old when Abraham and Sarah had a son, Isaac. Sarah did not want Isaac to be brought up in the same house with Ishmael, and when Ishmael was sixteen, she urged Abraham to send Ishmael and Hagar away. Abraham did not want to do this, for he loved Ishmael. An angel appeared to Abraham, however, and told him it was all right to have Hagar and Ishmael go away, for God would make the children of Ishmael into a great nation (Gen. 17:20).

When Ishmael and his mother went into the wilderness, he almost died of thirst. Then an angel of God appeared to his mother and assured her that God would care for them (Gen. 21:9-21).

Ishmael and his mother went on living in the wilderness, where he became a skilled hunter with bow and arrow. He married an Egyptian woman and had twelve sons and a daughter.

When his father, Abraham, died, Ishmael went back to Canaan and helped Isaac with the funeral (Gen. 25:7-18).

Ishmael died when he was 137 years old. He had become the ancestor of the people known as the Ishmaelites. All Arabs claim to be descendants of Ishmael.

ISHMAELITES *(ISH-may-lites)*

were the descendants of Ishmael, the son of Abraham and Hagar. They lived mostly in the desert areas and became known, like Ishmael, for their skill with bows and arrows.

Some Ishmaelites bought Joseph from his brothers and took him to Egypt.

All Arabs claim to be descendants of the Ishmaelites (Gen. 37:25-28).

ISRAEL *(IZ-ray-el)*

has several meanings.

1 *Israel* is another name for Jacob, the son of Isaac. An angel changed his name to Israel after an all-night wrestling match.

2. *Israel* also refers to the Hebrew people, who were called to a special relationship with God: He would be their God and they would be His people. In the New Testament, Christians are called the new "Israel of God"—people with a special relationship to God (Gal. 6:16).

3. *Israel* was often used as the name of the northern kingdom between 930 and 722 B.C. This kingdom, which included ten of the original twelve tribes, was also called Ephraim—the name of one of the strongest tribes.

After the northern kingdom was conquered by Assyria in 722 B.C., the term Israel was used for the southern kingdom, made up of the tribes of Judah and Benjamin. The southern kingdom was usually called Judah, however. The words *Jew* and *Jewish* come from Judah.

4. *Israel* also refers to the land called Canaan in the Old Testament. This includes what is now known as Israel.

The history of the. people known as Israel (the Hebrews) started with the time of Abraham, about 2000 B.C.

Abraham, his son Isaac, and Isaac's son Jacob are the ancestors or founders of the Israelites.

The chart on page 169 shows some of the main events in the history of Israel.

ISSACHAR *(ISS-uh-car)*

was the ninth son of Jacob and the forefather of one of the twelve tribes of Israel.

We know very little about him, except that he and his wife and children went to Egypt with his brothers and father. His descendants left the slavery of Egypt with Moses and the other Israelites.

Some of his famous descendants include Deborah (the judge) and two kings of Israel—Baasha and Elah.

Jesus—Son of God, our Savior—explained to people such as Nicodemus who God is and how to be right with him.

173

JABIN *(JAY-bin)*

was the name of two Canaanite kings of Hazor, a city in northern Israel.

The first King Jabin led an army from his own city and several surrounding cities to fight Joshua. However, Joshua and his army won, and King Jabin was killed in the battle (Josh. 11:7-10).

The second King Jabin conquered much of Israel. When Deborah was judge, she brought together soldiers from several tribes of Israel and defeated Jabin's army (Judg. 4:1-24; 5:1-31).

JACOB *(JAY-kub)*

was the younger of twin sons born to Isaac and Rebekah. His name was later changed to Israel, and from that name came the word *Israelites*. All Hebrew people (Israelites) are descendants of Jacob.

Jacob and his twin brother, Esau, didn't get along when they were young. Because Esau was born first, he was supposed to get the birthright—a special blessing from his father. Jacob wanted that birthright.

One day when Jacob was fixing food for himself, Esau came home tired and hungry. He asked Jacob for some of the food. "Sell me your birthright, and I will give you some food," Jacob answered.

Esau agreed. "After all," he said, "I'm about to die of hunger. My birthright will do me no good if I'm dead."

Jacob never told his father, Isaac, what he had done. When Isaac was getting old and blind, he decided it was time to give the special birthright blessing to Esau. He asked Esau, who was a good bow-and-arrow hunter, to kill an animal and fix his favorite food (Gen. 25:27-34).

Rebekah, Jacob's mother, heard Isaac talking to Esau. She wanted Jacob to

Jacob's mysterious wrestling match at the brook.

have the birthright, so she quickly fixed Isaac's favorite food. She told Jacob to put on Esau's clothes. Esau had more hair on his body than Jacob did, so Rebekah fastened some goat skin on Jacob's hands so he would feel hairy.

Then Jacob pretended he was Esau, took the food to his blind father, and received the special blessing (Gen. 27:1-41).

Esau was so angry when he learned what Jacob had done that he threatened to kill him. Jacob left his home in Beersheba to visit his uncle, Laban.

One night on his way, Jacob dreamed he saw a ladder reaching to heaven, with angels walking up and down (Gen. 28:10-22). At the top of the ladder was God, who said to him, "The land on which you lie I will give to you and to your descendants. I am with you and will keep you wherever you go."

Jacob called the place where he slept Bethel, meaning, "the house of God."

At his uncle's home, Jacob met Rachel and wanted to marry her. Laban said he would have to work seven years to earn Rachel as his wife. At the marriage, his bride wore the customary heavy veil. After the marriage, Jacob found he had married Leah, Rachel's older sister, instead! Laban said older daughters had to marry first and Jacob would have to work another seven years to marry Rachel. Jacob did (Gen. 29:15-30).

After he had stayed with Laban for 20 years, Jacob took his family back to Beersheba (Gen. 32:3-19). A messenger met him saying that Esau was coming to meet him with 400 men. Jacob was sure he and his family would all be killed. That night he had another meeting with God—he seemed to be wrestling with someone all night (Gen. 32:24-30). When morning was dawning, God told him that his name would be changed to Israel, which means "he who strives with God."

When Jacob finally met Esau, it was a friendly meeting. Jacob settled in Shechem, in Canaan. He had twelve sons—for whom the twelve tribes of Israel are named. One son, Joseph, was sold into slavery by his jealous brothers, but he later became the ruler of Egypt.

At a time of famine, Jacob and his other sons and families moved to Egypt, where Joseph was in charge of distributing grain. Jacob died in Egypt.

JAEL *(JAY-el)*
was a woman who killed Sisera, the commander of forces fighting against Israel when Deborah was judge (Judg. 4:11-21).

JAIRUS *(jay-EYE-rus)*
was the ruler of a synagogue whose twelve-year-old daughter was raised from death by Christ.

Jairus himself went to Jesus seeking help for his sick daughter. But before Jesus arrived at Jairus's home, messengers came saying the girl had died.

Jesus insisted on going anyway, and when He arrived, the people were weeping and mourning. Jesus sent everyone out of the house except Jairus and his wife and Peter, James, and John. Jesus took the girl's hand and commanded her to rise. She was immediately made well.

See Matthew 9:18-26; Mark 5:21-43; Luke 8:40-56.

JAMES
was a common Jewish name in the time of Christ. Three important men in the New Testament were named James. Two of the twelve apostles were named James.

1. Perhaps the most famous was the apostle James the son of Zebedee; his brother was the apostle John. He was a fisherman in Galilee when he was called to follow Jesus. He was one of the three most well-known disciples—Peter, James, and John. These three were with Jesus at several important moments—such as Jesus' time on the mountain of transfiguration where Jesus' appearance was changed (Mark 9:2-9); when Jesus prayed in Gethsemane before His crucifixion (Matt. 26:36-46); and when Jesus raised the daughter of Jairus from death (Mark 5:37-43).

This James was killed by Herod Agrippa I in A.D. 44 (Acts 12:1-3).

2. Another apostle named James was the son of Alpheus. He is mentioned only in the lists of the disciples. Nothing further is known about him (Matt. 10:3; Acts 1:13).

3. Another James was the half brother of Jesus. He probably wrote the Book of James in the New Testament. James and his other brothers were not followers of Christ during His life (John 7:5). But after

Jesus rose from the dead, they became believers and were in the upper room waiting for the coming of the Holy Spirit.

Jesus appeared to James in a miraculous way after the resurrection (I Cor. 15:7). James became a leader in the church in Jerusalem. He was in charge when Paul and Barnabas came to Jerusalem to discuss the serious problems arising when Gentiles became believers in Christ (Acts 15:1-21). Should the Gentile believers follow Jewish practices about food and religious ritual?

James said he thought Gentiles should be asked only to stay away from certain practices that offended Jewish believers.

James's advice was followed.

When Paul returned to Jerusalem after his third missionary journey, he went to tell James what God was doing in other areas (Acts 21:17-19).

James was stoned to death by the Jewish high priest in A.D. 62, according to the Jewish historian Josephus.

JAMES, LETTER OF

was probably written by James the brother of Jesus. It is written in high-quality Greek, and James probably had the help of an excellent secretary. This short book tells believers they must do more than talk about their faith—they must *do* what

Jairus could do nothing for his daughter—except call for Jesus.

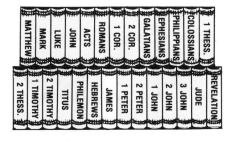

is pleasing to God.

James is very plain about the things that do not please God. He says the true believer should be careful about what he says. The Christian should not bless God and curse people. Christians are not to honor people because they are rich. Everyone is to be treated alike.

James urges Christians to pray for each other, to resist temptation, to be humble before God, to seek wisdom from God, and to realize that every good thing we have is a gift from God.

This book shows the difference between true religion and false religion. Beliefs don't mean anything unless they make us act better. "Faith, by itself, if it has no works, is dead" (Jas. 2:17).

JASON (JAY-sun)

was a Christian man at Thessalonica who invited Paul and Silas to stay at his house while they were preaching.

Some of the Jews who were jealous of

177

JEHOIAKIM *(juh-HOY-uh-kim)*

was the eighteenth king of Judah. He ruled from 609 to 598 B.C. (II Kings 23:34—24:6; II Chron. 36:3-8). He became king when his brother was taken captive by Pharaoh Neco, the ruler of Egypt. Neco made Jehoiakim king of Judah and told him what to do. Jehoiakim had to tax the people very heavily and give the money to Neco.

His name was originally Eliakim, but it was changed to Jehoiakim by Neco. Jehoiakim was a cruel and godless king during his eleven-year reign. He is best remembered for the scornful way he treated the prophet Jeremiah. Jeremiah had prophesied that Babylon would conquer Judah. When the king's princes heard about the prophecy, they told Jeremiah and his scribe, Baruch, to hide. One of the princes took the prophecy and read it to King Jehoiakim.

When the king heard something he didn't like, he cut out those parts with his knife and threw them into the fire (Jer. 25, 26, 36). God told Jeremiah to rewrite the prophecy and to include in it that

Jehoiakim would be taken captive and die in disgrace.

While Jehoiakim was king, the Babylonians captured most of Israel, and Jehoiakim then had to take orders from Nebuchadnezzar. Later, Jehoiakim tried to rebel against Nebuchadnezzar, but he was taken captive and killed, just as Jeremiah had prophesied.

Paul's success in winning converts gathered a crowd and attacked Jason's house. Paul and Silas were not there at the time, so the mob took Jason and some of his friends to the city judge and accused him of harboring criminals who were teaching there was another king, Jesus. This made it sound as though Paul and Silas were trying to overthrow the government.

The judge "took security" from Jason. This probably meant he made Jason promise that Paul and Silas would leave the city and not come back again. See Acts 17:1-10.

JAVELIN (see *Weapons*)

JEHOIACHIN *(juh-HOY-uh-kin)*

was next to the last king of Judah (II Kings 24:8-15). He was eighteen years old when his reign began in 598 B.C., and it lasted only three months and ten days. During this time he kept up the wicked practices of his father, the former king.

He was taken captive by Nebuchadnezzar to Babylon, where he lived the rest of his life. He was in prison for thirty-seven years. Then he was freed and given an allowance on which to live (II Kings 25:27-30).

JEHOIAKIM (see box at left)

JEHOIADA (juh-HOY-uh-duh)

was a high priest and uncle of Joash, a king of Judah. When Joash was a baby, Jehoiada and his wife rescued him from being killed by his grandmother. She became ruler of Judah when Joash's father, King Ahaziah, died. She reigned for seven years.

During these seven years Jehoiada and his wife hid Joash, and no one else knew he was alive. When he was seven years old, Jehoiada told the palace guards that the king's son, rightful heir to the throne, was alive. Jehoiada planned with them to have the boy crowned king when Queen Athaliah was not around. The plan worked.

Jehoiada became an important adviser to Joash. Jehoiada directed the destruction of many of the images and altars to the false god Baal. Jehoiada and Joash also arranged to have the temple repaired.

Because of his importance and his good work, Jehoiada was buried among the kings when he died at age 130.

See II Kings 11:1—12:16; II Chronicles 22:10—24:16.

JEHORAM (juh-HOR-um)

also known as Joram, was the name of one king of Israel and one king of Judah, both of whom lived and reigned about the same time.

1. Jehoram was the tenth king of Israel, reigning from 852 to 841 B.C. (II Kings 3:1-3). He is most remembered for his many meetings with the prophet Elisha (II Kings 3:9-24; 6:24—7:20). Elisha disliked him because he was an idol worshiper like his parents, Ahab and Jezebel.

Elisha, however, faithfully prophesied God's word to Jehoram, telling him how God would save him and his army from their enemies. Once the enemy thought that pools of water were blood; another time they heard the sound of armies attacking them, and they ran.

Jehoram later was killed by an arrow shot by Jehu, who became the next king of Israel (II Kings 9:14-26).

2. Another Jehoram was the fifth king of Judah, reigning from 848 to 841 B.C.. He married Athaliah, the wicked daughter of Ahab and Jezebel. Although Jehoram's father had been a godly king, Jehoram began worshiping idols when he became king at age thirty-two. He had all of his brothers killed so they could not threaten his rule. The prophet Elijah sent him a letter saying that because of his wickedness he would die of a terrible disease.

Part of the people under his rule, Edom and Libnah, rebelled against him. Later the Philistines and Arabs invaded Judah and carried away all of Jehoram's belongings and also his sons and wives. Jehoram did die of a painful disease. At his death, no one honored him as they usually honored kings.

See II Chronicles 21:1-20.

JEHOVAH (juh-HOVE-uh)

is one of the names for God. The Jews had a special name for God that was so sacred they would not even say it out loud. When reading the Old Testament,

JEHU *(JEE-hoo)*
was the name of two important men in the Old Testament.

1. Jehu was the eleventh king of Israel. While he was serving in the army, he was chosen by God to take the place of King Joram, the son of the wicked Ahab. The prophet Elisha told a younger prophet to go to the army post where Jehu was stationed and anoint him king of Israel (II Kings 9:1-13).

The prophet told Jehu that he must strike down the rulers who were relatives of Ahab (II Kings 10:1-27). Jehu did as he was told. Joram was killed and so was the wicked Jezebel, wife of Ahab.

Jehu was king for 28 years. He stopped the worship of Baal among the people. However, he still allowed the worship of golden calves, and this displeased God (II Kings 10:29).

We remember Jehu partly because he drove his chariot "furiously" (II Kings 9:20).

2. Jehu was an Old Testament prophet who denounced Baasha, king of Israel, and Jehoshaphat, king of Judah (II Kings 16:1-4; II Chron. 19:1-3).

they would substitute another more general name *(Lord)* for their special name for God.

Originally, all Hebrew words were written without vowels. A name such as Peter would be written PTR. The special name for God was written YHWH. Because the Jews never said the name, they eventually forgot how to pronounce it. Hundreds of years later, the vowels for *Adonai*, the Hebrew word for "Lord," were used with the letters YHWH, and from these two Hebrew words (the consonants of one and the vowels of the other) came the word *Jehovah* that is used in some translations of the Bible. Most translations now use the word *LORD* in capital letters for the Jewish special name for God.

JEREMIAH *(JER-uh-MY-uh)*
was one of the greatest Old Testament prophets and one of the most unpopular. He spent much of his time in prisons or hiding from angry kings. He was a prophet during the reigns of five kings of Judah—Josiah, Jehoahaz, Jehoiakim, Jehoiachin, and Zedekiah—a period of forty years.

God called him to be a prophet when he was a young man, but Jeremiah told God he was too young and not a good speaker (Jer.1:4-10). God said He would put His words in Jeremiah's mouth, and Jeremiah must speak them.

The messages God gave Jeremiah made people angry. He told people God was judging them for their idolatry and evil acts, and that a great power from the north would soon come and conquer them. When Jehoiakim was king, he became so angry at Jeremiah's prophecies that Jeremiah was arrested and threatened with death (Jer. 26:1-11). With God's help, he escaped. Later God told him to prophesy that destruction was coming to Judah. He was called a traitor and put in stocks. He was finally released with orders not to speak his terrible prophecies anymore.

But God still spoke to him, so Jeremiah put his words in writing instead, with the help of his friend, Baruch. Baruch gave them to a young man to read aloud at a house near the temple. The listeners were so shocked that some of them took the writings to King Jehoiakim. He listened as they were read to him and then cut them up and threw them into the fire. He ordered Jeremiah arrested. However, Jeremiah and Baruch went into hiding, and no one could find them.

The next king was 18-year-old Jehoiachin. Soon Nebuchadnezzar, king of Babylon, came with his army, took the young king captive, and left King Zedekiah in charge of Judah.

Meanwhile, God told Jeremiah and Baruch to rewrite all the prophecies that wicked King Jehoiakim had burned in the fire.

Zedekiah thought he could escape from the rule of Babylon if he made friends with Egypt (the enemy of Babylonia). Jeremiah heard about Zedekiah's plans and warned him not to do it, but that he should save the lives of his people by surrendering to Nebuchadnezzar.

Again Jeremiah was considered a traitor for giving that advice and was placed in a dungeon half-full of mud (Jer. 38:1-13).

Then, Nebuchadnezzar's army surrounded Jerusalem. The people tried to hold out against the army, but they ran out of food and water. Finally the city was defeated, and Nebuchadnezzar's army destroyed everything—including the beautiful temple of Solomon.

Many people of Judah were killed; others were forced to go to Babylon as exiles. The old and sick were allowed to stay in the battered city. Jeremiah was left in Jerusalem with the others.

The few that were left later decided to go to Egypt and try to make new lives for themselves there. They forced Jeremiah to go with them. In Egypt Jeremiah continued his prophecies, urging the people to turn away from idolatry and worship God again. In Egypt, Jeremiah finally died.

JEREMIAH (JER-uh-MY-uh), BOOK OF

is the longest prophetic book in the Old Testament. Even though the Book of Isaiah has more chapters, they are shorter than the chapters in the Book of Jeremiah.

It was written by the prophet Jeremiah about many events in his life and in the history of Judah (the southern kingdom) between 625 and 580 B.C. The book also gives many of the prophecies and sermons that Jeremiah spoke and wrote. However, things are not written in the

Jericho is not only the world's oldest city, it is the lowest—1,300 feet below sea level.

order in which they occurred.

The book seems to be arranged roughly this way:

1. Jeremiah's prophecies and sermons about Judah (chapters 1—25)

2. Events in the life of Jeremiah (chapters 26—45)

3. Jeremiah's prophecies about other countries (chapters 46—51)

4. The fall of Jerusalem and events that followed (chapter 52)

Although Jeremiah's prophecies were usually about the bad things that would happen to Judah and other countries, he also wrote about a New Covenant that God would make with His people. God would write His Law in their hearts, and He would forgive their sins. This new covenant is mentioned in several places in the New Testament.

See Jeremiah 31:31-34; Hebrews 8:7-13; 10:15-18.

JERICHO *(JER-ih-ko)*

is the oldest known city in the world—dating 5,000 years before the time of Abraham! It is located about one mile southeast of where the city was in Old Testament times.

Jericho is famous because its walls fell down after Joshua and his army marched around it for seven days (Josh. 6). At the command of God, Joshua and his men destroyed everything in the city. The city was not rebuilt for more than 500 years. Then it again became an important city. Later it was again destroyed.

The Jericho of the New Testament is near the modern town of Jericho. It was a great city, built by Herod as his winter capital because it has a tropical climate. Jesus often taught and healed there (Mark 10:46-52). Zacchaeus, who climbed a tree to see Jesus, lived in Jericho (Luke 19:1-10). Jesus' famous story about the good Samaritan is placed on the lonely winding road between Jerusalem and Jericho—a distance of about twenty miles (Luke 10:29-37).

JEROBOAM *(jer-uh-BOH-um)*

was the first king of the northern kingdom (Israel), ruling from about 931 to 910 B.C. He began as a government official under King Solomon (I Kings 11:28). He helped stir up anger against Solomon over the high taxes the people had to pay.

Jews often go to pray at Jerusalem's Dome of the Rock (upper right) and the Wailing Wall (lower right).

While walking one day, he met the prophet Ahijah. The prophet tore his mantle (robe) into twelve pieces and gave ten pieces to Jeroboam. Ahijah said this meant that soon Israel would split into two separate nations—one with ten tribes, the other with two—and that Jeroboam would become leader of the larger one (I Kings 11:29-39). The prophet told him he should obey God's laws.

After King Solomon's death, the prophecy came true, and the people of the ten tribes asked Jeroboam to become king (I Kings 12:20). He did; however, he forgot about obeying God's laws. For example, God had said that once a year all Israelites were to worship at the temple in Jerusalem. But Jerusalem was in the two-tribe section, and Jeroboam didn't want his people leaving his territory to worship. So he built two places of worship in his country—one at Dan, another at Bethel (I Kings 12:26-31).

Also, Jeroboam "decorated" his new houses of worship with golden calves and said, "Behold your gods, O Israel, who brought you up out of the land of Egypt." Faithful priests refused to serve at these altars, so Jeroboam got new priests and served as a priest himself.

Once while serving as a priest, a prophet told him that God would judge him for what he was doing. Jeroboam got angry, pointed at the man, and ordered him arrested. The hand that pointed suddenly went dead (I Kings 12:32—13:10)! Jeroboam pleaded with the prophet to ask God to heal him. The prophet did, and Jeroboam was healed.

But Jeroboam did not return to worshiping God. Instead he led his people to worship false gods.

JERUSALEM (juh-ROO-suh-lem)

is the most famous city on earth and in all of history. Its name means "city of peace," and if you visit Jerusalem today, probably at least one person will say to you, "Pray for the peace of Jerusalem."

Jerusalem has not been a city of peace, for it has been involved in many wars and been destroyed several times. But unlike most ancient cities, Jerusalem has always been rebuilt on exactly the same place.

Jerusalem was the capital of Israel under David and Solomon. In this city, Solomon erected his beautiful temple to God. After Israel was divided into northern and southern kingdoms in 930 B.C., Jerusalem continued to be the capital of Judah, the southern kingdom.

The city was destroyed by King Nebuchadnezzar in 586 B.C. when the southern kingdom was defeated and many of its people taken into exile in Babylon.

About 538 B.C. some Jews were able to return to Jerusalem and start to rebuild the temple. Nehemiah led the rebuilding of the walls of the city, beginning about 445 B.C.

During the next 500 years, Jerusalem was ruled by a number of countries including Greece, Persia, Egypt, Syria, and finally, Rome. It was during the Roman rule that Jesus visited Jerusalem several times and once wept about how it wouldn't listen to His message. He was finally crucified there. After He rose from the dead, He appeared to His disciples in Jerusalem and went back to heaven from a hill near the city.

The first Christian church was formed in Jerusalem after the Holy Spirit came upon the disciples during the feast of Pentecost.

The city was completely destroyed by the Romans in A.D. 70. After it was rebuilt beginning in A.D. 136, it came under the control of many rulers.

Most recently, the entire city came under the control of the modern nation of Israel in 1967. Today it is considered a sacred city by Jews, Christians, and Muslims. The Muslim Dome of the Rock (where Abraham is said to have offered his son as a sacrifice to God) now stands on part of the area where the temple once stood.

Jerusalem in the Bible has many names that show its special meaning to Jews and Christians. It is often referred to as "the city of God," "the holy mountain," and "Zion." *Jerusalem* is also used as a word picture of heaven, where God lives with His people. Hebrews 12:22 speaks of the "heavenly Jerusalem."

JESSE (JESS-ee)

was the father of King David. Jesse was a shepherd, and young David was taking care of some of his father's sheep when the prophet Samuel came and told Jesse that God had told him to anoint one of his sons as the next king of Israel. David was so young that at first Jesse did not even call him in from the fields to meet Samuel. See I Samuel 16:1-13.

JESUS (JEE-zus) CHRIST

is the most important person in the Bible. Although He was born in about 5 B.C. and was crucified about A.D. 30, the Bible says He lives forever because He is God.

The name *Jesus* is the same as the Old Testament name *Joshua*, meaning "the Lord is my salvation." Jesus is also called Messiah. In Hebrew this means "the anointed one." The word *Christ* comes

from the word *anointed* in Greek. Jesus is called Christ and Messiah because He was anointed or chosen by God for His special work as Savior of the world.

Most of what we know about Jesus' life on earth is found in the four Gospels in the New Testament—Matthew, Mark, Luke, and John. These writings tell us that Jesus was born in Bethlehem, a small village about 4-1/2 miles south of Jerusalem. This was the same village where King David had been born more than a thousand years earlier. Jesus' mother was Mary, a young Jewish girl who was engaged to marry Joseph, a carpenter of Nazareth, a small town about ninety miles north of Jerusalem.

An angel appeared to Mary and told her she would have a son. God by a miracle would cause her to become pregnant (Luke 1:26-38).

At the time of Jesus' birth, a huge star appeared in the sky. Wise men hundreds of miles away considered the star a sign that a great new king was being born. They made a long journey to follow the star and find the new king (Luke 2:1-7; Matt. 2:1-12).

When King Herod the Great heard about the wise men coming to look for a newborn king, he was afraid this new king would try to take his throne from him. So he ordered all baby boys in and around Bethlehem to be killed. However, God warned Joseph in a dream that he and Mary and the baby should go immediately to Egypt (Matt. 2:13-15). In this way, Jesus' life was saved. A few years later, King Herod the Great died, and Joseph and Mary and Jesus went home to

Nazareth in Galilee.

Although the new rulers appointed by the Roman governor were Jewish, the Jewish people hated them. The Jews wanted to be free to rule themselves and to set up a great kingdom like they had when David and Solomon had been their kings. They believed the Old Testament promised a Messiah (a person anointed by God) who would drive out the hated Romans and restore a new kingdom for them.

When Jesus was about thirty years old, He began to preach and teach. He often taught in synagogues in the small cities. His twelve special disciples and others (including some women) walked with Him from town to town.

Jesus' teachings were different from those of other Jewish teachers and priests. He told interesting stories and used plain words. The people liked to hear Him teach. As more and more people wanted to hear Him, Jesus had to teach outdoors on hillsides and beaches.

The people soon learned that Jesus could perform miracles (Mark 3:1-12). He healed people who had terrible diseases. He fed thousands of people with just a few loaves of bread and a few fish; He made a terrible storm go away. Because of these powers, many people wanted to make Him king of their country (John 6:15). They were sure that He would be able to defeat the hated Romans.

But that was not the kind of king Jesus came to be. His kingdom was one in which God ruled the hearts of people, who then tried to do God's will. Slowly the religious leaders of His time, the Pharisees, became more and more angry with Jesus. They became angry because He was friendly with people who clearly were sinners. One man who became one of His disciples had been a tax collector for the hated Romans. Also, He and His disciples did not keep the hundreds of religious rules the Pharisees thought were important.

And the leaders didn't like some of the things Jesus taught. He said He could forgive sins; they said, "Only God can do that!" So the Pharisees, scribes, and chief priests began to figure out ways to have Jesus put to death by the Romans.

The disciples were still loyal to Him, even though they did not understand many of the things Jesus was saying and doing. He told them that they must be servants of others. (They thought Jesus was going to become king, and they would be officers in His government.) Even though He told them that He was going to suffer and die, they didn't really believe it.

Finally one of His own disciples, Judas, helped the religious leaders have Jesus arrested (Matt. 26:47-50). He was tried by the Jewish council (Sanhedrin) on charges that He blasphemed God. Because the

council could not sentence anyone to death, He was taken to the Roman governor, Pilate, who sentenced Him to be crucified.

On the day we now call Good Friday, Jesus was crucified as a criminal along with two thieves. Even on the cross, He thought about others. He asked John to take care of His mother. He told one of the thieves that He would be in heaven with Him. He prayed for the soldiers who had crucified Him and for the people who had wanted all this to happen. After six hours of suffering, He died (John 19:17-30; Luke 23:32-49). The disciples were frightened and disappointed. They thought it was the end of all their dreams.

But on the third day, Jesus rose from the dead and appeared again to women who were His followers, and to the disciples (Matt, 28:1-15; Luke 24:1-11; John 20:1-31). For forty days, Jesus appeared occasionally to His followers, talked with them, and taught them. Then He ascended in a cloud to heaven, telling them that He would send "another Comforter"—the Holy Spirit—to be their teacher (Matt. 28:16-20; Acts 1:1-11).

He told them they were to go all over the world, teaching and baptizing people, and that He would be with them.

And the disciples did as Jesus told them. They told the story of forgiveness through Christ to people all over the known world. Today, Jesus' followers are doing the same thing, because Jesus has given them new life and made them part of His great kingdom of God. We enter His kingdom when we come under God's control and try to do what He wants. Jesus asked His followers to pray that God's kingdom would come and His will would be done on earth as it is in heaven.

JETHRO *(JETH-row)*

was Moses' father-in-law. Moses lived with him in Midian or the Sinai Peninsula and shepherded his sheep for forty years before he went back to Egypt to lead the Israelites out of slavery.

When Moses was leading the Israelites in the wilderness, Jethro came to visit him. He saw how overworked Moses was as he tried to govern and lead the people. He suggested that Moses appoint judges to help him in less important matters. Moses took his advice (Exod. 18).

JEW

at first referred to anyone who belonged to the tribe of Judah, one of Israel's twelve tribes.

But in the New Testament and even now, it means anyone who traces his ancestry to the Israelites or who is a follower of the Jewish religion.

JEZEBEL *(JEZ-uh-bel)*

was the wicked wife of Ahab, king of the northern kingdom. She brought the worship of the pagan god Baal into Israel and had 450 prophets of Baal eating in her palace. To please her, King Ahab built a temple and an altar to Baal (I Kings 16:32). She ordered all the prophets of God to be killed (I Kings 19:2).

The prophet Elijah had a famous contest with these prophets of Baal on Mount Carmel (I Kings 18:19). The false prophets were defeated and killed. After that contest, Jezebel ordered Elijah to be killed, but he escaped.

Elijah prophesied that God's judgment would fall on her and King Ahab. Ahab died in battle, and Jezebel died when she was thrown from a window in her palace (I Kings 22:34-40; II Kings 9:30-37).

JEZREEL *(JEZ-reel)*

was a city about sixty miles north of Jerusalem where King Ahab had a palace. Near the palace, a man named Naboth had a vineyard that King Ahab wanted for his vegetable garden (I Kings 21:1-16). When Naboth refused to sell it, Jezebel, the wicked wife of Ahab, arranged to have Naboth killed so Ahab could get it.

After Ahab's death in battle, Jezebel continued to live in the palace in Jezreel. She died by being thrown from the window (II Kings 9:30-37).

JOAB *(JO-ab)*

was commander of David's army. He was a skilled fighter, but he was also a cruel man. He killed Abner, the commander of an opposing army, who was trying to make peace with David (II Sam. 3:20-30). When Absalom, David's son, led a rebellion against David, David ordered that Absalom was not to be killed. However, Joab killed him anyway (II Sam. 18:9-15).

David then made Amasa commander of his army instead of Joab. Joab pretended to be Amasa's friend—and then one day suddenly stabbed him to death (II Sam. 20:4-10).

When David was dying, Joab supported Adonijah as the next king instead of Solomon. After Solomon was made king, he ordered Joab to be killed (I Kings 2:28-34).

JOASH *(JO-ash)*

was the name of three important people in the Old Testament, including one king

Joash was only seven years old when he was brought out of hiding and crowned king of Judah.

of Israel and one king of Judah.

1. Joash, the ninth king of Judah, ruled for forty years, from 835 to 796 B.C. (II Chron. 24:1-24). When he was a baby, everyone else in the royal family, including his father, was murdered. He was saved by his aunt and uncle, who hid him for seven years. Then he was brought out and crowned king. At first he took advice from his godly uncle, the high priest, and ruled well. Later he began to worship idols.

When Zechariah, the son of the priest, told him he was doing wrong, he had Zechariah killed. Joash was wounded in a battle with the Syrians, but he was killed in his own bed by his servants because he had ordered Zechariah killed.

2. Joash, the twelfth king of Israel, was also called Jehoash (II Kings 13:10-19; II Chron. 25:17-24). He was king for sixteen years, from about 799 to 783 B.C. Although he worshiped idols, he seemed to be a successful king. At one time, the king of Judah challenged him to war, and Joash tried to discourage the idea. When the king of Judah insisted on war, Joash led his army in a stunning defeat of Judah. Joash was a friend of the prophet Elisha.

3. Joash, the father of Gideon (Judg. 6: 28-32). When Gideon tore down the altar to Baal in his hometown, the townspeople wanted to kill him. But Joash said, "If Baal is a god, he ought to be able to protect himself!"

JOB *(jobe)*

was a man who was wise, rich, and good. Then suddenly terrible things happened to him. His ten children were all killed in a tornado. He lost all his wealth. And he became ill with a painful skin disease.

Three friends came to visit him, and they all tried to explain why these dreadful things had happened. They said it was because Job had some sin in his life and God was punishing him. His wife and friends all thought the same thing.

Job insisted it was not true, but none of them believed him. Job became very discouraged and angry with God for letting such bad things happen, but he still believed in God and trusted Him. Job realized that his trust in God did not depend on the things that happened to him.

God restored Job's health, made him twice as rich as he had been before, and gave him ten more children.

JOEL *(jole)*

was an Old Testament prophet who wrote a short book. No one knows exactly who he was or when he wrote. We do know that he wrote about a terrible plague of locusts that had invaded the land, stripping the crops and ruining orchards (Joel 2:8, 9). Joel told the people that the locusts had come as a punishment because they had not been faithful to God. The locust plague was said to be a time of judgment.

The most famous part of Joel's prophecy is a section the apostle Peter quoted on the Day of Pentecost: "It shall come to pass afterward that I will pour out my spirit on all flesh; your sons and your daughters shall prophesy, your old men shall dream dreams, and your young men shall see visions"(Joel 2:28-31).

JOHN THE APOSTLE

was known as "the disciple whom Jesus loved." He was involved in the writing of five New Testament books—the Gospel of John, I John, II John, III John, and Revelation.

John was a fisherman when Jesus called him to become a disciple. Jesus nicknamed him "Son of Thunder" (Mark 3: 17). This probably meant that when John was young, he did things on the spur of the moment and had a hot temper. He is the only one of Jesus' disciples known to have lived to old age. When he was older, he was known for his gentleness and loving spirit.

He was one of the three disciples—Peter, James, and John—who were very close to Jesus and saw Him do some miracles that no one else saw, such as raising the daughter of Jairus from the dead. Jesus took these three with Him into a garden to pray just before His trial and crucifixion. John was the only disciple who the Bible says watched the crucifixion. Jesus saw him and asked him to take care of His mother (John 19:26, 27).

After Jesus returned to heaven, John stayed in Jerusalem and became one of the leaders of the Christians there. He may have been the same John who was exiled much later on the island of Patmos because of his faith (Rev. 1:9). There God gave John visions. He wrote them in what we know as Revelation—the last book of

One day as John was baptizing, Jesus came and asked to be baptized.

the Bible. John was probably later released from Patmos and died in the city of Ephesus when he was an old man.

We don't know exactly when he wrote the parts of the New Testament that carry his name.

JOHN THE BAPTIST

was a prophet who was a cousin of Jesus. His parents, Zacharias and Elizabeth, were quite old when he was born (Luke 1:5-25, 57-80).

When he was a young man, he began to preach in the wilderness near the Jordan River just north of the Dead Sea. There he lived simply, eating locusts and wild honey, and wearing rough garments of camels' hair. He told his listeners that they must repent of their sins, treat people fairly, and share what they had with others. Many thought John was the coming Messiah, but he told them, "No. Another is coming who is mightier than I."

John baptized those who wanted to turn to God and change their ways. One day as John was baptizing, Jesus came and asked to be baptized. At first John refused, but Jesus insisted. Afterward a voice from heaven said, "This is my beloved Son, with whom I am well pleased (Matt. 3:1-17)."

Some of John's followers became disciples of Jesus after John told them that Jesus was the "Lamb of God who takes away the sin of the world" (John 1:29).

Some months later, John the Baptist was imprisoned by Herod Antipas, the ruler of Galilee. John had said that Herod was wrong to have married the wife of his half brother. While in prison, John sent some of his friends to ask Jesus if He really was the promised Messiah (Matt. 11:2-15).

Jesus sent word back: "Go and tell John what you hear and see; the blind receive their sight, and the lame walk, the lepers are cleansed and the deaf hear, and the dead are raised up and the poor have the good news preached to them."

After the messengers went back, Jesus told His disciples that there had been no prophet greater than John the Baptist.

John was killed after Herod's step-daughter asked for his head as a reward for her dancing at one of Herod's banquets (Matt. 14:1-12; Mark 6:14-29).

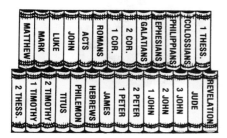

JOHN, GOSPEL OF

is one of the four New Testament books that tell about the earthly life of Jesus Christ. This Gospel was written by one of Jesus' disciples, the apostle John, probably when he was an old man. It was probably written after the other three stories of the life of Christ—Matthew, Mark, and Luke.

The apostle John tells many things about the life of Christ that the other three do not. Most of John's Gospel is about Jesus' teachings, travels, and miracles in Judea. (The other Gospels tell more about Jesus' ministry in Galilee—the northern part of Palestine.) These are some of the miracles that are described *only* in the Gospel of John:

Turning water into wine at a wedding (John 2:1-11)

Healing a lame man at the pool of Bethesda (John 5:1-18)

Healing the man who had been blind from birth (John 9:1-41)

Raising Lazarus from the dead (John 11:1-44)

John's Gospel also tells many teachings of Jesus that are not in the other Gospels. These include His sermon about the Bread of Life and His teaching that He is the Good Shepherd.

John tells the readers that Jesus is God. In the very first sentence of his book he calls Christ "the Word" and says, "The Word was God."

When Jesus had His last supper with His disciples before His death, He gave them many important lessons. These are recorded in John, chapters 13 to 17, and most of these teachings do not appear in the other Gospels.

The apostle John said in John 20:31 that he wrote this story of the life of Christ so that the readers would "believe that Jesus is the Christ, the Son of God, and that believing you may have life in his name."

We can be very thankful John wrote his story of Jesus' life, filling in many details that had not been included in the other accounts.

JOHN, FIRST LETTER OF

is a kind of sermon written between A.D. 85 and 100 by a disciple of Jesus, the apostle John. It was probably sent to the churches in Asia (now Turkey) where John lived toward the end of his long life.

In this sermon-letter, John reminded the readers that there were some teachers traveling around who said they were followers of Christ but were actually teach-

JONAH

JONAH *(JO-nuh)*

was an Old Testament prophet who had to be swallowed by a huge fish before he was willing to obey God. His story is told in the Book of Jonah.

When God called him to preach in a Gentile city, Nineveh, in about 745 B.C., Jonah did not want to go. He was afraid the people would repent and God would spare the wicked city. Jonah wanted God to destroy it because it was an enemy of Israel (Jonah 1:1-3).

Instead of going to Nineveh as God commanded, Jonah took a ship going in the opposite direction—to Tarshish, probably a city in what is now southwestern Spain. During a violent storm at sea, the sailors prayed to their heathen gods to save them. They felt the storm was due to some wicked person on board. They decided it was Jonah, and Jonah admitted it probably was his fault. He told them to

Jonah was headed across the Mediterranean Sea when the storm hit.

throw him overboard (Jonah 1:4—2:10). God sent a huge fish to swallow Jonah whole. Alive inside the fish, Jonah prayed to God, and after three days the fish vomited him up near the shore.

Jonah was now willing to go to Nineveh. Just as he thought, the people listened to his message and repented (Jonah 3). That made Jonah so angry that he went outside the city, sat down under a large plant, and complained to God (Jonah 4). The next day the plant withered, and Jonah was so hot he asked God to let him die.

God said Jonah cared more about the plant over his head than he did about all the people in Nineveh.

The Book of Jonah shows that God was concerned for all the people of the world—not just the Israelites, who were His chosen people.

ing things that were not true.

These teachers taught at least three false things:

1. that they knew some things other Christians did not know (I John 2:4).

2. that Jesus had never been truly human. They did not believe that Jesus had come "in the flesh" (I John 4:2).

3. that they never really sinned (I John 1:10).

John told his readers that all of those teachings were wrong. He also reminded them that anyone who says he is a believer in Christ must live right—he cannot just go on sinning as if it didn't matter. He said that Christians must love God and treat each other lovingly because "God is love."

JOHN, SECOND LETTER OF

is addressed to a Christian woman and her children. The apostle John wrote that he had met some of her children and he was glad they were following Christ. He warned the woman about teachers who said they were Christians but taught wrong things. John said she should not invite them into her home. He encouraged her to love other Christians and to follow the teachings of Christ.

JOHN, THIRD LETTER OF

was written by the apostle John to his friend Gaius, who was a leader in one of the churches. John praised Gaius for inviting some of the Christian traveling teachers to stay in his home. He also said Diotrephes, another man in the church, was not pleasing God by the way he was treating John and some other Christians.

JONAH (see box at left)

Jonathan once gave David a secret message while pretending to practice shooting arrows.

JONATHAN (JON-uh-thun)

was the oldest son of King Saul. He was David's best friend, and was a skilled and courageous soldier (I Sam. 14:1-45).

When his father, King Saul, saw that David was popular among the people, he hated him so much he plotted to kill him. Jonathan tried to show his father that he had no reason to kill David. But Saul's jealousy was so intense that he refused to listen to Jonathan. Jonathan warned David of Saul's plan to kill him, and this helped David escape (I Sam. 20:18-42).

Jonathan knew that David would become the next king of Israel even though, as Saul's oldest son, he should have been the next king. The love of David and Jonathan for each other was so deep that jealousy never hurt their friendship (I Sam. 18:1-3; 20:17).

At the end, Jonathan and King Saul were both killed in the same battle with the Philistines (I Sam. 31:1-6). Later King David wrote a song in Jonathan's honor (II Sam. 1:19-27).

JOPPA (JOP-uh)

was an ancient seaport very near where Israel's largest city—Tel Aviv—now stands. Joppa is now called Jaffa and is really a suburb of Tel Aviv.

The old Joppa was a walled city that existed before the time of Moses. It was the city where Jonah caught a ship for Tarshish when he was trying to run away from God's command (Jonah 1:3).

Joppa is mentioned in the New Testament as the city where Peter raised Dorcas to life (Acts 9:36-43). It was also where Peter saw a vision that made him

JORDAN

is the name of an Arab nation today and is also the name of an important river.

1. The modern nation of Jordan includes lands that the Bible calls Gilead, Ammon, Bashan, Edom, and Moab. Jordan's people are mostly Muslims.

2. The Jordan River was the most important river in Israel's history. It begins in the mountains north of the Sea of Galilee, runs into the Sea of Galilee, then out and down to the Dead Sea, where it ends. Because it is so winding, it actually travels about 200 miles to cover its 65-mile route. It is not a river that can be used for shipping. It has too many rapids and is only three to ten feet deep.

The nation of Israel had to cross the Jordan going into Canaan (Josh. 3—4). God miraculously made it possible for

Near this spot in the Jordan, Jesus was baptized.

them to cross over on dry land.

John the Baptist did his preaching in the wilderness along the Jordan River (Matt. 3:1-5), and Jesus was baptized there by him (Matt. 13-17).

realize the Gospel was for Gentiles as well as Jews (Acts 10).

JOSEPH OF ARIMATHEA
(AIR-im-uh-THEE-uh)

was a rich Jewish man who was a member of the ruling council when Christ was crucified. He secretly believed in Jesus, but was afraid to tell others. After Christ died on the cross, Joseph asked Pilate for permission to remove the body. He helped place Jesus' body in a new tomb he owned. See Matthew 27:57; Mark 15:43; Luke 23:50-53; John 19:38-41.

JOSEPH,

husband of Mary, was a carpenter who lived in Nazareth. When Mary was pregnant, an angel told Joseph that the Holy Spirit was the father of the child to be born, and Joseph should go ahead and marry her. He was with Mary when Jesus was born in a stable in Bethlehem.

Joseph was warned in a dream that Herod would try to kill the young child, and that they should go immediately to Egypt. The family stayed there until King Herod died. Then they all returned to Nazareth, where Joseph taught Jesus the carpenter trade. Joseph is last mentioned in the Bible in the story of the family trip to Jerusalem when Jesus was twelve.

Most scholars believe Joseph died before Jesus began His ministry.

See Matthew 1:18-25; 2:13-23; Luke 2:41-52.

JOSEPH,

son of Jacob, is one of the most important people in the Old Testament. His story explains how the Israelites became slaves to the Egyptians.

Joseph's father, Jacob, was ninetyyears old when Joseph was born, and Jacob favored Joseph over all his other sons. The older brothers were jealous and sold Joseph as a slave to a caravan of strangers going to Egypt (Gen. 27:12-36). They made their father think that Joseph had been killed by a wild animal.

Meanwhile, Joseph was sold to Potiphar, an officer of the Pharaoh. Joseph proved so trustworthy and skillful that he was given much responsibility. Later he was thrown into prison because Potiphar's wife lied about him (Gen. 39).

In prison, Joseph became known as a man who could tell what dreams meant. He was finally called to tell the Pharaoh what one of his dreams meant (Gen. 41:1-49). As a result, he was released from prison. Joseph later became the chief ruler of the land—second to the Pharaoh himself.

Several years later, the brothers of Joseph came to Egypt to buy grain (Gen. 42:1—45:20). They met Joseph, but did not recognize him. Joseph put them through several tests to see if they were still cruel and thoughtless. Their actions showed that they had changed. Joseph then told them who he was and invited them to bring their father and their families to live in Egypt.

Many years after their deaths, new cruel pharaohs came into power. They made slaves of the descendants of Joseph and his brothers.

JOSHUA *(JAH-shoo-uh)*

was Moses' assistant and military commander through Israel's forty years in the wilderness after the escape from Egypt. When Moses died just before Israel was ready to begin its conquest of Canaan,

Joshua was appointed the new leader (Num. 27:15-23).

He was already at least seventy years old at that time. He led the battle against the city of Jericho and many other campaigns (Josh. 6). He also assigned specific areas to the tribes and encouraged each to drive out the remaining Canaanites in their areas. Joshua then dissolved his top command post and retired to an area near Mount Ephraim. He died at age 110.

The Book of Joshua tells about the campaigns of the Israelites in conquering Canaan and explains how the land was divided up among the various tribes. The book begins with Joshua taking over after Moses' death and ends with the death of Joshua.

The first twelve chapters tell about the conquest of Canaan. Chapters 13 to 22 tell how it was settled and how disagreements were worked out. Chapters 22—24 tell how Joshua, when he was nearing death, called all the leaders of Israel together and reminded them of all that God had done for them (Josh. 23:1—24:28). He encouraged them to worship only God and to do all that God commanded. The leaders promised, "The Lord our God we will serve, and his voice we will obey." Joshua took a huge stone and put it in the sanctuary of God at Shechem as a reminder of their promise.

JOSIAH (jo-SY-uh)
was the sixteenth king of Judah and one of the most godly kings in the Old Testament.

He became king when he was eight years old, after his father had been killed by slaves in the palace. The people were worshiping idols and building altars to pagan gods. Worship of the Lord had almost been forgotten. Josiah's father, the previous king, had encouraged idolatry.

When Josiah was only sixteen, he began to change all that. He ordered his men to break down the images and the altars to foreign gods. When he was twenty years old, he pushed his reform to other areas.

But the most important event occurred when Josiah was twenty-six. At that time some repairs were being made in the temple of God, and the priest discovered the Book of the Law that had not been seen or read for years. After getting the advice of the prophetess Huldah, Josiah gathered all the leaders and many of the people of Judah to stand together in the temple while the Book of the Law was read to them. Josiah decided to try to do all that the book commanded.

He ordered that the Passover feast should be held again. The Passover had not been observed for hundreds of years. Second Kings 23:25 says about Josiah, "Before him there was no king like him, who turned to the Lord with all his heart and with all his soul and with all his might, according to all the law of Moses; nor did any like him—arise after him."

Josiah was killed in a battle with Egypt in 609 B.C. when he was thirty-nine years old. After that, many people returned to their old ways and forgot about worshiping God. Twenty-three years after his death, the kingdom of Judah was conquered by Babylon.

See II Kings 22:1—33:30; II Chronicles 34, 35.

JUDAH (JOO-duh)
was one of the twelve sons of Jacob and the head of one of the tribes of Israel. When his other brothers wanted to kill Joseph, it was Judah who persuaded them

Joseph's brothers never expected to find him in such a high position in Egypt.

It was Judas who led the soldiers to capture Jesus.

to sell him as a slave instead. Judah was an ancestor of King David and of Jesus Christ (Gen. 37:12-27; 38:1-26).

JUDAH *(JOO-duh)*, **KINGDOM OF**

was the southern kingdom when the Israelites divided into two separate countries after the death of King Solomon. The kingdom of Judah included most of the land assigned to the tribes of Judah, Simeon, and Benjamin, and also the kingdom of Edom.

This kingdom began in 930 B.C. and lasted until the capital city, Jerusalem, fell to the Babylonians in 586 B.C. The cities of Judah were destroyed at that time, and most of the leaders were forced into exile in Babylonia. They were free to live as they chose, but they could not return to Judah.

About forty years later, Babylonia was conquered by Persia. The Persian king, Cyrus, allowed the Jews to return to their own land if they wanted to. At least 43,000 went back to live and to rebuild the city of Jerusalem.

The word *Jew* comes from *Judah*.

JUDAH *(JOO-duh)*, **TRIBE OF**

descended from Judah, the son of Jacob. When Joshua led the Israelites into Canaan, the tribe of Judah was assigned the land between the Dead Sea and the Mediterranean Sea. It was one of the largest territories, nearly forty-five miles wide and fifty miles long. The tribe of Simeon was assigned a large area south of Judah, but a lot of it was almost desert land. Over a period of hundreds of years, the tribe of Simeon became a part of Judah. King David came from the tribe of Judah, and so did Mary and Joseph.

JUDAS *(JOO-das)*

was a popular name among Jews of Christ's time. Several are mentioned in the New Testament.

1. Judas, the brother of Christ. He is probably the "Jude" who wrote the Letter of Jude—one of the shorter books of the New Testament. He is mentioned in Matthew 13:55.

2. Judas, one of the apostles—the one who betrayed Jesus. In Acts 1:13 this Judas is called "Judas the son of James" (RSV) or "Judas the brother of James" (KJV). Nothing else is known about him.

3. Judas Iscariot *(iss-KARE-ee-ut)* is the disciple who betrayed Jesus. He served as treasurer for the disciples (John 13:29). Although they trusted Judas, Jesus knew all along that Judas would betray Him (John 6:64).

When a woman came and put expensive ointment on Jesus' feet, Judas complained that the money it cost could have been used to feed many poor people (John 12:3-8). However, he did not really care about the poor—he just wanted the money.

We do not know why Judas finally decided to lead the enemies of Jesus to Him (Matt. 26:47-50). The Bible says the chief priests paid him thirty pieces of silver. After Jesus was arrested, Judas felt so guilty for what he had done that he took the money and tried to give it back to the priests, but they refused it. He finally threw it on the floor of the temple (Matt. 27:3-5). Then he went and hanged himself.

JUDE

is one of the shorter books in the New Testament. This letter was probably written by one of the half brothers of Jesus, who did not believe in Jesus until after the resurrection.

In this short letter, Jude warns the readers to look out for false teachers who say it is all right to do bad things and to live as you please (Jude 3, 4, 16). Jude condemns grumblers, people who are always complaining, boasters, immoral people, and those who flatter others to get them to do what they want.

Jude writes that Christians must stay close to Christ and obey Him (Jude 20).

The most familiar part of Jude is the lovely benediction that is often repeated at the close of a church service (Jude 24, 25). It begins: "Now to him who is able to keep you from falling and to present you without blemish before the presence of his glory. . . ."

JUDEA *(JOO-DE-uh)*

is the Old Testament name for the part of Palestine to which many Jews returned after they had been exiled in Babylonia. Since most of these people were from the tribe of Judah, the land was called Judea.

In the New Testament, *Judea* refers to the southern part of Israel. It extended from the southern part of the Dead Sea north about sixty miles. It included Bethlehem, Jerusalem, and Jericho.

JUDGE

was a government official who had different duties at different periods of history. In the time of Moses, judges settled arguments among the people (Exod. 18:13-23).

When the Israelites had settled in

Canaan after the death of Joshua, judges were the chief rulers of various tribes or groups of tribes. They not only ruled during peacetimes but they were leaders in wars. Some of the prominent judges were Deborah, Gideon, and Samuel (Judg. 4:4, 5; I Sam. 7:15-16).

After Israel got a king as the chief ruler, judges again became those who settled disputes and took care of official business. Six thousand Levites were appointed to be officers and judges (I Chron. 23:2-4).

JUDGES, BOOK OF

tells what happened to the Israelites during the 350 years before Saul became king.

The Israelites began to forget God, who had led them out of Egypt into their promised land. They began to worship idols and other false gods like those of the neighboring countries. The Book of Judges also tells how the twelve tribes fought against each other. Each tribe seemed more concerned about itself than about the nation of Israel as a whole.

There were several small nations or groups of people still in Canaan who often made war against the Israelites. They included the Philistines, the Hittites, the Amorites, and several other groups. Sometimes, when the Israelites had a hard time with their enemies, they called on the Lord for help. God would raise up a judge to lead them and to defeat the enemy. But after the judge died, they would go back to their sinful ways. The Book of Judges tells about thirteen such leaders.

The book describes some of the cruelty of the Israelites when they left the worship of God and turned to idols. They became as evil and cruel as the people of the pagan neighboring countries.

Judges 2:11-19 is a summary of the whole Book of Judges.

JUDGMENT

is a word that appears often in the Bible.

In the Old Testament it often meant God was punishing a person or a nation for disobeying Him. God often "judged" the Israelites by letting an enemy country conquer them or oppress them.

In the New Testament, *judgment* is used differently. Sometimes it means to criticize or condemn someone. Jesus said Christians are not to judge each other (Matt. 7:1). However, we are to examine and judge ourselves (I Cor. 11:27-31). God's judgment also means God is examining our actions day by day, recognizing what is good and what is sinful. This is happening now—in the present.

Judgment also refers to the end of the world as we know it, when God will judge (or punish) sin, reward those who have lived for God, and Christ will rule completely (Matt. 12:36).

JULIUS CAESAR

(JOOL-yus SEE-zur)

was the founder of the Roman Empire. He was born about 100 B.C. and became a government official when he was a young man. As he was being promoted to higher offices, the self-governing Roman republic was growing weaker. Caesar was able to gain more and more power until he became absolute ruler.

In 44 B.C., he was stabbed to death. The rulers who followed him took the name *Caesar* as a title to show that they, too, were emperors.

When the twelve spies came back to Kadesh, they brought back beautiful fruit from the promised land. But they also brought back stories of the giants they had seen.

K

KADESH and KADESH-BARNEA *(KAY-dish bar-NEE-uh)*

are both names for a city about 100 miles southwest of Jerusalem in what we call the Sinai Peninsula. This city was an oasis in the wilderness.

The Israelites camped here while waiting to enter Canaan after leaving Egypt. When they reached this point, Moses sent twelve spies to scout out the promised land. Although the Lord wanted the people to go on in, they would not. They were afraid, because the spies reported there were giants in the land. Because they rebelled, the Lord made them wander 40 more years in the wilderness (Num. 13—14; Deut. 1:19-28; Josh. 14:6-8).

Moses' sister, the prophet Miriam, died at Kadesh-barnea and was buried there (Num. 20:1). Near Kadesh, Moses struck

Israel's first king, Saul, was anointed by Samuel.

a rock from which God then gave water to the complaining Israelites (Num. 20:11). Later, Kadesh-barnea was the southern border of Judah (Joshua 15:3).

KIN, KINSMEN

are people who are family or relatives. In ancient time a kin had the right to get revenge for a wrong done to one of his relatives or to pay his debt for him.

KING

is a man who rules a country and its people. Often the king was thought to be stronger or smarter than most people.

After the people of Israel first settled in Canaan, they did not have a king. They were ruled by judges, who made necessary decisions. But all the countries—and even some of the cities—around Israel had kings. And the people complained that they wanted one too (I Sam. 8:4-22).

The prophet Samuel warned the Israelites that God did not want them to have a king. The Lord wanted to be their only ruler. An earthly king would not always serve them well. "This is how a king will act," Samuel said. "He will tell you all what to do, and he will send your sons off to war."

But the people would not listen. "No!" they said, "we will have a king over us!"

So God told Samuel to appoint Saul as king. After Saul, David became king, and after David, Solomon. These were the greatest kings of Israel. Most of the time they led the people in honoring God.

But some of the later kings of Israel and Judah became very wicked and encouraged the worship of false gods. A few kings were good, leading the people back to the worship of God, who was the true King of Israel.

In the New Testament, Jesus is called our King. He rules over all people and all of creation. He leads a battle against death that He will win. He will be the all-powerful, wise, loving King of the universe through all eternity.

See I Corinthians 15:24-28.

KINGDOM OF GOD

means God's rule over people and places. In the Old Testament, the people over whom God ruled was Israel (I Chron. 28:5). In the New Testament, the Kingdom people are Christians. When we say that Jesus is our Lord, we are saying that He is the King of our lives. Jesus taught us to pray, "Thy kingdom come, thy will be done on earth as it is in heaven" (Matt. 13:31-33; Mark 4:26-32; Luke 10:9; 13:18-21). This means we are praying that all people will recognize God as King and obey Him.

The words *kingdom of God* and *kingdom of heaven* mean the same thing. The Jewish people said *"kingdom of heaven"* because they felt God's name was too sacred to speak.

The Bible speaks of an earthly *kingdom*

of God and a heavenly kingdom. God will finally remove evil from all of His creation. Then His Kingdom (both earth and heaven) will be free from all sin (Luke 22:18; II Tim. 4:18; II Pet. 1:11).

KINGS, FIRST BOOK OF

is an Old Testament book that tells the story of Israel's kings from Solomon (about 970 B.C.) to Ahab (851 B.C.). First Kings tells about the plan for and the building of Solomon's temple. It includes a long dedication of the temple as well as Solomon's prayer dedicating all the people to the worship of God (I Kings 8:1-61).

First Kings also tells how the kingdom of Israel was divided into two kingdoms, Israel (northern kingdom) and Judah (southern kingdom), after the death of Solomon. The two kingdoms were rivals. A few of the kings who ruled were good. Many were wicked and worshiped false gods (I Kings 12:1-20).

First Kings tells how God sent prophets such as Elijah to call the people and the kings back to the Lord. Elijah's messages and the miracles God performed for him are recorded in I Kings (I Kings 17—21).

KINGS, SECOND BOOK OF

is an Old Testament book that continues the history of the two kingdoms, Israel and Judah, from about 850 B.C. until their fall. The northern kingdom (Israel) was defeated and taken captive by Assyria in

It was a joyful day when the ark left Kiriath-jearim.

722 B.C. (II Kings 17). The southern kingdom (Judah) fell to Babylon in 586 B.C. (II Kings 24:8—25:30).

Several prophets proclaimed God's judgment and warning to these kings of Judah and Israel. These prophets included Elisha, who took on Elijah's cloak as Elijah was taken into heaven. Other prophets during this time were Amos and Hosea in the northern kingdom and Obadiah, Joel, Isaiah, Micah, Nahum, Habakkuk, Zephaniah, and Jeremiah in the southern kingdom.

All these prophets continually repeated that God's judgment was coming. The reasons were that God's people no longer worshiped the true God and that their lives were not pleasing to God. Once in a while the people repented but later slipped back to their old ways.

The prophets' warnings came true. All God's people became exiles in foreign lands.

KIRIATH-JEARIM
(KUR-yath JEE-o-rim)

was a fortress-like city about twelve miles west of Jerusalem. About 1050 B.C. the Philistines captured the ark of the covenant in a battle with the Israelites. Later they returned it to Kiriath-jearim. The ark stayed in a specially built house for twenty years, until King David brought it back to Jerusalem in great pomp and ceremony (I Sam. 6:21—7:2; II Sam. 6:1-15).

KISHON (KEY-shun),
KISON (KISS-un)

are both names for a brook in the mountains of what is now northwestern Israel near Lebanon. During the winter, the melting snows from the mountains make it dangerous to cross. It must be forded only at special places.

On the banks of the Kishon, the army of Deborah and Barak defeated the Canaanites led by Sisera. Many of the Canaanite soldiers were washed away by the raging Kishon when their chariots got bogged down in the mud and water. This was proof to the Israelites that God was with them in the battle.

See Judges 5:21.

KISS

in Bible times as today, was a sign of love, greeting, or respect. It was a common greeting between male relatives as well as between male and female relatives and between friends. Often one kissed on the cheek, forehead, or beard, but lips, hands, and even feet were kissed also. While kissing usually showed affection, it was sometimes a formal part of a blessing and of anointing a king in Old Testament times (Gen. 27:26, 27). In the New Testament, a kiss became the usual greeting between believers in the early church (Rom. 16:16).

Probably the most famous kiss in the Bible is the one Judas gave to Jesus in the garden of Gethsemane. While it seemed to be a greeting, it really was a sign to soldiers that this was the man they were to arrest (Matt. 26:48, 49; Mark 14:44, 45; Luke 22:47, 48).

KNOWLEDGE, TREE OF

was a special tree in the garden of Eden set apart by God to test the obedience of Adam and Eve. He told them not to eat its fruit, but they ate it anyway.

There was probably not much special about the fruit—the sin was in disobeying God's command. After they ate, Adam and Eve had a knowledge of evil that they did not have before.

See Genesis 2:9, 17; 3:1-19.

KORAH (KOR-uh)

was the name of several people in the Bible, of which these two are the most important:

1. A Levite whose descendants were doorkeepers and musicians in the tabernacle and the temple. Some of the Psalms (42, 44—49, 84, 87—88) were written by Korahites and were probably sung by a Korahite choir (Num. 26:9-11).

2. A man who, with two of his friends, led a rebellion against Moses during the Exodus (Exod. 6:24; I Chron. 6:22). God caused the earth to open and swallow the three men and their followers. This was a dramatic warning to the other Israelites against rebelling.

The stranger at the well turned out to be a servant of Laban's and Rebekah's great-uncle, Abraham.

LABAN *(LAY-bun)*

was the grand-nephew of Abraham. Laban's family had stayed near Haran when Abraham left to follow God to the promised land.

Years later, Abraham wanted a wife for his son Isaac. He sent his most trusted servant back to his relatives near Haran. When the servant met a young woman named Rebekah near a well, he felt she would be just the right bride for Isaac (Gen. 24:29-50). Laban was Rebekah's brother, and when he saw the bracelets the servant had given Rebekah, he hurried the servant into his house. He gave him food and did everything he could to please him. When the servant told Laban about Abraham and Isaac, Laban quickly approved the marriage of his sister.

After many years, Jacob, the son of Rebekah and Isaac, ran away to Haran because his brother, Esau, was very angry with him (Genesis 29—30). Jacob fell in

207

love with Laban's daughter Rachel. He agreed to work for Laban seven years in order to earn Rachel as his bride. But Laban tricked Jacob and sent Leah, his older daughter, to be Jacob's wife instead. Jacob asked to work seven more years in order to have Rachel as his wife also. Laban agreed, and Rachel and Jacob were married. After the second seven-year period, Jacob worked for six more years. When he decided to leave, he said to Laban, "Let me have the speckled and spotted goats and the black sheep from your flocks for my wages for these years."

Laban said, "Good! Let it be as you said." But Laban removed all the speckled and spotted goats and the black sheep before Jacob had a chance to collect them. But Jacob was just as tricky. He waited for the next generation to be born and then chose out the animals Laban had said he could have. Finally, Jacob outwitted Laban and returned to his own country.

LADDER

is mentioned in the story of Jacob's dream at Bethel. In his dream Jacob saw a ladder between heaven and earth. Angels were going up and down the ladder, letting him know that God loved him and would take care of him. The ladder Jacob dreamed about probably looked like a wide staircase. See Genesis 28:12-17.

LAMB

is a young sheep (see *Animals*).

Lambs were eaten only on very special occasions. Meat was scarce, and to kill an animal before it had given birth was wasteful. For that reason, a person in Bible times would show great love and respect to God by giving a lamb as an offering.

Giving a lamb as a sacrifice meant giving the very best to God (Gen. 4:4; 22:7).

A lamb was always sacrificed as a part of the Passover feast (Exod. 12:3-13). The Jews celebrated Passover because God freed them from slavery in Egypt.

Lamb is also a word picture for Jesus' offering Himself to free us from sin. The Bible calls Jesus the Lamb of God.

LAMB OF GOD

is a New Testament name for Jesus. That name was especially meaningful to people in Jesus' day because Jews sacrificed lambs as part of many worship services. The term *Lamb of God* described Jesus' mission: to sacrifice Himself for our sins.

When John the Baptist saw Jesus, he shouted, "Behold, the Lamb of God, who takes away the sin of the world!"(John 1:29).

The apostle Peter wrote, "You were ransomed with the precious blood of Christ, like that of a lamb without blemish or spot."(I Pet. 1:18, 19).

In the Book of Revelation, *lamb* is often a word picture for Jesus. That book shows Jesus as the Lamb of God, who will rule heaven and earth and see that sin is forever destroyed (Rev. 5:12-13; 7:14; 13:8; 22:1, 3).

LAMENTATIONS
(LAM-en-TAY-shuns)
is an Old Testament book of poems. Jeremiah wrote them about 580 B.C., after

A stone lamp from Old Testament times.

LAMP

is a container that gives light (Matt. 5:15). Lamps were usually shallow bowls with one side slightly pointed to hold a wick. Some had handles, and some had tops with small holes where the olive oil (used for fuel) was poured in. Lamps were made from clay or bronze. Every house had several lamps. Usually one was kept burning all the time to light the others when it became dark.

Lamp and *light* are used often in the Bible as word pictures. Christ is called a light that shines in the darkness (John 1:5). God's Word is called a lamp (Ps. 119:105; II Pet. 1:19). Since lamps were very important in helping people see where to go in the darkness, these word pictures showed that Christ Himself is the way to God, and God's Word helps people know what to do.

Jerusalem was destroyed. Babylon had captured Judah and taken many of the people away. The people left in Jerusalem were suffering. Although they worked very hard, many were hungry. Their friends and families were far away. They didn't know what might happen next.

The prophet Jeremiah suffered with them. He put his and their feelings into words in the poems in Lamentations. Even when Jeremiah was very discouraged, he was able to write about God's great faithfulness.

Jeremiah said the people in Jerusalem knew that their troubles were the result of their own wickedness and turning away from God. They admitted their sin. They knew God was right when He said they were bad and needed to be punished. They had been warned by the prophets that God's judgment was coming.

Jeremiah asked God for forgiveness and mercy. He said that although nations become powerful and then get weak, God remains the same.

But thou, O Lord, dost reign forever;
Thy throne endures to all generations.
Lamentations 5:19

Jeremiah's poems were a comfort to the people.

LAMPSTAND

was a tall holder on which a lamp was placed so it would be high and give more light. Usually lampstands used in Bible times were made of pottery, but a few were made of metal. Often they were decorated. A special kind of lamp-

stand was the menorah, which had places for seven lamps or wicks. Menorahs were probably used for light in the temple. After the destruction of the temple, Jewish people used menorahs to help them remember temple worship.

LANGUAGES OF THE BIBLE

were Hebrew, Aramaic, and Greek. Most of the Old Testament was written in Hebrew, which was also the language spoken by the Israelites for most of that time.

Parts of the Old Testament and some words of the New Testament were written in Aramaic. This was the language spoken by the people in the later periods of the Old Testament and during the time of the New Testament. It is similar to Hebrew.

Most of the New Testament was written in Greek, the language most widely spoken in the Roman Empire. All educated people read and spoke Greek. Greek is a complicated language and can express many ideas.

Jesus probably knew all three languages. He probably spoke Aramaic at home, learned Greek from townspeople as He grew up, and studied Hebrew in the early religious classes all Jewish boys were given. The apostle Paul also knew those three languages.

The people in the Middle East spoke many languages. Words and phrases from Egyptian, Syrian, Persian, and Latin appear at times in the Bible. The inscription above Jesus' cross was in Hebrew, Greek, and Latin so everyone could read it.

LAST SUPPER

is the name of the last meal Jesus ate with His disciples before His crucifixion.

It happened on Thursday evening of Passover Week in an upper room of a house in Jerusalem.

Almost everything about it was unusual, starting earlier in the day, when Jesus sent Peter and John to find a place for the meal. He told them to enter Jerusalem and then follow a man carrying a water pitcher. When the man got to his house, the two disciples were to ask to use one of the rooms for the evening. Everything happened as Jesus had described.

After the Passover meal was finished, Jesus gave a lesson in humility by washing the disciples' feet, which was really a slave's job. Jesus also said clearly that Judas was going to betray Him. Judas then got up and left. Jesus shocked Peter, who thought of himself as one of Jesus' best friends, by telling him he would soon refuse to admit that he even knew Jesus.

Sometime during the evening, Jesus shared some broken bread and some wine with the disciples. This was a picture of His death the next day, when He Himself would be broken for all people.

Jesus and the disciples sat and talked together a long time that evening. They finally sang a hymn and then left for the garden of Gethsemane.

See Matthew 26:17-30; John 13—14.

LAVER *(LAY-ver)*

was a bowl for washing. In Old Testament times, lavers were placed between the door of the tabernacle or Temple and the altar. Priests washed their feet and hands in the lavers before they worshiped God. This washing was to picture being cleansed from sin. In the temple, the lavers were decorated and were so large that they were placed on stands. Some-

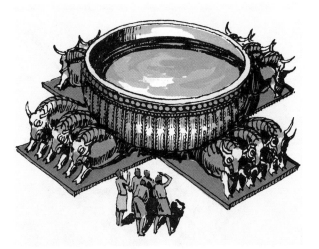

times animals for sacrifice were also washed with water from these lavers. See Exodus 30:17-21; I Kings 7:23-47.

LAW

is a word that means several things in the Bible, depending on what the particular writer is talking about. Here are some of the meanings:

1. Instruction about God and directions for how we are to live. Psalm 119:97 says, "Oh, how I love thy law! It is my meditation all the day." *Law* in the Psalms usually refers to all the teachings in the first five books of the Old Testament.

2. The Ten Commandments and other related laws in the Old Testament about our relationships with God and other people (Genesis, Exodus, Leviticus, Numbers, Deuteronomy).

3. The Old Testament laws about sacrifices for sin and priestly offerings, as well as the Ten Commandments (Exod. 20:3-17).

4. The New Testament, especially the Book of James, speaks of a new "law" or principle—the law of liberty in Christ (Jas. 1:25; 2:12). Christians are to be controlled by this "law of liberty."

Parts of the Old Testament have detailed instructions that told how Hebrews were to eat, dress, build houses, and worship. Even today some Jewish people live by these laws. For example, one food law said they were not to eat meat and dairy products in the same meal. So if you were to order steak in a restaurant in Jerusalem, you could not have butter for your bread at the same meal (although you could have margarine).

The Old Testament Law had many rules about the religious services of the Israelites (Lev; Gal 3:21; Heb. 10:1). Many of these, such as the sacrificing of lambs, were pictures of the salvation that God would provide through Jesus Christ. The New Testament Book of Hebrews says that these Old Testament sacrifices and the laws about them are no longer needed. Now we have a better way. Christ has fulfilled the Law for all who accept Him.

Jesus also repeated and deepened the moral principles of the Ten Commandments (Matt. 22:36-40). Those who follow Jesus are to obey His teachings.

LAZARUS *(LAZZ-uh-rus)* OF BETHANY

was a special friend of Jesus. He was the brother of Martha and Mary. Jesus had often visited at Lazarus's house in Bethany, a village about two miles from Jerusalem.

On one visit Jesus found Mary and Martha crying because Lazarus had died. Both Martha and Mary knew of Jesus' power, so each of them said, "Lord, if you had been here, my brother would not have died."

But Jesus told them, "I am the resurrection and the life." Then He went to the

LAZARUS *(LAZZ-uh-rus),*

was a sick beggar with ugly sores on his body. He was the main character in a story Jesus told. Lazarus had been so poor that he didn't have enough to eat. He begged for food at the door of a rich man who had plenty to eat and even wasted some. The rich man never gave Lazarus a good meal and he didn't do anything about his painful sores.

Both Lazarus and the rich man died, and in the next life their places were just the opposite. Lazarus lived next to the father of the Jewish people, Abraham. His life was now comfortable and happy. The rich man was uncomfortable and unhappy, and he was in pain. Now the rich man became the beggar, asking Abraham to let Lazarus bring him a drink. But Abraham said, "Son, remember that in your life you received lots of good things. Lazarus had only bad things. Now you are separated from each other by too great a distance for anyone to come and help you."

Lazarus was a beggar because he was too sick to work..

The rich man wanted Abraham to send Lazarus back to warn the rich man's five brothers not to make the same mistakes he had made. Abraham refused, saying that if the brothers did not listen to the clear teachings of Moses and other prophets, they would not listen to someone who came back from the dead.
See Luke 16:19-31.

tomb of Lazarus. "Lazarus, come out!" Jesus shouted. Lazarus came back to life after having been dead four days; he walked out of the tomb.

Later, the chief priests wanted to kill Lazarus because so many people heard about the miracle and were believing in Jesus.
See John 11:1-46; 12:9-11.

LEAH *(LEE-uh)*

was Jacob's first wife. She was the mother of Reuben, Simeon, Levi, Judah, Issachar, Zebulun, and Dinah. Jacob's second wife was Rachel, Leah's younger sister.

Jacob had worked for seven years in order to marry Rachel, but Laban, the women's father, sent Leah to the wedding instead. Jacob was disappointed but he worked another seven years for Rachel. Although Leah knew she was not the favorite, she was loyal to Jacob. She went with him to Canaan when he left Laban's house. See Genesis 29:21-30; 35:23.

LEAVEN *(LEV-un)*

is the ingredient in bread that makes it rise or expand. *Leaven* is also used in the Bible as a word picture for ideas or influences that grow or spread.

Sometimes *leaven* is used to mean a good influence (Matt. 13:33; Luke 13:20, 21). For example, Jesus compared the kingdom of God to leaven. Silently, steadily, the Kingdom grows just as bread dough rises.

More often *leaven* is a picture of a bad influence (Matt. 16:11). For example, Jesus said the wrong teaching of the Pharisees was like leaven. Keeping leaven out of bread was a picture of people keeping sin or evil out of their lives. That was one reason the Jews always ate unleavened bread at their Passover meals (Exod. 12:33, 34; 13:7-10). The other reason for eating unleavened bread at Passover was that it reminded the Jewish people of how the Israelites had to leave Egypt in a hurry. They had to be ready to go when God commanded them. They could not wait for the bread to rise.

Jesus ate unleavened bread the night He was betrayed (Mark 14:12, 22).

LEBANON

was the name of a mountain range; it is now in the southern part of the country also called Lebanon. *Lebanon* means "the white" and probably refers to the snow that covers the tops of the mountains most of the year. The high, rugged peaks are famous for their beauty. Tall trees from these mountains, called the cedars of Lebanon, were used to build the temple of Solomon.

See I Kings 5:1-18.

LEEK (see *Plants*)

LENTILS (see *Plants*)

LEPROSY (see *Diseases*)

LETTER

is a written message. Both the Old Testament and the New Testament contain letters (Est. 1:22; 3:13; Jer. 29:1-28; Acts 15:22, 23). Generally, letters and epistles are the same thing, but some people would say letters are written for one person, while epistles are meant to be shared and read by many people.

Letter in the Bible can also mean a single letter of the alphabet, or any small detail, as in "letter of the law."

LEVI (*LEE-vie*)

was Jacob and Leah's third son. His descendants were the Levites—the tribe from which all priests came. Levi took part in a bloody revenge against the men of the city of Shechem (Gen. 34:25-31; 45:1-7).

Levi and his brothers were jealous of their younger brother Joseph (Gen. 37:4, 28; 42:6). They sold Joseph as a slave. Later, in Egypt, Levi and his brothers had to bow down to Joseph, who had become an important man.

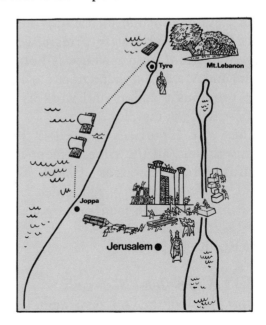

Levi became a common Jewish name. It was the second name for the apostle Matthew.

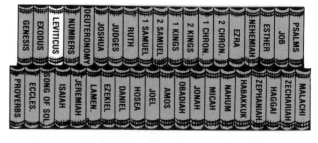

LEVITES *(LEE-vites)*

were the descendants of Levi, the son of Jacob and Leah. During the Exodus from Egypt, when the people wanted to worship false gods, Moses asked, "Who is on the Lord's side?" Immediately, the sons of Levi volunteered to help him. He said to them, "Today you have ordained yourselves for the service of the Lord." Moses gave them this blessing for being loyal.

The Levites became the tribe from which all the priests came. All priests had to be Levites, but not all Levites were priests. Those who were priests were descended from Aaron, who was both a Levite and Moses' brother. Other Levites were religious teachers and workers in the tabernacle or temple.

When the Israelites settled in the promised land, all the tribes except the Levites were given areas of land. The Levites were given forty-eight cities scattered throughout the land so they could minister to all the people.

See Exodus 32:25-29.

LEVITICUS *(luh-VIT-eh-cuss)*

the third book of the Old Testament, has been called "the priests' handbook," because it sets down rules for religious ceremonies as well as for everyday life. It is named for the tribe of Levi, from which all priests of Israel came. Leviticus was written by Moses while the Israelites wandered in the wilderness before they entered the promised land.

The first seven chapters told the priests how to offer sacrifices for their sins and for the sins of all the other people. Other chapters gave rules about what food to eat, about keeping clean, about how to observe the sabbath, and about doing right or wrong acts. Chapter 16 was especially important; it described what had to happen on the Day of Atonement, when the high priest entered the holy of holies.

In Leviticus, God again promised to be with His people: "I will make my abode among you. I will walk among you, and will be your God, and you shall be my people."

The word *holy* is used again and again in Leviticus to describe God and to show the people what God wanted them to be like. God told them that keeping all these commands and ceremonies were part of living as God's people should.

LIBERTY

means freedom, the opposite of slavery. In the Bible it means physical freedom from being the slave of another person, or freedom from being a slave to sin.

Slavery was common in ancient times, and the Bible treats slavery as a fact of life. A slave could be given liberty and become a free person but this was not as common as it should have been.

Liberty from sin comes through accepting Christ as Savior and becoming free to live as He wants us to live. As Romans 6:18, 22 tells us, liberty comes from choosing a new master.

LIFE

may mean either physical life or spiritual life. Both kinds of life come from God.

When God first created people, He breathed into Adam the breath of life (Gen. 2:7). Physical life is God's precious gift to each person. God forbids any person to take another person's life (Gen. 9:5; Exod. 20:13; Lev. 24:17).

While a healthy physical life is important, a healthy spiritual life is even more important. Spiritual life is a gift from God also (John 3:36; 5:24; Rom. 6:23; I John 5:12). New life begins when a person commits himself in faith to Christ and asks Jesus to be the Savior of his or her life. It is a life of friendship with God that will last forever.

LIFE, BOOK OF

is a word picture of the heavenly record of those who are in fellowship with God while they are on earth. The Bible says that only those whose names are in the book of life will get to enter heaven. See Philippians 4:3; Revelation 20:11-15.

LINEN

is a cloth or thread made from flax. It was fine and expensive fabric in Bible times, worn by wealthy people and by the priests in the temple (Lev. 6:10). Jesus

was buried in linen and put in a rich man's tomb (Matt. 27:59). When the Book of Revelation says that in heaven Christians will be dressed in fine linen, it shows they will wear the very best—probably what they could not afford on earth (Rev. 19:8). Revelation also says the linen robes of the Christians stand for their good deeds.

LINTEL *(LIN-tul)*

is the board or stone across the top of a door or window. The lintel supports the wall above it. On the first Passover, every Israelite family brushed the blood of the Passover lamb on the front lintel of their house. See Exodus 12:22, 23.

LIVER

is a large organ inside human and animal bodies. It is part of the system that digests food. Heathen people used animal livers to try to tell the future or find out other secrets (Ezek. 21:21). Some Bible writers saw the liver as the place where deepest sorrows were felt (Lam. 2:11 (KJV).

LOCUST (LOW-cust)

is an insect much like a grasshopper. It was very common in Bible lands. Locusts would gather in large groups and travel long distances, eating everything. Locusts were the eighth plague God sent to Egypt before the Israelites were freed. Locusts were also eaten for food. The Old Testament Book of Joel was written after crops in Israel had been destroyed by locusts.

LOINS (loynz)

are the middle part of the body, between the ribs and the hips. People wore wide belts around their loins and fastened swords there when they had to fight battles. So having your loins "girded" meant you were ready for action. Sometimes people wrapped sackcloth around their loins to show they were in mourning because someone had died or they had sinned. Because the reproductive organs are in the loins, children were said to have come from their parents' "loins."

LORD

in the Bible usually refers to God the Father, or Jesus Christ. However, it is sometimes used for kings, slave owners, or leaders. *Lord* is used for one who has respect, power, and authority. Men who were called lord in ancient times had to be obeyed by those under them. Sometimes any person who deserved respect would be called lord. When the word *Lord* is applied to God, it shows that He is the owner and ruler of the whole earth. People who follow Him are to obey and respect Him.

In the Old Testament some translations print the word in capital letters—LORD—when the word is the special covenant name (Yahweh) that the Israelites had for God. This word was so sacred to the Israelites that they did not even pronounce it. They substituted another word meaning "lord" or "master." The American Standard Version uses the word Jehovah for this special covenant name for God. In Psalm 97:5, both words for *lord* appear. You can look up this verse and see how your translation shows the difference between the two words.

See Isaiah 1:24; Romans 10:9; I Corinthians 6:11.

LORD OF HOSTS

is a special Old Testament name for God. It shows His control over all the angels in heaven as well as His followers on earth. Often the name gives the idea of God and all the forces of righteousness going into battle against evil. See I Samuel 1:11; Psalms 24:10; 59:5; 84:1, 3, 12.

LORD'S DAY

is the day set aside to honor the Lord Jesus Christ. Because Jesus rose from the dead on the first day of the week (Sunday), many early Christians used that day to worship and remember Him. Other things made this day special. After His resurrection, Jesus appeared to His disciples on the first day of the week (Luke 24:13-49; John 20:1-25). The coming of the Holy Spirit at Pentecost was on the first day of the week while early Christians were meeting together to honor Christ (Acts 20:7; I Cor. 16:1, 2). The vision John received before he wrote the Book of Revelation came on the Lord's Day (Rev. 1:10).

LORD'S PRAYER

is the name Christians have given the prayer Jesus taught His disciples. They had asked, "Lord, teach us to pray."

The model prayer Jesus gave them begins, "Our Father who art in heaven." This short, beautiful prayer shows that believers may pray to their heavenly Father, asking Him to complete His plans in the world and to meet their needs. This prayer shows how much we must depend on God.

See Matthew 6:9-13; Luke 11:2-4.

Our Father which art in heaven, hallowed be thy name. Thy kingdom come. Thy will be done in earth, as it is in heaven. Give us this day our daily bread.

And forgive us our debts, as we forgive our debtors. And lead us not into temptation, but deliver us from evil: For thine is the kingdom, and the power, and the glory, for ever. Amen.

(Matt. 6:9-13)

LORD'S SUPPER

is a celebration when Christians proclaim Jesus' death and resurrection from the dead. It reminds us that all Christians are part of God's family and that we look forward to the time when Christ will fully rule all of the universe.

The Lord's Supper was started at the last Passover feast Jesus ate with His disciples, the night before He was crucified. As they were eating, Jesus took some bread, broke it into pieces, and told His disciples to eat it. "This is my body," He said. Then He gave them some wine and told them to drink it. "This is my blood," He said. Breaking the bread and pouring the wine were pictures of what would happen the next day, when Jesus' body would be broken and His blood shed for all people. Jesus told the disciples they should meet together often to share such a meal and remember Him. He promised He would be present with them in a special way when they did this.

Christians through the centuries have continued to take part in the Lord's Supper. It is a time to remember what Christ has done for us and to renew our promise to obey Him.

See Matthew 26:26-28; Mark 14:22-24; Luke 22:17-19; I Corinthians 10:16, 17; 11:23-34.

LOT

Abraham's nephew, went with Abraham from Ur to their new home in Canaan. They and their families and herds traveled a long way together, and they seemed to get along well. But after they reached Canaan, problems arose. Their herdsmen quarreled. Abraham decided that he and Lot must have separate land. Abraham took Lot to a high place and asked him to choose. "If you take the right hand, then I will go to the left," Abraham said.

Selfishly, Lot chose the land that looked better for his cattle. But that selfish decision led to trouble for Lot and his family. His land lay near the wicked cities Sodom and Gomorrah. Lot and his family later moved to Sodom. Lot faced many problems living there, and finally God destroyed the cities for their wickedness. But God spared Lot, leading him and his family away just in time.

See Genesis 11:31; 13—14.

LOT'S WIFE

Lot and his two daughters barely escaped the fire that destroyed Sodom.

LOT'S WIFE

ran with her husband and daughters from the wicked city of Sodom when God told them He would destroy it. Because their family had been the only righteous people in the city, God wanted to spare their lives. "Flee for your life; do not look back or stop anywhere in the valley," the angels had told them.

But Lot's wife disobeyed the angels' command. As she looked back to watch fire and brimstone fall on the cities of Sodom and Gomorrah, she was destroyed also. Her body turned into a pillar of salt.

See Genesis 19:15-28.

LOVE

is what the Christian faith is all about (Matt, 5:43-48; 22:37-39; I Cor. 13; I John 3:14). Love is more than just a feeling of being attracted to someone or of feeling happy with someone—as we do with fam-ily, friends, or pets. It means choosing to be kind and helpful to others even though we may not want to. It is doing for other people what we would like to have them do for us.

Love between a husband and wife is a promise to care for each other and do everything possible to help the other person. This love-promise brings tenderness, joy, excitement, and a sense of how good it is to be together. It also helps husbands and wives go through times of trouble together. When this attitude is shared with children, a family becomes a true place of love.

The Bible says God is love and that all real love comes from God (John 3:16; 17:26; I John 4:8, 16). God shows His love for us by caring for us all the time. He also showed it by sending His Son, Jesus, to take away our sins. Jesus Christ is the highest example of love, both in His life

218

on earth and in His death for us.

God's power helps us love others. The Bible speaks of "brotherly love," which is being concerned for others who need something we can give (John 13:35; I John 2:10-18). They may be people we have never met. Christ said we are to love even our enemies.

The Christian church is built on God's love for us and on the special love Christians have for each other. Jesus said, "By this all men will know that you are my disciples, if you have love for one another."

LUKE

was a well-educated Gentile doctor. He wrote two New Testament books, the Gospel of Luke and the Acts of the Apostles. He traveled with the apostle Paul, who called him the "beloved physician" In Colossians 4:14. his writing style shows he watched for details and was accurate, traits he may have learned as a doctor.

Scholars believe he may have come from Macedonia (northern Greece). Tradition says he was martyred in Greece.

LUKE, GOSPEL OF

is the third book in the New Testament. It is the story of the life of Jesus written about A.D. 60 by the doctor Luke. Although he was not one of the twelve disciples and probably did not know Jesus while He lived on earth, Luke was a close friend of the apostle Paul and got much information for his Gospel from him. He no doubt also talked to Mary, Jesus' mother, and probably to Mary and Martha of Bethany. He wrote his Gospel for Gentiles, because Luke himself was a Gentile and because Paul was an apostle to the Gentiles. Luke's purpose was to record in an orderly way exactly what Jesus said and did. He was writing for people who had just heard of Jesus.

After a short introduction, Luke records the life of Jesus step by step, beginning before He was born. He tells about the angel's visit to Mary, Mary's answer, and the full story of the birth of Jesus. This is the only Gospel that tells anything about the boyhood of Jesus. Then comes His baptism, His public ministry, and finally His death, resurrection, and ascension.

Throughout the book, Luke shows Jesus' concern for all people: rich and poor, Gentile and Jew. He also points out the many times Jesus prayed—at His baptism, after cleansing the leper, before calling His disciples, on the Mount of Transfiguration, on the cross, and at His death.

LYDDA *(LID-uh)*

was a village, sometimes called Lod, about thirty miles northwest of Jerusalem. Jews returning after the Babylonian Exile settled there for a while (Ezra 2:33; Neh. 7:37). Peter helped the people in a church there (Acts 9:32-38).

LYDIA *(LID-ee-uh)*

a well-to-do businesswoman in Philippi, was Paul's first convert in Europe. She heard about Jesus as she and other women were praying by a river. She believed what Paul told her about Christ. After her whole family and her servants believed and were baptized, she invited Paul and his traveling companions to stay at her home. The church at Philippi met at her house. See Acts 16:13-15, 40.

LYING

is any action or word that is meant to deceive or fool someone else. God is truth, and He expects His people to speak the truth (John 1:17; 14:6; Rom. 3:4). Satan is the father of lies, and those who tell lies are giving support to Satan (John 8:44). All types of lying are condemned in the Bible, but especially bad is "bearing false witness"—telling something untrue about another person in order to hurt him (Exod. 20:16).

LYSTRA *(LISS-truh)*

was a Roman colony in the land that is now Turkey. Paul healed a crippled man there, and came back to the city several times on his missionary journeys. Timothy came from Lystra. See Acts 14:1-11; 16:1.

When God spoke to Moses from a burning bush, He gave him a difficult job: to lead the Israelites out of slavery in Egypt.

MACCABEES *(MAK-uh-beez)*, REVOLT OF THE

was a revolution led by Jewish patriots in 168-167 B.C. to make Syria stop persecuting the Jews in Israel. The revolution brought some freedom for the Jews.

A priest named Mattathias and his sons were the leaders of the revolt. One of the sons, Judas, was called Maccabee (meaning "Hammerer") because of his fighting ability. Later all the men in the revolt were called Maccabees. Judas and

his band of Jews camped in the mountains and fought against the Syrians who occupied their country. They also fought against those Jews who sided with the Syrians. The Maccabees tore down pagan altars and asked other Jewish people to join them. Syria sent in its army, and the Maccabees insisted they would "either live nobly or die nobly." They defeated the Syrian army.

After driving away the Syrians, Judas Maccabee worked to restore true worship in Palestine. He cleansed the temple from pagan worship and began proper sacrifices to the Lord. An eight-day celebration called Hanukkah dedicated the temple to right worship.

Their troubles did not end, but the Jewish people remember the Maccabees as heroes. Their story is told in two books called I and II Maccabees. These books are a part of the Roman Catholic Bible.

MACEDONIA *(mass-uh-DOE-nee-uh)* was a Roman province in New Testament times. A kingdom in the northern part of modern Greece, it was the first part of Europe to hear about Christ. The apostle Paul visited Macedonia many times. Paul first traveled to Macedonia after he had a vision. "Come over to Macedonia and help us," the man in the vision said. Paul left right away and landed at Philippi, the leading city in Macedonia. There he met Lydia, and when she accepted Christ, the first church in Europe began. See Acts 16:9, 10.

MAGI *(MAY-jie)* is a name used for the wise men from the East who came to Bethlehem to honor the baby Jesus. See Matthew 2.

MAHLON *(MAY-lon)* was Ruth's first husband, an Israelite who married her in Moab and died about ten years later. See Ruth 1:2, 5; 4:9. 10.

MAID, MAIDEN means either a young unmarried woman, or a female servant, or both.

MALACHI *(MAL-uh-kie)* was the prophet who wrote the last book of the Old Testament. He lived around 450 B.C. and warned against sin and turning from God. He predicted that those who were not true to God would be

judged, and he promised blessing for those who repented.

The book asked questions to make the people think about their lives. Malachi criticized priests for being careless in conducting worship. He condemned the people who were not giving God their tithes and were using defective animals for sacrifices. He asked them to return to obeying the Law.

Malachi looked forward to the Messiah, who would be God's "messenger of the Covenant" and would cleanse and purify God's people. "The Lord whom you seek will suddenly come to his temple," Malachi said in 3:1-3. "But who can endure the day of his coming, and who can stand when he appears? For he is like a refiner's fire . . . and he will purify. . . ."

Although Malachi preached about judgment, he reminded the people that the Lord cared for them. The book begins with "I have loved you, says the Lord." And it ends with a promise of the coming Messiah: "But for you who fear my name the sun of righteousness shall rise, with healing in its wings."

MAN

in the Bible is a word that often means all people—men and women. God made man to love and worship Him. Genesis 5:2 says, "Male and female he created them, and he blessed them and named them Man when they were created."

Man can also mean a person of the male sex. All persons—men and women—were created like God with thoughts, feelings, and a will God made people to be His special friends. This makes people different from animals. Men and women are responsible for taking care of Planet Earth.(Gen. 1:27. 28).

MANASSEH *(muh-NASS-uh)*

was the name of two men in the Old Testament.

1. Joseph's oldest son, who was born in Egypt (Gen. 41:51; 48:5, 19). His grandfather Jacob adopted him, and he became head of one of the twelve tribes of Israel.

2. An evil king of Judah (II Kings 21:1-17; II Chron. 33:1-20). Son of King Hezekiah, he began to rule in 687 B.C. when he was only twelve years old. At first Manasseh was too young to control the people in power, and they started the country worshiping idols. But as he grew up, Manasseh did things even worse. He built altars to Baal and to the sun, moon, stars, and planets. He put a heathen altar inside the temple. He punished people or prophets who remained true to God. After God allowed him to be captured and taken to Babylon, he repented of his evil work. But it was too late. He had already brought his country, Judah, to its downfall.

MANASSEH *(muh-NASS-uh)*, TRIBE OF

was one of the twelve tribes of Israel that left Egypt for Canaan. The people in the tribe were descendants of Manasseh, Joseph's son who was adopted by Jacob. When they got to Israel, half of the tribe settled east of the Jordan River and half crossed over. Those on the west side were given good land, and they were important among the twelve tribes. Their land stretched from the Jordan River to the Mediterranean Sea through the middle of Canaan. They later became part of the northern kingdom of Israel. Those who stayed on the east side became idol worshipers. All of the tribe of Manasseh were later taken away as prisoners to Assyria. See Joshua 17:7-10.

MANGER (MAIN-jur)

is a box built at the right height to feed cattle or horses. It was usually filled with straw, hay, or oats. The most famous manger was the one where the baby Jesus was laid when He was born in Bethlehem. See Luke 2:7, 12, 16.

MANNA (see box at right)

MANOAH (muh-NO-uh)

was Samson's father. He and his wife had wanted a child for a long time. One day an angel appeared to Manoah's wife and told her that she would have a son, and she should dedicate him to the Lord as a Nazirite. Manoah asked God to send the angel again so they could ask him what to do with their son. When the angel came, he repeated his instructions. He proved he was an angel by going up toward heaven in the flame of the altar Manoah prepared. The angel's word came true. A son—Samson—was born, and Manoah and his wife raised him according to the strict Nazirite laws. See Judges 13.

MANTLE (MAN-tul)

was usually a loose cloak without sleeves worn like an overcoat. In II Kings 2:8-14, Elijah's mantle was given to Elisha as a

sign that he would become a prophet after Elijah's death.

MARK, GOSPEL OF

is the second book of the New Testament. It's the shortest of the Gospels and records Jesus' actions more than His words. John Mark wrote this Gospel in Rome about A.D. 65-70. Many scholars think that Mark wrote down much of the material that the apostle Peter used in his preaching. It was probably the first of the Gospels to be written.

Mark did not write about Jesus' birth or childhood. The story starts with Jesus as a grown man meeting John the Baptist. This Gospel tells about Jesus' temptation, His work in His home region of Galilee, and His choosing and training of disciples. It describes many of Jesus' miracles and shows that Jesus was a helper of others as well as master of the universe.

But when Jesus' work of healing and teaching was coming to an end, He began to prepare His disciples for the future. Mark wrote what Jesus taught about the troubles that lay ahead. He recorded Jesus' last supper with His disciples, Jesus' arrest in the garden of Gethsemane, and His death on the cross. Mark ended his Gospel with Jesus' resurrection from the dead. In the last chapter, an angel talks to Mary, Mary Magdalene, and Salome and gives this promise: "Do not be amazed; you seek Jesus of Nazareth, who was crucified. He has risen, he is not

MANNA *(MAN-uh)*

was a food God provided for the Israelites while they wandered in the wilderness. In a miraculous way, manna appeared fresh every night on the ground so the people could gather it in the morning. They could use it in many ways. They could grind it up and make cakes, or they could boil it like cereal. The Bible says it looked like white seeds or flakes and tast-

ed like wafers made with honey. See Exodus 16:13-21, 31-36; Numbers 11:7-9.

here. . . . Go, tell his disciples and Peter that he is going before you to Galilee; there you will see him, as he told you."

The last twelve verses in Mark are often printed in small type at the end of the book. This is because some of the oldest Greek copies we have of this Gospel do not include those verses. Most scholars believe the last twelve verses were added later by someone else.

MARK, JOHN

was the writer of the second Gospel and a friend of Peter. He traveled with Paul and Barnabas on their first missionary journey. John was his Jewish name; Mark or Marcus was his Roman name. In the New Testament, he is called Mark, John Mark, and John.

Mark's mother, Mary, lived in Jerusalem in a large house. She was a Christian, and when Mark was a young man, he met many of the early Christian leaders (Acts 12:12). Peter referred to him as "my son" in I Peter 5:13 because of their close friendship.

Mark started out with Paul and Barnabas on a missionary journey but did not finish it, perhaps because of home-

sickness or some disagreement with Paul (Acts 12:25; 13:13; 15:36-41). Mark went along with Barnabas on his next journey and proved himself. Later Paul highly recommended Mark as a good Christian worker. Mark spent some time with Paul in Rome, and it was probably there he wrote the Gospel that has his name (Philem. 24; II Tim. 4:11).

MARKETPLACE

was the center of town life in Bible times.

The Middle East today still has open marketplaces.

People bought and sold supplies, met friends, hired workers, and gathered for meetings and discussions. Court cases were often tried in the marketplace. Paul and Silas were brought to the rulers in the marketplace in Philippi and then were attacked by the crowds gathered there.

Paul often preached in marketplaces on his missionary journeys.

See Acts 16:19-23; 17:17.

MARRIAGE

began in the garden of Eden as a way for human beings to give and receive love and companionship. Genesis 2:24 says, "A man leaves his father and his mother and cleaves to his wife, and they become one flesh."

Marriage also is intended to provide a loving place for children.

The model God gave in Genesis, before people sinned, was for one husband and one wife (I Cor. 7:4). In Old Testament times, Hebrew men, like the pagan men around them, often had more than one wife The Bible never says this is good; it simply tells what the people did. In fact, the Old Testament tells many stories about problems that arose when men had more than one wife.

The Bible gives many instructions about marriage. Husbands and wives are to love each other; submit to each other; enjoy each other; respect each other.

Marriage is sometimes used in the Bible as a picture of God's relationship with His people (Eph. 5:21-33). In the Old Testament, God is pictured as the husband and the Hebrew people as His wife. Christ gave himself for the church as husbands are to give themselves for their wives. Wives are to be subject to their husbands as the church is subject to Christ.

MARS HILL

was a little hill in downtown Athens near the temple to the ancient Greek gods. The Greek council met there in New Testament times, and Paul was brought there to explain his message. Paul delivered a famous sermon there, and part of it is found in Acts 17:16-34.

MARTHA *(MAR-thuh)*

was a close friend of Jesus. She and her brother Lazarus and sister Mary lived in Bethany, just two miles outside of Jerusalem. Jesus often visited them for meals, and Martha seemed to be the hostess on these occasions. John 11:5 records that "Jesus loved Martha and her sister and Lazarus," showing how close this family was to Him. See Luke 10:38-42; John 11:1-44.

MARTYR *(MAR-tur)*

is a person who is killed or made to suffer greatly because of his beliefs. Stephen was the first Christian martyr. Most of the apostles and many other early Christians were martyred because they would not give up their faith in Christ. The Bible says many more will give their lives for Christ before the time of the final judgment. See Acts 6:8—7:60; 22:20; Revelation 6:9-11.

MARY, MOTHER OF JESUS

was a godly woman. When the angel Gabriel told her she would give birth to God's Son, she asked, "How can this be?" The angel explained that God would work a miracle through her, and the child to be born would not be Joseph's son, but the Son of God (Matt. 1—2; Luke 1—2). She responded with a beautiful hymn of praise. Shortly after that she married Joseph, a carpenter to whom she was engaged. Mary remembered all the wonderful events surrounding Jesus' birth and probably shared them later with the apostles and the Gospel writers.

When Jesus was twelve years old, Mary and Joseph were amazed that Jesus taught the teachers in the temple.

Years later, at a wedding in the village of Cana, she asked Jesus to perform His first miracle (John 2:1-11).

When Jesus was being crucified, He took special notice of His mother, who had come to be with Him at His death (John 19:25-27). He asked His disciple John to care for her. (Joseph apparently had already died.) Later, Mary seems to have been active in the early church (Acts 1:14).

MARY MAGDALENE

(MAG-duh-leen)

was a woman from whom Jesus cast out seven demons (Mark 16:9; Luke 8:2). She was also the first person to whom Jesus appeared after His resurrection. She was a devoted follower of Jesus. She was called "Magdalene" because she came from the town of Magdala on the Sea of Galilee. Like Jesus, she was a Galilean.

MARY OF BETHANY

the sister of Martha and Lazarus, was a close friend of Jesus. Jesus often visited her family home in Bethany, just two miles from Jerusalem. Mary liked to sit with the disciples and listen to Jesus teach. When Martha scolded her for not helping prepare a meal, Jesus said, "Mary has chosen the good portion" (Luke 10:38-42). Mary also watched as Jesus brought her dead brother Lazarus back to life (John 11:2-31).

Another time Mary was so filled with love for Jesus that she poured expensive perfume on His feet (John 12:1-8). Jesus appreciated her gift and told those around Him that this was a sign He was being prepared for burial.

MASTER

was a name for Jesus used in the New Testament, especially in the Gospel of Luke. The name showed respect for Jesus as a teacher and guide.

MATTHEW *(MATH-you)*

was a tax collector before he became one of Jesus' disciples. He was also called Levi. He wrote the first book of the New Testament, the Gospel of Matthew. He was well prepared to write a story of Jesus' life, because tax collectors were skilled at writing and keeping records, and because Matthew was with Jesus during all of Jesus' public life.

Matthew met Jesus while he was collecting taxes for King Herod Antipas in Galilee. Tax collectors were very unpopular. They were working for the Roman Empire that loyal Jews hated. Plus, tax collectors were often dishonest, taxing more than they had to and keeping the extra money themselves.

Matthew was busy at his work when Jesus walked up to him and said, "Follow me" (Matt. 9:9; Mark 2:14; Luke 5:27). Matthew left his business and followed Jesus. Later he had a dinner party at his home for his tax collector friends and Jesus (Matt. 9:10-13; Luke 5:29-32). Outsiders were upset that Jesus associated with such unpopular people. Jesus replied, "Those who are well have no need of a physician, but those who are sick." Matthew never went back to his tax collecting. Instead he followed Jesus.

MATTHEW (MATH-you), GOSPEL OF

is the first book of the New Testament. It is the life story of Jesus written by his apostle Matthew. It was written especially for Jewish readers.

This Gospel often shows that Jesus fulfilled the Old Testament prophecies. "That it might be fulfilled" is a common expression in Matthew. This book shows that Jesus was the King the Jewish people had been looking for. Matthew traced

It was very early on the first day of the week when Mary Magdalene took her spices to the tomb of Jesus.

Jesus' ancestors back to King David, and then back to Abraham, the father of the Hebrew people. Matthew told about the birth of Jesus and the visit of the Eastern kings to honor Him.

Matthew included several collections of things Jesus taught. These are placed among the stories of His healings and other good works.

The first group of sayings is about what it means to follow Jesus. This includes the well-known Sermon on the Mount in chapters 5 to 7.

The second group of teachings is in chapter 10. Jesus told the twelve apostles what He expected of them and what they should expect when they went out to preach about Christ and His kingdom.

The third section of sayings is about the kingdom of God. It is a series of stories in which Jesus compared His kingdom to seeds that a farmer sows, to a hidden treasure, and to a net thrown into the sea. These stories appear in chapter 13.

Other stories and teachings about what the kingdom of God means appear throughout the rest of the book. The largest collection is in chapters 24 and 25. Chapters 26—28 tell about the Last Supper, the arrest, the trial, death, and resurrection of Jesus. Matthew's Gospel ends with the Great Commission, given by Jesus just before He was taken to heaven. "Go therefore and make disciples of all nations, baptizing them in the name of the Father and of the Son and of the Holy Spirit, teaching them to observe all that I have commanded you; and lo, I am with you always, to the close of the age."

MATTHIAS *(muh-THIE-us)*

was chosen to take the place of Judas Iscariot. The eleven apostles first chose two men who met the requirements: Matthias and Joseph Justus. Both men had been with Jesus and the other apostles since the time of Jesus' baptism. Then the apostles prayed, "Lord, who knowest the hearts of all men, show which one of these two thou hast chosen to take the place in this ministry and apostleship." The Lord chose Matthias, and he began the work of an apostle. Matthias is never mentioned again in the New Testament. See Acts 1:15-26.

MEALS

and eating customs varied in Bible times, but generally people ate two meals a day. Workers did not eat breakfast but often took some bread and cheese with them to work. Then one light meal was eaten sometime between 10 o'clock and noon just before a midday rest from the hot sun. Then a large meal was eaten in the evening. This was a time for fellowship and having guests. Banquets and feasts were always held in the evening. At ordinary meals women ate with the men, but only men were invited to banquets.

Meals were made up of three kinds of food: vegetables (including grains), fruits, and animal foods (lamb, calf, and milk products). The poor people, however, rarely ate meat. The main food of the poor was bread, which they ate at every meal. Sometimes honey or oil was mixed

Jesus ate with Matthew and his friends—whether the Pharisees liked it or not.

in the bread dough.

Knives, forks, or spoons were not used. Dinner was usually one main dish, with everything cooked together in the same pot. People dipped bread into the pot or used their fingers.

In Abraham's time people usually sat on the ground for meals. But in New Testament times people stretched out on the floor or on couches around three sides of a large, low, square table, leaving the fourth side free for serving. Usually guests would recline at a right angle to the table, supporting themselves on their left elbow so their right hands were free

for eating.

Giving thanks before meals was expected. Jesus gave thanks before feeding the 5,000 and at the Last Supper. See Genesis 18:8; Matthew 15:36.

MEASURES

were not as exact in ancient times as they are today. People then were satisfied with round numbers. They often measured things in "handfuls"—the amount one could hold in his hand. On page 231 are some of the measures mentioned in the Bible compared approximately to our measures today.

Hebrew Measurements

Hebrew Measurements	U. S. Measurements	Metric Measurements
Liquid Measures:		
log	2/3 pint	.313 liter
hin 12 logs	1 gallon	3.8 liters
bath 6 hins	6 gallons	22.7 liters
cor, homer 10 baths	60 gallons	226.8 liters
metretal, firkin	10 gallons	38.37 liters
Dry Measures:		
kab, cab	1.16 quarts	1.28 liters
omer, issaron 1-4/5 cabs	2.09 quarts	2.3 liters
seah 3-1/3 omers	2/3 peck	5.81 liters
ephah 3 seahs	1/2 bushel	17.6 liters
lethech	2-1/2 bushels	88.1 liters

homer, cor 2 lethech
          10 ephahs
          100 omers
	5 bushels	176.2 liters

bushel	7-1/2 quarts	8.3 liters
measure	1 quart	1.1 liters
pot	1 pint	.55 liters
Distance Measures:		
finger 3/4 inch		19 millimeters
handbreadth, palm, 4 fingers	3 inches	76 millimeters
span 3 handbreadths	9 inches	.22 meters
cubit 6 handbreadths	18 inches	44 meters
reed 6 cubits	9 feet	2.64 meters
fathom	6 feet	1.82 meters
stadium, furlong	606 feet	184.7 meters
mile	5,280 feet	1.48 kilometers

Area Measures:
acre, yoke—the area oxen could plow in one day (5/8 acre)

MEDES (meeds)

were the people of the land of Media (what is today the northwest part of Iran). A fierce, warlike people, they were important during the Old Testament times. They often joined with the Persians to fight the Assyrians and the Egyptians. Israel was sometimes part of their battleground.

Darius the Mede was the first ruler of the Medo-Persian Empire after it defeated Babylon. Daniel worked under Darius for about nine years, and Darius was kind to Daniel.

See Isaiah 13:17; Daniel 5:31; 6:8, 12; 8:20.

MENE, MENE, TEKEL, AND PARSIN *(MEE-nee, TEE-kul, PAR-sun)* (or **UPHARSIN**)

were mysterious Aramaic words that were suddenly written on the wall of King Belshazzar's banquet hall while he was giving a great feast. The guests were merrily drinking wine from golden cups taken from the temple in Jerusalem. When they saw the words, they were shocked. The terrified king called in his wise men to interpret the words, but they could not. Then the queen suggested they bring in Daniel, one of the captives from Israel. She had heard that he could interpret dreams.

Daniel told the king what the words meant:

"God has numbered the days of your kingdom and brought it to an end.

"You have been weighed in the balances and found wanting.

"Your kingdom is divided and given to the Medes and Persians."

That very night King Belshazzar was killed.

See Daniel 5.

MEPHIBOSHETH
(muh-FIB-uh-sheth)

also called Meribaal, was the crippled son of Jonathan, David's friend. Jonathan was killed in battle when Mephibosheth was five years old. A nurse grabbed the boy and ran from Jerusalem to keep him safe from the fights over who would be the next king. In her rush, she dropped him and crippled him for life.

After David was settled on the throne, Mephibosheth was brought to him. David remembered his friendship with Jonathan and invited Mephibosheth to live in the palace. Even though he was King Saul's grandson and might have claimed to be king, Mephibosheth remained loyal to King David. David realized Mephibosheth's loyalty and accepted him as a friend.

See II Samuel 4:4; 9; 16:1-4; 19:24-30.

MERCY SEAT

was a beautiful slab of gold on top of the ark of the covenant. On it stood the two golden cherubim. The ark sat inside the holy of holies in the tabernacle and temple. On the annual Day of Atonement, the mercy seat was sprinkled with the blood of the sacrifice to wipe away the sins of the high priest and the sins of all the Israelites. See Exodus 25:17-22; 26:34; 37:6-9; Leviticus 16:2, 13-15.

MESSIAH *(muh-SIE-uh)*

is the Hebrew word for "anointed one." It applies in a special way to Jesus. Old Testament priests, prophets, and kings were all anointed with oil in a ceremony dedicating them and their work to God. Even the bowls and other parts of the tabernacle were anointed to set them apart for God's purposes.

God revealed that He would send a Messiah, an "anointed one," to bring peace and to establish His kingdom. The Jewish people looked forward to the day when this Messiah would come and deliver them.

But many Jewish people misunderstood the Messiah's work. They expected a political leader who would help them defeat their Gentile rulers. Instead, God was sending a spiritual Savior who would give meaning to life on earth and through all eternity. The Messiah was a suffering servant who would bring more than earthly blessing (Isa. 53).

The disciples realized that Jesus Christ was the Messiah, God's special anointed

"I am the Messiah," Jesus told a woman at the well.

Mephibosheth was welcomed into David's palace.

one, who would fulfill God's purpose. When Andrew told his brother Peter about Jesus, he said, "We have found the Messiah" (John 1:41).

When Jesus first began to teach and preach, He showed the people in His hometown that He was the Messiah (Luke 4:16-21). He went to the synagogue and read a passage about the anointed one from Isaiah 61:1-2. Then He said, "Today this scripture has been fulfilled in your hearing."

Even though Jesus was careful not to give people the wrong idea that He would help overthrow the Roman government, they kept thinking He would. When He died on the cross, they could not understand what was happening. Only after Jesus rose from the dead, and after the Holy Spirit came at Pentecost, did the disciples begin to understand that Jesus was a spiritual Messiah.

Christ is the Greek word for Messiah. Whenever the New Testament refers to Jesus as Christ, it is saying that He is the Messiah.

METHUSELAH
(muh-THOO-zuh-luh)
lived longer than anyone else in the Bible. He died at age 969, just before God sent the Flood. Noah was his grandson. See Genesis 5:21-27.

MICAH *(MY-cuh)*, BOOK OF
is an Old Testament book written by the prophet Micah just before the Northern Kingdom was conquered in 722 B.C. In his book, Micah preached against the sins of the people. But he also told how God would some day bless His people.

Micah said that God was angry with the people for worshiping idols, taking advantage of the poor, and refusing to obey God. He said both the northern Kingdom (Samaria) and the southern Kingdom (Jerusalem) would fall before their enemies.

Against this gloomy background, Micah told about God's plan for the world. The Messiah would come to fulfill God's plan. Micah 5:2 says Bethlehem would be the place where the ruler of Israel would be born. Micah reminded everyone that although God sees the sins of His people, He loves and forgives those who repent. Micah 7:18 declares, "Who is a God like thee, pardoning iniquity and passing over transgression?. . . He does not retain his anger for ever because he delights in steadfast love."

MICHAEL *(MY-kul)*
is an archangel whose name means "Who is like God?" Michael is most concerned with caring for God's people, the Jews. He fights against the wicked, even Satan himself. See Daniel 10:10-21; Jude 1:9; Revelation 12:7.

MICHMASH *(MICK-mash)*
sometimes spelled Michmas, was a city on a high hill about eight miles northeast of Jerusalem. It controlled an important pass between the Jordan valley and western Israel. In this pass, during a battle between Israel and the Philistines, Saul's son Jonathan led the Israelites to victory. See I Samuel 13—14.

When the Philistines finally captured Samson, they blinded him and made him push a millstone.

MIND

to ancient people, was not simply another word for brain. Translators often use the word *mind* to mean the center of the whole person.

Bible writers often used heart to refer to the center of thinking and deciding.

MINISTER *(MIN-uh-stir)*

means "to serve." It also refers to a person who serves. Today it usually means a person whose life is dedicated to service for God and who earns his living in this service (I Cor. 9:14). The apostle Paul

MIDIAN *(MID-ee-un)*

was the son of Abraham and his second wife, Keturah. The Midianites, his descendants, were wealthy nomads who lived east of the Jordan River and down into the Sinai Peninsula (Exod. 2:15-21; 18:1-11). Moses married a Midianite, Zipporah.

When the Israelites were in the wilderness after they left Egypt, the Midianites seemed friendly to them. Many years later they became enemies. Two hundred years after Israel settled in the promised land, the Midianites gained rule over them for a few years. They made life miserable for the Israelites, raiding their villages and trampling down their crops. God chose Gideon to drive the Midianites out (Judg. 6—7).

MILLS and MILLSTONES

were used to grind grain into meal or flour. Two round, heavy stones rotated against each other as people (usually women) turned them with a handle. Some mills were so big that oxen were used to turn them. The sound of the mill grinding in the morning was the sign of prosperity, according to Jeremiah 25:10.

When a wedding feast ran out of wine, Jesus miraculously made some more—out of water.

Miriam's mother made a basket for baby Moses—and it saved his life.

said that those who are called by God to spend their lives proclaiming the Gospel should earn their living that way (I Tim. 1:12; II Tim. 1:11).

Paul wrote to Timothy that he had been appointed by God for this kind of service.

MIRACLE

is a wonderful happening done by the power of God. Miracles may be beyond the known laws of nature, but they are not magic. Miracles depend on God's will and His power, not on any magic formula. The one who works the miracle does so through God's power. Miraculous displays of God's power are found throughout the Old Testament, especially during the times of Moses, of Elijah and Elisha, and of Daniel.

The greatest miracles in all of history

came during the lifetime of Jesus Christ. Jesus spoke a great deal about the reign of God. The miracles Jesus worked were samples of what it will be like when God's reign in the world is complete and all evil and sin are destroyed.

MIRIAM *(MEER-ee-um)*

was an Old Testament prophet and poet. She was the sister of Moses and Aaron. As a young girl she looked after the baby Moses when he was hidden in a basket in the Nile River to keep him safe from the Egyptians (Exod. 2:4, 7, 8). When an Egyptian princess found Moses, Miriam offered to find a nurse for the baby. The nurse was Moses' mother, so even though Moses belonged to the princess, his mother raised him as a Hebrew.

As an adult, Miriam joined Moses and

Aaron on the Exodus of the Israelites from Egypt. After escaping from the Egyptians in the miraculous crossing of the Red Sea, Miriam composed a song of praise to the Lord and led the other women in celebrating the victory (Exod. 15:20, 21).

From the beginning of the Exodus, Miriam was respected as a prophet. Later prophets identified her as a leader of the Hebrews. But Miriam and her brother Aaron criticized Moses for choosing a wife they didn't think was suitable (Num. 12:1-15). For this unwise criticism Miriam was cursed with leprosy. But Moses prayed for her, and God said Miriam would have to stay outside the camp for seven days. The whole march was delayed because of her illness. Then the Lord healed her. When she died, she was buried at Kadesh (Num. 20:1).

MISSIONARY JOURNEYS

were travels of Paul and other early disciples to spread the Gospel throughout Greece and Asia Minor (now Turkey). Paul made three missionary journeys. On the first he went through the island of Cyprus and then to the southern coast and inland plateau of Asia Minor (Acts 13—14). On the way he began churches; on the way back to Jerusalem he visited the churches he had started, to encourage and help them.

On Paul's second trip, he went to Greece—Athens and Corinth—by way of Macedonia (today's northern Greece). He stayed in Corinth a year and a half before returning to Jerusalem and Antioch. See Acts 15:36—18:22.

On his third journey, he visited most of the same churches again and collected money to help poor Christians at Jerusalem (Acts 18:23-21:16).

MITE (see Money)

MOAB (MOE-ab)

was the nation that descended from Lot's grandson Moab. These people lived east of the southern part of the Dead Sea, and they were constant enemies of the Israelites. When the Israelites were leaving Egypt for the promised land, the Moabites refused to let them pass peacefully through their land (Judg. 11:17, 18;

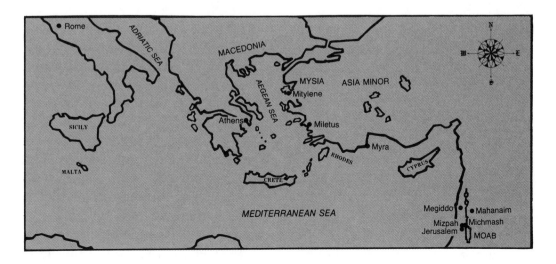

Num. 22:1—25:9). Although they couldn't conquer Israel, they did make trouble. They sent young Moabite women into the Israelites' camp to tempt the men into worshiping idols. God was angry and sent a plague upon Israel as punishment.

Moses died on Mount Pisgah in Moab. Joshua was chosen on the nearby plains to be Israel's next leader.

Almost a hundred years later, the Moabites joined the Ammonites and the Amalekites and ruled over Israel for eighteen years. Finally Ehud, a man from the tribe of Benjamin, killed the Moabite king, and the Moabite army went home (Judg. 3:12-25).

Some events in the Book of Ruth took place in Moab, and Ruth herself was a Moabite. This story took place in a time of peace between Israel and Moab.

But trouble began again around 850 B.C. King Ahab had demanded heavy tribute (a kind of tax) from Mesha, the king of Moab. Mesha rebelled, and Kings Jehoram of the northern kingdom and Jehoshaphat of Judah defeated Moab and ruined the land (II Kings 3:4-27). Moab never again became a strong nation.

MOLECH *(MOE-leck),*
MOLOCH *(MOE-lock)*
was an ugly heathen god to whom people were sometimes sacrificed. He was worshiped by the Ammonites before Israel came to Canaan. Sometimes heathen people killed their own children and placed the bodies in the arms of the idol. Moses told the Hebrews they were to have nothing to do with this horrible god. See Leviticus 18:21; 20:1-5; Psalm 105:35-42.

MONEY
in very early times was pieces of metal, often in the shape of jewelry, especially bracelets. The owner could trade a piece of metal or a whole bracelet for the goods he needed. Perfumes and ointment were also used for trade.

The first coin mentioned in the Old Testament, the shekel, means "weight." The value of the metal money depended on how much it weighed.

About 700 B.C. coins with some imprint or stamp began to be used. The Hebrews at first used the coins of the Assyrians or Babylonians, but later they made their own coins of metal stamped with an official seal.

Some of the coins most often mentioned in the New Testament are:

Denarius was a Roman coin made of silver. It was about the size of our dime. It was worth a day's wages of a poor worker. Some translations use *penny* or *pence* for this coin, but it was worth much more than our modern penny. A denarius often had the picture of the Roman emperor stamped on it. In Matthew 22:15-22, Jesus said that by looking at the coin anyone could see that it belonged to Caesar.

Drachma was a Greek coin worth about the same as a denarius. A drachma was usually stamped with a picture of a Greek god, animal, or other object. The drachma is the coin mentioned in Luke 15:8.

The two sides of a shekel coined about 140 B.C.

Farthing was a Greek coin of little value. It was worth two mites. Some translations use *penny* for farthing. A farthing is mentioned in Matthew 10:29 and Luke 12:6.

Mite was the Jewish coin of least value. It was made of copper. Two mites were worth one farthing or one penny. This was the coin the woman placed in the temple offering (Mark 12:42;Luke 21:14).

Pound was equal to about 50 shekels, or the wages of a poor man for 50 days. When Jesus told a parable about a man giving his servants one, five, and ten pounds to invest, he was speaking of large sums of money (Luke 19:11-26).

Pence, Penny refers to the Roman denarius, worth about a day's pay for a poor working man.

Shekel was a Jewish coin about the size of a nickel. A picture of a pot of manna was imprinted on one side and the picture of a flowering rod on the other side. A shekel was worth about the same as a Roman denarius—the wages of a poor working man for one day.

Talent was worth 3,000 shekels—the wages of a working man for almost ten years. When Jesus talked about talents in His parables, He was speaking of huge sums of money (Matt. 18:23-35; 25:14-30).

MONEY CHANGER

a man who sat at a table in the temple court during New Testament times, was like a banker in some ways. He exchanged foreign coins for the Jewish coins the priests demanded in temple worship. Often money changers made a large profit, because they were not afraid to cheat. Jesus said they had made the temple a den of thieves, and He chased them out after

His triumphal entry into Jerusalem. See Matthew 21:12; Mark 11:15.

MOON

was one of the earliest ways of measuring time. A month was measured by time from full moon to full moon. Some heathen people worshiped the moon, but Hebrews were told not to worship the sun, moon, or stars. See Deuteronomy 4:19.

MORDECAI *(MOR-duh-kie)*

was a Jewish hero of the Book of Esther. He was a cousin and adviser to Queen Esther. Mordecai and Esther lived in Susa, the Persian capital, about 486-465 B.C. After Esther became the king's wife, Mordecai saved the king's life by warning him of a plot against him.

Haman, the king's chief minister, became furious with Mordecai for not bowing to him as he rode through the streets. Haman devised a plan that the king approved to have all the Jews killed, and he built a gallows especially for Mordecai. Neither Haman nor the king knew that Queen Esther was Jewish. Mordecai went into mourning for his people, wailing and wearing sackcloth and ashes. He told Esther she should reveal to the king that she was Jewish and try to get the king to give some protection to her people. When Esther told the king what Haman's plot was, Haman was hanged on his own gallows. Mordecai then replaced Haman as chief minister to the king. See Esther 2—10.

MORIAH (muh-RIE-uh)

was the place where God told Abraham to offer Isaac as a sacrifice. Isaac was spared, however, when God provided an animal for the sacrifice. The exact location is not known, but many people believe this is the same Mount Moriah on which Solomon built his temple—a rock-like hill in the center of Jerusalem today. See Genesis 22:2; II Chronicles 3:1.

MOSES (MOE-zus)

is the man most often mentioned in the Old Testament. He was the leader of the Hebrews in their escape from Egypt (Exod. 2:1-10). He also received the Ten Commandments and the Old Testament Law from God. He is considered the founder of the Jewish religion.

Moses was the son of Hebrew slaves in Egypt (Exod. 2:1-10). Just after he was born, the Pharaoh ordered that all male Hebrew babies were to be killed. Moses' mother made a waterproof basket, placed her baby son in it, and hid it in the rushes near the shore of the Nile River. She told her daughter, Miriam, to watch it. The basket and baby were found by an Egyptian princess, who adopted Moses. She hired Moses' mother to take care of him while he was young. In this way, Moses grew up understanding the beliefs and customs of both the Hebrews and the Egyptians.

When Moses was forty years old, he had to flee from Egypt because he killed an Egyptian while trying to defend an Israelite slave. Moses lived in the wilderness for another forty years. Then God spoke to him from a bush that looked like it was on fire but never burned up (Exod. 3:2—4:17). God told Moses that he was to lead the Israelites out of their slavery in Egypt to a promised land that God would give them.

Moses said he could not lead because he was not a good speaker. But God told him his brother Aaron would be his helper and do the speaking. It took ten terrible plagues sent by God on Egypt before the Pharaoh said the Israelites could leave. Even then he changed his mind and sent his army to bring them back. God defeated the Pharaoh by opening the Red Sea for the Israelites to go through safely, then closing it on the Egyptian army that tried to follow them (Exod. 12). So the Israelites escaped.

During their forty years in the wilderness, God guided the people with a cloud during the day and a pillar of fire at night. But the people constantly grumbled and complained that Moses had led them out of Egypt to die in the desert. Many times Moses was discouraged. Sometimes he disobeyed God. But he was still a great leader. He had to organize a mass of people, settle their arguments, answer their complaints, and try to teach them how to worship God. God gave Moses instructions about building a tabernacle as a place of worship. He gave Moses laws so the people would know how to live.

Moses and all the adults who left Egypt were not permitted to enter the promised land because of their earlier sins of doubting and disobeying God.

*The people walked
on dry ground
across the Red Sea.*

Just before Moses turned over the leadership of the nation to Joshua, he gave a great speech. He reminded the Israelites of how God had led them through their years in the wilderness and how they had often failed to obey God. He reminded them of the Ten Commandments and other instructions God had given them. He emphasized that God expected love and obedience from them—not grumblings and complainings. He told them how important it was to keep God's law and to teach it to their children. Most of the Book of Deuteronomy is a record of Moses' final speech (or speeches). See Deuteronomy 1—33.

Moses died at age 120 and was buried in the land of Moab (Deut. 34). Moses is often mentioned in the New Testament as the giver of the Law that Christ came to fulfill.

MOUNT OF OLIVES
(see *Olives, Mount of*)

MOURNING *(MORN-ing)*
is showing sadness or sorrow, usually at a person's death.

When people in Bible times learned of a death or other tragedy, they often tore their clothes (II Sam. 1:2). Sometimes mourners sprinkled dust or ashes on their heads (Josh. 7:6). People often wore clothing made of coarse material (such as goat hair) as a sign of mourning (Isa. 22:12). Another mourning custom was to cover your head with a heavy veil (Jer. 14:3).

When people wanted to show they were sorry for their sins, they often showed it in these same ways.

After a person died, friends and relatives would mourn for a week or longer. They would cry loudly around the body (Luke 8:52, 53). Sometimes extra mourners would be hired to help the family express grief. Musicians might play mournful music (especially on the flute) to show the family's sadness. Some of these customs are seen in the story of the death of Jairus's daughter (Mark 5:21-24,35-43)

MURDER
means to kill someone on purpose. It is a horrible sin, and God says in the sixth commandment, "Thou shalt not kill." (Exod. 20:13). The Living Bible properly translates this, "You must not murder."

Murder is not the same as manslaughter. Manslaughter means to kill someone accidentally. In the Old Testament a person accused of killing someone could flee to a City of Refuge. If he could prove he had not killed on purpose, or that he had not killed anyone at all, he was protected there from revenge. A person accused of murder could not be found guilty unless two witnesses had seen him do it (Num. 35: 30-31; Deut. 17:6, 7). If a person were found guilty, he would be put to death.

MURMUR
means constant complaining or grumbling. Murmuring is often spoken so low and so unhappily that the words are hard to understand.

MUSIC
was an important part of life in Bible times, from birth to death. People used music to celebrate and to mourn, to praise God and to praise their heroes. Music made everyday work more pleasant.

Music was important in the worship of the Hebrews. The temple had an orchestra. The Levites were the temple singers and musicians. They often used singers and instruments together. Some parts of the Bible were meant to be sung. The Psalms are the best known songs, but other songs are found throughout the Old and New Testaments.

Many of the introductions to the psalms give instructions about how they are to be sung. Psalm 61 and several others use a Hebrew word that means "with stringed instruments." Psalm 5 says, "for the flutes." We aren't sure of the meaning of some of the words. *Alamoth,* in the introduction to Psalm 46, means "maidens." It probably meant that it was to be sung by women's voices only. Many psalms tell which melodies should be used. Psalm 22 says the tune should be "The Hind of the Dawn." Psalm 45 is supposed to be sung to "Lilies." These tunes, of course, were not written down, so we have no way of knowing what they were.

MUSICAL INSTRUMENTS

were important in Bible times. Here are some of the most common ones:

Bells were small jingles attached to the hem of the high priest's garments. When he moved, they rang to call attention to the sacred work the high priest was doing.

Clarinet, called a flute in some translations, was something like today's clarinet but much simpler. It was used at weddings, banquets, and funerals. Matthew 9:23 shows that it was played along with the wailing of mourners at a funeral.

Cymbals, used only in religious ceremonies, were similar to today's cymbals. Psalm 150 talks about "loud cymbals" and "high-sounding cymbals." The loud cymbals were larger, played with both hands. The smaller high-sounding cymbals were played with one hand by attaching them to the thumb and middle finger.

Flute was an instrument with a shrill sound, made of a hollow reed, bone, or piece of wood. It was not considered proper for use in religious services.

Gong, made of brass, was used at weddings and other happy times. Paul refers to its loud noise in I Corinthians 13:1.

Harp was made of wood with twelve strings. The musician picked the strings with his fingers. The harp was one of the most important instruments in the temple orchestra.

Lyre *(LIE-ur)* was a square or triangle-shaped instrument. Like the harp, it was made of wood, but it usually had ten strings instead of twelve and was plucked with a small pick instead of the fingers. The lyre was smaller in size and higher in pitch than the harp. It made a sweet, soft sound. It was one of the temple orchestra instruments. David played a lyre to soothe Saul in I Samuel 16:23.

Oboe was a double reed instrument similar to the modern oboe. It had two pipes, which could be blown separately or together. It was used for Passover festivals and other special ceremonies.

Organ was a skin-covered box with ten holes. Air was forced through to make the sound, which was regulated by the holes. It made a loud sound and was used in the temple to call priests and Levites to their duties.

Pipe was a shepherd's pipe or flute that was played to express wild joy or great sorrow. It was not used in the temple orchestra, but the psalmist encouraged its use in worship in Psalm 150:4.

Psaltery was another stringed instrument, but it was different from both the harp and the lyre. The psaltery had ten

strings and was similar to today's zither. It was often played with the harp and lyre.

Shofar, a curved ram's horn, is still used in Jewish worship today. Shofars were part of the temple orchestra, and a shofar was blown by the priests as a signal in religious ceremonies. It is still used that way today: to announce events such as the Jewish New Year and the beginning of each sabbath. The Israelites blew shofar horns as the walls of Jericho fell down.

Tambourine, or tof, was a small drum made from a wooden hoop and animal skins. (There were no bells attached as on our modern tambourines.) It beat the rhythm for dances, joyful occasions, and religious ceremonies. Both King David and the prophet Miriam played the tambourine when they wanted to show their delight in the Lord's care for them.

Timbrel *(TIM-brul)* was a small drum, something like a tambourine but without any jingles attached. It was used to provide rhythm for dances and celebrations. It was usually played by women.

Trumpet was a straight tube about eighteen inches long ending in a bell shape, made from either copper or silver. There were always at least two trumpets played at each temple service—and sometimes as many as 120. Trumpets and shofars were blown to begin important events.

MUSTARD (see *Plants*)

NAAMAN *(NAY-uh-mun)*

was a commander of Syria's army. But he had the disease of leprosy.

His wife's young Hebrew slave said there was a prophet in Israel who could heal Naaman. So he went to the home of Elisha. Elisha did not come out of his house to see Naaman. He sent a message that if Naaman would dip seven times in the Jordan River, he would be healed.

Naaman was angry. He said if he was supposed to dip in the river himself, his own country had better choices to offer

Noah's building project didn't make much sense—until it started to rain.

than the Jordan. However, Naaman's servants urged him to follow Elisha's directions. He did and was healed.

He went back to Elisha and promised not to offer sacrifices to any god but the Lord. He tried to give Elisha some expensive gifts, but Elisha refused them.

See II Kings 5:1-27.

NABOTH (NAY-buth)

was an Israelite who had a good vineyard next to King Ahab's palace in Jezreel. Ahab told Naboth he wanted the land for a vegetable garden and would pay him for it or give him another vineyard somewhere else.

Naboth said no. He had inherited that land from his father, and he wanted to keep it.

When Ahab told his wife, Jezebel, about the vineyard, she said, "I'll get it for you." She arranged to have some men accuse Naboth of cursing God and the king. Because of these charges, Naboth was stoned to death.

When Ahab went to claim the vineyard, he met the prophet Elijah, who told him God would judge him for what he had done to Naboth.

See I Kings 21.

NAHUM (NAY-hum)

was an Old Testament prophet who wrote a short book. Nothing else is known about the man except that he came from the town of Elkosh—the location of which is not known either.

His book is full of poetic, powerful word pictures about God's strength and goodness (Nah. 1).

Nahum prophesied the defeat of Nineveh, the capital of Assyria (Nah. 3). At this time in history (sometime between 663 and 612 B.C.) the Assyrians were threatening the kingdom of Judah. The idea that Nineveh could ever be defeated seemed impossible. But Nahum's prophecy came true in 612 B.C., when Nineveh was conquered by Babylon.

NAOMI (nay-OH-mee)

was the mother-in-law of Ruth. She and her family lived in Moab for a while. After Naomi's husband and Ruth's husband (Naomi's son) died there, Naomi and Ruth returned to Bethlehem, Naomi's former home. Naomi helped Ruth meet and marry Boaz and took care of Ruth and Boaz's baby boy. See Book of Ruth.

NAPHTALI (NAF-tuh-lie)

was the sixth son of Jacob, and the ancestor of the tribe of Naphtali (Genesis 30:7, 8). This tribe settled in good land west of the Sea of Galilee (Josh. 19:32-39). That part of the kingdom of Israel was conquered by the Syrians, and many of its people were sent into exile in 733 B.C. (I Kings 15:20; II Kings 15:29).

NATHAN (NAY-thun)

was a prophet of God who was a counselor to King David. When David wanted to build a house of worship for God, he talked with Nathan (II Sam. 7). That night God spoke to Nathan. Nathan was to tell David that David's son was to build the temple, not David. When Nathan delivered the message, David accepted it as God's will.

Several years later, King David wanted to marry Bathsheba He arranged to have Bathsheba's husband killed in battle. Nathan then told him that God would judge him for his sin(II Sam. 12:1-25).

When David was an old man and soon to die, Nathan learned that Adonijah, one of David's sons, was plotting to become king instead of Solomon. Nathan told David, and then, following David's orders, Nathan and others quickly arranged for Solomon to be made king (I Kings 1:8-53).

Nathan also wrote a history of the reigns of David and Solomon, but no copies of his work have been saved (I Chron. 29:29; II Chron. 9:29).

NATHANAEL (nuh-THAN-yul)

is listed in the Gospel of John as one of Jesus' disciples. He is mentioned only in the Gospel of John, but some scholars think he is the same as the person who is called Bartholomew in the other Gospels.

Nathanael was brought to Jesus by Philip. After Nathanael talked with Jesus, he was convinced that Jesus was the Son of God. See John 1:43-51.

NAZARENE (NAZ-uh-reen)

was a person who lived in the town of Nazareth in Galilee. Jesus lived there as a child, so He was called a Nazarene. In New Testament times, Christians were sometimes called Nazarenes because they were followers of Jesus. See Matthew 2:23; Acts 24:5.

NAZARETH (NAZ-uh-reth)

was the town in Galilee where Jesus lived

The hills of Nazareth are filled with limestone caves; perhaps Joseph and Mary lived in one.

during His childhood and youth (Luke 2:39, 51).

Early in His ministry, He preached in the synagogue in Nazareth, but the people became so angry with Him that they wanted to kill Him (Luke 4:16-30). Jews who lived other places thought Nazareth was a city of low moral and religious standards (John 1:46).

Today Nazareth is a large city, and most of the people who live there are Arabs.

NAZIRITE (NAZ-uh-rite)

was a Hebrew man or woman who took a vow to commit himself or herself to God

Nebuchadnezzar was furious when his wise men couldn't tell him what he had dreamed.

in a special way for a certain length of time (Num. 6:1-21). The time could be anywhere from thirty days to a lifetime. While under the Nazirite vow, persons were not to eat anything made with grapes, they were not to cut their hair, and they were not to touch a dead body.

There are only two examples in the Bible of lifelong Nazirites: Samson and Samuel (Judg. 13:7; 16; 17; I Sam. 1:11). Many scholars believe John the Baptist was also a Nazirite (Mark 1:6; Luke 1:15).

Some scholars think that Paul took a Nazirite vow for a short time and completed it in Cenchreae, where he cut his hair again (Acts 18:18).

NEBO *(NEE-bo)*

was the name of the mountain from which Moses saw the promised land (Deut. 34:1). Nebo was also a town near Mount Nebo (Num. 32:3; Isa. 15:2).

NEBUCHADNEZZAR
(NEB-uh-kad-NEZ-er)

was the king of Babylon during its time of greatest glory. He ruled from 605 to 562 B.C. He made the city of Babylon beautiful; his hanging gardens became world-famous. He installed irrigation systems and built a strong defense system.

His armies invaded Judah three times—in 605, 597, and 586 B.C. In 597 the armies came into the city of Jerusalem and took most of the furnishings of the temple back to Babylon (II Kings 24:1—25:21; II Chron. 36:6-21). Thousands of Israelites were forced to leave their country and go to Babylon to live. These included the leaders and educated people of Judah.

Among those forced to leave were the prophet Daniel and his three friends, Shadrach, Meshach, and Abednego (Dan. 1:1-21). They were brought to the palace to be educated as advisers for the king. Twice Nebuchadnezzar had dreams that only Daniel was able to interpret (Dan. 2:1-3; 4:1-37). Nebuchadnezzar respected Daniel and his friends and gave them important jobs in his government.

In 586 B.C. Nebuchadnezzar's army again came to Jerusalem, this time destroying the city and the famous temple Solomon had built. More Israelites were forced to leave Judah and go to Babylon to live.

Nebuchadnezzar was a proud, power-hungry king. He once set up a huge golden image and ordered everyone to worship it. When Shadrach, Meshach, and Abednego disobeyed the command, they were thrown into a furnace so hot that it killed the men who threw them in (Dan. 3). But God kept the three safe, and they came out unharmed. Nebuchadnezzar then issued another order saying that no one could speak a word against the God of these Hebrews.

The second dream that Daniel interpreted foretold that Nebuchadnezzar would have a mental illness. He would be so sick that for seven months he would think and act like an ox instead of a human. All this came true.

When Nebuchadnezzar recovered from his illness, he worshiped the true God (Dan. 4:34-37). He died in 562 B.C. after being king for forty-three years.

NEGEB *(NEG-eb)*

was a dry, hilly area south of Judea.

The Negeb is so dry that the people have to keep moving in search of water.

Abraham went toward the Negeb when he first came to Canaan (Gen. 12:9). This area was part of the promised land and was originally assigned to the tribe of Simeon (Josh. 19:8).

The area is now known as the Negev in modern Israel. It has few inhabitants except Bedouin (Arab) nomads, who use it to pasture their flocks. Water is scarce and the land is not good for farming.

NEHEMIAH *(NEE-huh-MY-uh)*

was the governor who led the rebuilding of the walls of Jerusalem and much of the city. He also restored the worship of God among the people.

Nehemiah's work began in 445 B.C.—more than 100 years after Jerusalem had been destroyed by Nebuchadnezzar, king of Babylon. After Babylon conquered Jerusalem, Persia defeated Babylon. Nehemiah was a descendant of people who had been taken as exiles from Jerusalem.

Nehemiah held an important position in the court of Persia's King Artaxerxes. He was cupbearer—the one who served wine at the king's table. Nehemiah asked the king to let him return to Jerusalem to rebuild the walls of the city. The king not only gave him permission, but later appointed him governor of the area (Neh. 2:1-8).

Nehemiah was a talented organizer. He ordered needed supplies and assigned various groups to build certain parts of the wall. The people trusted him and were willing to work hard for him. They rebuilt the walls in fifty-two days.

The work was hard, and it was even harder because some enemies of the Israelites tried to stop the work This group was led by two men, Sanballat and Tobiah (Neh. 4, 6). They were afraid the country of Judah would become powerful again. Nehemiah ordered half the people to stand guard with swords and shields while the others worked on the wall.

When the wall was finished, Nehemiah gathered all the people together (Neh. 8). Ezra the scribe read the Law of Moses to them. For many years, most of the people had not worshiped God. Nehemiah and Ezra taught them to observe the sabbath and feast days and to restore other parts of their worship (Neh. 13:15-22).

The Book of Nehemiah tells the last events of Jewish history recorded in the Old Testament.

NERO (see box at right)

NEW TESTAMENT
(TEST-tuh-ment)

is a collection of twenty-seven books or documents written about the life of Christ, the early church, and the Christian faith. They were written between the years A.D. 50 and 90. *Testament* means "agreement" or "covenant," and these books are called the New Testament because they are about the new agreement or new covenant God made with people through the life, death, and resurrection of Christ. People can have a new life of fellowship with God by faith in Christ.

There are four kinds of books in the

NERO (NEE-row)

was probably the emperor (Caesar) of Rome who had both Paul and Peter killed.

He began as a good ruler in A.D. 54. We know the apostle Paul appealed his case to the emperor and was taken to Rome in A.D. 60. It is possible that Paul appeared before Nero and was freed, perhaps in A.D. 62 or 63.

Nero's later rule of terror and cruelty began about A.D. 63. He had his own mother put to death, as well as some of his most trusted advisers. In A.D. 64 a large part of the city of Rome burned. Many thought that Nero had ordered the burning of the city. To draw suspicion away from himself, Nero accused the Christians of starting the fire. This became an excuse to begin a terrible persecution of Christians. Some were burned as torches in Nero's own gardens; others were crucified or thrown to wild beasts. Probably both Peter and Paul were included at this time.

Paul is brought to trial before the emperor Nero.

The Roman Senate finally decreed that Nero should die. But before the decree could be carried out, Nero ordered the death of many senators and in A.D. 68, he killed himself. See Acts 25:10, 11.

New Testament:

1. The Gospels. Each of these was written by a different author, *Matthew, Mark, Luke, and John.* Each one tells about Jesus Christ's life, teachings, death, and resurrection.

2. The Acts of the Apostles. This book tells about the early church, its leaders, and how It spread from Jerusalem around the then known world within thirty years. Luke wrote the Book of *Acts.*

3. The Letters. There are twenty-one1 letters: *Romans; I and II Corinthians; Galatians; Ephesians; Philippians; Col-ossians; I and II Thessalonians; I and II Timothy; Titus; Philemon; Hebrews; James; I and II Peter; I, II, and III John; and Jude.* They were written mostly to specific churches, but some were written to Christians everywhere. They explain important truths of the Christian faith. Thirteen of the letters are believed to have been written by the apostle Paul. Others were written by James, John, Peter, and Jude. We do not know the writer of some letters, such as Hebrews.

4. The Book of Revelation. John wrote this book, which begins and ends like a

Nicodemus first came to see Jesus at night.

letter and has seven short letters in chapters 2 and 3. However, most of the book is called an *apocalypse*—a writing that involves visions about the end of this world and about the next world. The apocalypse in *Revelation* tells how God is going to defeat sin, remove all evil, and live with His people forever. The visions include such things as living creatures, beasts, seals, trumpets, bowls of judgment, a dragon, and a beautiful city that will never be destroyed.

The books of the New Testament are not arranged in the order in which they were written or in the order of the events they describe but by subject matter.

NICODEMUS *(NICK-uh-DEE-mus)*

was one of the Pharisees who belonged to the ruling Jewish council called the Sanhedrin. Nicodemus wanted to know what Jesus taught. Because the Pharisees were enemies of Jesus, Nicodemus had to come to see him secretly at night (John 3:1-5). Jesus told him that he must become a whole new person—he had to be born again.

When the Sanhedrin wanted to condemn Jesus without a fair trial, Nicodemus objected (John 7:45-52). But he was afraid to be an open follower of Jesus until after Jesus died. Then Nicodemus boldly showed that he was a disciple by helping to bury Jesus' body in the tomb (John 19:38-42).

NILE RIVER

is the third longest river in the world. Only the Amazon and the Mississippi are longer. It runs nearly 2,500 miles through the middle of Africa to Egypt and the Mediterranean Sea.

A very wide plain along the coast of Egypt is flooded each July by the Nile River. This flooding makes the land good for farming. Without the Nile River, the country of Egypt could not have survived. The seven years of famine in Joseph's time were probably caused when the Nile did not flood as usual.

NINEVEH *(NIN-uh-vuh)*

was one of the oldest cities of the world. It was founded by Nimrod the famous hunter (Gen. 10:11). Archaeological digging has shown that people lived there as early as 4500 B.C. When it was the capital of the empire of Assyria, it had beautiful palaces for its kings, temples for its pagan gods, and a canal thirty miles long that ran from a dam to the north (II Kings 19:36, 37).

In the Bible Nineveh is best known as the city to which Jonah went to preach (Jonah 1:2; 3:2, 3; 4:11). The people repented when Jonah warned them that God would destroy the city, and the city was spared. It was finally destroyed in 612 B.C. by the Babylonians, Medes, and Scythians.

NOAH *(NO-ah)*

was a good man who continued to do right when everyone around him was doing wrong (Gen. 6:9). The Bible says Noah "was blameless" and "walked with God." The other people were so evil that God sent the Flood to destroy everyone except Noah and his family. God told Noah the Flood was coming and instructed him to build a huge boat, or ark, so he and his family could be saved (Gen. 6:13-22). Noah and his three sons spent many years building the ark. When it was completed, Noah's family went into the ark. Noah also brought into the ark a male and female of every known animal and bird.

Then the rains began (Gen. 7:1—8:19). It rained for forty days—almost six

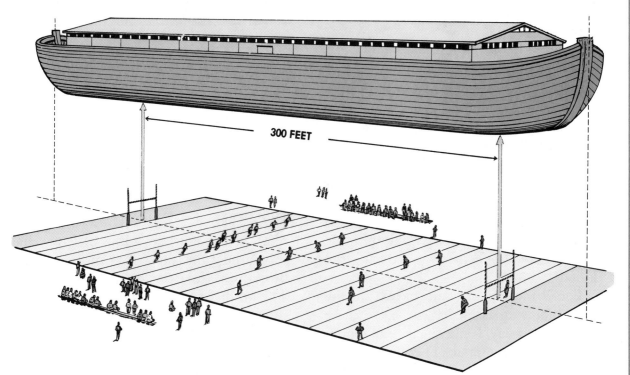

Noah's ark was longer than a football field.

weeks—until everything was flooded and the people and animals left outside were drowned. Noah and his family and the animals stayed in the ark almost a year. They had to wait until the land was dry enough so they could walk on the ground, build houses, and grow food again.

One of Noah's first acts when he got out was to build an altar to worship God (Gen. 8:20).

After the Flood, God made a covenant, or agreement, with Noah (Gen. 9:9-17). God promised He would never again send a flood to destroy all living things. As a proof of His promise, God sent a rainbow across the sky.

Noah lived for 350 years after the Flood; he died when he was 950 years old.

The New Testament says Noah was a preacher, or herald, of righteousness (Heb. 11:7).

NOAH'S ARK

is the boat God told Noah to build so he could escape the coming Flood (Gen. 6:14-16). The Book of Genesis says the boat was to be 450 feet long (longer than a football field), 75 feet wide, and 45 feet high. It had three decks, or levels. It was to be made of gopher wood. (Bible scholars are not sure what kind of wood this was.) A model of the boat shows that it was not made to be a sailing ship but more like a large barge. Its only purpose was to stay above the water during the Flood.

The Bible says it came to rest on the "mountains of Ararat." (Gen. 8:4). There is in present-day Turkey a range of mountains known as Ararat. These mountains might be the place mentioned in the Bible, but we do not know for sure. Some

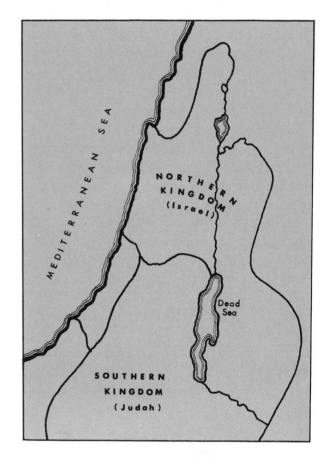

explorers have seen what they thought looked like a large boat under the ice on one of these mountains. Groups of explorers have tried to climb the mountains to find out for sure if a boat is there, but so far there is no final proof that what people have seen is Noah's ark.

NORTHERN KINGDOM

refers to the northern tribes of Israel that separated from the tribes of Judah and Benjamin after the death of Solomon. The northern and southern kingdoms had separate kings and sometimes fought each other. The northern kingdom was also known as Israel and as Ephraim (the name of one of the strongest tribes). Its capital was Samaria.

The southern kingdom was known as, Judah. Its capital was Jerusalem.

The northern kingdom was defeated by Assyria in 722 B.C., and many of its people were sent as exiles into Assyria.

NUMBERS

were very different in Bible times. Our use of numerals l, 2, 3, 4, 5, 6, 7, 8, 9, and 10 did not begin until about A.D. 600. People in Bible times counted as we do, but as far as we know, they did not use numerals. In most of the Hebrew Old Testament, numbers were written out as words, such as "seventy-two" or "one hundred eighty-seven thousand."

The Greeks in New Testament times used the letters of the alphabet for their numbers. The first letter, *alpha*, meant "1;" the second letter, *beta*, meant "2," and so forth.

Some numbers had special meaning. From very early times, seven was a sacred number. God created the earth in seven days. The feast of unleavened bread and the feast of tabernacles lasted seven days. The candlestick in the tabernacle had seven branches; the priests walked around Jericho seven times; John wrote to seven churches in Revelation. There are many such examples. Seven seems to mean something that is complete or whole.

Twelve is also a special number. There were twelve tribes of Israel; there were twelve apostles.

Forty seems to be a general figure meaning a long period of time. It rained for forty days at the Flood of Noah; the Israelites were in the wilderness forty years; Moses was on the mountain for forty days; Christ was tempted for forty days.

NUMBERS, BOOK OF

contains the story of the trials and victories of the Israelites from the time they escaped slavery in Egypt to the time, forty years later, when they entered the promised land.

In the Hebrew Bible, this book is called "In the Wilderness," which describes what it is about. The name *Numbers* comes from the Greek translation of the Old Testament. The ancient translators called it *Numbers* because the beginning of the book and the end of the book tell the number of males over twenty years of age; there were about 600,000 (Num. 1:1-46; 26:1-62). They were counted to see how many men there were who could be in an army if the Israelites needed one. Therefore women, children, and priests (Levites) were not included in the count.

The Book of Numbers tells how twelve men were sent to spy out the promised land (Num. 13). Two of the spies, Caleb and Joshua, believed God would help the Israelites conquer the land. God was pleased by their faith. But ten of the men came back saying that the people were so big and strong the Israelites would never be able to conquer them. After they had heard what the spies said, most of the Israelites said they would rather go back to Egypt. Because of their lack of faith, God said they would have to live in the wilderness for forty years (Num. 14).

That would be long enough for the fighting men of that generation to die and a new group to grow up.

When the Israelites heard God's punishment, they insisted on going immediately to fight in Canaan even though Moses told them they must not. They fought one battle but were defeated.

Moses was the leader of the Israelites during the time of the Book of Numbers. The book tells how God helped Moses and the people live in the wilderness. God let them know He was with them by putting a fire over the tabernacle at night and a cloud by day (Num. 9:15-23). When the cloud moved, they were to move their camp to wherever the cloud led them. Numbers tells how the people were to camp in an orderly way. It tells how they were to divide the land when they arrived in Canaan.

Near the end of the book is the story of some of the battles the Israelites fought on the east side of the Jordan River—land not thought of as part of Canaan. The people of three tribes, Reuben, Gad, and Manasseh, had many cattle, and they asked for permission to build their homes on the east side of the Jordan (Num. 32). Moses said they could if they would promise to help the rest of the Israelites in their battles to win the land of Canaan.

Numbers also tells the strange story of the prophet Balaam and how God would not let him prophesy against the Israelites (Num. 22—25).

Numbers 6:24-26 is a beautiful prayer that is often used as a benediction in church services today.

The Book of Numbers shows how God took care of His people even when they disobeyed Him. It shows how much He cared about all the details of their lives. It also shows how God punished sin.

God's people in the Old Testament both thanked the Lord and asked His forgiveness through offerings.

OATHS

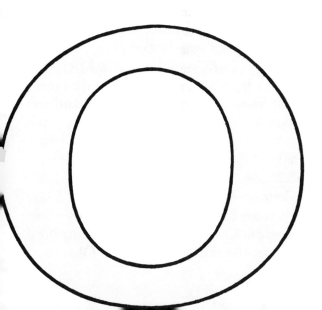

are solemn vows that people make to promise that what they say is true. In Bible times, there were several methods of taking oaths. Sometimes a person said something like "as the Lord lives." They meant that their words were as dependable as the fact that God is alive. Other times a person made a signal, such as raising his hand toward heaven. In our country, we use oaths in court cases, where a person places his hand on the Bible and says, "I swear to tell the truth, the whole truth, and nothing but the truth, so help me God."

In Jesus' time, Jews had some oaths that were considered binding and others that were not. Jesus talked about these in Matthew 23:16-22. He also said that those who are His disciples should not need oaths—everything they say should be completely honest, without any special oath. See Matthew 5:33-37.

OBADIAH (OH-buh-DIE-uh)

was the prophet who wrote the shortest book in the Old Testament. We know nothing else about him; we are not even certain when the book was written.

The twenty-one verses in Obadiah are about the nation of Edom. These people were descendants of Esau, Jacob's brother. Their country was south of the Dead Sea. Even though the people of Edom and the people of Israel were distant relatives, they were usually enemies. The Edomites sometimes fought with the Philistines against the Israelites.

Obadiah said that the people of Edom would be punished by God for being proud and for joining other nations in trying to destroy God's people. He reminded the Edomites that all the earth belongs to God and that someday God would rule it.

OBED (OH-bed)

was the son of Ruth and Boaz. He was the grandfather of King David. See Ruth 4:17.

OBEDIENCE

means doing what we're told to do. We are commanded to be obedient to God in every way (I John 5:2). Romans 1:5 says part of faith is obedience. Children are told to obey their parents and to honor them (Eph. 6:1, 2).

OCCUPATIONS
(ock-you-PAY-shuns)

are the jobs people do to earn a living. Jobs in Bible times centered mostly around farming, building and repairing homes, government, armies and defense, and religious life. Like today, a man or woman might earn money in two or three ways at the same time. There were very few big businesses, but many people ran small businesses from their own homes.

People were divided generally into two groups—those who were free and those who were slaves. The slaves usually worked side by side with their masters in the fields, or in the business of the master, but all the money went to the master. Slaves sometimes had important positions in the house—but they were still slaves.

The following list includes many of the ancient occupations. There were probably many other occupations that are not mentioned in the Bible.

Apothecary (see *Perfumer*)

Archer (ARCH-ur) was a soldier who used a bow and arrow as his weapons. First Samuel 31:3 tells that King Saul was wounded by a Philistine archer. Egyptian archers wounded King Josiah so badly that he died, according to II Chronicles 35:23, 24.

Armor-Bearer (ARE-mur-BARE-ur) was a personal servant of an army commander. Armor-bearers are mentioned only in the early part of the Old Testament—never in the New Testa-ment. For a short time, David was the armor-bearer for King Saul, according to I Samuel 16:21.

Artificers (see *Craftsmen*)

Bakers were people who cooked bread. In ancient cities, bread dough was pre-pared at home and the loaves taken to large city ovens for baking. This saved fuel and kept individual homes from get-ting so hot.

Beggars asked others for food or money. Many people in Bible times never had jobs. They lived from what others gave them. Beggars were often crippled or blind, and thus could not work.

Brickmakers were important in Bible times. Building with sun-dried bricks was very common. Even though Israel had many stones, bricks were often used to build city walls. In Bible times, bricks were made from wet clay mixed with straw or other vegetable materials. The clay mix was made into bricks either by hand or in a wooden mold. The Israelites in Egypt were forced to make bricks and to gather their own straw for them (Exod. 5:6-9).

Butler (see *Cupbearer*)

Centurion *(sen-TOUR-ee-un)* was a com-mander of 100 men in the Roman army.

Chamberlain *(CHAYM-bur-len)* had charge of a king's house. He made sure that everything was done properly and according to social custom.

Clerk usually refers to the town clerk. The town clerk mentioned in Acts 19:35 was a man of authority and influence, probably the chief officer of the town of Ephesus. Such a man would keep records, write down the laws passed by other groups, and be the go-between for the Roman government and the city council.

Craftsmen were skilled in certain trades.

Coppersmiths made tools, cooking utensils, and other things. They used not only copper but also other metals.

Counselor *(KOWN-suh-lur)* usually refers to an important man in govern-ment, one who helped the king make decisions.

Craftsmen were skilled in certain trades—carpentry, wood carving, tent making, leatherwork.

Cupbearer was a palace official who served wine to the king. He was a loyal man whom the king trusted.

Custodian *(kuh-STOW-dee-un)* was a male slave who looked after the son of his owner. He walked to school with him and took care of him in other ways until the son was sixteen years old.

Diviners *(dih-VINE-urs)* seemed to have some secret knowledge about what would happen in the future. Diviners were often involved in witchcraft or demon power.

Dyers *(DIE-urs)* colored woven cloth. They got their colors from natural sources—red came from worms, blue from the rind of pomegranates, purple from certain shellfish.

Farmers threshed wheat by driving oxen over it; then they used the wind to separate the chaff from the grain. What a contrast to modern machinery!

Elders *(ELL-durs)* were older men who usually ruled villages. This practice was used in the Old Testament and was carried over in part to the New Testament. The Sanhedrin that ruled Jerusalem was this type of government. When churches were formed, elders were appointed for each congregation (Acts 14: 23).

Farmers grew crops for people to eat. More people were farmers than any other occupation. Many men who were soldiers or had some other occupation also worked as farmers (see *Agriculture*)

Fishermen worked along every lake, river, or sea to catch fish. They fished mostly with large nets but also with hooks and spears. Fishing at night was common on the Sea of Galilee.

Fullers washed or bleached clothing. Both men and women were fullers. The soaps used by ancient people to clean and whiten cloth often smelled bad. So the fuller's shop was usually outside the city, where the smells wouldn't bother so many people.

Gatekeepers or **Porters** were in charge of gates to the city, or gates to the temple, or even gates to a sheepfold. They served as guards, opening the gates only to those who had a right to come inside.

Herdsmen cared for oxen, sheep, goats, or camels. Usually a herdsman did not own the animals but was hired to look after them. He would protect them from wild beasts and make sure they had pasture for grazing.

Herald *(HAIR-uld)* was a town crier who went through the streets shouting the king's commands.

Hunters were common from earliest times, when people hunted to get food. Later, hunting became a recreation. Men hunted with bows and arrows. They also used nets and cages to catch ducks, quail, and partridges. For large animals such as wolves, bears, and lions, hunters often dug pits, covered the holes with brush, and waited for the animals to fall in.

Husbandman *(HUZ-bund-mun)* means the same as farmer.

Innkeepers rented overnight lodging to travelers. Their lodging places were more like campgrounds than hotels. Sometimes an inn was only a large courtyard with a fence, gate, and well. A few inns had buildings with rooms.

Judges performed several kinds of work. In the Book of Judges, a judge was the chief leader of the land—the military commander and the highest official.

Later in Israel, judges were those who decided court cases. These judges usually held court in the square inside the city gates, although Samuel traveled from city to city to hold court sessions.

Lawyers knew a great deal about the laws of the Old Testament.

Magicians practiced superstitious ceremonies to try to make things happen. They had many books about sorcery. Magic was condemned by the Old Testament and by the early church in Acts 19:19.

Magistrates *(MAJ-iss-traits)* were the highest ruling officials in each Roman colony.

Maids were usually female slaves. Fathers sometimes gave maids to their daughters as part of a marriage dowry.

Masons worked with stone. Their skill was important, since most buildings in Israel were made of stone.

Merchants were men or women who bought things in one place and sold them in another. Sometimes they traveled to distant places to buy goods people might want and then sold them from door to door. Often they set up a shop in the large city market and sold their goods there.

Midwives were women who helped whenever a baby was being born. Midwives are mentioned in Exodus 1:15-20.

Miners worked to get iron, copper, and other metals out of the ground. Mining was not common among the Hebrews.

Minstrels were musicians who played for special occasions. The prophet Elisha once called for a minstrel to play for him (II Kings 3:15). Minstrels were often hired to play at weddings or funerals.

Money Changers were Jews in New Testament times who sat in the temple court and exchanged other kinds of money for temple (Jewish) money. They sometimes charged unfair prices. Jesus drove them out of the temple and said they had made the Lord's house into a "den of thieves" (Matt. 21:12, 13; Mark 11:15).

Musicians included singers and those who played cymbals, harps, pipes, or trumpets. Music played an important part in the life of Israel. Fifty-four psalms were written "to the chief musician" or choirmaster.

Nurses did more than care for the sick. They were often a kind of tutor and helped raise children.

Officers were people who held any official position. They usually had the

Merchants sometimes traveled to distant places to sell their goods.

authority over others.

Overseers were people with some authority over others.

Perfumers made perfumes, drugs, or healing oils. Most of their work involved making things with pleasant smells to overcome the many bad smells of the average village.

Physicians *(fih-ZIH-shuns)* treated the sick with salves, mineral baths, and medicines.

Plowman (see *Farmer*)

Porter (see *Gatekeeper*)

Potters made cooking and storage pots from clay. Many clay pots were needed in Bible times because they broke easily. Metal pots were very expensive. Pottery making was considered a low-class trade, and potters often lived in the poorest parts of the city. But the Bible sometimes uses *potter* as a word picture of God and His creative work (Isa. 64:8; Rom. 9:20, 21).

Preachers announce news, usually messages about God. In II Peter 2:5, Noah is called a "preacher of righteousness." Paul said that he was appointed a preacher (I Tim. 2:7). In Bible times, preachers had to have strong voices, since they often spoke outdoors.

Priests *(preests)* offered sacrifices and did religious duties. From the time of Moses to the New Testament, Hebrew priests were descendants of Aaron. Pagan religions also had their own priests.

Procurators *(PRAH-cure-ay-turs)* were governors of Roman provinces. They were appointed by the Roman emperor.

Prophets *(PRAH-fits)* and **Prophetesses** (PRAH-fih-tess-ez) were men and women who spoke for God to the people. They delivered God's message, calling people to repent and live a holy life. The message often included God's future blessing or judgment.

Publicans *(PUB-lih-kunz)* were Jewish men who worked as tax collectors for the Roman government. They often tried to collect as much money as they could. They were considered traitors by the Jewish people.

Rabbis *(RAB-eyes)* were Jewish teachers of the Old Testament Law and traditions.

Recorder (see *Clerk*)

Refiners *(re-FINE-urs)* were those who worked with metals. Sometimes they melted gold and silver to make it purer, and sometimes they extracted metals from iron and bronze ores.

Ruler of the Synagogue was responsible for making sure the synagogue was ready and prepared for services.

Sailors worked on the cargo ships that sailed the Mediterranean Sea.

Seller or **Salesperson** (see *Merchant*)

Schoolmaster (see *Custodian*)

Scribes wrote letters and kept accounts for someone else, like a secretary.

In the New Testament, scribes were men who studied the Old Testament Law and the Jewish traditions so they could tell others what was permitted and what was not permitted. They were men of great influence and were given the best seats at feasts and in the synagogue.

Seers were able to predict future events. Samuel called himself a seer (I Sam. 9:19).

Senators (see *Elders*)

Sergeants *(SAHR-jents)* worked with the chief Roman officers. They carried out the punishment the officers ordered.

Servants were under the authority of someone else. Sometimes servants were slaves; often they were not.

Sheepmasters were shepherds who *owned* their sheep. They did not take care of someone else's flocks.

Shepherds took care of sheep, either their own or someone else's. Since sheep are affectionate animals that never fight and need protection from wild animals, shepherds cared deeply about their sheep, knew them all by name, and saw that they were fed and brought safely to the fold at night.

Silversmiths made objects out of silver. They refined the ore and formed the finished objects. They made musical instruments, decorations, and furnishings for the tabernacle and temple. Pagan silversmiths made many idols. Acts 19:23-41 tells about one pagan silversmith who tried to stop Paul's preaching at Ephesus.

Singers were important in Jewish worship. Nehemiah 7:67 mentions a temple choir of 245 men and women.

Slaves were persons owned by someone else. The owners completely controlled them. Sometimes Hebrews who could not pay their debts became slaves to the person to whom they owned money. Hebrew fathers might sell their own children as servants or slaves. Hebrews also got slaves through conquering other countries. And, in turn, Hebrews sometimes became slaves when other countries conquered them. Slavery led to evil in both Old and New Testament times. Eventually, the message of the Gospel helped people see how wrong slavery was.

Smiths worked in stone, wood, or metal. They were so important to a nation that conquerors sometimes took the smiths as captives to weaken their defeated enemy.

Soldiers were those paid for defending their country. In the time of Moses and Joshua, every man above the age of twenty was a soldier and had to be prepared to fight whenever he was needed. Until the

Shepherds brought their sheep safely back to the fold at night.

time of King David, all soldiers were foot soldiers. Later they began using chariots and horses.

Sorcerers *(SOR-sir-ers)* claimed they could foretell the future with the aid of evil spirits. God warned His people to stay away from sorcerers (Mal. 3:5).

Spinners made thread from flax, wool, or cotton. From their thread people wove cloth.

Stewards *(STEW-urds)* were managers of household business. Jesus told a parable about a steward who wasted his employer's belongings (Luke 16:1-3).

Stonecutters worked in quarries or cut stones for buildings such as the temple in Jerusalem. First Kings 5:15 says Solomon had thousands of stonecutters working on the temple.

Tanners made leather out of animal hides. This was considered by the Jews as an "unclean" occupation, so tanners usually lived outside of towns.

Taskmasters assigned work to those under them.

Tax Collectors (see *Publicans*)

Teachers in New Testament times

In the wilderness, weavers and dyers made colorful curtains for the tabernacle.

were the rabbis in the synagogues. They conducted school to teach children to read and write. The rabbis also taught adults about the Old Testament Law.

In the Christian church there were some traveling teachers, who went from church to church to help people learn more about the Gospel.

Tentmakers made tents from hair, wool, or animal skins. In New Testament times, it was the custom for every Jewish boy to have some trade. Paul was a tentmaker. So were his Christian friends, Priscilla and Aquila (Acts 18:1-3).

Tetrarch *(TEH-trark)* was a ruler of a small section in the Roman Empire. He was often called king, even though he ruled for the emperor of Rome.

Tiller (see *Farmer*)

Town Clerk (see *Clerk*)

Treasurer was an important officer in ancient cities. He was in charge of the money that came in from taxes and the money that was paid out.

Tutor (see *Custodian*)

Wardrobe Keeper was a servant in the king's house who had charge of the king's robes. They were probably kept in a special room.

Watchman of the City patrolled the streets to protect people. His job was something like today's policeman, except that as he walked through the streets, the ancient watchman also called out the approximate hour of midnight (they had no clocks or watches) and the time called "cock-crow."

Weavers made cloth or rugs from the thread or string made by the spinners. Weavers were usually women, but some men were also weavers.

Witches and **Wizards** both practiced witchcraft and said they could communicate with demons and the spirits of the dead. Witches were women; men were wizards. Witchcraft is always condemned in the Bible.

OFFERINGS *(OFF-ringz)* and OBLATIONS *(oh-BLAY-shunz)*

are gifts to God. They show a person trusts God and wants to do what He commands. The Old Testament Law gave a long list of instructions about how offerings were to be made, when they should be given, and for what purpose.

Offerings were usually animals or other food, and most offerings were burned on an altar in the tabernacle or temple. Animal offerings always involved blood and were a symbol of sins being forgiven by death. Christians believe that Jesus Christ was the final, once-for-all sacrifice to bring forgiveness of sins to all who believe in Him.

Some of the offerings mentioned in the

Old Testament are these:

Burnt Offerings were burned upon the altar in the temple or tabernacle. These offerings might be bullocks, lambs, rams, or goats. The animal had to be in perfect condition. Blood was sprinkled around the altar, and the entire animal (except the skin) was burned up in the fire. Burnt offerings were always for sin.

Drink Offerings were a pouring out of liquids—usually wine and oil (separately or mixed together)—as an offering. They were always given with other sacrifices—never alone.

Evening Sacrifice refers to one of the daily sacrifices made to God in the tabernacle or temple. Every morning and every evening an animal was burned as a sacrifice to God. With it was offered a cereal offering and a drink offering. Details are given in Numbers 28:3-8.

Meal, Meat, or **Cereal Offerings** all refer to vegetable offerings. These were a mixture of fine flour, oil, and flavorings made into bread or cakes. Sometimes these offerings were burned at the altar. Other times, part was burned and the rest was given to the priest.

Peace Offerings were given to renew fellowship with God. There were three kinds of peace offerings:

1. Thank offerings for some unexpected blessing of God.

2. Votive offerings to go along with a vow made to God.

3. Freewill offerings given as an expression of love for God.

Peace offerings could be any animal normally used for sacrifices. No birds could be used. In peace offerings, the breast and shoulder of the animal were given to the priest. The blood was sprinkled on the altar and the fat was burned. The person who made the offerings and his friends ate the rest of the meat. They ate "before the Lord" in the tabernacle or temple. Eating it there showed that God was a guest at the meal.

Sin Offering could be a bullock, a male or female goat, a female lamb, a dove, or a pigeon. The sin offering was for sins that affected the life of the person who did them.

Trespass or **Guilt Offering** was a ram or a male lamb. This offering was given to God when a person had hurt someone else by his sin—as in stealing. In such cases, the person not only had to make a trespass offering to God but also had to pay back what he had stolen or make up in whatever way possible the wrong he had done.

Wave Offerings and **Heave Offerings** refer to the motions made by the priest when a peace offering was given. A wave offering meant that the breast of the animal was placed in the high priest's hands and "waved" before the Lord to show that it had been given to God's representative—the priest. In the heave offering, the right thigh of the animal (the choicest part) was treated in a similar way as the wave offering, and the then eaten by the priests.

OFFICER (OFF-uh-sur)
is a person who had some position of leadership, usually for a king or ruling group. In the Old Testament, those who gave orders to the Hebrew slaves in Egypt were called officers. There were officers in the army and in the palace of the king. In the New Testament, guards of prisons were called officers in Luke 12:58. Those who came from the chief priests and Pharisees to arrest Jesus in the garden of Gethsemane were also called officers. See Luke 12:58; John 18:3, 18,22.

OIL
is often mentioned in the Bible and usually refers to olive oil. Oil was important in cooking and in medicines (Exod. 29:2). Oil was also used in very simple lamps to give light in homes and in the tabernacle at night. Most lamps were small containers of clay with a wick lying in oil.

Oil was used as a soothing salve to help wounds heal; it was also a cleanser to wipe away the dust of the roads. People often poured oil on the heads of important visitors to make them feel better (Ps. 104:15). The Twenty Third Psalm mentions this custom—"Thou anointest my head with oil."

Oil was often used in ceremonies to anoint men chosen for some special task or honor. Kings were anointed like this, and so were priests and prophets (I Kings 19:15, 16; Exod. 29:1-9).

OLD TESTAMENT
is the first part of the Bible. It has thirty-nine books or separate writings. These books tell some of the things that happened from the time God created the world until the time of Ezra and Nehemiah—about 400 B.C.

Except for the first eleven chapters of Genesis, the Old Testament tells mostly about the Hebrews, starting with Abraham, whose story begins in Genesis 12.

The books in the Old Testament are not arranged in the order of the events they describe. For instance, Ezra and Nehemiah were the last Old Testament books written, but they were placed about halfway through the Old Testament.

The Old Testament is arranged instead by subject matter and by the type of writing. **Genesis, Exodus, Leviticus, Numbers,** and **Deuteronomy** tell about the Hebrew nation from the beginning until the time the Israelites were ready to enter Canaan with Joshua as leader. These first five books are called the Law. They give the details of the old covenant—the agreement God had with Moses and the Hebrews telling what He expected of them. These books tell about the commandments, the sacrifices and feasts, the foods the people were to eat, how they were to treat each other, and how they were to live in the land God was giving them.

The next group of twelve books, sometimes called the books of history, tell what happened to the Hebrew people from the time they entered Canaan until about 400 B.C. The books of **Joshua, Judges, I** and **II Samuel,** and **I** and **II Kings** tell about the Israelites in their relationship with other countries; they especially point out whether the people obeyed God or turned from God to worship idols.

The books of **I and II Chronicles** tell about many of the same things that are recorded in I and II Kings. But Chronicles tells only about the happenings in the southern kingdom (Judah), while I and II Kings tell about both Judah and Israel, the northern kingdom.

Ruth shows us a good side of the people during one period of the judges.

Ezra and **Nehemiah** tell about life in Jerusalem when some of the Hebrews returned from exile in Babylonia.

Esther tells about life in Persia for those who did not return to Israel after their Exile.

Five books of poetry appear next in the Old Testament. These are **Job, Psalms, Proverbs, Ecclesiastes,** and the **Song of Solomon.** However, there are several other books of prophecy that are all or nearly all poetry. These include Isaiah, Jeremiah, Joel, Lamentations, Amos, Obadiah, Micah, Nahum, Habakkuk, and Zephaniah.

After the poetry books come the books of the major prophets. These books are Isaiah, Jeremiah, Lamentations, Ezekiel, and Daniel. After these come twelve short books known as the minor prophets: Hosea, Joel, Amos, Obadiah, Jonah, Micah, Nahum, Habakkuk, Zephaniah, Haggai, Zechariah, and Malachi.

All the books of prophecy—major prophets and minor prophets—are writings of men whom God used to warn people of judgment if they did not worship God and obey His commands. While some of the prophets' messages were aimed at the nations around Israel, most of them were meant for the nation of

Israel. Many of their writings, however, are about ideas and attitudes that apply to people of all times—including our own. Some of the writings of the prophets also apply in a special way to the coming of Jesus Christ—either the first time when He came to die for the sins of the world, or His future return when He will come again to rule the world.

The Old Testament laid the foundation for the time when Jesus would come and teach more about God. The Old Testament tells about God's concern for the Hebrew nation and His instructions on how they were to live and worship. The Old Testament shows how the people did not keep God's commands. Instead they often worshiped idols like the nations around them did. Even the kings often worshiped idols and punished the prophets God sent to warn the people of their sins. Finally God allowed pagan nations to defeat Israel and carry many of the people off to other countries as captives.

Some say these olive trees outside Jerusalem are 2,000 years old—the original garden of Gethsemane.

Eventually, about 536 B.C., some Jews came back to Jerusalem to rebuild the Temple. In 450 B.C., Nehemiah returned to lead the people in rebuilding the walls of the city.

The New Testament (or New Covenant) clearly completes the Old Testament (or Old Covenant). Jesus Christ came to give Himself as the sacrifice for the sins of all men. He was what all the sacrifices of the Old Testament had been leading up to.

OLIVES, MOUNT OF

is sometimes called Olivet. It is not really a mountain but rather a rounded ridge east of Jerusalem that stands higher than other parts of the city. The valley of Kidron lies between the city walls and this mountainous ridge. The ridge is about a mile long with four small peaks on it.

In New Testament times, the area was something like a park of Jerusalem. It was a wooded area where people came to get away from the heat and crowds of the city.

Many important Bible events took place on this ridge. Jesus often taught His disciples there (Matt. 24:3—25: 46). The garden of Gethsemane, where Jesus prayed before His crucifixion, is somewhere on the hill (Matt. 26:30-46). Jesus began His triumphal entry into Jerusalem from this place on the Sunday before His crucifixion (Matt. 21:1-3; Mark 11:1-9; Luke 19:29-40).

The ridge was important in the defense of Jerusalem. When the Romans destroyed the city in A.D. 70, the soldiers camped on this hill, where they could get a good view of the city.

Today, the Mount of Olives is heavily

ORNAMENTS *(OR-nuh-muntz)*
in the Bible were decorations on clothing, houses, temples, or tools. Ancient people were very artistic and often made beautiful carvings, jewelry, paintings, and other handwork.

Among the wealthy, clothing was beautifully embroidered. Those who could afford them wore gold necklaces, earrings, rings, bracelets, and buckles. Jewelry was also made of silver and other less expensive materials.

Even tools and weapons were often carved and decorated.

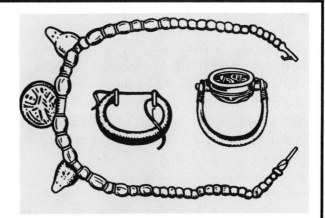

Both the Old and New Testaments warn against too much emphasis on jewels and fine clothing. Christians should work instead for inner beauty.
See Isaiah 3:18-23; I Timothy 2:9, 10.

---

populated with hotels, homes, businesses, and Hebrew University.

OMEGA (see *Alpha*)

OMER (see *Measures*)

ORPAH (OR-puh)
was the sister-in-law of Ruth. Both Ruth and Orpah were Moabite women who married sons of Naomi after Naomi and her husband came to Moab. All the men in the family died, and Naomi decided to go back to Bethlehem, where she had lived before. Both Orpah and Ruth decided to go with her. Naomi told them to stay among their own people. Orpah followed her advice, but Ruth insisted on going with her mother-in-law to Bethlehem. Ruth later became the great-grandmother of King David. See Ruth 1:1-14.

ORNAMENTS (see box above)

OVENS
in Israeli homes were usually barrel-shaped, two or three feet across the middle, and made of baked clay. Fires were made with dry grass, bushes, or animal dung mixed with straw. Bread dough was pushed against the walls and baked very quickly. Large cities often had central ovens to which many women took their bread to be baked, so that their homes would not get so hot.

PALESTINE

PALESTINE *(PAL-uh-stine)*
is the ancient name of an area about seventy miles wide and 150 miles long between the Mediterranean Sea and the Jordan River. It is about the size of the state of Vermont. *Palestine* is a general name that applies to most of what is now Israel. In the Old Testament it was sometimes called Canaan.

Although Israel is small, it has great variations in climate. Along the northern coast, the climate is moderate—something like that of New York City.

Jerusalem, thirty-four miles inland, has a climate more like that of Tennessee or northern Georgia. Jericho is only fifteen

Paul often told crowds about the day God stopped him on his way to Damascus to arrest Christians.

miles from Jerusalem, but it is 700 feet below sea level, and its climate is tropical.

Although all of Israel is hilly, the northern part has the most rugged hills. The central part has the best farmland. Even though this area has many hills, there are fertile valleys between the hills, and the climate is good for farming. Much of southern Israel has so little rainfall that it is barely usable for grazing sheep and camels. There is some land around wells that can be farmed.

In Bible times, fishing was an important part of life, especially around the Sea of Galilee. The Jordan River, although it was too shallow and had too many rapids for boats and shipping, was also important in the life of the people. It flows from the Sea of Galilee to the Dead Sea sixty-five miles away, but the river is so winding that it actually runs 200 miles. Along the river, there was fertile land on which the people grew good crops.

PAPHOS (PAY-fus)

was the capital city on the west end of the island of Cyprus in the Mediterranean Sea. Paul visited this city on his first missionary journey. At Paphos, a Roman official named Sergius Paulus became a Christian, and a false prophet was blinded for a while. See Acts 13:4-12.

PAPYRUS (puh-PIE-rus)

was a tall plant that grew in water and swampy places. It was made into sheets for writing. Although our word *paper* comes from *papyrus*, papyrus was not paper.

To make writing material from papyrus, ancient people took the inside of the papyrus stalk and cut it into thin strips. These strips were criss-crossed on top of each other with some kind of glue and then left under something heavy to make them stay together. When the sheets were dry, they were polished with stone and glued together to form rolls or scrolls for writing.

Papyrus was also used to make light boats or canoes. The little basket in which the baby Moses was placed in the Nile River was probably made of papyrus, although the word used in Exodus 2:3 is "bulrushes."

PARABLE (PAIR-uh-bul)

is a story that teaches a lesson. Each parable usually points out *one* spiritual truth and teaches a lesson by comparing one situation with another. Jesus often taught with parables. Usually His parables were easily understood by His listeners, but sometimes He had to explain what they meant.

Perhaps Jesus' most famous parable is about the Samaritan who helped the man who was robbed and beaten (Luke 10:29-37). Jesus told this parable to show how persons ought to treat their neighbors.

PARCHMENT (PARCH-ment)

was an expensive writing material made from the skins of sheep or goats. It was made by removing the hair from the skins, soaking them in lime, and then stretching them on frames. The skins were finally rubbed smooth with chalk or pumice stone.

Parchment lasted much longer than papyrus. For this reason, scribes often used parchment in making copies of Old Testament writings.

When Paul wrote his second letter to Timothy, he told him to "bring the parchments." He may have been asking for

copies of the Old Testament writings. See II Timothy 4:13

PASSOVER FEAST (see *Feasts*)

PATMOS *(PAT-mus)*

is the small island where John was exiled about A.D. 95. The Roman emperor Domitian sent him there because of his Christian faith. While John was there, God sent him remarkable visions. John wrote these visions in a letter he sent to seven churches—the Book of Revelation, the last book in the Bible.

The island of Patmos is only about 16 square miles and is located about thirty-five miles off the coast of Asia Minor (now called Turkey). The island is now known as Patino. See Revelation 1:9.

PATRIARCHS *(PAY-tree-arks)*

were the men who founded the Hebrew nation. It usually refers to Abraham, Isaac, and Jacob. Sometimes the sons of Jacob are included, and Paul calls David a patriarch (Acts 2:2). See Acts 2:29; 7:8, 9; Romans 9:5; 15:8; Hebrews 7:4.

PAUL

is, next to Jesus Christ, the outstanding character in the New Testament. Although he was a devout Jew, he became the apostle to the Gentiles—the man God used more than anyone else to spread the Christian message around the world of that day. He was the author of thirteen New Testament books.

Paul's Hebrew name was Saul, but after he became a believer in Christ, he began to be known as Paul.

Saul grew up in a strict Jewish home in Tarsus, a Roman city in what is now southeastern Turkey (Acts 22:3; 26:4, 5). Tarsus was strongly influenced by Greek culture and learning. There Saul learned to understand Gentile thought and culture. This helped him later when God called him to preach the Gospel to Gentiles. He could speak and write fluently both in the Jewish language (Aramaic) and the Greek language of the Gentile world. In Tarsus, he also learned a trade—tent making.

When Saul was in his early teens, he was sent to Jerusalem to study under a famous teacher, Gamaliel. He mastered the Old Testament and became devoted to his Jewish faith. When he was about thirty years old, he watched with approval as Jews stoned to death Stephen, the first Christian martyr.

Then Saul decided to try to stop Christianity (Acts 8:1-3; 9:1, 2). He headed for Damascus to persecute Christians. But on the way, Jesus appeared to him in a blinding vision, asking, "Saul, Saul, why do you persecute me?" Saul realized he had been wrong, and gave himself fully to Christ (Acts 9:1-22). After being blind for three days, Saul received his sight through Ananias, a Christian sent by God.

Then he went to Arabia to study, to meditate, and to let the Spirit of God teach him how Christ was the Messiah promised in the Old Testament that he knew so well (Gal. 1:13-17).

He began preaching in synagogues and met with threats upon his life. Eventually Barnabas, a Christian leader from Jerusalem, asked him to come to Antioch, where a new church was growing (Acts 11:25, 26). The two men worked with the church there for more than a year.

About A.D. 48, the church at Antioch sent Saul, Barnabas, and John Mark (nephew of Barnabas) on a trip to Cyprus and parts of Asia Minor (now Turkey) (Acts 13:1—14:28). (About this time, Saul's name was changed to Paul.) They began in a city by preaching in Jewish synagogues. Often, after a few weeks

Suddenly Saul saw a bright light and fell to the ground.

PAUL

they were forced to leave the synagogue and meet elsewhere. Opposition was so bad in Lystra that Paul was stoned and dragged out of the city, where he was left for dead. But God spared his life; he recovered, and the next day he went on to Derbe, another city.

Later Paul and Barnabas returned to Antioch, where they told how God was working among Gentiles and how new churches were beginning.

While in Israel, Paul met with other apostles at Jerusalem to try to decide how the new Gentile Christians should fit in with the Jewish Christians (Acts 15:1-35; Gal. 2:1-10). The Jewish Christians believed that Gentile Christians must keep the Old Testament Jewish Law. After long discussion, the disciples agreed that Gentile Christians did not have to keep the Jewish Law, but they should not do some things that were particularly offensive to Jewish people.

When Paul and Barnabas were ready to make their second missionary journey, they had a serious disagreement. Barnabas wanted to take John Mark along again, but Paul said no because Mark had gone home halfway through the first trip. Finally, they decided that Barnabas and Mark should go back to Cyprus, and Paul should take Silas and go to cities in Asia Minor and Greece.

In his second missionary journey, Paul visited some of the churches he had started on his first journey and also went on to preach at Troas, Philippi, Thessalonica, Berea, Athens, Corinth, Ephesus, and Cenchreae (Acts 15:36—18:22). Then he returned to Antioch.

After a short time, he began his third journey, returning to many of the same cities again (Acts 18:23-21:26). In some he stayed for long periods of time. He lived at Ephesus for three years. He was eager to show that Gentile Christians and Jewish Christians were part of the same faith, so he encouraged the new churches to collect money for Christians in Jerusalem who were in need. He decided to take the offering to Jerusalem himself.

When he arrived, he was arrested on false charges of defiling the temple by bringing a Gentile into it (Acts 21:27—28:30). A Jewish mob would have killed him if he had not been rescued by a Roman officer.

When the Roman officer learned that some Jews planned to kill Paul, he sent Paul to Caesarea, the city where the Roman ruler of the area lived. Paul was held in jail there for two years awaiting trial. During this time, he got to explain his faith to Felix and Festus, two Roman governors, and to Herod Agrippa, the Jewish puppet king of Galilee (Acts 24:1—26:32). When Paul saw that he could not receive a fair trial, he appealed to Caesar. This meant his case would be determined by Emperor Nero himself. Paul could do this because he was a Roman citizen.

Paul was sent to Rome as a prisoner about A.D. 60. The ship was wrecked in a storm, but the group finally arrived in Rome (Acts 27:1—28:10). Paul was treated well and was allowed to live in his own rented house with a soldier guarding him. His friends visited him (Acts 28:30, 31). As a prisoner, he wrote several letters that are in our New Testament: Colossians, Philemon, Ephesians, and Philippians.

The letters of Paul to Timothy and Titus show that Paul was released by Nero probably in the spring of A.D. 63. He returned to some of the churches he

Paul spent a lot of time teaching people about Jesus. He often taught in the synagogue.

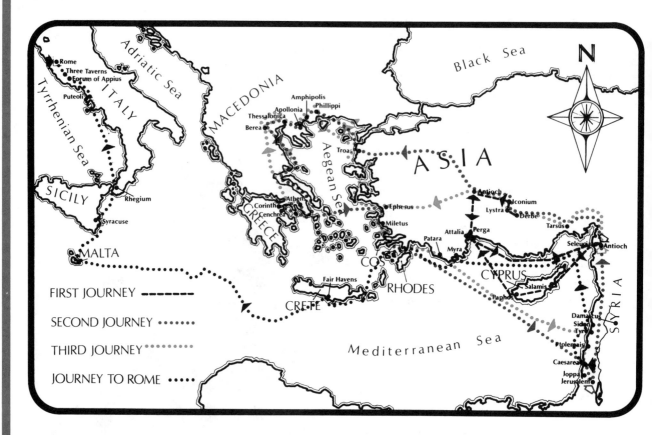

FIRST JOURNEY – – – –
SECOND JOURNEY ••••••
THIRD JOURNEY •••••••
JOURNEY TO ROME ••••

began. But by A.D. 64, Paul was again in prison in Rome. He was apparently executed in A.D. 66 or 67 as part of Nero's persecution of Christians.

Paul was one of the world's great thinkers, but he was also a man of practical common sense. He loved his own Jewish people very much, but he gave his life to bring the Gospel to non-Jews. He had a physical ailment that he called his "thorn in the flesh." Scholars do not know what the ailment was, but it made him realize how dependent he was on God's help at all times.

Paul, more than any other person, helped the Christian church to understand the Christian message of salvation by faith in Jesus Christ. He also taught that God expected believers to live honestly and lovingly with all people.

PENTATEUCH *(PEN-tuh-tuke)*

is a name given to the first five books of the Old Testament: Genesis, Exodus, Leviticus, Numbers, and Deuteronomy. *Pentateuch* is a Greek word meaning "five volumes." The Hebrew word for these books is *torah*, meaning "the law" or "the teaching." These books tell about the time from Creation to the death of Moses.

PENTECOST *(PEN-tuh-cost)*

was originally a Jewish feast called "First Fruits" or "Feast of Weeks." This feast was celebrated fifty days after the feast of Passover.

Pentecost is known among Christians as the time when the Holy Spirit was given in a special way to the Jerusalem disciples, who were celebrating the Jewish feast of Pentecost. As the believers were together, they heard a sound like a strong wind and saw something that looked like tongues of fire on each person. Then they began to speak in languages they had never learned. Visitors attending the feast from distant places heard about the works of God in their own native languages. On that day, about 3,000 people became Christians.

See Exodus 34:22; Deuteronomy 16:9-11; Acts 2:1-42.

PERGA *(PUR-guh)*

was a large city in Asia Minor (now called Turkey). Paul and Barnabas went through the city twice on their first missionary journey, going and returning. At that time, Perga had a huge temple to the Greek goddess Artemis. Today the city is known as Murtana. See Acts 13:13; 14:25.

PERSECUTE *(PUR-see-cute)*

means to try to harm or destroy, sometimes by injury or torture. Usually people are persecuted because of their beliefs. Prophets were sometimes persecuted in the Old Testament. Daniel, for example, refused to stop praying to God and was therefore thrown into a den of lions.

In the early church, Christians were often persecuted because they would not say, "Caesar is Lord." The New Testament teaches that Christians should be prepared for persecution.

See Luke 21:12; II Timothy 3:12.

PERSIA *(PUR-zhuh)*

refers both to a specific country and to an empire that was very strong during one period of Old Testament history. The country was the part of the Middle East roughly similar to the present country of Iran.

The Persian ruler Cyrus began building the Persian Empire in 559 B.C. Persia defeated Nebuchadnezzar and the Babylonians and became the ruling empire from about 539 to 331 B.C. During this period, Persia controlled not only Israel but also Egypt and eastern Greece. In 539 B.C., Cyrus permitted many of the Jews who had been captured earlier to return to Israel and rebuild the temple and the city of Jerusalem.

Persia was finally defeated by Alexander the Great of Greece.

The Book of Esther was written about the reign of Ahasuerus, king of Persia.

See II Chronicles 36:20-23; Ezra 1:1-8; 4:3-24; 6:1-12; Book of Esther.

PETER, THE APOSTLE

was the leader of the twelve disciples and later a leader in the early church. He is always named first in the lists of the twelve disciples (Luke 5:1-10). His original name was Simon. Jesus gave him the name Cephas or Peter, which means "rock." He was originally a fisherman who lived in Capernaum in Galilee. He was married, but we know nothing about his wife or whether they had children (Mark 1:30; I Cor. 9:5).

PETER

Peter first met Jesus along the shore of the Sea of Galilee. He and his brother, Andrew, both left their work of fishing to follow Christ.

Many stories in the Gospels show Peter to be full of energy, a man who often seemed to act before he thought. He sometimes bragged, as when he told Jesus that all others might turn away from Him, but he never would. Within a few hours, Peter was denying that he even knew Jesus. Later, realizing what he had done, he wept (Matt. 26:31-35, 69-75; Mark 14:27-31, 66-72; Luke 22:31-34, 54-62; John 18:15-18; 25-27).

Peter was the first of the disciples to recognize and say that Jesus really was the Messiah, the Son of God (Matt. 16:13-20). But a few minutes later, Peter talked when he should have kept quiet. Jesus told His disciples that He would go to Jerusalem and die there, and Peter told Jesus to stop talking like that!

Peter's love for Jesus, however, was very deep. He tried to defend Jesus when the soldiers came to arrest Him (Luke 22: 47-51; John 18:10, 11). He cut off the ear of one of the men, but Jesus healed it. Peter was one of two disciples who ran to the tomb on Easter morning and found that Jesus' body was gone (John 20:1-10).

When the Holy Spirit came at Pentecost, after Jesus had gone to heaven, Peter explained to the crowd what was happening (Acts 2:14-42). As the result of Peter's first sermon, 3,000 people became believers.

Peter was involved in many miracles after Pentecost. A lame man was healed at the temple gate (Acts 3:1-26). When Peter explained that the miracle was done by the power of Christ, he was arrested and put in prison (Acts 4:1-22; 5:12-41; 12:1-19). This was the first of several times that Peter was imprisoned.

God sent a special vision to Peter to show him that the Gospel was for the Gentiles as well as Jews. As a result, he went and preached to Cornelius and his family, who were among the earliest Gentile believers (Acts 10:1—11:18).

Peter is the major person in Acts 1—12. Beginning in Acts 13, more is told about Paul than about Peter. Because of this, little is known of Peter's later life, but he seems to have traveled widely preaching primarily to Jews.

Peter wrote two books in the New Testament. First and II Peter are letters to Christians in Asia Minor (now Turkey) to help them stand strong in Christ in spite of persecution.

Most scholars believe that Peter eventually went to Rome, where he was martyred in the persecutions ordered by the Emperor Nero.

PETER, FIRST LETTER OF

was written by the apostle Peter between A.D. 62 and 69 to Christians in northern Asia Minor (now Turkey). Peter may have visited some of these Christian groups earlier, but the apostle Paul had not.

Peter wrote this letter to encourage the Christians to have joy and trust God even though they would be facing persecution. Many scholars think Peter was in Rome when he wrote this letter and could see that Emperor Nero's persecution of the church would probably spread to other areas. He tells Christians to look forward to the time when Christ will return. However, since Christ suffered while He was on earth, Christians too must be prepared to suffer for Him. Meanwhile, they should live for God, do what is right,

The man who was once lame, praised God after he was healed.

show love to one another, and obey the laws of the land. Leaders of the church should be examples to others.

PETER, SECOND LETTER OF

was written under the direction of the apostle Peter to warn about false teachers. Peter knew he would not live much longer, and he wanted the readers to beware of those who taught wrong things. He warned that false teachers would say that Christ will not return a second time, but Christians should not believe such teachers. He also said that the person who really knows Christ in a true way will practice self-control and live a godly life.

PHARAOH *(FAY-roh)*

was the title of the rulers in ancient Egypt, just as *president* is the name of the top official in the United States. Moses was raised in the home of the Pharaoh of his time (Exod. 1—15). Later God sent terrible plagues upon Egypt because the Pharaoh would not let the Israelites leave his country, where they had become slaves.

PHARISEES *(FAIR-uh-seez)*

were the strictest and most influential group of Jews in the time of Jesus. They studied the Old Testament and were determined to keep every rule in it. Many traditions and interpretations of the

Old Testament had grown through the centuries, and the Pharisees tried to follow these too. They did not associate with others who did not share their ideas, and they often looked down on other Jews.

Because they put more emphasis on keeping rules than on loving people, they did not approve when Jesus made friends with those whom the Pharisees called "sinners."

Pharisees disliked Jesus especially because He did not follow their very strict laws of keeping the sabbath (Matt. 12:1-14; Luke 5:21). They objected when Jesus healed people on the sabbath, because that was "work." Jesus often condemned their wrong attitudes (Matt. 9:10-13; 23:1-36). Some of the leaders of the New Testament church had once been Pharisees—men such as the apostle Paul, Nicodemus, and probably Joseph of Arimathea (Mark 15:42-46; Luke 23:50; John 3:1-15; Acts 26:5; Phil. 3:4-6).

PHILEMON *(fuh-LEE-mun)*

was a Christian man in Colossae. The apostle Paul wrote him a short letter that is now a part of our New Testament.

Philemon had a slave named Onesimus who ran away and probably went to Rome, where he met Paul and became a

Pharisees often made a big show of their praying.

Christian. Paul sent Onesimus back to Philemon with this letter. It is a loving letter, telling Philemon to receive Onesimus not as a slave but as a brother in the Lord. Paul told Philemon to charge anything Onesimus owed to Paul's account. Paul also told Philemon how helpful Onesimus had been to him in prison.

PHILIP (FIL-up)

is the name of two important people in the New Testament:

1. Philip, the apostle or disciple of Jesus, who brought Nathanael to Jesus. Later on, he also brought some Gentiles to meet Jesus. Philip is not mentioned in the Bible after the time of Pentecost, but tradition says he did missionary work in Asia Minor (now Turkey). See Matthew 10:23; John 1:43-51; 6:5, 6; 12:20-23; 14:8-14; Acts 1:13.

2. Philip, the deacon and evangelist, was a Greek-speaking Jew who was one of the seven deacons appointed to help take care of food for widows in Jerusalem (Acts 6:1-6; 8:4-40; 21:7-10). After Stephen was stoned, the deacons became evangelists or missionaries. Philip went to the city of Samaria to preach. Many people believed in Christ, and God did some miracles of healing through Philip.

When God called him to go to a desert road, he met an Ethiopian man who was reading the Book of Isaiah in a chariot. Philip sat down with him and explained that Jesus was the Messiah about whom the prophet Isaiah had written. The Ethiopian believed in Christ, and Philip baptized him. Then "the Spirit of the Lord caught up Philip; and the eunuch saw him no more." Philip was soon found preaching in other towns.

Philip later lived in Caesarea, where he was an evangelist. Paul often stayed with him when he traveled to Caesarea. Philip had four unmarried daughters who prophesied. The Bible tells nothing more of Philip's later life.

PHILIPPI (FIL-uh-pie or fuh-LIP-eye)

was a major city in northeastern Macedonia, an area that is now part of Greece. Philippi was a Roman colony. Many retired Roman soldiers lived there, and the people had all the legal rights of Roman citizens.

Philippi was a city of mixtures: the languages and culture were Greek; the government was Roman; the religions included the worship of Greek, Roman, and Egyptian gods plus emperor worship.

This city was the first place in Europe to hear the Gospel. Paul went to Philippi on his second missionary journey after

God sent him a vision of a Macedonian man saying, "Come over and help us."
See Acts 16:1-40; Philippians 4:2, 3.

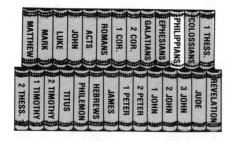

PHILIPPIANS *(foh-LIP-ee-onz)*, LETTER TO

was written by the apostle Paul to the church at Philippi. He thanked the believers for sending one of their members, Epaphroditus, to visit Paul in prison and bring him a gift of money (Phil. 4:10-20). It was the only church from which Paul ever accepted such a gift.

Epaphroditus became sick while he was with Paul and almost died. After he recovered, Paul sent him home to Philippi with this letter, telling the Philippians to receive Epaphroditus with joy and to show honor to him, for he had risked his life in the service of Christ (Phil. 2:25-30).

Paul had a closer relationship with this church than with any other. His love for the Philippians shows clearly in this letter. He wrote of his joy in remembering them and of their joy in the Lord. The idea of joy or rejoicing appears sixteen times in this short letter—even though Paul was in prison when he wrote it.

He reminded the Philippians of how Christ gave up the joys of heaven to become a man and die on the cross (Phil. 2:5-11). He reminded them how important it is for Christians to be content wherever God places them. And he said to think about things that are true, pure, lovely, and gracious (Phil. 4:8).

PHILISTINES
(FIL-uh-steenze or fuh-LIS-teenz)

lived along the coast of the Mediterranean Sea in southern Canaan and were wealthier and more advanced in using tools and crafts (particularly metals) than the Hebrews. They were usually enemies of the Israelites and fought many battles with them during the time of the Book of Judges—about 1400 to 1050 B.C.

These people were the enemies in many famous Bible stories. A Philistine woman, Delilah, tricked Samson into telling the secret of his great strength. The giant that David killed with a sling and a stone was a Philistine. The Israelites never fully conquered the Philistines.

PHINEHAS *(FIN-ee-us)*,

an Old Testament priest, was the son of Eli (see *Hophni and Phinehas*). See I Samuel 2:12-17; 4:1-22.

Delilah was the Philistine who trapped Samson.

"I am innocent of this man's blood," Pontius Pilate said as he washed his hands during Jesus' trial.

PILATE *(PIE-lut),*
PONTIUS *(PON-chos),*

was the governor of Judea during the time of Jesus' death. He was a Roman responsible for keeping peace among the Jews.

Pilate never got along well with the Jews. He did not understand them or their religion. The Jewish historian Josephus wrote that Pilate outraged the Jews by using temple money to build an aqueduct. He also brought shields decorated with figures of Roman emperors into Jerusalem.

When Jesus was brought to him, he realized that Jesus was innocent of the charges against Him. However, Pilate did not want to get into more trouble with the Jews, so he allowed Jesus to be executed because he did not want to lose his job.

He was removed from his position about six years later. History does not record what happened to him after that, although Christian tradition says he later killed himself.

See Matthew 27:1-31; Mark 15:1-15; Luke 23:1-25; John 18:28—19:6.

PILLAR OF FIRE AND CLOUD

was the sign God used to lead the Israelites through the wilderness (Neh. 9:19). God showed this miraculous sign to the Israelites as they were fleeing from the army of the Pharaoh (Exod. 13:21-22; 14:19-24). It continued to guide them all during the forty years before they entered Canaan. The cloud (in the daytime) and the fire (at night) were apparently shaped like a stone set upright.

During the Hebrews' forty years in the wilderness, God spoke to Moses many times from the cloud as it stood over the Tabernacle (Exod. 33:8-11). Moses would go into the tabernacle. Then the cloud would come down and stay at the door of the tabernacle as God spoke to Moses from it.

At the end of the forty years, when Joshua was ready to take over command from Moses, God spoke to both of them from the cloud in front of the tabernacle (Deut. 31:14-23).

The pillar is not mentioned after the death of Moses.

PLAGUES (playgz) OF EGYPT

were disasters sent by God to convince the pharaoh to let the Israelites leave Egypt. Although some of these plagues could be considered natural disasters, their timing was certainly arranged by God to fulfill His purpose for the Hebrews. There were ten plagues:

1. Water became blood (Exod. 7:14-24).
2. Frogs swarmed throughout all of the land (Exod. 8:1-15).
3. Swarms of lice (or gnats, or sandflies, or fleas) came (Exod. 8:19).
4. Swarms of flies came in great numbers (Exod. 8:20-32).
5. Cattle became diseased. The cattle of the Egyptians died, but none of the cattle of the Hebrews died (Exod. 9:1-7).
6. Boils or sores infected people and anmals. A fine dust settled over the land, and all the Egyptians and their cattle broke out in boils (Exod. 9:8-12).
7. Hail destroyed animals and crops (Exod. 8:13-35).
8. Locusts came and ate up the crops that were just coming out of the ground and had not been destroyed by the hail (Exod. 10:1-20).
9. Darkness covered the land for three days (Exod. 10:21-29).
10. The oldest child in each family and the firstborn cattle all died. The Israelites were protected by God from this terrible plague by sprinkling the blood of the Passover lamb on their doorposts. This was the beginning of the Passover feast, which is still celebrated to the present time. This plague finally convinced the Pharaoh to let the Hebrews go (Exod. 11:1—12:32).

PLANTS AND TREES

of many different types are mentioned in the Bible. The following is a list of some of them. Most can be identified as plants now growing around the Mediterranean or in other areas with similar climates. Some, however, are not known today by their biblical names, and scholars are not sure just what plants the Bible was referring to.

Acacia or **Shittah** trees still grow in the desert regions of Sinai and the Negev. Acacia wood is very hard and is orange-brown. The ark of the c ovenant and many other objects in the tabernacle were made of acacia or shittim wood, according to Exodus 25-27,30, and 35—38.

Almond trees blossom earlier than most fruit trees. Moses used almond sticks to test who was called to be the spiritual leader. Aaron's rod budded overnight and bore ripe almonds (Num. 17:1-11).

The design of the almond blossom was used to decorate the Israelites' golden candlesticks in the tabernacle (Exod. 25:33-36).

Apples are mentioned several times in the Old Testament, especially in the Song of Solomon. However, they may not be the kind of apples we know today, since apples grow only in remote places in Israel and are of poor quality. Scholars suggest that the fruit might have been the apricot or quince instead.

Barley was the most common grain grown in Israel. Most of the poor people used it for bread and cereal because it cost less than wheat.

Beans, especially dried beans, were a regular part of the diet of poor people in Israel. Dried beans were sometimes ground and mixed with grain to make bread (Ezek. 4:9).

Bulrush is the papyrus plant, a tall slender plant that grows in swampy places. The boat for the baby Moses was made from this plant (Exod. 2:3). Bulrushes were also used to make writing material before the days of paper.

Cassia (KASH-ee-uh) was a tree whose bark had a fragrant smell. Its small leaves were added to the oil used for anointing sacred things. It is described in Exodus 30:22-33.

Cedar (SEE-dur) Trees were often used in Bible times as building material. Cedar was also used to burn the sacrifices (Lev. 14:4-6; Num. 19:6).

Cinnamon (SIN-uh-mun) is a tree that grows about twenty feet high. The spice cinnamon comes from its inner bark. Cinnamon was used in the holy anointing oil in the Old Testament (Exod. 30:23) and in perfume.

Cucumbers were like our cucumbers.

Cummin was a plant whose seeds were used for seasoning food.

Cypress Tree in the Bible may or may not be the same as our cypress trees; authorities aren't sure. Some think the gopher wood Noah used to build the ark was cypress wood.

Fig Tree is the first known tree mentioned in the Bible. Genesis 3:7 says that

Bulrushes

One of the few remaining cedars of Lebanon.

Adam and Eve made aprons from fig leaves.

Figs were an important food for the Israelites.

For a person to "sit under his fig tree" was a sign of peace and prosperity. It is also a picture of deep thought, as in John 1:50, where Jesus said He saw Nathanael sitting under a fig tree.

Frankincense *(FRANK-in-sense)* is a tree in northern India and Arabia. When a cut is made in its bark, a resin comes out that is used in incense. It was used in the tabernacle and the temple. The wise men brought a gift of frankincense to the baby Jesus (Matt. 2:11).

Gall, the juice of the opium poppy, makes a person so sleepy he cannot feel pain. When Jesus was dying on the cross, He was offered a drink made of vinegar and gall (Matt. 27:32-34).

Grape (see *Vine*)

Herbs or **Bitter Herbs** were greens gathered fresh and eaten as a salad at the Passover. They may have included endive, chicory, lettuce, watercress, sorrell, and dandelions (Exod. 12:8; Num. 9:11).

Hyssop *(HISS-up)* is an herb plant something like marjoram. Its stem is hairy and holds moisture well. In the story of the Passover feast in Exodus 12:21, 22, the Hebrews were told to take a bunch of hyssop and use it as a brush to put blood on the lintel and doorposts. At the crucifixion of Jesus, John 19:29 says that Jesus was given vinegar on hyssop. This may have been the same kind of hyssop attached to a reed or stick, or it may have been a kind of sorghum cane stick that has a similar Latin name.

Lentils *(LEN-tulz)* were similar to today's lentils—a member of the pea family. The "pottage" that Jacob sold to Esau for his birthright was made of lentils (Gen. 25:34). Lentils are often mentioned as a food in the Old Testament.

Lilies that Jesus mentioned in Luke 12:27 may have meant any beautiful wild flowers, such as anemones or poppies, that grew freely along roadsides and fields in Israel.

Mustard Plants are mentioned in one of Jesus' parables. The mustard seed is small and grows rapidly into a large plant. Jesus used the mustard seed as an example of how the Kingdom of God grows. See Matthew 13:31, 32; 17:20; Mark 4:30-32; Luke 13:18, 19; 17:6.

Myrrh *(mer)* was a fragrant substance made from a plant. Used as part of perfume, it was among the gifts offered to the baby Jesus (Matt. 2:11). Myrrh was also used to embalm the body of Jesus (John 19:39).

Nard was a fragrant ointment made from the roots and stems of the spikenard plant. It was a favorite perfume of ancient people. It was very expensive because it had to be imported from India. This was the ointment Mary placed on the feet of Jesus, as told in John 12:3. Mark 14:3 tells of another time when nard was poured on the head of Jesus.

Nuts included both pistachio nuts and walnuts. Walnuts were eaten and also pressed to get oil.

Olive Trees were important to people in Israel. Olives were eaten for food, and olive oil was used in cooking, lamps, medicines, and ointments. Olive wood was used in carpentry. Olive trees grow well in the rocky soil, require very little water, and produce fruit for hundreds of years.

Onions were a favorite food of the Hebrews in Egypt. They are mentioned in Numbers 11:5.

Palm Trees were date palms. They have grown in Israel for at least 5,000 years. John 12:13 says that when Jesus rode into Jerusalem on the Sunday before His crucifixion, the crowds took branches of palm trees and went out to meet Him. The Christian church calls the Sunday before Easter "Palm Sunday."

Pomegranate *(PAHM-uh-GRAN-ut)* Tree gives a delicious fruit about the size of an apple. The fruit has many seeds. Pomegranate trees grew in the famous hanging gardens of Babylon.

Spikenard (see *Nard*)

Tares probably refer to weeds called darnel that grow in wheat fields. Because they look so much like wheat, tares were usually left until harvest time. Sometimes they were pulled out by hand; other times they were harvested with the wheat and then separated with a sieve. The seeds of tares were much

Hyssop

Myrrh

Pomegranate

Tares (above), wheat (below)

smaller than wheat and would go through the sieve, leaving only the wheat. Jesus talked about tares in Matthew 13:25.

Thistles are prickly plants. Many kinds grow in Israel.

Thorns are plants with sharp points. They are common in Israel and are mentioned several times in the Bible. The crown of thorns placed on Jesus before His crucifixion was probably made from a thorn bush now known as the Christ thorn.

Vine usually refers to a grapevine. The harvesting of grapes was always a time of festivals. Vineyards are mentioned often in the Bible.

Wheat was the most common cereal in Israel. The King James Version often calls wheat "corn."

PLOW

in Bible times was a wooden or metal tool that farmers used to break up the ground. Oxen usually pulled plows, and farmers guided them as they walked in back of the plow. The earliest plows were only forked sticks that scratched the surface of the ground rather than turning it over.

PLUMB *(plum)* LINE

is a cord with a stone or weight (called a plummet) tied to one end. Builders use plumb lines to test whether a wall is straight up and down. In the Bible, *plumb line* is sometimes used as a word pic-

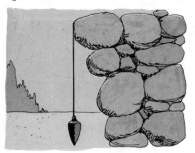

ture for the way God tests the uprightness of His people. See II Kings 21:13; Isaiah 28:17; Amos 7:7-9.

PONTIUS PILATE (see *Pilate*)

POOL OF BETHESDA

(buh-THEZ-duh) or
was a spring-fed pool surrounded by five porches. When the spring flowed, the

water in the pool bubbled. Many sick people gathered on the porches. They believed that the water could heal them when it was bubbling.

One sabbath as Jesus walked beside the pool in Jerusalem, He healed a man who had been ill for thirty-eight years. Some Jews were angry because Jesus healed on the sabbath. See John 5:1-16.

POTIPHAR *(POT-uh-fur)*

was one of the pharaoh's officers. Potiphar bought Joseph as a slave. Potiphar soon recognized Joseph's keen mind and organizing ability and placed him in charge of running his household. When Potiphar's wife falsely accused Joseph of molesting her, Potiphar put Joseph in prison. See Genesis 39:1-20.

POTTERY MAKING

was important to people during Bible times. Almost all containers were made from pottery, because wood and metal were very expensive. Potters made bowls, cups, cooking pots, lamps, ovens, and storage jars for water, grain, and other supplies.

Almost all pottery made during Bible

times was made on a potter's wheel. A lump of clay was thrown on the potter's wheel, and as the wheel turned, the potter formed the shape he desired with his hands. After it was partially hardened, he might put it on the wheel again to finish off any rough places. He also decorated the pot by painting it.

Finally the pot was fired in a kiln. This means it was baked a certain number of hours at very high temperatures. Firing was the most difficult job of the potter. The secrets of how to do it well were passed on from father to son.

The potter is sometimes used in the Bible as a word picture of God creating or making people as He wants them to be. See Jeremiah 18:1-6; Romans 9:20, 21.

PRAISE

refers to words or actions that give honor to someone—usually God. The words or acts show the deep feelings and thoughts of the one giving praise. In the Old Testament, praise often involved singing, dancing, "glad shouts," sacrifices, or gifts of thanksgiving in the temple or tabernacle. In the New Testament, praise to God is equally important. Hebrews 13:15 says that Christians are to "continually offer up a sacrifice of praise to God."

PRAYER

is conscious communication with God. But prayer is much more than asking God for things we want. Prayer includes praising God, giving thanks for His blessings, confessing our sins, asking God for help, and praying for other people.

Even though He was the Son of God, Jesus prayed often when He was on earth (Mark 14:32-42; Luke 3:21; 6:12, 13). He prayed when He was baptized, when He chose His 12 disciples, when He faced the crucifixion, and other times. When His disciples asked Jesus to teach them to pray, He gave them a sample prayer— "the Lord's Prayer" (Matt. 6:9-13).

The Bible teaches that when we pray we must have faith that God hears and

Caiaphas and the other priests put Jesus on trial illegally in the middle of the night.

will answer our prayers (Mark 11:24). We are to pray in Jesus' name, seeking the will of God (John 14:13, 14). The Holy Spirit will lead us in praying if we ask Him to. And we must have a forgiving heart, if we want God to forgive us (Mark 11:25, 26).

PRIESTS

in the Old Testament were the link between a holy God and sinful people.

Priests among the Hebrews began in the wilderness after the Israelites escaped from Egypt. Three kinds of priests are described in the Old Testament Book of Numbers.

1. **The high priest.** Aaron was the first high priest. He was a member of the tribe of Levi. All priests were descendants of Aaron, but the high priest was supposed to be the oldest male descendant of Eleazar, Aaron's son.

The high priest wore beautiful robes. The high priest, like other priests, offered sacrifices in the tabernacle and later in the temple. His most important work, however, came once a year on the Day of Atonement. On that day he put aside his beautiful clothes and put on plain linen clothes. Then he entered the holy of holies to sprinkle blood on the mercy seat of the ark of the covenant to atone for his sins and for the sins of the people.

2. **The priests.** The regular priests were all Levites, but they were also descendants of Aaron. The priests were divided into twenty-four groups. They took turns working in the tabernacle and later in the temple. They wore white linen robes. Only the priests could offer the sacrifices that the people brought to God. When King Saul and later King Uzziah offered sacrifices, they were punished by God (I Sam.13:8-15; II Chron. 26:16-21).

The priests were supported primarily by the offerings people brought to the tabernacle or the temple. Part of these offerings went to the priests and their families. The Israelites were required to give one-tenth of their earnings or harvest to the tribe of Levi, and one-tenth of that was given to the priests.

During some periods of Old Testament history, the priests also taught the Law of Moses to the people, and some priests served as judges. The Book of Numbers tells many of the other responsibilities of the priests.

3. The Levites. They were the descendants of Levi, one of the sons of Jacob, so they were one of the twelve tribes of Israel. When the Israelites came out of Egypt, the Levites were assigned to help the priests care for the tabernacle and later the temple. Some were responsible for the furniture of the tabernacle, others for all the screens, hangings, and coverings, and others for putting up the tabernacle or taking it down. After the temple was built, some Levites were singers and musicians, others were gatekeepers, porters, and assistants to the priests in offering sacrifices. During some periods Levites taught the Law of Moses and explained what it meant.

Levites were not given a particular part of the land of Israel as their own but were assigned instead to forty-eight cities where they could live and have some pastureland. The people of the other eleven tribes were told to give one-tenth of their income to the Levites for their service in the tabernacle and the temple. The Levites, in turn, were to give one-tenth of this to the priests.

Levites began their service when they

Priscilla, Aquila, and Paul made tents together for a while in Corinth.

were twenty-five years old and worked until age fifty.

In the New Testament, Christ is called the high priest who is superior to any high priest in the Old Testament (Heb. 3—10). He is the final link between God and people. When He sacrificed Himself for the sins of people, no further sacrifice by priests was needed.

In the New Testament all believers are called priests (I Pet. 2:5, 9; Rev. 5:9, 10; 20:6). We are called to be the links between God and people around us.

PRISCILLA (pris-SILL-uh)
AND AQUILA (uh-QUIL-uh)

were a Christian couple who were leaders in the early church. They were both tentmakers who moved from place to place around the Mediterranean Sea, teaching and preaching the Gospel wherever they went.

They first met Paul in Corinth, and Paul lived with them (Acts 18:1-3). Later they lived in Ephesus, where they taught Apollos more about the Gospel (Acts 18:24-26). They lived for some time in Rome, where they had a church meeting regularly in their home (I Cor. 16:19). Later they returned to Ephesus and again had a church in their home.

PRISON

was a place where a person accused or convicted of a crime was held. Often the prisoners in Bible times were beaten and then placed in chains or stocks (Acts 16:22-34). Often their food was only bread and water (II Chron. 18:26). Sometimes a prisoner who had not been proven guilty but was awaiting trial would be permitted to stay in his own house with guards to watch him (Acts 28:16).

This was true of Paul in Rome.

In ancient times, people were sometimes put in prison simply because they could not pay their debts. Jesus urged Christians to visit those in prison (Matt. 25:34-36).

PRODIGAL (PRAH-dih-gul) SON

refers to the story Jesus told about a son who spent all of his inheritance on foolish things. (*Prodigal* means recklessly wasteful.) Then he returned to his father to ask forgiveness. The father forgave him freely and had a party to celebrate his return. Jesus used the story to show that God freely and joyously forgives those

who confess their sin and return to Him. See Luke 15:11-32.

PROPHECY *(PRAH-fuh-see)*

is a message of God delivered by a prophet—a man or woman chosen by God. Prophecies in the Old Testament were meant to tell the Israelites or other people something God wanted them to know. Prophecy reminded people to worship God by telling them what God had done in the past, what He was doing in the present, and what He would do in the future.

The prophet Jeremiah once smashed a clay vessel to illustrate how God was going to have to break the people for their sin.

PROPHETS

were men and women in the Old and New Testaments whom God chose to deliver His messages to people. The pro-phets we remember best are Elijah, Isa-iah, Jeremiah, and Ezekiel, but there were many others, including Deborah and Huldah (Judg. 4, 5).

Prophets received their messages from God in many ways.

Sometimes God used dreams or night visions (Num. 12:6). Sometimes He used daytime visions, like the one Isaiah received in the temple (Isa. 6). And sometimes God spoke to His prophets directly, as He did when Isaiah was leaving King Hezekiah.

Prophets were often unpopular because they told of God's judgment. Jeremiah was imprisoned several times because he courageously spoke God's message to the people of his day.

Prophets such as Nathan, Isaiah, Jeremiah, and Ezekiel spoke to the kings of their time, often bringing messages of God's judgment for wrongdoing (II Kings 20:1-11).

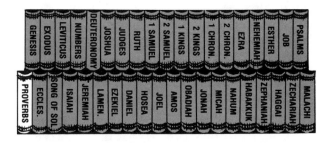

PROVERBS *(PRAH-vurbz)*, BOOK OF PROVERBS

is an Old Testament book of wise sayings. Many were written by King Solomon, the son of David. Some sections were apparently written by Agur (Prov. 30) and Lemuel (Prov. 31:1-9). There is no mention of these two men elsewhere in the Bible.

The main idea in this book is found in the words "The fear of the Lord is the beginning of knowledge; fools despise wisdom and instruction" (Prov. 1:7).

Most of the proverbs tell what a wise person does and contrasts his acts with those of a foolish person. For example, "A soft answer turns away wrath, but a harsh word stirs up anger" (Prov. 15:1). Most of the proverbs use contrast and show the difference between a person who tries to please God and a person who tries only to please himself.

PSALMS *(salmz)*

is an Old Testament book of 150 Hebrew poems of prayer and praise meant to be sung (some were to be accompanied by an orchestra).

Most scholars believe that many of the psalms came from David's time and later. The Psalms had their greatest use as a hymnbook when the Jewish people returned from exile in Babylon and rebuilt the temple.

The Psalms were divided into five "books." Most translations show these divisions.

Book I	Psalms 1—41
Book II	Psalms 42—72
Book III	Psalms 73—89
Book IV	Psalms 90—106
Book V	Psalms 107—150

The Psalms are a favorite part of the Bible for most people. The language is beautiful and majestic, but it is also very personal. The poems describe how people feel in times of thanksgiving, joy, sorrow, distress, or when they feel a guilty conscience.

Some of the psalms are called Messianic psalms because they seem to describe the coming of the Messiah, Jesus Christ.

Among the Messianic psalms are Psalms 2, 22, 72, and 110. When Jesus was dying on the cross, He quoted from Psalm 22:1.

Many Psalms are songs of praise to God for His majesty, love, and care. Many of our beautiful choir anthems are psalms set to music.

PUBLICANS *(PUB-luh-kunz)*

were men who worked as tax collectors for the Roman government. They agreed to collect a certain amount for the government. Anything they could get above that amount became their salary. Publicans were considered traitors by the Jewish people.

One of these tax collectors, Matthew, became a disciple of Jesus.

Jesus once told a parable about a publican and a Pharisee who prayed. In the story, the publican turned out to be a better person in the eyes of God than the Pharisee.

See Matthew 9:9; Luke 18:9-14.

PURIM *(POOR-im)*, PUR *(POOR)*

is a Jewish festival during February or March to celebrate the victory of the Jews over wicked Haman in the time of Queen Esther.

The feast is still celebrated today by Jews. Jewish families go to the synagogue to hear someone read the Book of Esther. People boo and shout whenever Haman's name is mentioned. Children often dress up in costumes to resemble the characters in the story. It is a time of joy. See Esther 9:2-32.

The queen of Sheba heard so many amazing things about King Solomon that she had to come visit him.

QUAIL (see *Birds*)

QUARRY *(KWOR-ee)*
means a place from which stones are taken for building, or it refers to the process of cutting or removing stones.

Archaeologists have found quarries dating back to Bible times. In one quarry, the limestone was relatively soft until it was exposed to air for a long time; then it became hard and durable. The workers made slits in the soft stone and then inserted wedges of wood. Then they poured water over the wedges. When the wood swelled the rock split into pieces that could be moved. Scholars think this may have been the way that huge stones were prepared for Solomon's temple.

See I Kings 6:7.

QUEEN

is used three ways in the Bible.

1. A queen could be the ruler of a land, such as the queen of Sheba, or Candace, queen of Ethiopia (I Kings 10:1; Acts 8:27). The Hebrews had one ruling queen, Athaliah, who ruled Judah for six years after the death of King Ahaziah, her son (II Chron. 22:10—23:15).

2. The wife of the king was also called queen. Queen Vashti and Queen Esther are both mentioned in the Book of Esther (Esth. 8:1-17). The wife of a king had no official power, although some queens had great influence—either for good or for bad. Jezebel, wife of King Ahab, used her influence to have Naboth put to death (I Kings 21). Queen Esther used her influence to save the Jewish people.

3. The mother of the king was also called the queen or the queen mother. The queen mother usually had more power than the wife of the king. Asa, the king of Judah, removed Maacah, his mother, from being queen because she made an awful image to worship (I Kings 15:13).

Many queen mothers are mentioned in the Bible.

QUEEN OF HEAVEN

was a female goddess that many Jews worshiped during the time of Jeremiah the prophet. Many scholars believe the Queen of Heaven was Ashtoreth, the goddess of love and fertility, who is often mentioned in the Old Testament. Other scholars believe the Queen of Heaven refers to some other goddess or to a particular star that people worshiped. Jeremiah told the people that God would judge them severely because they wor-shiped this false Queen of Heaven. See Jeremiah 7:18; 44:17-25.

QUEEN OF SHEBA

(see *Sheba, Queen of*)

QUIRINIUS *(kwih-RIN-ee-us)*

was the Roman governor of Syria when Jesus was born. He was appointed by the emperor of Rome and had been a military hero (Luke 2:1-3).

QUIVER *(KWIV-er)*

was a leather container for arrows. It was usually carried over the shoulder.

Quiver is sometimes used in the Bible as a word picture. Psalm 127:5 compares sons with arrows and says, "Happy is the man who has his quiver full of them." In ancient times, having many sons made a man important.

In Isaiah 49:2, God is compared to a quiver in which a person could hide and be safe.

QUMRAN (see *Dead Sea Scrolls*)

In 1947, a shepherd boy found jars containing ancient scrolls near Qumran. Pieces from 400 books were eventually recovered.

RABBI *(RAB-eye)*,
RABBONI *(ruh-BONE-eye)*
were Jewish words meaning "my master" or "my lord." They were terms Jews used for teachers, especially teachers of the Old Testament Law. Jesus' followers and others often used this title of respect when addressing Jesus. See Matthew 23:7, 8; John 1:38, 49; 3:2; 4:31; 6:25; 20:16.

RACHEL *(RAY-chul)*,
the beautiful favorite wife of Jacob, was the mother of Joseph and Benjamin. She was also Jacob's cousin and the daughter of crafty Laban.

She met Jacob after he fled from his brother Esau's anger. He had come to stay with his mother's relatives. As he got to know Rachel, he wanted to marry her. Laban told Jacob he had to work seven years to earn Rachel for a wife.

But Laban tricked Jacob and gave him Leah, his older daughter, instead. Then Jacob had to work another seven years to have Rachel as his second wife. After

Only Jewish boys got to attend the classes taught by the rabbi in Bible times.

297

another dispute with Laban, Jacob and his wives and children fled.

Rachel stole some household gods from her father and hid them, although Jacob did not know this. The gods would have given Rachel the right to her father's property. Eventually Laban and Jacob made peace with each other, and Laban allowed the whole family to return to Jacob's home area, Canaan.

Rachel and her first son, Joseph, were Jacob's favorites. Even though Jacob loved Rachel more than Leah, Rachel was jealous of Leah because she had many children while Rachel had only one. Rachel later had another son, Benjamin, but she died in childbirth as he was born. She was buried near Ephrath. Her tomb is on the road between Jeru-salem and Bethlehem, and many people visit it to honor her. See Genesis 29—31; 35:16-19.

RAHAB *(RAY-hab)*

one of the women mentioned in the genealogy of Jesus, was a prostitute who helped the Israelites in their battle for Jericho. She was a native of Jericho, but she let the Israelite spies stay in her home. Messengers from the king of the city told Rahab to turn the men over to them, but she hid them under stalks of flax on her roof. In return for their safety, Rahab asked the spies to protect her and her family during the Israelite invasion.

They agreed, and she helped them escape by letting them down over the walls of the city using a scarlet rope. The spies told her to hang the rope from her window so the Israelite soldiers would know which house was hers.

She followed their orders, and Joshua had Rahab and her family brought out of Jericho before the city was burned. Rahab

is mentioned among the heroes of faith in Hebrews 11.

See Joshua 2, 6; Matthew 1:5; Hebrews 11:31; James 2:25.

RAINBOW

is the arch of the seven colors of the prism often seen in the sky after or during rain. God gave the rainbow as His covenant to protect the earth from another flood. God gave this sign to Noah after the waters of the great Flood went down.

The prophet Ezekiel and the apostle John saw the rainbow as a sign of God's glory.

See Genesis 9:8-17; Ezekiel 1:28; Revelation 4:3.

REBEKAH *(reh-BECK-ah)*

was the gracious bride of Isaac. However, she later became the scheming mother of Jacob and Esau.

When Abraham wanted a bride for his son Isaac, he sent his servant Eliezer back to his relatives at Haran to find a suitable woman. There Eliezer met Rebekah at a well and asked her for some water. She not only gave him water, but she watered all his camels. This was a big job, because camels that have been traveling drink many gallons of water.

When Eliezer learned that this beautiful young woman was a relative of Abraham, he praised the Lord. He gave gifts of jewelry to Rebekah. She quickly ran to show her brother Laban and her father Bethuel the gold ring and two gold bracelets.

They invited Eliezer to their home to explain why he had come. He told them he was looking for a wife for his master's son. Laban and Bethuel asked Rebekah if she was willing to leave her home and marry someone she did not know. "I will go," she said. So Rebekah became the bride of Isaac.

But they had no children for twenty years. Finally God answered their prayers, and twins were born—Esau and Jacob. Although Esau was the firstborn, Rebekah loved Jacob more and wanted him to get the birthright that belonged to the firstborn. She planned a scheme for Jacob to fool his aging, blind father. The scheme worked, and Jacob got the birthright and the blessing that should have gone to Esau. Esau was so angry that Rebekah had to send Jacob back to Haran to stay with her family to be safe.

After her death Rebekah was buried near her husband and his family in a field called Machpelah. The burial place is now a part of the modern city of Hebron.

See Genesis 24:1—27:5; 49:31.

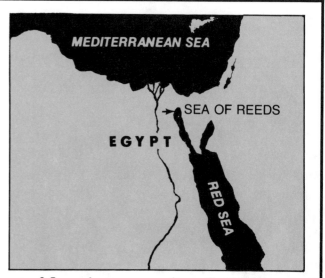

RED SEA

is a large body of water 1,300 miles long, stretching from the Indian Ocean up to the Suez Canal. Although the Red Sea is salty, its waters are green and clear, and many fish and other forms of life thrive there.

A marshy area that may have once been a northern finger of the Red Sea between the Mediterranean and the Gulf of Suez was important in the Old Testament. This area, more properly called the "Sea of Reeds," probably was the water God miraculously separated to let the people of Israel cross as they fled from the Egyptians. See Exodus 13:17—14:30.

REDEEMER (ree-DEEM-er)

is one of the special names for Jesus. (In the Old Testament, a redeemer was a person, sometimes a relative, who paid the price to buy a slave his freedom.)

Jesus is called the Redeemer because He freed us from the slavery of sin. We all have been slaves to sin, but Jesus "redeemed" us by dying on the cross for us. That was the price He paid. Now we can live as free children of God.

Old Testament prophecies sometimes use the name *Redeemer* for the coming Messiah.

See Isaiah 59:20; Ephesians 1:7; Colossians 1:14.

REDEMPTION (ree-DEMP-shun)

means paying the price for land or someone enslaved so that the land can be returned to its original owner, or the slave can be set free.

In the New Testament, *redemption* is a word picture to show how Christ, by His death and resurrection, "bought us back" from our slavery to sin.

On the cross, Jesus gave His life to set people free. Christ made possible a new life and new freedom to live as God's children. Because of Christ's redemption, we can live in friendship with God.

See Romans 3:24; I Corinthians 6:20; Galatians 3:13; Titus 2:14; Hebrews 9:12.

RED SEA (see box above)

REED

is a Babylonian measure about three yards long (see *Measures*).

REHOBOAM (ree-uh-BO-um)

was the foolish and luxury-loving son of King Solomon. He was king when the Israelites divided into two separate kingdoms—Judah and Israel.

When Rehoboam began to reign after the death of his father Solomon about 992 B.C., he wanted to raise the people's taxes.

But the people felt their taxes had been too high even under Solomon's rule. When Rehoboam consulted with his advisers, the older advisers told him to reduce taxes. But the younger advisers told him to be firm and to threaten more taxes to let the people know he was boss.

Rehoboam took the advice of the younger men and raised the taxes. The people of the northern part of the kingdom rebelled. Jeroboam, a young official who had worked for Solomon, became the leader of the northern ten tribes. Only the tribes of Judah and Benjamin stayed with Rehoboam.

Rehoboam was not able to reunite the kingdom. When he prepared to wage war against the north, the Lord stopped him. Israel became two nations: the northern kingdom, called Israel, and the southern kingdom, called Judah.

In the southern kingdom, Rehoboam welcomed the priests and Levites who were forced out by Jeroboam after he set up pagan worship. The southern kingdom also turned to idols soon after the kingdoms separated, and "there was war between Rehoboam and Jeroboam all the days of his life," according to I Kings 15:6.

See I Kings 12:1-24; 14:21-31; II Chronicles 11—12.

RELIGION (ree-LIH-jun)

is a system of faith and worship.

The word *religion* is not used in the Old Testament. Belief was not separated from actions. Old Testament people knew that each person should respond to God with his or her whole self.

In New Testament times, some people had the mistaken idea they could "believe" certain truths without having their beliefs change their lives. James, especially, insisted that "beliefs" without a life of helping others was no belief at all. "What is true religion like?" he asked. "Religion that is pure and undefiled before God and the Father is this: to visit orphans and widows in their affliction, and to keep oneself unstained from the world." See James 1:27.

REMISSION (ree-MISH-shun)

means pardoning or forgiveness. God remits our sins because of Jesus' death and resurrection. See Romans 3:25; Hebrews 9:22.

REMEMBRANCE (ree-MEM-brunce)

is an action or thing that makes us remembver a person or an event. The Lord often asked His people to do certain things to remind them of what He had done for them (Exod. 12:12; I Cor. 11:24).

REPENTANCE (ree-PENT-unce)

means sorrow for sin, and turning away from that sin to serve God and do right. Repentance involves:

1. admitting before God that what we did or said was wrong,

2. feeling sorrow for that wrongdoing and the hurt it caused God or others,

3. and most important, turning from wrong acts to right acts. As we turn away from sin, we turn back to God (Matt. 3:8, 11; 27:3, 4; Luke 3:3, 8).

Repentance is necessary for salvation (Matt. 3:2; 4:17; Acts 5:31; 11:18; 20:21; 26:20; II Peter 3:9). To accept Jesus' gift of new life, we must deal with sin in our lives. The Holy Spirit brings us to repentance and then leads us to ask forgiveness. God gives the repentant sinner new attitudes and new power to resist sin.

RESURRECTION

(rez-ur-RECK-shun)

means coming to life again after being dead.

Two kinds of resurrection are mentioned in the Bible. One is the kind Jesus gave to Lazarus when He brought him back from the grave after being dead four days (John 11:1-44). Jesus also raised from death the daughter of Jairus and the son of the widow of Nain (Mark 5:35-43; Luke 7:11-17). All of these people came back to the usual kind of physical life. And they all died again at the end of their earthly lives.

Another kind of resurrection will take place in the future—for all people who have ever lived on the earth (Dan. 12:2; Acts 24:15; Rom. 6:5; 8:11; I Cor. 15:12-57). Our new bodies will not be like our old bodies. They will be "spiritual bodies" that will never die. (The Bible views the real person as including both body and soul.) In this final resurrection, God's people will live forever with Him, while those who rejected Him will be forever separated from God.

RESURRECTION

(rez-ur-RECK-shun)

OF JESUS CHRIST

is the very center of the Christian faith. Because Jesus became alive again after death, believers in Christ know they, too, will live after death (Matt. 28; Mark 16; Luke 24; John 20).

Jesus had been put to death on a cross outside the city walls of Jerusalem. Many people had seen Him die, and a Roman soldier even used a sword to pierce His side to be sure He was dead. His body was taken to a cavelike tomb in a garden belonging to a wealthy follower. Guards were posted to be sure no one interfered with the body. Because Jesus died near sundown on the day that would begin the Jews' sabbath, the ancient burial customs were not completed that day nor the next day, for that was the sabbath itself. So on the third day some of the women who were His friends returned to do what was required for dead bodies. But there was no body! Instead, they found angels, who told them, "He is risen; go and tell his disciples."

Soon after His resurrection, Jesus appeared several times to His disciples. They were surprised, but they recognized Him. He was not a ghost. "See my hands and my feet, that it is I myself," He said to them. At least twice after His resurrection, Jesus ate with His disciples, showing that He was not just a spirit or a vision.

The resurrection of Jesus is a central theme of the New Testament. Paul wrote often about the power and purpose of the resurrection. Jesus Christ rescued us from the power of sin by dying on the cross; He showed His rule over the universe by rising from death. His resurrection was further proof that He was the Son of God.

Because of this glorious event, Christians know that they will receive new "spiritual" bodies like the one Christ had after His resurrection (Acts 1:15-22; 13:26, 27; Rom. 8:19-22; I Cor. 15:17-19). Christians also have the power of the risen Christ (the same power necessary to raise Him from death) available in their everyday lives and when they face death.

REUBEN *(ROO-ben)*

was the oldest of Jacob and Leah's sons. He saved the life of his younger brother

Mary Magdalene was the first person to see Jesus after He had come back from the dead.

303

Joseph when his other brothers wanted to kill Joseph (Gen. 37:19-22; 42:22, 37; 46:9). Reuben convinced them instead to sell Joseph into slavery in Egypt.

After Joseph became a powerful ruler in Egypt, Reuben and his brothers went to Egypt to get food because there was a famine in Israel. As the oldest of the brothers, Reuben was the spokesman. Before Joseph let his brothers know who he was, he tested them to see if they were still cruel and uncaring. Reuben showed his concern for his brothers and his father during this testing time.

After Joseph and his brothers were reconciled, Reuben and his family moved to Egypt with all of Jacob's descendants.

Reuben was the ancestor of the tribe of Reuben (Num. 1:21; 2:16; 32:1-33; I Chron. 5:25, 26; 12:37). When the Israelites left Egypt for the promised land 400 years later, the tribe had grown to more than 150,000. After the conquest of Canaan, the tribe of Reuben settled on the east side of the Jordan River. When the northern kingdom was defeated in 722 B.C., many of the tribe of Reuben were taken into exile in Assyria.

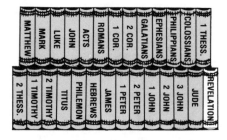

REVELATION, BOOK OF

is the last book of the New Testament. John wrote it on the island of Patmos, where he had been exiled because of his faith in Christ. Revelation tells how God gave John visions of the future church and the future earth. It is filled with strange word pictures using beasts, dragons, angels, thrones, scrolls, trumpets, and bowls. It is somewhat like the Old Testament prophecies of Daniel and Ezekiel.

John wrote specifically to the "seven churches that are in Asia," churches that were facing hard times around the close of the first century. He wrote to encourage them to stay true to their faith in Jesus Christ. He then tells of God's judgment upon the world to come, where the forces of Satan and evil are overcome in battle by Jesus Christ. Then a new heaven and a new earth are prepared, where God and His people enjoy each other forever. There is no night, no sadness, no evil. Those who have been faithful to God have only joy.

As he closes the book, John commands Christians to be faithful to God and to be ready for the return of Christ.

RHODA (ROAD-uh)

was a young servant girl in a house in Jerusalem where a group of Christians had gathered to pray for the release of the apostle Peter from prison. When she heard a knock at the gate of the house, she went to see who was there. When she heard Peter's voice, she was so surprised she forgot to open the gate! Instead, she ran inside to tell the others Peter had come. They insisted she must be imagining things. They did not believe her until they finally went to the gate, where Peter was still knocking. See Acts 12:12-16.

RIGHTEOUSNESS
(RIE-chuss-ness)

means living according to God's will. In

the Old Testament, God gave commands that He expected people to follow (Exod. 20:1-17; Deut. 6:5). But no person except Jesus Christ has ever lived up to all of God's holy law (Isa. 64:6; Rom. 3:19-26; 5:12-21). We all choose to sin at times, but God has made it possible for us to share in His righteousness (II Corin. 5:21; I John 1:7-9). Jesus Christ died for our sins; He atoned for our sins. When we accept this, He gives us His righteousness so we can have a loving relationship with God.

Christians seek Jesus' help to live righteously every day. We want to live up to our name *Christians* ("Christ's ones"). Christ's power and strength can help us live righteously.

RING

was a piece of jewelry with special authority in ancient times. Important people used rings as their signatures. A ruler would have his own sign on a ring, and every important document would be stamped or sealed with that sign. If the ruler gave an assistant his ring to use, he was giving him his authority.

Later, each household had a ring that represented the authority of that household. When the father placed a ring on the hand of his prodigal son, it showed that the son was fully restored to his place of authority in the family. (Luke 15:22).

ROMANS *(ROW-munz)*, LETTER TO THE

is one of the most important books of the Bible. It was written about A.D. 58 by the apostle Paul to Christians he had never met in the city of Rome.

In this letter, Paul explained more fully than anywhere else what it means to be

Rhoda was so excited she forgot to open the door.

"justified by faith." He explained that Jews and Gentiles alike are sinners and cannot by themselves meet God's stan-

dards. "All have sinned and fall short of the glory of God," Paul wrote.

But after showing how impossible it is for anyone to keep God's laws, Paul showed that God has freely provided a way to become righteous in God's sight. That way is through faith in Jesus Christ, God's Son. It is the way of "grace"—God gives us something we don't deserve. Paul explained that even Old Testament saints such as Abraham *believed* God—and that was considered "righteousness."

Paul was very careful to point out that although salvation is a free gift of God, it does not mean that Christians may go on sinning freely because God forgives them. Not at all, he said. We are to use the power of God's Spirit to defeat sin.

ROME, CHURCH OF

was started before the year A.D. 50. Although Christians were often persecut-

ROMAN EMPIRE

was the ruling government all around the Mediterranean from about 63 B.C. to A.D. 450.

It began as a small city-state in Italy and grew into an empire that controlled most of the world of that day. It reached from Britain, France, and Germany in the north to Morocco in Africa and east to what is now Turkey and Lebanon. As Rome conquered and controlled these areas, it brought some degree of peace that lasted about five centuries. This peace also permitted trade to flourish. Roman money became the common currency throughout the world.

In the time before Christ, the city-state had a form of democracy with a senate representing the citizens. Later the emperor became more and more powerful. By about A.D. 100, the emperor of Rome was even worshiped as a god in some places. The Romans insisted that everyone must say, "Caesar is Lord."

Because Christians would not do that,

THE ROMAN EMPIRE
in the first century.

the huge Roman Empire persecuted the tiny early church, and many Christians were thrown to the lions. But this seemed to make the church even stronger.

The peace and the ease of travel that Rome established helped the church to grow and spread throughout the world of that day.

Ruth gathered grain from the field of Boaz.
He had instructed his workers
to leave extra grain for her to pick up.

ed by the Roman government, the church survived and grew. Christians met in homes. By A.D. 95, Rome was a strong center of the Christian church.

After the Emperor Constantine became a Christian in the fourth century A.D.., the leader of the church became more and more powerful.

In our day, the Roman Catholic church is called the Church of Rome. Its leader, the pope, lives in a special part of Rome called Vatican City.

ROME, CITY OF

was the bustling capital of the Roman Empire. The city began about six centuries before Christ. Built on seven hills, Rome lies about ten miles up the Tiber River off the west coast of Italy. At the time of Christ, more than a million people lived there. By the third and fourth cen-

turies A.D., the city had lost its glory and had less than half a million people.

Most Roman emperors lived in the city of Rome, and some of them were considered gods by the citizens.

Early Christians were severely persecuted in Rome. Many were killed. Christians sometimes hid and worshiped in tunnels called catacombs beneath the city. Most scholars believe that the wicked city John wrote about in Revelation 17 and 18 was the city of Rome.

Nevertheless, the Gospel of Christ lived on, and Rome, the wicked city, became an important Christian center.

RUTH, BOOK OF

is an Old Testament book that tells the story of a romance between a foreign widow and her former husband's relative in the time of the judges. The story took

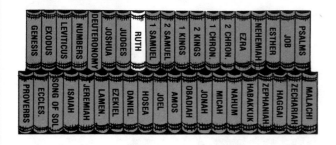

place sometime between 1300 and 1010 B.C.

Naomi and her husband went to live in Moab during a famine in Israel. After the famine was over, Naomi's husband died, and she wanted to return home. Ruth, a Moabite woman, had married Naomi's son, but he had also died. Now Ruth and Naomi had only each other to love. So Ruth left her own country to return to Israel with her mother-in-law. As they started back to Bethlehem, Ruth showed her love to Naomi by vowing never to leave her.

When the two widows arrived in Bethlehem, it was harvest time. To get food, Ruth arranged to work as a gleaner—one who picked up what the threshers dropped or left in the fields. She worked for Boaz, a relative of Naomi. Boaz saw the young widow working hard in the field and began asking questions about her. Eventually Boaz and Ruth were married and had a son, Obed, whom Naomi helped care for.

Ruth stayed in Israel, accepting the country as her own. She was the great-grandmother of King David and is listed in Matthew 1:5 as one of the ancestors of Jesus.

SABBATH *(SAB-buth)*

was and is the weekly day of rest and worship for the Jews and some Christians. It is observed on the seventh day of the week (Saturday).

After Christ rose from the dead on the first day of the week (Sunday), Christians began to gather on Sundays to celebrate Christ's resurrection (Acts 20:7; I Cor. 16:1-2). In Jerusalem, where most of the Christians were Jewish, they also worshiped in the synagogue and rested on Saturday. However, as the Christian and Jewish faiths became more separate, most

Christians kept Sunday as their holy day and gradually gave up observing Saturday as the sabbath. Some Christians today,

Stephen was not afraid to tell the Sanhedrin that they had often refused to listen to God.

however, believe that Saturday is still the proper day for worship.

The idea of the sabbath goes back to Creation. The Bible says, "God blessed the seventh day and hallowed it, because on it God rested from all his work which he had done in creation." (Gen. 2:3). Keeping the sabbath was one of the Ten Commandments given to Moses (Exod. 20:8-11; 16:23.30; 34:21; Deut. 5:12-15). God meant for the sabbath to be a day of rest, worship, and remembrance that He brought Israel out of slavery in Egypt.

During the 500 years between the close of the Old Testament and the coming of Christ, Jewish scribes tried to clarify what could and could not be done on the sabbath. Jesus regularly worshiped in the synagogue on the sabbath. He sometimes ignored the long list of rules if they interfered with His helping people. He healed people on the sabbath, although the strict Pharisees insisted this was "work" and against the Law (Matt. 12:1-14; Mark 2:23—3:6; Luke 6:1-11; John 5:1-18). Jesus replied that the sabbath was made to benefit people.

SACRIFICE (SAK-rih-fice)

in the Bible is an offering or gift of something valuable to God. Sacrifices have been a part of religions from the beginning of time. Cain and Abel, the first sons of Adam and Eve, brought sacrifices to God; so did Noah (Gen. 4:3-5; Gen. 8:20).

When Moses led the Israelites out of Egypt, he told the people what sacrifices God wanted. The sacrifices outlined in Exodus, Leviticus, Numbers, and Deuteronomy were followed by the Hebrews until the destruction of the temple in A.D. 70. The Jews since then no longer offer sacrifices.

The Book of Hebrews says that after Christ's great sacrifice of Himself for our sins, no further sacrifices for sin were necessary. However, the New Testament says we should offer to God a "sacrifice of praise" (Heb. 13:15). We should also offer ourselves as a "living sacrifice to God" (Rom. 12:1).

SADDUCEES (SAD-you-seez)

were a group of Jewish priests who, during New Testament times, were loyal to the Roman government. The Sadducees were largely a political party made up of wealthy priests. Usually the high priest (who was appointed by the Romans) was a Sadducee. When the New Testament speaks of "chief priests," it refers to Sadducees. Although the Sadducees were small in number, they were very influential. Sadducees were a part of the Sanhedrin, the ruling council of Jerusalem.

Sadducees differed from other Jewish groups in the following ways:

1. They stressed the first five books of the Old Testament, but they did not observe many of the traditions that the Pharisees accepted.

2. They did not believe that bodies will be resurrected. It is not clear whether they believed in life after death.

3. The Sadducees did not believe in angels or spirits (Matt. 22:23; Mark 12:18; Luke 20:27; Acts 4:2; 23:8).

When Jesus began His ministry, the Sadducees ignored Him. But when people began to think of Jesus as a teacher with authority, the Sadducees were angry (Matt. 21:23; Luke 19:47; 20:19, 27-40). Later they joined the scribes and the Pharisees in trying to destroy Jesus.

After the death and resurrection of Jesus Christ, the Sadducees opposed the

Christians. They put the apostles in prison, but God delivered them.

There is no record in the New Testament of any Sadducees becoming Christians.

SALVATION (sal-VAY-shun)

has a broad meaning. The word comes from the idea of being saved from or delivered from some serious disease or some physical or spiritual danger. Today it usually refers to a person's being saved through Christ from the penalty and power of sin.

Often in the Old Testament, salvation referred to a person or a group being saved from physical danger. When the Israelites were crossing the Red Sea in their escape from Egypt, and the pharaoh's army was close behind them, Moses said, "Fear not, stand firm, and see the salvation of the Lord" (Exod. 14:13). The "salvation" in this case was the destruction of the Egyptian army in the Red Sea.

The New Testament records only one time when Jesus used the word *salvation* (Luke 19:9). He said to Zacchaeus, the tax collector, "Today salvation has come to this house . . . for the Son of man came to seek and to save the lost." Jesus obviously meant a spiritual salvation, for Zacchaeus was not in any physical danger, nor was he physically lost.

The apostle Paul makes clear that spiritual salvation means being delivered from *sin*—both its power over our lives and the judgment it brings from God. This kind of salvation comes through faith in Jesus Christ, who gave His life so we could enter into the new life He made possible (Rom. 1:16). Salvation begins when we give ourselves to Christ, but it is a process

that continues throughout our lives.

SAMARIA (suh-MAIR-ee-uh)

is the name of both a city and an area in Israel. It is not always clear in the Old Testament whether a verse refers to the area or to the city.

During most of the 210-year history of the northern kingdom (Israel), the city of Samaria was its capital. For this reason, the name *Samaria* often refers to the whole northern kingdom. King Omri made Samaria the capital city of Israel about 880 B.C. Later his son, King Ahab, built an elaborate palace there, decorated with so much ivory that it was called "the ivory house" (I Kings 16:24, 28; 22:38-39). Ahab and his wife, Jezebel, made it a place of luxury and idol worship.

The city was finally destroyed by the Assyrians in 722 B.C. after a three-year siege. Most of it was burned. It was later rebuilt.

In the New Testament, *Samaria* refers to an area about forty miles wide and thirty-five miles long right in the middle of Israel. Judea was south of it and Galilee was north. The people who lived in Samaria did not follow the same rules of Judaism as the people in Judea and Galilee. Terrible hatred existed between

Samaritans and the other Jews of Israel during the time of Christ. For this reason, most Jews would not travel through Samaria; they would take a much longer route so they wouldn't have to go through this province.

Jesus, however, traveled through Samaria, and on one such trip He had an important conversation with a woman at a well (John 4:3-6).

SAMARITANS *(suh-MAIR-ih-tunz)*
were people who lived in Samaria, a province in Israel between Judea and Galilee.

SAMSON *(SAM-sun)*
was an Old Testament judge who had unusual God-given strength—but who was not very wise spiritually.

An angel told Samson's mother that she and her husband would have a son who should become a Nazirite (Judg. 13:2-25). (Nazirites spent their lives dedicated to God. They did not cut their hair, drink wine or anything with alcohol in it, or eat food God said was not clean.) The angel said Samson would help free Israel from its Philistine rulers.

When Samson was grown, he married a Philistine woman. At the week-long wedding feast, Samson gave a riddle to thirty men who were guests (Judg. 14:1—15:20). If they could answer the riddle, he would provide each of them with two new outfits of clothing. If they could not, they would have to give him sixty new outfits.

When the men could not guess the riddle after several days, they told Samson's wife she would have to get the answer or they would burn down her father's house. She tricked Samson to get the answer.

Samson was so angry that he went out and killed thirty men to get their clothes to give to the guests. Then he went back to his parents' house.

When he later returned, he found that his wife had been given to another man. This made Samson even angrier. He caught 300 foxes, tied their tails together with flaming torches, and let the foxes loose in the Philistine grain fields. The grain harvest was destroyed.

In revenge, the Philistines burned Samson's wife and her father. Samson then killed more Philistines.

The Philistines came out to capture him, and Samson killed 1,000 of them with the jawbone of a donkey.

Later Samson met a woman named Delilah. The Philistines offered her much money to find out what made Samson strong. Delilah coaxed Samson until he finally told her he would lose his strength if his head were shaved (Judg. 16:1-22).

When the Philistines tried to capture Samson, he simply ripped loose the city gates.

While Samson slept, the Philistines shaved his head. His God-given strength left him. The Philistines then poked out his eyes and made him work in a prison.

During one of the feasts for their pagan god, Dagon, the Philistines brought Samson out of prison to make fun of him. Standing between the two pillars, Samson prayed to God for the strength to push them down. As the walls and ceiling fell, thousands of Philistines were killed—and so was Samson (Judg. 16:23-31).

SAMUEL *(SAM-you-ull)*

was a prophet, a priest, and the last judge of Israel.

He was born in answer to the prayers of his mother, Hannah, who promised that if God would give her a son she would dedicate him to the Lord (I Sam. 1:9-20). To keep her promise, Hannah brought young Samuel to the tabernacle, where he grew up under the care of the priest Eli (I Sam. 1:21-28; 3:1-21).

Later, as a prophet, priest, and judge, Samuel told the Israelites they must stop worshiping false gods (I Sam. 7:3-15). He called all the people to a meeting at the city of Mizpah, where he offered a sacrifice to God and asked Him to forgive the people.

The Philistines heard of the meeting and decided to attack the Israelites at Mizpah. Samuel prayed, and God sent such a severe thunderstorm that the Philistines got their orders mixed up. The Israelites went after them and defeated them.

For most of his life, Samuel was the spiritual and political leader of the Israelites. When he was an old man, the Israelites told Samuel they wanted a king to rule them. God told Samuel they could

Samuel grew up in the tabernacle, helping Eli the priest. It was there that God spoke aloud to him one night.

have a king, but they should know that a king would cause them a lot of trouble. At God's directions, Samuel anointed Saul as the first king of Israel (I Sam. 8:4-22; 9:15—10:1).

When King Saul did not follow God's commands, Samuel warned him that God would make someone else king.

God told Samuel to anoint David as the new king. Later, when Saul was trying to kill David, David stayed at Samuel's home.

All of Israel was sad when Samuel died (I Sam. 25:1).

SAMUEL, FIRST BOOK OF

is one of two books called Samuel in our modern Bibles. However, the two parts were one book until about 200 B.C., when the Bible was translated into Greek. The translators then divided it into two parts, and it is now known as I Samuel and II Samuel.

Although the books are named after Samuel, who was a judge, prophet, and priest, no one knows who wrote them.

First Samuel tells the history of the Israelites from the birth of Samuel to the death of King Saul.

At God's command, Samuel anointed Saul to be the first king. But when Saul disobeyed God, God told Samuel to secretly anoint David as king. Saul had loved David. However, after David killed the giant Goliath, David became so popu-

lar with the people that Saul was overcome with jealousy.

David was also good friends with Jonathan, Saul's son, and this made Saul even more jealous. After Saul tried to kill David, David fled to the wilderness. Saul and his army followed, but were never able to capture him. Several times, David could have killed Saul, but he refused to do so.

Meanwhile, Saul and his army were also fighting the Philistines, and in one battle, Saul, Jonathan, and his two brothers were all killed. The story of Saul's death completes the book of I Samuel.

SAMUEL, SECOND BOOK OF

tells what happened during the reign of David as king. These events include: David capturing Jerusalem and making it his capital city, warring with the Ammonites and the Syrians, plotting the death of Uriah—the husband of beautiful Bathsheba—because David wanted to marry her, fleeing from Absalom (David's son) who led a rebellion against his father, and ordering a census that displeased God. When David built an altar to offer sacrifices, God stopped the disease which He had sent on Israel as punishment. Later this place of sacrifice became the place where Solomon's temple was built.

SANHEDRIN (san-HEE-drun)

was the highest Jewish council of men who governed the Jewish people in Israel in New Testament times. They were subject to the Roman rulers, but they had the final say in religious matters, in collecting taxes, and in some criminal cases.

The current high priest served as president. The seventy members included for-

mer high priests, heads of important families in Jerusalem, and leading scribes and Pharisees. Historical records do not show exactly how members were chosen or how long they served.

The Sanhedrin usually met in one of the temple buildings or courts every day except the sabbath or feast days.

The Sanhedrin could pass a death sentence on a prisoner but could not carry it out without permission of the Roman ruler. That is why Jesus had to be brought before Pilate as well as the Sanhedrin. The Sanhedrin told Pilate a lie about Jesus—that He taught people that He was a king and they should not pay taxes to Rome.

The power of the Sanhedrin ended after Jerusalem was destroyed in A.D. 70.

See Mark 14:53-65; 15:1-11; Luke 23:1-12; Acts 23:1-10.

SAPPHIRA (see *Ananias*)

SARAH (*SAIR-uh*)

was the wife of Abraham. She became the mother of Isaac when she was ninety years old. In the New Testament she is called the mother of all believers (Gal. 4:21-31).

At first her name was Sarai. God promised Abram, in Mesopotamia, that he and Sarai would be the parents of a nation of people. He told them to move south to Canaan, but they went instead to Egypt because there was a famine in Canaan (Gen. 11:29—12:20).

Years went by, and still Sarai did not have a child. So she followed the land's custom and gave her servant, Hagar, to Abram as a second wife (Gen. 16:1-16; 21:1-14). Hagar had a son, Ishmael.

But God told Abram again that he and Sarai would have a child who would be the ancestor of a whole nation. God then changed Abram's name to Abraham, and Sarai's to Sarah, or "mother of a multitude" (Gen. 17:15-19).

One day, the Lord visited Abraham and Sarah's tent. While Sarah was inside preparing food for them, she heard the Lord tell her husband that she would have a son soon. Sarah laughed to think of having a child in their old age (Gen. 18:1-15).

However, God kept His promise, and Sarah at age ninety gave birth to a boy. He was named Isaac, which means "laughter" (Gen. 21:1-8).

Sarah and her servant, Hagar, didn't always get along well. Sarah didn't want her son Isaac to play with Hagar's son, Ishmael, so she convinced Abraham to send Hagar and Ishmael away.

Sarah died when she was 127, and Abraham buried her in a cave in a field he bought.

SATAN (*SAY-tun*)

is the enemy who opposes God and man. He does not have a physical body. The Bible uses many names for him—the devil, the evil one, the deceiver of the world, the father of lies, Beelzebub, the old serpent, and the prince of the power of the air.

Jesus Himself was tempted by Satan in

King Saul could not stand to see the crowds praising David and decided to kill him.

the wilderness following His baptism (Matt. 4:1-11). Judas betrayed Jesus after Satan entered into him (Luke 22:3; John 13:27).

The apostle Paul said that Satan sometimes disguises himself as an angel of light (II Cor. 11:14).

The Bible does not say directly where Satan came from, but he was already In the garden of Eden when Adam and Eve were created. Although the serpent is not called Satan, he used that creature to tempt Eve (Gen. 3:1-15).

Satan is the ruler of a kingdom made up of demons. He hates God and tries to destroy God's work. The Book of Revelation pictures Satan and his angels as finally being destroyed (Matt. 25:41; Rom. 16:20; Rev. 20:7-10).

SAUL

was the first king of Israel. When the prophet Samuel anointed him king, Saul was a tall, handsome young man who knew how to work hard (I Sam. 9:10). He was humble and did not consider himself worthy to be king. God used him to win some battles against the Philistines, one of Israel's toughest enemies.

But although Saul was brave, he did not become a good king. After David killed Goliath, Saul became very jealous of David's popularity and tried to kill him, even though David was close friends with Saul's son Jonathan (I Sam. 18:6-16). Several times Saul and his army set out to find and kill David (I Sam. 19:11—20:34; 23:19—24:22; 26:1-25). But David, who now also had a small army of faithful followers, always escaped.

Saul also was impatient and did not always obey God's clear commands. Once he acted like a priest and made a sacrifice to God instead of waiting for the priest Samuel to make the sacrifice (I Sam. 13:8-13). Another time he disobeyed God and kept some things he had found in the camp of the Amalekites after they were defeated (I Sam. 15:1-29). God had said he was to destroy everything.

Finally, in a battle with the Philistines, Saul and his three sons were killed (I Sam. 31). The Philistines, to show how they hated Saul, hung the bodies on the walls of one of their cities and placed Saul's armor in the temple of their heathen god. However, some brave Israelites risked their lives to rescue the bodies and give them a proper burial (I Sam. 11:1-11).

SAUL (New Testament) (see *Paul*)

SAVIOR (*SAVE-yur*)

is someone who saves or delivers others from evil or danger.

The Old Testament nearly always speaks of God as the Savior of His people (Isa. 43:11; 45:21; 60:16). He saved His people from Egyptian slavery and delivered them from enemies in many other ways.

In the New Testament, *Savior* usually refers to Christ saving us from sin (Luke 2:11; John 4:42; Titus 1:4; 2:13; 3:6; I John 4:14). When the birth of Christ was announced to the shepherds, the angels said, "For to you is born this day in the city of David a Savior, who is Christ the Lord."

God is our Savior, for He is the one who planned our salvation; Christ is our Savior, for He died for our sins (I Tim. 1:1; 2:3; 4:10; Titus 1:3; 2:10; 3:4).

SCEPTER (*SEP-ter*)

was a rod or baton that symbolized the authority of a ruler. Some scepters were long and thin like a curtain rod; others were short and flat. King Ahasuerus held out his scepter to Queen Esther to show that she had his permission to speak.

SCHOOLS

are rarely mentioned in the Bible. What we know about education in Bible times comes mostly from other very old writings that have been found by archaeologists.

So far as we can tell, the Jews who came back to Israel from exile in Babylonia about 450 B.C. started synagogue schools, where boys were taught to read and write and to understand the writings of the Old Testament. (Girls did not go to school.) The Jewish scribes or rabbis (meaning "teachers") were in charge. If there were more than twenty-five boys in the school, an assistant helped. If anyone misbehaved, he was punished. Learning was mostly by memorizing.

If boys wanted more education than they received at the synagogue school, or if they wanted to become scribes themselves, they found a teacher they liked and studied with him. The apostle Paul studied with one such teacher—the famous Gamaliel. See Luke 8:1, 2; Acts 22:3.

SCORPION

(*SKOR-pea-un*)
is a poisonous insect that looks like a tiny lobster. In its tail is a poisonous stinger that can kill small animals and be very painful to humans. See Deuteronomy 8:15; Ezekiel 2:6; Revelation 9:10.

SCRIBES

were important religious leaders of the Jews from the time of Ezra (about 450 B.C.) through the New Testament period.

Ezra was the most famous scribe of the Old Testament (Ezra 7:6-11). He and other Jews who came to Israel from exile in Babylonia taught the Law of Moses to the people. They also copied the Old Testament writings and handed them down from one generation to another.

By New Testament times, the scribes were mostly Pharisees. They were known as the men who best understood the Law of Moses and could tell common people what they could and could not do as devout Jews. They taught children and adults in the synagogue schools. They often served as judges in Jewish courts. However, they were supposed to make their living some other way, so most of them had some trade.

Jesus accused them of greed, however, so they probably were getting fees for their teachings in some way (Matt. 9:3-7; 23:2-31; Mark 2:6-12; 3:22-30; 7:1-13; 12:38-40; Luke 20:46). Jesus also accused them of pretending to be holy when they really were not.

The New Testament scribes were Jesus' worst enemies and played an important part in His death (Matt. 20:18; 26:57; 27:41; Mark 11:18; 14:1; 15:1, 37; Luke 23:10).

SCRIPTURES (SKRIP-churz)

in the New Testament is a word that refers to scrolls of the Old Testament. When Jesus and Paul spoke of the Scriptures, they meant these scrolls (Matt. 21:42; Mark 14:49; Luke 4:16-21; John 5:39; 13:18; Rom. 4:3; I Tim. 5:18). After the writings that form the New Testament were collected and recognized as having authority, Christians began speaking of both the Old and New Testaments as "Scripture."

SCROLL

was an ancient form of book. In Bible times, books were made of papyrus or parchment (made from animal skins) glued together to form long rolls. Some were twenty to thirty-five feet long. Each end was fastened to a stick, and the scroll was rolled up so that the beginning of the scroll was on the right and the end on the left—because the Hebrew language reads from right to left. Jesus read from this kind of scroll in Nazareth.

Scrolls are still used today for reading the Old Testament in Jewish synagogues.

See Luke 4:16-20.

SCROLLS, DEAD SEA
(see *Dead Sea Scrolls*)

SEA, BRONZE or MOLTEN or BRAZEN

was a huge bronze basin 18 feet across and 7-1/2 feet high, holding about 12,000 gallons of water. It sat in the temple on a base of twelve bronze statues of oxen. The priests washed in it.

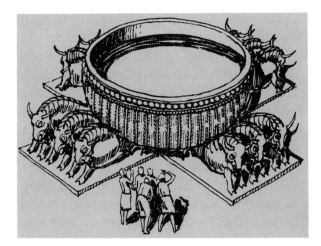

When the Babylonians conquered Jerusalem in 586 B.C., they broke the basin and took the pieces to Babylon.

See I Kings 7:23-26; II Kings 25:13; II Chronicles 4:6.

SEA OF GALILEE
(see *Galilee, Sea of*)

SECOND COMING OF CHRIST
is referred to nearly 300 times in the New Testament.

The night before Jesus was crucified, He told His disciples He would return (John 14:3; Acts 1:11). When He ascended to heaven, two angels told the disciples that Jesus would come again in the same manner as they had seen Him go.

Although sincere Christians differ about when and how the Second Coming will occur, most agree that Christ will return in a way that will be clearly visible to people, and that it will be an event of great joy to all believers. The Second Coming will be the climax of all Christ's work on earth (I Thess. 4:13-18; II Thess. 1:6-12; Rev. 19:11-27). God and those who love Him will finally live together in fellowship forever and ever.

SEPTUAGINT *(SEP-too-uh-jint)*
was the first and most important translation of the Old Testament from the Hebrew into the Greek language. It was completed sometime between 280 and 180 B.C. in Alexandria, Egypt.

Septuagint means "70," and the translation got that name because tradition says seventy men worked on it.

The translation was made because many Jews had moved away from Israel and knew Greek better than Hebrew.

SEPULCHRE *(SEP-ul-ker)*
is another word for tomb.

SERAPHIM (see *Angels*)

SERMON ON THE MOUNT
is the name usually given to the teachings of Jesus recorded in Matthew 5—7.

Given during the first year of Jesus' public ministry, the teachings seem to be addressed mostly to the disciples, although a crowd was also present. They explain the high ideals that followers of Christ should have.

Many of the sayings in this section are repeated in other parts of the Gospels. Since Jesus taught in many places, He no doubt repeated His teachings over and over. Some scholars believe this "sermon" is more a collection of Jesus' teachings than a sermon delivered at one time.

SERPENT *(SER-punt)*
in the Bible seems to refer to a poisonous snake. *Serpent* is often used as a word picture for sin or for something evil.

In the story of the temptation of Adam and Eve in the garden of Eden, a serpent tempted Eve.

319

See Genesis 3:1-14; Psalm 58:4; II Corinthians 11:3; Revelation 20:2.

SETH

was the third son of Adam and Eve, born after Cain killed Abel. Seth lived 912 years and had many sons and daughters. See Genesis 4:25, 26; 5:6, 7.

SEVEN CHURCHES (see box below)

SHADRACH (SHAD-rak), MESHACH (MEE-shack), and ABEDNEGO (uh-BED-nee-go)

were the names of Daniel's three friends who were thrown into a furnace.

The three young men had been taken from Judah to Babylon when King Nebuchadnezzar invaded Israel in 605 B.C. They were soon chosen, along with Daniel, to be trained for three years in the king's court.

King Nebuchadnezzar made an image ninety feet high, which all his officers were to worship. When Shadrach, Meshach, and Abednego refused, the king had them thrown into a fiery furnace.

Then an amazing thing happened. As the king looked into the furnace, he said, "I see four men loose, walking in the midst of the fire, and they are not hurt; and the appearance of the fourth is like a son of the gods."

The king called the men—and they walked out unharmed. The king then ruled that no one was to speak a word against the God of Shadrach, Meshach, and Abednego.

The king then gave the three men even higher positions in his kingdom. See Daniel 1—3.

SHEBA (SHEE-buh), QUEEN OF

was the ruler of the Sabean kingdom in Arabia, about 1,500 miles from Israel, during the time of Solomon.

She came to see King Solomon, probably on a trading mission as well as to ask questions to test his wisdom. When she saw his great wealth and his wisdom, the

SEVEN CHURCHES

were the churches in Asia (now Turkey) to whom the Book of Revelation was written. These churches were in large cities—Ephesus, Smyrna, Pergamum, Thyatira, Sardis, Philadelphia, and Laodicea—probably cities that the writer, John, had visited. Each of the seven churches was given a specific message in the Book of Revelation, but they were also told to read what the Spirit of God said to the other churches. The whole book was written to all of them. See Revelation 1:4—3:22.

As the king looked into the furnace, he said, "I see four men loose, walking in the midst of the fire."

Bible says "there was no more spirit in her." Solomon and the queen exchanged lavish gifts, probably made trade agreements, and then she returned to her own country.

See I Kings 10:1-13.

SHEEPFOLD

was a large pen to protect sheep and to keep them from getting lost at night. Sheepfolds were only walls made of stones. Often the top of the walls were covered with thorns to keep out robbers. There was no roof.

Several flocks would be kept in the same sheepfold at night, with one person guarding the door. Each shepherd knew his own sheep, and they knew him.

See John 10:1-16.

SHEM

was the oldest son of Noah. His brothers were Ham and Japheth. He seems to have been the ancestor of all Semites, including the Hebrews. He helped to keep his father Noah from being disgraced when Noah became drunk. See Genesis 9:18-23.

SHIPS AND SAILING

were not a part of the life of most Hebrews in Old Testament times. The

Israelites were farmers rather than sailors, because they had no harbors.

Most of the Mediterranean coast was usually controlled by their enemies, the Philistines and the Phoenicians, who were the main shipbuilders and sailors of the Mediterranean world.

The New Testament mentions Galilean fishing boats and merchant ships. The Galilean boats had small sails and oars, and could carry about twelve men and a load of fish. Jesus sometimes preached from these boats (Luke 5:3; Mark 4:1).

Ships were important to Paul's journeys (Acts 27; II Cor. 11:25). There were no special ships for passengers, so Paul traveled on merchant ships that carried grain and other cargo.

SHOWBREAD

were twelve loaves of bread, representing the twelve tribes of Israel. The loaves were placed on a special table in the tabernacle (later the temple) each Sabbath by the priests. This bread was also called the "Bread of the Presence," referring to the presence of God.

The twelve loaves were arranged in two rows on a table in the holy place. When fresh loaves were brought each sabbath, the old loaves were removed and could be eaten only by the priests (Exod. 25:30; Lev. 24:5-9; I Chron. 9:32).

SILAS *(SY-luss)*

was one of Paul's companions on his second missionary journey. He is sometimes called Silvanus. He was a Jew and a Roman citizen. The church in Jerusalem sent Silas with Paul and Barnabas to the Christians in Antioch to explain the decisions that had been made about Gentile Christians keeping the Jewish Law (Acts 15:22-41).

Silas later returned to his home in Jerusalem while Paul and Barnabas stayed in Antioch. However, when Paul and Barnabas separated, Paul chose Silas to go with him on the second missionary journey.

Silas was imprisoned and beaten with Paul in Philippi (Acts 16:19—17:15). They then went on to Thessalonica. After a three-week stay there that ended in a riot, they continued on to Berea. Silas and Timothy stayed in Berea for a short time, while Paul went on to Athens.

Silas and Timothy joined Paul in Corinth and stayed there for some time. From Corinth, Paul wrote two letters back to the church at Thessalonica. Silas is mentioned in both of them (he is called Silvanus). Scholars believe Silas may have helped Paul in writing these letters (II Cor. 1:19; I Thess.1:1; II Thess. 1:1).

Silas helped Peter write I Peter—by

A strange girl followed Silas and Paul in Philippi.

serving as his secretary (I Pet. 5:12).

SILOAM *(sy-LOH-um)*

is a pool or reservoir that still exists in Jerusalem. Jesus healed a man who was blind by putting clay on his eyes and telling him, "Go, wash in the pool of Siloam."

The pool was built in the time of Hezekiah, who was king of Judah from 716 to 687 B.C. The main source of water for Jerusalem was then the spring of Gihon, outside the city walls. In time of war, an enemy could cut off the city's water supply and make the city surrender. So Hezekiah built a tunnel 1,750 feet long that channeled the water from the spring into the city and into a pool or reservoir that was called the pool of Siloam.

See II Kings 20:20; II Chronicles 32:4, 30; Isaiah 22:9-11; John 9:1-12.

SILVER

has been known from very early times. It was used as money and also to make things: cups and crowns for kings and nobles, jewelry, idols, and the trumpets, bowls, and other furnishings in the tabernacle and temple.

Silver was refined in furnaces.

See Genesis 24:53; 44:2; Leviticus 27:16; Numbers 10:2; 7:13, 19; Zechariah 6:11; Acts 19:24.

SIMEON *(SIM-ee-un)*

was the name of three important people, one in the Old Testament and two in the New Testament.

1. Simeon was the second son of Jacob by his first wife, Leah, and was the founder of one of the twelve tribes of Israel (Gen. 29:33).

2. Simeon in the New Testament was an aged, godly man who met the baby Jesus and His parents in the temple. He said the Holy Spirit had promised him that before he died he would see the Messiah. See Luke 2:25-35.

3. Simeon, or Symeon, is another name for Simon Peter, Jesus' disciple. See Acts 15:14.

SIMON *(SY-mun)*

was a common name in New Testament times. It was the name of two of Jesus' twelve disciples. It was also the name of one of Jesus' brothers and of several other New Testament people.

1. One disciple was Simon Peter, the brother of Andrew. He was one of the best-known of the disciples (see *Peter*).

2. Another disciple was Simon the Cananaean, which means the Zealot. The Zealots were a Jewish political party who wanted to overthrow the Roman government. This Simon is not mentioned after the death and resurrection of Christ

Simeon met the baby Jesus and his parents in the Temple.

(Luke 6:15; Mark 3:18).

3. Simon, a half brother of Jesus, is mentioned in Matthew 13:55 and Mark 6:3.

4. Simon of Cyrene was the man who was forced to carry Jesus' cross on the way to the crucifixion, according to Matthew 27:32; Mark 15:21; Luke 23:26.

5. Simon of Bethany was a man who had leprosy. Jesus visited his home, we are told in Matthew 26:6-13 and Mark 14:3-9.

6. Another Simon was a Pharisee who invited Jesus to have dinner in his home. He found fault with Jesus for permitting a woman to put expensive ointment on His feet. The story is in Luke 7:35-50.

7. Simon Magus was a magician in Samaria. He became a believer in Christ through Philip, who came and preached the Gospel. Then Peter and John came, laid their hands on the new believers, and they received the Holy Spirit. Simon was so impressed that he offered Peter and John money if they would give him that kind of power. Peter rebuked him for thinking he could buy the gift of God with money (Acts 8:9-24).

8. Simon the tanner lived at Joppa, on the Mediterranean coast. Peter was staying with him when he had the vision of a sheet coming down from heaven. The story is told in Acts 9:43-10:23.

SIN

is any act or thought that is contrary to God and His will. When we sin, we sin against God, who is perfect (Jer. 3:25; 14:7, 20).

Sin separates us from God. Every person beginning with Adam, has sinned (Isa. 53:6; Rom. 3:23; 5:12). We have all chosen to behave and think in ways that are contrary to God and His will. Our sin has separated us from the deep friendship with God that He meant for us to have. God has never turned away from us, but we have turned away from God.

This attitude of ignoring God causes us to do foolish and wrong things. Sin makes us feel guilty because we know we are not being what God intended us to be.

Some people try to ignore their feelings of guilt or try to blame someone else. But that only increases the sense of loneliness and separation from God. The final penalty for sin is eternal separation from God.

A better way is for us to turn to God, asking Him to forgive our sin. God knew that we could never get rid of our sin or our guilt alone. But because He wants us to be free to love Him and be friends with Him, He sent His Son, Jesus Christ, to die for our sins so the penalty of our sin can be removed (Matt. 1:21; John 1:29; I Cor. 15:3; II Cor. 5:21; I Pet. 2:24; 3:18).

As we confess our sin to God and turn to Him, God gives us new life and new power to overcome sin (I John 1:7-9; Ps. 51:10; Rom. 6:14). We may never be perfect, but our new life in Christ makes us want to do right rather than wrong. We may not fully conquer sin, but sin will no longer fully conquer us.

SINAI (SI-ni), MOUNT

also known as Mount Horeb, is the place where Moses went to receive the Ten Commandments from God. It is also the place to which Elijah fled to escape the anger of Jezebel. We are not sure of the exact location of this mountain, but most scholars believe it is one of the mountains in the southern part of the Sinai Peninsula.

See Exodus 19; I Kings 19:1-8.

Earthquakes shook Mount Sinai several times.

SISERA (SIS-er-uh)

was captain of an army of Canaanites who fought the Israelites over a twenty-year period. The Canaanites were difficult to fight, for they had 900 chariots of iron, and the Israelites had none.

Deborah and Barak gathered men from other tribes to fight Sisera's forces and defeated his army. Sisera fled on foot, hiding in the tent of a woman named Jael. While he slept in her tent, she killed him.

See Judges 4:1-22.

SKULL, PLACE OF (see *Golgotha*)

SLAVERY

was practiced in all of the Mediterranean area in Bible times. In the Old Testament period, Hebrews had slaves and sometimes were slaves. However, most slaves were *temporary* rather than permanent slaves.

The most common form of slavery among Hebrews was debt-slavery. If a

325

they won a war, used the captured soldiers as slaves. Most of such men were "state slaves"—they belonged to the king and had to build roads, erect fortresses, and work in royal industries.

In New Testament times, slavery still existed but was not as common in Israel as in surrounding countries.

None of Jesus' disciples were slaves or slaveholders. Jesus taught by word and example that we should freely serve each other and should treat every other person as we would like to be treated (Matt. 7:12; 20:25-28; Luke 6:31; 22:24-27).

SLING

was a weapon carried by shepherds to throw stones or clay pebbles at animals that were attacking their flocks or cattle. Slings were sometimes used by soldiers.

The sling was made of two narrow strips of leather joined in the middle by a wider piece where the stone was held. The shepherd tied one end to his wrist. The other end was held in his hand. The sling was then skillfully swung around and the loose end released to make the stone fly.

David killed the giant Goliath with such a sling (I Sam. 17:40-50). Men with slings were a regular part of the armies of Israel. Seven hundred left-handed men in

The Jewish people have never forgotten their years of slavery in Egypt.

man could not pay his debts, he, his wife, and his children could be forced to become slaves of the person to whom he owed money. Old Testament Law said they could be held as slaves for only six years, regardless of how much they owed (Exod. 21:1-27; Lev. 25:39-55; Deut. 15:12-18).

Sometimes Hebrews were captured in war and carried away to other countries as slaves. Sometimes the Hebrews, when

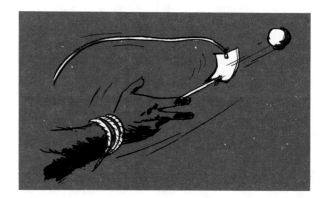

the tribe of Benjamin were once said to be so good with slings that they "could sling a stone at a hair, and not miss." (Judg. 20:16)

SODOM (see box below)

SOLOMON *(SAHL-uh-mun)*
was the third and last king of the united kingdom of Israel, reigning from 970 to 930 B.C. (I Kings 1:11—2:12). He was the son of King David and Bathsheba.

He was known for his great wisdom and his ability as a leader and administrator. He developed a strong army, brought the Israelites into a unified nation instead of a group of twelve tribes, and built a nation larger and more prosperous than at any other time in its history. He was a skilled diplomat who maintained peace with the countries around him.

He is most remembered for the beautiful temple to God that he erected, based on plans of his father, King David (I Kings 6:1-38; 7:15-51; I Chron. 28:11-19). It took seven years to build. It was the first temple Israel had, and it replaced the simple tabernacle, where the people had worshiped for about 400 years (I Kings 8).

Solomon started his reign with great promise. He asked God for wisdom and God gave him his request.

He is thought to have written the books of Proverbs, Ecclesiastes, Song of Solomon, and Psalms 72 and 127.

However, as Solomon became richer, he turned away from God (I Kings 3:1; 11:1-13). He married many foreign wives. Eventually he also worshiped their gods and built temples for them. Because he built such ornate palaces for himself, he had to tax the people heavily, and they became dissatisfied (I Kings 7:1-8; 10:18-21). After his death, the unified kingdom fell apart and was never established again.

SON OF GOD
is a term used in the New Testament to show that Jesus was the unique Son of God—God's revelation of Himself on earth.

Although Jesus did not describe

SODOM *(SOD-um)*
was the name of a city God destroyed for its wickedness during the time of Abraham. Scholars do not know where the city was located, for no genuine traces of it have been found.

Lot and his family got out of Sodom just in time.

Lot and his family went to live in Sodom after he separated from Abraham. Later, God told Abraham He was going to destroy Sodom and Gomorrah because the people were so wicked. Abraham pleaded with God, and for the sake of Abraham, God warned Lot to take his family and flee. Then God destroyed the city. Lot, his wife, and two daughters fled, but Lot's wife looked back—and turned into a pillar of salt.

See Genesis 18:16—19:29.

When the priests moved the ark into Solomon's new Temple, it was a day of great rejoicing.

Himself as the Son of God, He agreed that He was when others called Him that (Mark 14:61, -62). When the high priest asked, "Are you the Christ, the Son of the Blessed?" Christ answered, "I am."

At Jesus' baptism, and also on the Mount of Transfiguration, a voice from heaven said, This is my beloved Son." (Mark 1:11; 9:7).

Jesus taught the disciples that His relationship to God was different from their relationship to God. He spoke of "my Father" rather than "our Father" Only when He was teaching the disciples to pray did He say, "Our Father."

Jesus stated clearly that "I and the Father are one" and that "I am in the Father and the Father in me." He also said, "He who has seen me has seen the Father." (John 5:18; 10:30; 14:9-11).

The Gospel of John and the Letters of John often speak of Jesus as God's Son. The most well-known passage is John 3:16.

Paul spoke of Jesus as the Son of God in his preaching and his letters (Acts 9:20; Rom. 1:2-4).

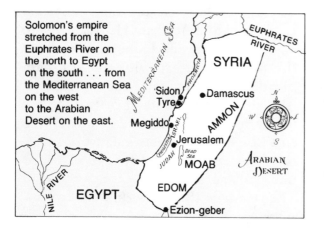

Solomon's empire stretched from the Euphrates River on the north to Egypt on the south . . . from the Mediterranean Sea on the west to the Arabian Desert on the east.

SON OF MAN

was Jesus' favorite name for Himself. It is used 78 times in the Gospels. With this term, Jesus identified Himself as a true man as well as being the Son of God. He often spoke of Himself this way when talking about the need to suffer and to give His life for the sins of all people.

See Mark 8:31; 9:31; 10:33; 14:41; Luke 18:31-33; 21:27, 28; John 13:31.

SONG OF SOLOMON

is a beautiful love poem in the Old Testament. It is sometimes called the Song of Songs, perhaps because it was a favorite. Some scholars thought it was a word picture of God's love for Israel, or Christ's love for the church.

Now, however, most scholars agree that it was meant to be a lovely poem showing the beauty of human love between a man and a woman.

SOUL

is often used in the Bible about the part of a person that is not physical. In Matthew 10:28 Jesus told His listeners not to fear those who are able to kill the body but cannot kill the soul. They were to fear God instead, who is able to destroy both body and soul.

In other places in the New Testament, *soul* refers to the whole living part of a person. Sometimes the Bible speaks of both soul and spirit, but they usually seem to mean much the same thing.

SOUTHERN KINGDOM

refers to the kingdom of Judah. After the death of Solomon, the kingdom of Israel was divided into two parts: the northern kingdom (Israel), composed of ten tribes, and the southern kingdom (Judah), composed of two tribes—Judah and Simeon, plus a small part of Benjamin. The southern kingdom was less than half the size of the northern kingdom, and much of its land was desert. It had a population of only about 300,000.

At first Judah tried to force the northern kingdom to reunite with it, but could not.

The northern kingdom was defeated by Assyria in 722 B.C. The southern kingdom lasted until 586 B.C., when it was finally conquered by Babylon and many of its people were carried away into exile.

SPIES

in Bible times went to enemy territories to find out about military strength or to spread rumors that would hurt the enemy.

Moses sent spies into Canaan. The chief priests sent spies to find some charges against Jesus.

See Numbers 13:1-33; Joshua 2:1-24; Luke 20:19, 20.

SPIRIT

refers to the inner part of a person rather than His physical body. Jesus said, "God is spirit," showing that God does not have a physical body as we have. Sometimes spirit is used in the New Testament as that part of a person that is able to have fellowship with God. See John 4:24; Romans 8:15-16.

329

SPIRIT, HOLY (see *Holy Spirit*)

SPIRITUAL GIFTS

refer to callings, talents, or abilities that God gives to His people for two purposes:

1. To help other Christians develop in their faith. The Bible term is "edifying the church."

2. To help win others to belief in Christ as Savior (see I Cor. 14:21-25).

Some of the gifts Paul mentions in his letters are: prophecy, teaching, helping, speaking in tongues, hospitality, working miracles, healing, and being a pastor, evangelist, administrator, or apostle.

The New Testament teaches that we Christians are responsible to God for the gifts He gives us, and we are to use them to benefit each other. Paul teaches that many gifts are needed if "the body" (the church) is to grow in a balanced way.

See Romans 12:6-8; I Corinthians 12, 14; Ephesians 4:7-13.

What was the bright star that the wise men followed? Astronomers still don't know for sure.

SPOILS

were the goods taken from an enemy after a battle. In Old Testament times, the conquering army regularly took all jewelry, possessions, cattle, men, women, and children. The captives usually became slaves; the goods were divided up among the conquerors and those who stayed home.

Israel and the nations around it all followed this practice. In Israel, part of the spoils were usually offered to God.

See Numbers 31:26-27; II Kings 14:14.

STAFF and ROD

mean the same thing. It was a shaft of wood used for support in walking or climbing. The staffs or rods of Moses and Aaron were used by God to work miracles. A staff was often a sign of authority. A shepherd used his rod or staff to beat off attacking animals or to rescue lost

After the Lord worked a miracle victory for Jehosaphat and his people, it took them three days to carry away the spoils.

STEPHEN (*STEE-vun*)

was the first Christian known to die for his faith. He was a member of the early church in Jerusalem and one of seven men chosen to be in charge of giving food and money to poor widows.

Stephen did miracles and spoke about the power of Christ. But he let the Holy Spirit speak through him.

Those who listened became so angry they took him outside the city and stoned him to death. Saul, who later became the apostle Paul, watched and agreed to his death.

After Stephen's death, all Christians were persecuted. Many had to leave their homes in Jerusalem, but they carried the gospel wherever they went, and the church began to spread through other parts of Israel.

See Acts 6:1—4.

sheep. He also used his staff to count the sheep every day.

See Exodus 7:9-20; 8:16, 17.

STAR OF THE EAST

is mentioned in Matthew 2:2 as the light that guided the wise men to Bethlehem.

Many astronomers have tried to figure out what caused this star to shine at that time in such a distinctive way, since the movement of most stars is so exact that their positions can be determined for centuries ahead or centuries past.

One idea is that it was the result of a conjunction of the planets Jupiter and Saturn that is known to have occurred about 7 B.C. It could also have been a supernova—a faint star that suddenly becomes brighter and then fades slowly for no known reason. Whatever the star was, God, who controls the universe, planned whatever was necessary to make it shine at the right time.

See Matthew 2:1-12.

STEPHEN (see box above)

STOCKS

were wooden frames in which a prisoner's hands and feet were locked, often in a painful position with legs stretched apart.

The prophet Jeremiah was locked in stocks, and so were Paul and Silas in the prison in Philippi.

See Jeremiah 20:2, 3; Acts 16:23-34.

STONING

was the usual Hebrew method of killing someone who had disobeyed certain parts of the Jewish Law, such as offering human sacrifices or idolatry (Lev. 20:2; Deut. 13:6-10).

STOVES

in Israel were usually made of clay. They were round and wide enough at the bottom to put in the dry grass, sticks, and sometimes charcoal that were used for fuels. The stove was shaped smaller at the top—just large enough to hold a pan or pot. Air vents at the bottom kept the fire going.

Wealthy people had stoves that were small metal containers in which charcoal was burned.

SYNAGOGUE *(SIN-uh-gog)*

is a place where Jews meet together to

In the Middle East today, bread is sometimes baked on small, flat stoves on the ground.

read the Old Testament and to worship God. Many historians believe that synagogues began after the Jewish people were taken into exile in Babylonia in 597 B.C. They had no temple there, but they began to gather together on the sabbath to read and worship. synagogue can refer both to the building in which they met and to the people who met there.

By New Testament times, synagogues were common throughout the Mediterranean area wherever there were ten or more Jewish families in a city.

Most synagogues were simple buildings, unlike the temple in Jerusalem. Each synagogue had a wooden chest in which the Old Testament scrolls were kept wrapped in a linen cloth. The persons who read from the scrolls stood on some kind of platform.

The people usually sat on benches along the sides of walls. Sometimes there was a gallery or balcony where the women sat. Some scholars think that in some synagogues women were seated on one side and men on the other, or women were seated in a separate room. In some areas, women may not have been permitted in the synagogue at all.

SYRIA *(SEER-ee-uh)*

in Bible times was an area north of Israel. It covered most of the land south of modern Turkey, north of the Sea of Galilee, west of the Arabian Desert, and east of the Mediterranean Sea. The modern nation of Syria covers some of the same territory.

Damascus was Syria's most active city in Bible times, and it is the capital of modern Syria. The Arabic language is the common language used in Syria now. The apostle Paul was converted in Syria near Damascus (Acts 9).

Syria was usually richer, larger, and more powerful than Israel, with abundant fruits, farms, and flocks of sheep and goats. It has been famous for silk, wool, and metal.

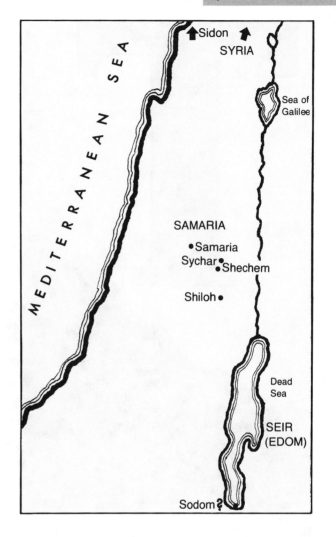

TABERNACLE

T

TABERNACLE *(TAB-er-nack-ul)*
was the Israelites' sacred tent for worship.
They used it during their wanderings in the
wilderness on their Exodus from Egypt and
for many years after they conquered
Canaan. Moses and the Israelites built it as

"God's house"—where God revealed Himself and lived among His people. It was used for worship and sacrifice until it was replaced by King Solomon's temple.

God said the tabernacle was to be built from materials that people gave. The Israelites brought gold, silver, and bronze metals; blue, purple, and scarlet fabrics; fine linen; goat's hair, goatskins, rams' skins; acacia wood; oil for the lamps; spices and incense; onyx stones and other valuable gems. They brought their gifts to Moses so he could supervise the building of a place of worship worthy of the God who had brought them out of slavery.

The tabernacle stood in an enclosure or court about 150 feet long and 75 feet wide. The walls of the court were made of linen draperies, fastened to posts of bronze. In this courtyard the people worshiped God. They never entered the tabernacle itself. Near the center of the courtyard stood the altar of burnt offerings, where priests offered the sacrifices the people brought.

The tabernacle itself was about 45 feet long and 15 feet wide—no bigger than an average classroom, only longer and narrower. It was made from cloth drapes and animal skins held up by acacia wood supports. Only the priests entered the tabernacle. A heavy curtain embroidered with red, purple, and blue cherubim divided the tabernacle into two smaller rooms.

The room nearest the entrance was called the holy place. It had an altar for incense. It also had golden candlesticks with seven branches and a table for special bread called showbread. The table was acacia wood overlaid with gold. Twelve loaves of bread were placed in two heaps on the table. Fresh bread was placed there every week. This was also called "the table of the Presence," because it reminded Israel of God's daily care in providing their food.

The room beyond the holy place was called the holy of holies. Only the high priest could enter this room, and he went in only once a year on the Day of Atonement. On that day he offered a sacrifice for the sins of the people and of himself.

The holy of holies contained the ark of the covenant, a small box made of wood covered with gold. Inside the ark were three things: the tablets of the Law given to Moses on Mount Sinai, a sample of the manna that Israel ate in the wilderness, and Aaron's rod that had budded with flowers. The ark was very sacred. Only certain Levites could carry it when the tabernacle was moved.

When the tabernacle was taken apart for moving, the ark and the two altars were carried by Levites. The rest of the tabernacle was folded up and placed in six covered wagons, each drawn by two oxen. For thirty-five years during the wilderness wanderings, the tabernacle stayed at Kadesh. In Joshua's time the tabernacle was settled in Shiloh.

The tabernacle was a symbol to the people of God's presence with them. The ark represented God's presence and forgiving love. The twelve loaves of showbread stood for the twelve tribes of Israel. The candlestick pictured the light of God's Word and will. The incense reminded the people of prayer rising toward God.

See Exodus 25—27, 35—40.

TABITHA (see *Dorcas*)

TABLE OF SHOWBREAD

a gold-covered table in the holy place of

the tabernacle, held twelve loaves of bread that were changed weekly. It was also called "the table of the bread of the Presence" and reminded the twelve tribes of ancient Israel of God's daily care for them. See Leviticus 24:5-9.

TABLES OF THE LAW

were stone slabs or tablets on which Moses received the Ten Commandments from God. When Moses brought them down from his meeting with God on Mount Sinai, he found the Israelites worshiping a gold calf they had made in the forty days while he had been gone. In anger, Moses threw down the tablets, breaking them.

God called Moses to cut two new slabs of stone and take them up the mountain to receive the Law again. This time Moses put the tables of the Law into the ark of the covenant. The ark was placed in the tabernacle and later in King Solomon's temple.

The tables were finally lost forever

when the temple was ruined by the Babylonians in 586 B.C.

See Exodus 24:12-18; 32:15-20; 34:1-35.

TALMUD *(TAHL-mud)*

is a collection of Jewish stories, teachings, traditions, comments about, and interpretations of the Old Testament that were gathered and written down between A.D. 250 and 550.

At first the Talmud was oral teachings to help the Jewish people interpret the Old Testament Law. Later it included teachings to interpret the rest of the Old Testament. As the collection of teachings grew over the centuries, it became necessary to write them down.

Through the centuries the Talmud has had a great influence on Jewish people, and they rank it second in importance to the Old Testament itself.

TARES (see *Plants*)

TARSUS *(TAR-sus),*

a city ten miles from the northeast coast of the Mediterranean Sea, was the birthplace and early home of the apostle Paul. Although it was located in what is now Turkey, it was then the capital of the Roman province of Cilicia. During Paul's time the city had a famous university, and the people were greatly influenced by Greek thought. Tarsus was also famous for its goat's hair cloth. People from Tarsus were very proud of their city, as we can see in Paul's boast in Acts 21:39.

TAX

means money paid by citizens to support their rulers. Taxes were collected both by the government and by the religious authorities in Bible times. Early Old

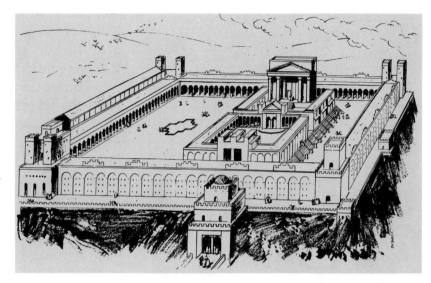

The New Testament temple was built by Herod the Great.

Testament taxes included a half shekel yearly for the support of the tabernacle (Exod. 30:13-15). Both rich and poor paid the same tax. After the Israelites demanded a king, the people had to pay heavy taxes, just as Samuel had warned (I Sam. 8:11-18). King Solomon put such heavy taxes on the people that after he died the northern tribes revolted, and the kingdom was divided.

During New Testament times the Roman rulers of Israel used local Jewish people to collect taxes for them. These men agreed to collect a certain amount for the government. Anything additional became their salary. That way tax collectors could make big profits for themselves. A census for taxation brought Mary and Joseph to Bethlehem at the time of the birth of Christ. Jews paid taxes on personal property, produce grown in the field, items bought and sold, customs at seaports and city gates, and, in Jerusalem, on houses. During this time the Jews also continued to pay the annual half shekel temple tax.

TEACHER

is a name used often as a title of respect for Jesus in the New Testament. Jesus was considered a leader of His group, and His teaching was recognized as having authority. Even those who opposed Him called Him "Rabbi" (teacher) (Mark 12:14).

Some leaders of the early church were also called teachers (Acts 13:1). Teachers proclaimed the Gospel, repeated Jesus' teachings so Christians could hear them, and taught about Jesus and the Old Testament.

TEMPLE *(TEM-pul)*

was the permanent place of Jewish worship through much of the Old Testament and New Testament period. Between 950 B.C. and A.D. 70, three different temples were built on the same hill in Jerusalem—Mount Moriah, the place where Abraham was going to sacrifice Isaac.

1. King Solomon ordered the building of the first temple in 950 B.C. to replace the tabernacle (II Sam. 7; I Kings 6—8; II

The idea of building a temple was David's, but his son Solomon carried out the plans.

Chron. 2—7). Its basic floor plan resembled that of the tabernacle. It took seven years to build the temple itself, and thirteen more to finish the other buildings that were part of the complex. Babylonians destroyed this temple in 586 B.C. when they burned Jerusalem. Nothing remains of King Solomon's temple, so we don't know exactly what it was like. The Old Testament, however, does have many details about the temple.

The whole temple complex was beautiful. Many of the furnishings were made of gold or bronze. The nation of Israel was very proud of this great temple. Unfortunately, between 950 and 586 B.C. some of the wicked kings allowed pagan worship inside this temple that had been dedicated to God. Other kings took treasures from the temple to pay off foreign attackers. King Josiah removed the pagan altars, cleaned up and repaired the tem-

ple, and restored it to its proper use (II Kings 21—23). But the temple was finally plundered and destroyed by the Babylonians in 586 B.C.

2. The Restoration Temple was built by Zerubbabel, the governor of the Jews returning from Babylon, and Jeshua, the high priest (Ezra 1—8). It was completed in 515 B.C. No description of this temple exists, but it probably followed the same pattern as Solomon's. Although it was beautiful, it was much simpler and less expensive than Solomon's. Some Jews wept because it was so modest compared to Solomon's temple. The returning Jews had little money for the building.

3. The third temple, Herod's temple, was begun about 20 B.C. It was a rebuilding of the old structure, piece by piece, without disturbing temple worship. It took more than forty-six years to build. This was the temple in which Jesus worshiped.

Herod's temple was burned and destroyed along with the rest of Jerusalem in A.D. 70 by Roman armies. But the foundation of one wall remains today; it is called the Western Wall, or "Wailing Wall," at which Jews in Jerusalem often worship and pray.

The writer of Hebrews says that Christ fulfilled all the requirements of the Old Testament sacrifice and worship needed in the temple (Heb. 7—10). Christ brings a better way to approach God, and each believer becomes a "temple" where Christ dwells (I Cor. 6:19).

TEMPT

has both a negative and a positive meaning in the Bible. The negative meaning is to try to make a person do something wrong. The positive meaning is to test a person to improve his spiritual strength.

Satan tempts us to do evil, sometimes working through our own desires. Satan first appeared in the form of a serpent. He appealed to Eve's taste, sight, and pride. Eve believed Satan rather than God and yielded to temptation.

Satan used these same ideas to tempt Jesus in the wilderness. But unlike us, Jesus resisted all temptation.

Although we often fail, God offers help when we are tempted. First Corinthians 10:13 says, ". . . God is faithful, and he will not let you be tempted beyond your strength, but . . . will also provide the way of escape, that you may be able to endure it."

This verse may also involve another meaning of temptation—testing. God wants us to be strong in faith. To produce that strength, He sometimes allows obstacles in our paths to build up our "spiritual muscle." He tested Abraham by asking him to be willing to give up his son, and he tested Job by taking away everything he owned James 1:12 tells us that if we endure the test, we will receive the crown of life which God has promised to those who love Him.

Although testing may seem unpleasant, the results are good. We have a closer relationship with God, and we know we have passed the test.

TEMPTATION OF JESUS

is the 40-day period Jesus spent in the wilderness just after His baptism. At the end of this time, Satan tried to tempt Him to do wrong.

Jesus had been fasting—eating little or nothing. Naturally, He was hungry. Satan first suggested to Jesus that He turn stones into bread so He could eat. Satan

was really saying, "Use Your power to live the way You deserve."

Jesus showed that obeying what God says is more important than eating. He answered, by quoting part of Deuteronomy 8:3, "It is written, 'Man shall not live by bread alone, but by every word that proceeds from the mouth of God.'

Then Satan took Jesus to a very high mountain and pointed out the magnificent kingdoms of the world. "All these I will give You," he said, "if You will fall down and worship me." Satan was telling Jesus that He could control all of the world without having to suffer on the cross—*if* He would only show respect to Satan.

But Jesus answered, "Begone, Satan! for it is written, 'You shall worship the Lord your God and him only shall you serve' "(a quotation from Deuteronomy 6:13).

In another temptation, Satan took Jesus to the highest part of the temple. He suggested that Jesus jump off to prove that the angels would catch Him in time to escape injury. By this, Satan was saying, "Why spend all that time teaching,

preaching, healing, and helping people? Just jump off the temple. After the angels rescue You, everyone will know God sent You. Do what you want to do. Get what You want the easy way."

Jesus again answered by quoting the Old Testament. "It is written, 'You shall not tempt the Lord your God.' "(Deut. 6:16). He knew people must not tempt God to see whether He will rescue them from their own foolishness.

Jesus resisted all of Satan's temptations, setting a pattern for us in overcoming similar temptations. His resistance also showed that He was the Son of God.

See Matthew 4:1-11; Mark 1:12, 13; Luke 4:1-13; Hebrews 2:18; 4:15.

TEN COMMANDMENTS

a list of rules of conduct given by God through Moses, showed God's people how He wanted them to live. The first four commandments discuss how people should live in relationship to God. The last six discuss how people should live with each other.

God called Moses to the top of Mount Sinai early in the Israelites' journey from Egypt. On two tablets of stone, God wrote these rules as a covenant or agreement between Himself and the people He had chosen as His own. These Ten Commandments have become the standard of behavior for much of the world.

• Commandment 1: "You shall have no other gods before me," guarantees the worship of the one true God.

• Commandment 2: "You shall not make for yourself a graven image," guards against worshiping idols.

• Commandment 3: "You shall not take the name of the Lord your God in vain," protects against dishonoring God's name or using it in a meaningless or disrespectful way.

• Commandment 4: "Remember the sabbath day, to keep it holy," provides a special day each week for worship.

• Commandment 5: "Honor your father and your mother," shows God's desire for close, loving families where members respect each other.

• Commandment 6: "You shall not kill."

• Commandment 7: "You shall not commit adultery."

• Commandment 8: "You shall not steal."

• Commandment 9: "You shall not bear false witness against your neighbor."

• Commandment 10: "You shall not covet," warns against wrong desire for things that don't belong to us. If we envy other people's money, clothes, popularity, or skills, this desire can lead to breaking other commandments and can cause pain both to ourselves and others.

When we live by these commands, we enjoy a happier, healthier relationship with God and other people. However, no one has ever kept all these commandments all his life. That's why God offers salvation freely by believing in Jesus Christ. Jesus is the only person who has ever lived up to God's high standards. By faith, we can share some of His power to carry out what we know God wants us to do.

See Exodus 20:2-20; Deuteronomy 5.

TENT

a movable shelter made of cloth or skins supported by poles, was the regular living place of many Old Testament people and of shepherds and soldiers in the New Testament. Most tents in Bible times were made of strong goat's hair cloth.

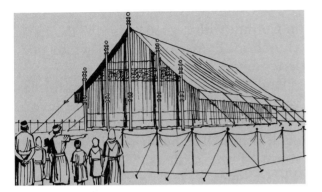

Often the covering appeared striped because of the addition of patches over worn or torn places. People slept inside on coarse straw mats and cooked on stoves that were only a group of stones at the tent entrance, or a hole in the ground.

The tabernacle used by Israel in the wilderness was a kind of tent.

TENT OF MEETING
(see *Tabernacle*)

TESTAMENT *(TESS-tuh-ment)*
in the Bible usually refers to an unbreakable agreement or covenant between God and His people.

The two parts of the Bible—the Old Testament and the New Testament—are named for the two covenants God made with His people. In the Old Testament, God made a covenant with the Israelites (stated at Sinai and repeated later) that if they would obey Him and follow His commands, they would be His people (Jer. 31:31-34). In the New Testament, God put into operation a new covenant that He had first revealed to Jeremiah. In the new covenant, salvation is by faith in Jesus Christ. Through Christ our sins are forgiven, and every person, whether Jew or Gentile, can by faith become a member of God's family. God's Law is written in our hearts; we obey it because we want to, not because we have to.

The word *testament* in our day and among the Greeks in New Testament times refers to the unbreakable written instructions a person gives about who should have his property when he dies. We call this a "will" (Gal. 3:15, 16). The apostle Paul compared God's covenant with Israel with a will, which cannot be changed after the person dies. Paul showed that Christ's coming does not destroy the Old Testament covenant but rather fulfills it.

When Christ ate the Last Supper with His disciples, He took a cup of wine and said, "This cup is the new covenant [testament] in my blood" (I Cor. 11:25). Christ's coming was the beginning of a new spiritual inheritance for those who accept Him.

TESTIMONY *(TEST-ih-MOAN-ee)*
has several meanings in the Bible. In the Old Testament it often refers to the Law of God or to all the teachings of the Old Testament (Ps. 119:14, 22, 24, 31, 36). Other times it refers to the actual tablets of stone on which God wrote the Ten Commandments for Moses. These were later stored in the ark of the covenant. For this reason the ark was often called "the ark of the testimony," and the tabernacle was sometimes called the "tabernacle of the testimony" (Exod. 30:6; Num. 1:50, 53).

In the New Testament, *testimony* usually refers to giving proof or evidence that something is true (John 3:32, 33; 21:24; Acts 22:18). This is our usual meaning when we speak of giving a testimony for Christ.

THADDAEUS (THAD-ee-us)

was one of Jesus' twelve disciples. In some lists he is called Judas the son of James. The writer of the Gospel of John was careful not to get him mixed up with Judas Iscariot, who betrayed Jesus. Little is known about Thaddaeus except that he traveled with the other disciples. See Matthew 10:3; Mark 3:18; Luke 6:16; John 14:22; Acts 1:13.

THEOPHANY (thee-AH-fun-ee)

is a visible appearance of God in the Bible. God usually appeared as a human being or an angel. Before sin came, God visited often with Adam and Eve (Gen. 3:8). Once Abraham had a theophany in his tent in the desert (Gen. 18). God also appeared as an angel to Hagar, Sarah's maid, in the wilderness (Gen. 16:7-13).

THESSALONIANS
(thess-uh-LOW-nee-uns),
FIRST LETTER TO THE

is the thirteenth book of the New Testament. Paul wrote it to the church he had started in Thessalonica during a stay of only three weeks. His co-workers Silas (Silvanus) and Timothy had been with him. Paul had been forced to leave Thessalonica because of opposition from Jewish leaders. He went on to Berea, then Athens, and finally Corinth, but he sent Timothy back to Thessalonica from Athens. After Timothy returned to Paul in Corinth with a good report of the new church in Thessalonica, Paul wrote this letter to the Thessalonians.

Paul began by saying how thankful he was for these new Christians. He loved them and admired the love they had for each other. But he needed to correct some of their ideas. The people of Thessalonica were so excited about the promise of the Second Coming of the Lord Jesus that some had even given up their jobs. Paul wrote to tell them that no one knows for sure when Christ will come again (I Thess. 4:13—5:8). Some people will die before that day, but all Christians will share in the glory of Christ's return, for God will raise them up when He comes. Meanwhile, each person must live each day in a way pleasing to the Lord. That's the best way to prepare for His coming.

First Thessalonians is probably the earliest of Paul's letter that we have in the New Testament. It was written about A.D. 51.

THESSALONIANS, SECOND LETTER TO THE

was the second letter to the new Christians at Thessalonica from Paul and his co-workers Silvanus and Timothy. It was written a few months after the first letter. Paul wrote to encourage these new Christians to remain faithful to Christ. They were suffering harsh persecution. To keep them true, Paul said, "To this end we always pray for you, that our God may make you worthy of his call."

Then Paul told them more about the Second Coming of Christ. This added to what he had said in his first letter. He said that when Christ comes, Christians will receive rest, and their persecutors will be punished (II Thess. 1:5-11). Jesus will be glorified in His saints, and all believers will be filled with wonder.

He reminded them that no one knows when Christ will return (II Thess. 2:1-12). Before He comes, there will be even worse persecution. Someone who is anti-Christ will bring lawlessness to the world. Christians will suffer, but they must make a habit of living as directed by God's Spirit. That's how they will remain true both now and in the last days.

For that reason the people at Thessalonica were to encourage each other to live godly lives (II Thess. 2:13—3:18). They were not to allow idleness. People must work for a living. Those who didn't obey this were to be gently shown their error.

THESSALONICA
(thess-uh-low-NYE-kuh)
was the chief seaport of Macedonia. Sometimes called Salonika, it is now the second largest city in modern Greece.

In New Testament times it was an important trade city. Paul visited there on a missionary journey but had to leave after three weeks because of persecution. However, the church he started there grew vigorously. He later sent Timothy to help the new Christians. A few months after his visit, Paul wrote I and II Thessalonians to encourage the people and to explain to them some of the things that would occur before Christ came again. See Acts 17:1-10.

THOMAS (TOM-us)
was one of Jesus' twelve disciples. He was also called Didymus, which probably meant he was a twin. Although he is most remembered for his doubting, the

"Put your finger here, and see my hands," Jesus said to convince Thomas that He really was alive.

Gospels show he was deeply devoted to Jesus.

When Jesus went to Bethany to heal Lazarus, most of the disciples hesitated because they were afraid. They knew that Jewish leaders wanted to get rid of Jesus. Yet Thomas said, "Let us also go, that we may die with him" (John 11:16).

Later, Thomas showed his honesty and sincerity in the question he asked after Jesus foretold His coming crucifixion Thomas asked, "Lord, we do not know where you are going; how can we know the way?"(John 14:5).

Thomas was not with the other disciples when Jesus appeared after His resurrection. When Thomas heard about it, he said he would not believe unless he could see and feel Jesus' body Himself. Yet as soon as Jesus appeared, Thomas was convinced "My Lord and my God!" he said (John 20:24-29).

THORNS, CROWN OF
(see *Crown of Thorns*)

THRESHING

separates ripe grains from their stems and husks.

If the farmer was threshing only a small amount of grain, he beat the sheaves of grain with a rod or flail. For a larger quantity, he spread the sheaves on a large outdoor floor of stone or clay that was packed hard and smooth. Oxen pulled heavy wooden sleds over the grain. The pressure rubbed the kernels out of the husks. Then the farmer winnowed the grain by throwing it into the air so the wind would blow away the lighter chaff. The heavier grain fell back to the floor. If possible, farmers built their threshing floors on hilltops to catch the most wind.

In some countries, people still thresh grain this way.

THRONES

are special chairs for kings or other heads of state on official occasions. Because rulers sit on thrones, *throne* is often used as a word picture for authority and power.

Thrones were often beautifully decorated. Solomon's throne was made of ivory and gold (I Kings 10:18-20).

Old Testament worshipers thought of the ark of the covenant as "God's throne." In visions, Isaiah, Ezekiel, Daniel, and John all saw God on His throne reigning over the earth (Isa. 6:1-3; Ezek.1:4-28; Dan. 7:9-10; Rev. 4). The New Testament also speaks of Jesus sitting on a throne to judge and rule the world, and believers reigning with Him with justice and fairness (Rev. 2:26-28; 3:21; 20:4-6).

THUMMIN (see *Urim and Thummin*)

TIGRIS *(TIE-griss)* RIVER

is an important river about 1,150 miles long. It begins in mountains in Turkey, flows through modern-day Iraq, and empties into the Persian Gulf. The area between the Tigris and the Euphrates rivers is considered by many to be where civilization started.

TIMBREL (see *Musical Instruments*)

TIME

was not the same to ancient people as it is to us. They did not have clocks to tick off exact minutes. Instead, they noticed changes in nature: the sun determined night and day; the moon measured months; the movement in the sun's pat-

Two rows of carved lions led up to Solomon's majestic throne.

tern determined years. The hottest part of the day was noon. For many, many centuries, years were dated only in relationship to some great event, such as "two years before the earthquake" (Amos 1:1). This is one reason it is hard to know exact dates for the events recorded in the Bible.

Each country numbered its years from important dates in its own history. Some countries started their years in autumn, others in spring. Historians must match events in the Bible to events outside the Bible to figure out when something happened.

Although the Roman day began at midnight and was twelve hours long, the Hebrew day began at sunset and lasted twenty-four hours. In the New Testament, nighttime was divided into four "watches," according to the shifts when army guards and others had to stay awake

for protection. That meant the length of each watch varied during the seasons, according to how long it was dark. Midnight was always in the second watch. Dawn was in the fourth. For example, Matthew 14:25 tells us of Jesus coming to the disciples at the "fourth watch." That is, He came just before or at dawn.

TIMOTHY *(TIM-uh-thee)*

was a close friend and helper to the apostle Paul. He became the person Paul depended on the most to help churches that had problems. When Paul was in prison or faced other hardships, Timothy was the person he wanted most to see.

During the closing years of Paul's life, Timothy was in Ephesus, serving as pastor and leader of the churches there. Two books of the New Testament—I and II Timothy—are letters that Paul wrote to

345

The letters Timothy received from Paul are now part of our New Testament.

Timothy at Ephesus.

Things Paul wrote show that Timothy was naturally timid. But he apparently was so dependable and earnest in his work for God that he developed into an important leader in the early church.

Timothy was the son of a Gentile father and a Jewish mother, Lois (Acts 16:1-3; II Tim. 1:3-5). Paul called Timothy his "spiritual son." This probably meant that Paul helped Timothy become Christian.

Timothy joined Paul in Lystra on Paul's second missionary journey. After they were driven out of Thessalonica by Jewish persecution, Paul sent Timothy back to help the Christians there. Several times Paul sent Timothy to churches as his representative.

Timothy was with Paul during much of his third missionary journey. The second letter of Paul to Timothy was probably written while Paul was in prison in Rome, shortly before his death. In it he wrote, "Do your best to come before winter."

Paul clearly expressed his opinion of Timothy in Philippians 2:19-24. "I have no one like him, who will be genuinely anxious for your welfare. . . . Timothy's worth you know, how as a son with a father he has served with me in the gospel" (Phil. 2:19-22; I Tim. 4:12-15).

TIMOTHY, I and II

are personal letters from the apostle Paul to Timothy, who was serving as pastor or overseer of the church (or churches) at Ephesus. Paul and Timothy had a deep friendship, and these letters are full of personal encouragement and advice from Paul to Timothy.

First Timothy was probably written about A.D. 63, while Paul was in Philippi between his first and second imprisonments in Rome. He gave Timothy practical advice about qualifications for church officials, how to conduct worship, and how to deal with false teachings that come into the church. Paul also told Timothy what to do about some of the social problems in the church, such as the care of widows and children.

Paul explained again how God wants all people to be saved, and that Jesus is the mediator between God and people. He reminded him that Christ, the King of kings, will come again.

Second Timothy is the last known letter of Paul before he was executed in Rome. Writing from prison about A.D. 64, Paul knew he was near the end of his life. He wrote about Christ as the conqueror of death, and the joy he was going to have in being with Christ.

He urged Timothy to come to see him if possible, but he also urged him to study the Scriptures, to be faithful in his work in Ephesus, and to live in away that would glorify Christ. He warned Timothy that he probably would suffer persecution as Paul had.

TITHE *(tieth)*

means a tenth of one's income set aside for special use. Early in Bible times, people who worshiped God gave a tithe of their income as part of their worship. Abraham gave his tithe to Melchizedek, a priest of the Most High God (Gen. 14:17-20). After the Law of Moses was established, Israelites were expected to give a tenth to support the priests, Levites, and needy people (Deut. 14:22-27; Mal. 3:8-10). The tithe was sometimes crops and animals, sometimes money. People who gave food as a tithe sometimes ate it with the Levites in the place of worship after it had been offered to God.

In Jesus' time, tithing was strictly enforced for practicing Jews. In fact, the Pharisees insisted on tithing even the herbs they used to season their food (Matt. 23:23; Luke 11:42). But they were not always fair in everyday dealings with others. For this, Jesus condemned them.

Christians are told to give regularly to God's work and to help others, because we love God and know He will supply our needs (II Cor. 9:6-15).

TITUS *(TIE-tus)*

was a friend and helper of the apostle Paul (II Cor. 2:13; 7:5-16). He was a son of Greek parents, and he probably became a Christian after listening to Paul preach. Later, he went with Paul to Jerusalem to meet with Jewish Christians there. These Jewish Christians did not realize that a Gentile could become a Christian without becoming a Jew first. They wanted Titus to be circumcised as a sign that he accepted the Jewish religion. Paul said, "No, Titus does not have to be circumcised. He does not have to become a Jew first." This helped the new Christians realize that Christianity was larger than Judaism (Gal. 2:1-10). In time, Titus became so well accepted that he was given many responsibilities among the early churches.

Later, Titus became a Christian leader or pastor of the church on the island of Crete (Titus 1—3). The church had many problems. Paul wrote a letter to him there. This letter, the Epistle to Titus, is a part of the New Testament

TITUS *(TIE-tus)*, **LETTER TO**

is a letter from the apostle Paul to his friend Titus. Titus was a Christian leader or pastor on the island of Crete, where the church had many problems. Paul reminded Titus that pastors and leaders in a church must be holy people. They must be able to live happily with their own families if they are going to work

happily with the larger church family. They must be honest in all they do and not be lazy. In chapter 1, verse 16, Paul warned Titus to watch out for hypocrites, who "profess to know God, but they deny

TOMB

refers to a burial place, usually a natural or artificial cave. Early tombs were often natural caves in the rocky hills.

Many of the heathen nations around Israel built fancy burial places. Although Hebrew burial places were simple, they were very important to them. Abraham paid 400 shekels of silver for the field and cave that became the family burial place. That would equal thousands of dollars in our money. Old Testament people often were buried in vaults or caves with their ancestors.

In New Testament times, Jews were buried in caves in stone cliffs. Several bodies might be in each tomb. Each body was wrapped in graveclothes and prepared with spices. One opening was the entrance to all the ledges prepared for the bodies.

Tombs in Rome were called catacombs. These were large underground networks of caves and corridors. Niches in the walls served as ledges for bodies. Each niche

Lazarus may have been buried in this tomb.

could be sealed with bricks or a marble slab. When persecution was bad, early Christians hid in the catacombs.

him by their deeds."

The letter says Christ "gave himself for us to redeem us from all iniquity" and that the Holy Spirit has been given to us through Christ.

TONGUES OF FIRE

were among the signs of the Holy Spirit's coming on the Day of Pentecost. All of the disciples, the brothers of Jesus, and some of the women followers of Jesus had gathered together in Jerusalem. Suddenly a sound like a mighty wind filled the house. Something like tiny tongues of flames seemed to rest on each person in the room as they were all filled with the Holy Spirit. See Acts 1:14, 2:1-3.

TORAH *(TOR-uh)*

is the Hebrew word for the Law of God, and it refers to the first five books of the Old Testament. Other parts of the Old Testament Law were later also considered part of the Torah by the Jews. Taking care of the Torah was the responsibility of the Old Testament priests. Learning and reading the Torah is still important for Jewish people.

TOWER OF BABEL *(see Babel)*

TRADE

was important as early as Abraham's time. People traded food and furs for goods such as pottery and cloth at the local marketplace. Usually this was at a city gate. Sometimes each gate of a city was for one kind of item. Grains might be traded at one, livestock at another. In ancient Jerusalem, potters had their workshops near the southern part of the city. Bakers had their own street.

In earliest times, all trade was done

through barter. Later, metal pieces and jewelry began to be exchanged for products.

Gradually, trade with other countries and regions became important. Trade routes grew up between large cities, and small cities were born along these roads. As tradesmen made better products, their markets increased. They had more and more need for raw materials.

Ancient Israel exported mainly agricultural products. Olive oil, grains, resin, honey, dried nuts, wine, figs, raisins, and dates went at first to Egypt and Syria. Later Italy, Spain, and Asia Minor traded tin, lead, silver, and iron for Israel's goods. Israel produced some textiles but imported finer cloth from Egypt, Syria, and Phoenicia. When Solomon built the temple, he traded widely to get the best materials. Much trade was carried on by sea, especially with the Phoenicians, but

caravans across long land routes were also common.

By New Testament times, trade was regulated by Rome. Roman coins could buy products anywhere in the known world. Roman traders may have reached even India and Scandinavia. Israel was no longer an important trading country, except for the trade routes that crossed it.

Many cities in Asia Minor mentioned in the New Testament were important trade centers. Paul followed the usual trade routes on his missionary journeys, for they were the highways of his day. Many churches began in cities such as Thyatira and Laodicea that were famous for their trade. See Revelation 18:11-19.

TRANSFIGURATION

(tranz-fig-yur-AY-shun)

means a change in form or appearance. The word is used to describe the time when a dramatic change took place in Jesus' physical appearance as three of His disciples watched.

Shortly before His last trip to Jerusalem, Jesus took Peter, James, and John to a high mountain. As Jesus was praying, His face began to shine like the sun. His clothes became dazzling white. Moses and Elijah appeared and talked with Jesus about His coming death.

Peter became so excited. "Master, it is well that we are here; let us make three booths, one for you and one for Moses and one for Elijah," he said. But as Peter was speaking, a bright cloud surrounded them. A voice came from the cloud: "This is my beloved Son, with whom I am well pleased; listen to him."

The three disciples were overwhelmed. They kneeled with their faces touching the ground. But then Jesus came and

touched them. "Rise, and have no fear," He said. When they opened their eyes, they saw Jesus—all alone. Jesus told them they were not to tell anyone what they had seen until after His resurrection.

See Matthew 17:1-8; Mark 9:2-8; Luke 9:28-36.

TRANSGRESSION (see *Sin*)

TRAVEL

in ancient times usually meant walking. As people and animals made the same trips over and over, they wore paths. As more and more walked, these paths became roads. When people traveled on foot or rode camels or donkeys, it didn't matter much if roads had rocks and pebbles or were overgrown with weeks. But by the time of King Solomon, horses and chariots were used in travel, and roads became trade routes. They had to be cleared and straightened. Good roads brought business to people along the way.

Caravans passed along the "king's highway," a road that ran south from Damascus and through Israel east of the Jordan River. Another road, "the way of the sea," passed the west coast of Lake Galilee on

mile trip from Nazareth to Bethlehem took five days' travel time. Mary and Joseph were required by Jewish Law to take the baby Jesus from Bethlehem to the temple in Jerusalem—five miles away—before He was forty days old. The trip they later took to Egypt was more than 200 miles each way. Although they probably had a donkey, they no doubt walked most of the way.

As Jesus grew, He made many trips from Nazareth to Jerusalem. His parents were devout Jews. They would go to the temple several times a year. To avoid robbers and to make the trip more pleasant, many people walked together, singing and talking with each other. This is why Jesus' parents did not miss Him on the trip back from Jerusalem when He was twelve years old.

its way to the sea. It followed the Mediterranean shore south to Egypt. All this time, of course, the common people traveled by foot.

In Israel, all religious Jews made at least one trip every year to Jerusalem, usually at Passover time. From Galilee, it took several days for people to walk to Jerusalem. Thieves hid along the way to rob travelers.

By New Testament times the Romans had improved roads throughout the empire. Although the roads were safer, robbers still threatened. Jesus' story of the good Samaritan shows how common robbery was.

When Jesus was born, the seventy-five-

TREASURY

Israelites used tree limbs to build small shelters for the feast of tabernacles each year.

There were many sailing ships on the seas. Their main purpose was to carry goods, but sometimes they carried passengers. When Jonah in the Old Testament and Paul in the New Testament wanted to take a ship, they looked for a cargo ship. They paid the captain to take them along. But the captain was always more interested in his cargo than in his passengers.

Paul is the best-known traveler in the Bible. His missionary journeys—by foot and by boat—are recorded in the Book of Acts. But other early Christians—Philip, Peter, Priscilla and Aquila—also moved around the known world. Travel was not easy or pleasant for any of them.

See Luke 2:1-5, 22, 41-51; Matthew 2:13-15.

TREASURY

is a place where valuable things are kept or placed. In the temple where Jesus worshiped, tithes and taxes were paid at the treasury, or collection box. Jesus once sat near the treasury as He watched a poor widow bring her offering. See Deuteronomy 28:12; Mark 12:41.

TREES

were plentiful in some parts of ancient Israel and scarce in others. There are more than 300 references to trees in the Bible. Scholars have identified more than twenty-five kinds of trees that grew there. Israelites used tree limbs to build booths or small shelters for the feast of tabernacles each year.

The people often waved branches of palm trees, willows, and leafy trees as a sign of rejoicing.

Some groves of trees were used as places of pagan worship. During the years between A.D. 70 and 1900, most trees in Israel were cut down. Thousands of new trees have been planted in Israel since 1948.

TREE OF KNOWLEDGE

was a special tree that grew in the middle of the garden of Eden. God commanded Adam and Eve not to eat its fruit, because they would then know good and evil—they would know what sin was. But Adam and Eve did eat some of the tree's fruit. Then they knew that sin was disobeying God's command. After they ate, they were ashamed both of what they did and of who they were. Their sin led to death for themselves and all people since then. See Genesis 2:8—3:7.

TRIAL OF JESUS

was in two parts—first before the Jewish leaders, then before the Roman authorities.

After His arrest in the garden of Gethsemane, Jesus was immediately brought to Jerusalem, to the court of the religious authorities called the Sanhedrin. Caiaphas, the high priest, was in charge of the trial. Caiaphas and his followers were jealous of Jesus and His popularity with the people. They feared an uprising against the Romans that would destroy their influence. They found people who would tell lies about Jesus so they could have an excuse to get rid of Him. As people accused Him, Jesus remained silent.

Finally the high priest said to Jesus: "Are you the Christ, the Son of the Blessed?"

Jesus answered, "I am." By saying this, Jesus affirmed that He was the Son of God. The Jews considered this blasphemy, and for blasphemy a man should be put to death.

Caiaphas tore his robe as he said to the Sanhedrin, "You have heard His blasphemy. What is your decision?"

"He deserves death!" they answered. They and the guards spit at Jesus, hit Him, and made fun of Him.

But the Jewish government had only limited power under Rome. These leaders could not execute Jesus. So the Sanhedrin sent Him to Pilate, the Roman governor. There they accused Jesus of treason—of saying He was a king.

To the Romans this would be a serious

Roman soldiers were ordered to crucify Jesus.

crime, for it could mean Jesus was trying to stir up a rebellion.

"Are you the King of the Jews?" Pilate asked Jesus.

"You have said so," Jesus answered. Jesus stayed silent during the rest of the questioning. Pilate didn't think Jesus was a threat to the emperor, but Pilate did not want the Jewish leaders to be angry at Him. So he thought of a way to sidestep the problem. Jesus was from Galilee—an area under the rule of a half-Jewish puppet king named Herod Antipas. Herod happened to be in Jerusalem right then, so Pilate sent Jesus to him.

But Herod only sent Him back. Then Pilate had another idea. During the Passover feast, the custom was to release a Jewish prisoner. If the Jews chose Jesus for release, it would solve his problem.

But the crowd was stirred up by the Jewish leaders. The people shouted, "Release to us Barabbas." Barabbas was a murderer and a revolutionary.

"Then what shall I do with Jesus who is called Christ?" asked Pilate.

"Crucify, crucify Him," screamed the mob. Pilate tried whipping Jesus. He hoped this cruelty would be enough for the crowd. But even when the people saw Jesus beaten and bleeding, they ranted on. They wanted Him dead.

Pilate washed his hands to try to show the guilt was not his. Then he delivered Jesus to be crucified.

See Matthew 26:57—27:26; Luke 22:54—23:25; John 19:1-15.

TRIUMPHAL ENTRY

was Jesus' kingly entrance into Jerusalem on the Sunday before His crucifixion. He came riding a colt, a sign that He was on a mission of peace, not war. Conquering generals rode on a horse or in a chariot.

As Jesus entered the city from the Mount of Olives, His followers shouted and sang, "Blessed is the King who comes in the name of the Lord!" Some cut palm branches and laid them as a carpet for the colt to walk on. Some even spread their clothes in the road. Their enthusiasm filled the city. Each Palm Sunday we remember that day.

See Matthew 21:1-11; Mark 11:1-11; Luke 19:28-44; John 12:12-19.

TYRE (tire)

was an island city along the coast of what is now Lebanon. About fifty- miles north of Nazareth, Tyre was a center of trade in ancient times and was famous for the purple dyes produced there.

Ships from Tyre sailed all around the Mediterranean.

During some of the Old Testament period, Tyre was a kingdom by itself and threatened Israel. Later Tyre fell to Assyria, then Egypt, Babylonia, and Persia. Three chapters of the Book of Ezekiel prophesy the fall of Tyre. See Ezekiel 26—28

Jesus once visited the area of Tyre and healed the daughter of a Greek woman (Mark 7:24-31).

Paul once stayed there for seven days with Christians. When he left, he and the Christians from Tyre, including children, had a prayer meeting together on the beach (Acts 21:3-7).

When you stand on the Mount of Olives today, this is how the city of Jerusalem looks.

Ur of the Chaldees, where Abraham grew up, was famous for its worship of the moon-god.

UNCLEAN

refers to thoughts, acts, people, places, and foods that are displeasing to God. Either they are contrary to God's specific commands, or they involve moral wrongdoing.

In the Old Testament, *unclean* usually referred to certain meat that the Israelites were forbidden to eat, or to people who were "unclean" because they had touched a dead body, had bodily discharges, or had leprosy.

Unclean foods in the Old Testament were certain meats (Lev. 11). Animals were considered good for food and therefore "clean" if they both chewed the cud and had parted hoofs. These included oxen, sheep, goats, and deer. Animals or birds that fed on dead animals were not to be eaten. Such unclean birds of prey included the vulture, sea gull, hawk, ostrich, and bat.

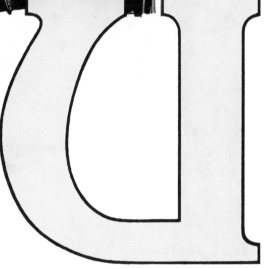

Only fish with fins and scales could be eaten; crabs, eels, and clams were forbidden.

Insects that had two legs for leaping as well as four regular legs were considered clean. This meant most insects such as grasshoppers could be eaten, but no others. All lizards were considered unfit to eat as well as rodents and other animals with four paws.

Even clean animals could become

Lepers were called unclean and were separated from all other people They had to wear torn clothes and cry, "Unclean, unclean," whenever someone without leprosy came near them.

As Jesus traveled to Jerusalem, He met ten lepers. Having compassion on them, He healed them. But only one leper came back to thank Him (Luke 17:11-19).

unclean. The Hebrews could not eat any animal that died of natural causes or had been killed by another animal.

A person could become unclean for several reasons (Lev. 12, 15; Num. 9:1-13). Anyone who touched a dead person was unclean for seven days and had to have special washings on the third and seventh days to become clean again. A woman who had a baby was unclean for a week or two weeks, depending on the sex of the baby. Then she had to offer a young pigeon or a turtledove as a sacrifice.

Bodily discharges in men or women made them unclean. Special bathing and clothes washing was necessary to be considered clean once more.

After Christ died and rose again, these regulations about uncleanness faded away. God sent a special vision to Peter to show him that all foods were now "clean." In Acts 15:28, 29, only four restrictions were given to new Christians: eat no food offered to idols, eat no blood, eat no animal that has been strangled, and keep away from sexual immorality.

The prophets also spoke about unclean thoughts. Isaiah said he lived among people with "unclean lips," referring to thoughts and words that were contrary to the holiness of God (Isa. 6:5; Gal. 5:19-21; Eph. 5:5).

In the New Testament, *uncleanness* refers either to such things as eating wrong foods or to moral sins. Jesus cast out unclean spirits (demons), who caused people to do evil (Matt. 10:1; Mark 3:11).

UNFORGIVABLE SIN

is mentioned several times in the New Testament. Jesus said, "Whoever speaks against the Holy Spirit will not be forgiven, either in this age or in the age to come."

The work of the Holy Spirit is to make people aware of who Christ is and how our sins can be forgiven through Him. If a person throughout his life "speaks against" the Holy Spirit, he is saying he does not want Christ's remedy for his sin. For this reason, his sin is unforgivable, because he is refusing the cure or forgiveness that Christ came to make possible.

John 3:16, 18 says that a person who believes in Jesus has eternal life, and "he who believes in him is not condemned; he who does not believe is condemned already."

See Matthew 12:32; Mark 3:29; Luke 12:10; Hebrews 10:26-29; I John 5:16.

UNLEAVENED *(un-LEV-und)* BREAD

is bread made without yeast. Unleavened bread does not rise. On the night of the Passover, the Hebrews prepared a quick meal of roasted lamb and unleavened bread. They took some of the unleavened dough with them in their packs. At the Passover feast, which is still observed today by Jews, they eat unleavened bread to remind them of how God delivered His people out of Egypt. See Exodus 12:1-28.

UPPER ROOM

is the place where Jesus had His last supper with the disciples before His crucifixion. It may have been the same upper room where the disciples met together to pray after Jesus ascended into heaven.

It probably was a second-floor room built on the flat roof of the home of a friend of Jesus. Such rooms were commonly used as guest rooms and often had outside stairways.

See Mark 14:12-25; Luke 22:7-13; Acts 1:12-14.

UR

was the city where Abraham was born and grew up. It was near the north end of the Persian Gulf in what is now Iraq.

Ur was a center of advanced learning in Abraham's day; it had libraries, schools, and many temples to pagan gods. The people worshiped the moon-god Nanna. They built a large temple and tower (called a ziggurat) to their god. People also kept small idols in their homes. These things are not mentioned in the Bible, but archaeologists discovered them as they dug up the ruins of the old city.

Ur was also a trading center. Ships carried alabaster, copper ore, ivory, gold, and hard woods to trade at Ur.

God called Abraham out of Ur and sent him to the land of Canaan.

See Genesis 11:28, 31; 15:7; Nehemiah 9:7.

URIAH *(your-EYE-uh)*

the Hittite was the husband of Bathsheba and a loyal soldier in King David's army. When King David committed adultery with Bathsheba, she became pregnant. David used several tricks to try to make it look as though Bathsheba's baby was Uriah's baby. But the tricks didn't work.

After a special meal and a long talk, Jesus and His disciples left the upper room.

Finally, David told the commander of his army to put Uriah in the front lines, where he would be likely to be killed. Uriah was killed, and David later married Bathsheba, but he was punished by God for his sin. See II Samuel 11:1—12:15.

USURY *(USE-your-ee)*

means charging for the use of money. We call it interest charges on loans or charge accounts.

In the Old Testament, the Hebrews were told not to charge interest to other Hebrews, because those who borrowed were usually poor (Exod. 22:25; Deut.

23:19). Hebrews were supposed to share what they had with their poor. However, they could charge interest to non-Hebrews.

When the Jews were in exile in Babylon, they ignored God's commands about helping the poor and not charging interest (Neh. 5:10, 11; Ezek. 18:5-13). When they returned with Nehemiah to rebuild the walls of Jerusalem, they kept on charging interest on loans. Nehemiah urged them to stop.

In the New Testament, most businesses charged interest. Jesus did not condemn this practice in His parable of the owner who gave his servants money to invest (Matt. 25:14-30).

UZZAH *(UZZ-uh)*

was a Hebrew who died suddenly after he touched the ark of the covenant. (The Old Testament Law in Num. 4:15 said no one was to touch it.)

The ark had been kept in Kiriath-jearim, in the house of Abinadab, Uzzah's father. King David wanted to bring it to Jerusalem, the capital of Israel, so he and many Israelites went to Kiriath-jearim to get it. They put the ark on a new cart pulled by oxen. Uzzah and his brother, Ahio, drove the cart. During the journey, the oxen stumbled, and Uzzah reached out to steady the ark. He died immediately.

David and the other Israelites were too frightened to take the ark on to Jerusalem. They left it at another man's house for three months before they came back to get it.

See I Chronicles 13:1-14.

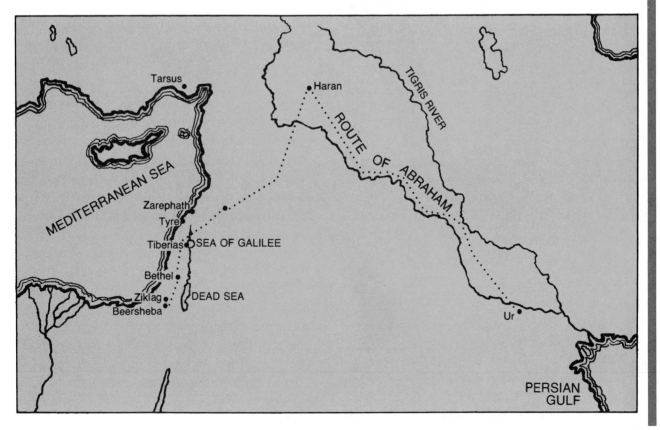

King Ahab could not keep his eyes off Naboth's vineyard next door. Finally, the king had him killed in order to get it.

reign, he held a huge banquet for the princes and army chiefs in his kingdom. There was much drinking and merriment. On the seventh day of the feast, when the king and many of the guests were quite drunk, the king ordered Queen Vashti to come and show off her beauty to the men.

Queen Vashti was having a separate banquet for the women, and she refused.

The king and his counselors were very angry. They said Vashti was setting a bad example for other wives, who might think they, too, could disobey their husbands. (In that time, wives were thought of as part of their husbands' possessions.)

They advised King Ahasuerus to remove Vashti from being queen and look

VASHTI *(VASH-tee)*

was the beautiful wife of Ahasuerus (also called Xerxes I), the pagan king of Persia from about 485 to 465 B.C.

During the third year of Ahasuerus's

for a new queen to take her place. The king followed their advice and chose Esther as the new queen (see *Esther*).

See Esther 1:5-20.

VEILS *(vales)*

in the Old Testament were thin scarves or shawls covering the face. They were usually worn by women. Rebekah covered herself with a veil before she met Isaac. Tamar tricked Judah, her father-in-law, by disguising herself with a veil.

Moses' face shone brightly after he received the Ten Commandments on Mount Sinai, and he hid his face behind a veil. The apostle Paul used the idea of Moses' veil as a word picture of something that hides the truth.

The Revised Standard Version and some other translations speak of veils in I Corinthians 11:2-10, where Paul gave instructions about how men and women were to pray and prophesy in public meetings. The Greek word for *veil* is not used, however; instead, there are phrases such as "down from the head" and "authority upon the head." So we are not sure whether Paul was referring to some sort of head covering or perhaps a particular long hairstyle.

See Exodus 34:33-35; I Corinthians 11:2-10; II Corinthians 3:12-16.

VEIL OF THE TEMPLE

was a pair of thick curtains about eighteen inches apart that hung at the entrance of the holy of holies in the temple (Exod. 26:31-33; 36:35). The veil hid the ark of the covenant and the mercy seat from the view of the people (also see *Temple*).

The curtains were woven with blue, purple, and scarlet thread with pictures of cherubim worked into them.

In the early days, no one could go behind the veil except the Levitical priests (Num. 18:7; Lev. 16:2-28). Later, only the high priest could enter behind the veil, and even he could go only once a year—on the Day of Atonement.

At Jesus' death, the veil in the temple was ripped by a miracle from top to bottom (Matt. 27:51; Mark 15:38). This act showed that because of Christ's death, all people could now come into God's presence by faith in Jesus Christ (Heb. 10:20).

VERSIONS OF THE BIBLE

refers to translations of the Bible from its original languages (Hebrew, Aramaic, Greek) to languages of today. New versions of the Bible are written to help make the meaning clear. Through the last five centuries, people have translated the Bible into many languages.

The Old Testament was first written in Hebrew. The Septuagint version of the Old Testament was used in Jesus' day. It was a translation into Greek from the Hebrew (see *Septuagint*).

The New Testament was written first in Greek. By A.D. 250, both Old and New Testaments had been translated into Latin. But it was a poor translation. In A.D. 382, a scholar named Jerome began work on a revision. His work became known as the Latin Vulgate Bible. This was the translation used by the Roman Catholic Church for more than 1,500 years.

After Latin began to die as a language, some Christians believed the Bible was needed in the languages that people spoke. John Wycliffe translated the first English version of the Bible in A.D. 1382. He wanted the average person to be able to read and understand the Bible. His version was based on Jerome's Latin Vulgate.

After the printing press was invented, William Tyndale made a translation of the Bible that was printed in 1525. Many religious leaders did not believe common people should be able to read the Bible in their own language. They tried to stop Tyndale, but he paid no attention. He made another translation of the Bible, this time based on the Hebrew and Greek copies of the Bible.

In 1604, King James of England ordered that a new translation be made of the whole Bible, working from the original Greek and Hebrew as much as possible. He appointed fifty-four scholars to do the work. The King James Version was completed in 1611 and is still read widely today.

Since that time, many other versions of the Bible have been written. Some of the best known are the Revised Standard Version, the Good News Bible, the Living Bible, and the New International Version.

In 1947 the Dead Sea Scrolls were found. These included some Old Testament writings dated 200 B.C. to A.D. 100. These have been a great help in bringing modern translations closer to the original writings of the Bible.

VESSELS

are containers made to hold liquids or dry materials. In Bible times, vessels were made from pottery, straw, metals, leather, cloth, and wood.

Pottery was the most common. Baskets, metal containers, leather buckets and pouches, and cloth, wooden, and stone containers were also common. Vessels

Villages in Israel today sometimes look a lot like they did in earlier times.

made of alabaster often held perfume.

Leather was used for buckets to draw water from the wells. Leather vessels were used for wine.

In the New Testament, the word *vessel* is sometimes used as a word picture of people. Second Timothy 2:21 speaks of a purified person as "a vessel for noble use." First Peter 3:7 in the King James Version uses "weaker vessel" to mean woman.

VILLAGES

were usually located near larger cities. The villagers fled to the city in times of war. A village had no walls around it; it was only a cluster of small, one-room houses, often made of mud or grass.

In the New Testament, a village was sometimes defined as a place without a synagogue.

VINES grow grapes in VINEYARDS
(VIN-yerds)

Grapes were grown in ancient Egypt and Canaan even before Abraham's time. The hilly areas of Judea and Samaria were good for growing grapes.

A vineyard was usually surrounded by a wall of stones or thorny hedges to keep out wild animals.

Most vineyards had a tower for a watchman, a winepress hollowed out of rock, and a vat, which held the wine. Jesus once told a parable that described the planting of a vineyard.

Grapevines needed much care. Each spring they had to be pruned and the dead branches burned. Jesus used this as a word picture of how God helps each Christian become a better person.

During the harvest, sometimes the whole family guarded the vineyard against thieves.

The time of stamping out the juice was one of great happiness. The people sang as they crushed the grapes with their feet. The wine was kept in new goatskin bags.

Jesus called Himself the "true vine" and His disciples "the branches."

See Matthew 21:33-41; John 15:1-8.

VIRGIN (VIR-jin)

is a person who has had no sexual intercourse. Usually it refers to a woman, but Rev. 14:4 speaks of men virgins also.

In the Old Testament, girls wore certain clothes to show that they were virgins. David's daughter Tamar wore a long robe with sleeves, to show she was a virgin (II Sam. 13:18;).

Jesus told a parable about ten young virgins who went to a wedding feast (Matt. 25:1-13).

VIRGIN BIRTH

refers to the miracle of Jesus being born by the virgin Mary and the Holy Spirit.

An angel told her that the Holy Spirit would come upon her so that "the child to be born will be called holy, the Son of God." Jesus was not conceived as the result of sexual intercourse. See Matthew 1:18-25; Luke 1:26—2:7.

VISIONS *(VIH-zhunz)*

were the most common way God revealed truth to His prophets. A vision is something like a dream, except that it is given by God and reveals truth in pictures. Most prophets were awake and very alert when they received visions from God. Daniel was with others when he saw the vision God gave him (Dan. 10:4-8). His companions did not see it, but they felt great fear and ran away.

The apostle Paul saw Ananias in a vision coming to renew his sight (Acts 9:1-19). The Lord spoke in a vision to Ananias, telling him to go.

Cornelius, a godly Gentile man, had a vision instructing him to send for Peter.

At the same time, Peter received a puzzling vision in which a huge sheet came down from heaven with animals that Jews were forbidden to eat (Acts 10:1—11:18). God told Peter to "kill and eat." Peter did not understand the vision until Cornelius and his family and friends received the Holy Spirit. Then Peter realized that his vision showed that God would accept all people by faith in Jesus Christ.

The Bible mentions many other godly people and prophets who received visions. The prophet Isaiah had a remarkable vision of God (Isa. 6:1-13).

False prophets also claimed to have visions (Jer. 14:14; Ezek. 13:2-9). Jeremiah and Ezekiel said God would punish the false prophets with their lying visions.

VOWS

were a voluntary promise to God, made in hope of certain benefits. Jacob vowed to give a tenth of all he had to God, if God would be with him, provide for him, and bring him back home safely (Gen. 28:20-22).

Once a vow was made, it had to be kept or else it was sin. A vow had to be spoken out loud to be binding (Num. 30:1-16; Deut. 23:21-23).

In the New Testament, Jesus said everything His followers said should be just as binding as a vow. A simple yes or no should be enough. But if people did make vows, they must keep them faithfully. See Matthew 5:34-36; 23:16-22; Mark 7:10-13.

When farmers threw their crushed grain into the air so the wind would blow away the chaff, it was called winnowing.

WAGES

are the pay a person earns by working for someone else. Wages in the Bible are sometimes called "reward" or "hire."

Wages were not common in the Old Testament, because most work was done by family members. But Old Testament laws said that fair wages (such as food, clothing, or money) should be paid to hired workers such as farm helpers, shepherds, and fishing crews (Lev. 19:13). Pharaoh's daughter promised wages to Moses' mother for taking care of him.

In the New Testament, wages were commonly paid to workers. An employer would go to the marketplace in the morning and look for workers. At the end of the day, he would pay wages (usually very little) for their work. Jesus told a parable about this (Matt. 20:1-16).

Wages is often used as a word picture of getting what we deserve, especially for the bad things we do. The New Testament says that the "wages of sin is death,

365

but the free gift of God is eternal life in Christ Jesus our Lord" (Rom. 6:23). Every person earns or deserves death, but eternal life is a gift (not a reward or wage) from God.

WALLS

in Bible times were the major way of defending cities against attack. Every ancient city had huge walls made of mud, stones, or brick. Some of those walls are still standing today. See Deuteronomy 1:28.

Famous city walls in the Old Testament include Jericho's walls, which were wide enough to have houses built on top of them (Josh. 6), and the walls of Jerusalem, which were built and rebuilt many times (I Kings 3:1). Nehemiah had a group of Jews repair the walls of Jerusalem after the Exile.

New Testament cities also had walls. Paul escaped over the Damascus wall (Acts 9:23, 24).

WAR

was very common in ancient Israel, and the Israelites were often in battles against other people. They saw war as God's way

of giving them the promised land. Sometimes God did miracles to allow Israel to win battles, such as the time the sun stood still for Joshua (Josh. 10:12-14).

The Old Testament also states that God used wars to punish the Israelites for their idolatry and disobedience (II Chron. 36:15-21). The wars of Old Testament times were often vicious and cruel. Sometimes whole cities, including men, women, and children, were destroyed or taken into slavery by the armies that won the battles.

The Israelites had experienced the cruelties of war. Isaiah said the promised Messiah would be a "Prince of Peace," not war.

During the New Testament, the Roman Empire had established more peaceful times in Israel. But Jesus said there would be wars and rumors of wars until He returned to rule. In His Sermon on the Mount, Jesus said, "Blessed are the peacemakers, for they shall be called sons of God" (Matt. 5:9).

One of the important promises of the Old Testament is that God will make wars cease to the ends of the earth.

However, the Book of Revelation states that when Christ returns, He will Himself use war to bring an end of war, defeating the forces of evil (Rev. 19:11-21). Then the Old Testament promise "Neither shall they learn war and more" will be fulfilled (Ps. 46:9; Isa. 2:4; Mic. 4:3).

In our present sinful world, soldiers and policemen seem to be necessary to keep order. Misuse of their power, however, brings terrible results.

Paul used *war* and *weapons* as word pictures of the battles Christians must fight against evil spiritual forces. He said Christians should "put on the whole armor of God" to defeat Satan (also see *Weapons*).

WASHING

in the hot, dry, dusty land of Israel was important. The people usually washed their feet when they came in to a house, and also their hands and faces before they ate. Because water was scarce, few people could take baths; instead, they washed in the streams and small fountains.

In Old Testament times, washing was an important part of worship. A huge basin of water in the tabernacle reminded the people that God wanted them to be "clean," or free from sin. Priests washed themselves with great care before taking part in sacrifices. If things or persons were "unclean" in the Old Testament, they had to be washed before becoming "clean" again.

The idea of washing and being clean is also found in the New Testament. Jesus washed the disciples' feet at the Last Supper. In a spiritual sense, baptism is a sign that our sins have been "washed" away—or forgiven—by Jesus.

See Exodus 30:17-21; Isaiah 1:16; John 13:1-11; Titus 3:5; Hebrews 10:22.

WATCHES OF THE NIGHT

was a name for the hours of nighttime. In Bible times, most people started their day at sunrise and ended it with sunset.

In the Old Testament, the Jews divided their night into three watches: the beginning of the night ("evening"), darkness ("twilight"), and the end of the night ("dawn").

By the time of Jesus, the Roman way of counting watches was more common. Mark 13:35 lists them as (1) evening, (2) midnight, (3) the cock-crowing, and (4) morning.

See Exodus 14:24; Psalm 90:4; Luke 12:38.

WATER

is mentioned many times in the Bible. Because Israel had little rainfall, water was precious. Drinking water carried in goatskins was sold in the marketplace (Deut. 2:28). Wherever wells, fountains, and springs were found, people built towns. When rain fell, it was considered a blessing from God (Ps. 23:2). One of the plagues God sent upon Egypt was bad water.

Water was recognized by Old Testament writers as one of the essentials of life (Gen. 21:14). The Levitical priests used water in their worship ceremonies (Exod. 30:17-21).

Water is used in many word pictures in the Bible. It stands for the source of all life and for eternal life. Jesus talked to the woman at the well about the "living water" of eternal life (John 4:14).

Another word picture is found in Matthew 10:42, where it says we should offer "a cup of cold water" to people in need, meaning we should care for them and help them.

WATERPOTS

were clay pitchers used in ancient times by people who had to haul water from wells or springs to their houses or to troughs for their animals. Each clay pot held several gallons of water. At the wedding in Cana, Jesus performed His first miracle by turning the water in large waterpots (20-30 gallons) into wine. See Genesis 24:15-20 Luke 22:10; John 2:6-10.

WEALTH

in ancient times was associated with many servants, large herds of camels, sheep, or other animals, silver, gold, and other precious metals. Job, Abraham, Lot, Isaac, and Jacob were wealthy men (Gen. 13:2; Job 1:3). Wealth was considered a blessing from God (Deut. 8:17, 18).

God teaches that He is the giver of wealth. But He also teaches that wealth is to be shared with the poor and those in need.

Jesus told a parable about a wealthy man who trusted only in his riches (Ps. 52:7; Mark 10:17-27; Luke 12:13-21). He did not realize that his death would occur that very night. Through this parable, Jesus taught that a person should aim to please God rather than to pile up riches. The rich young ruler was an example of a person enslaved by his wealth.

James denounced rich men who cheated the people who worked for them (Jas. 5:1-6).

Paul wrote Timothy that the love of money is the root of evil (I Tim. 6:6-10). It is better, Paul said, to be content with what God gives.

WEAPONS

were used in Bible times to protect people from wild animals and robbers and also to fight wars. The Israelites were often involved in small- and large-scale wars. Sometimes one tribe fought another, or the southern kingdom fought the northern kingdom, or all the people fought other enemies such as the Assyrians and Babylonians.

Cities were usually walled and often built on hilltops so guards on the walls could see any approaching enemy.

The following list includes common weapons used in Bible times.

Armor for soldiers was usually made of leather coated with a thin layer of metal for added protection. Strips of the leather were fastened together to form a kind of sleeveless coat that was tied together at the back with leather strings. Sometimes soldiers wore a square of bronze over the chest under this armor as a kind of heart guard. Kings often had armor made with more metal.

When the word *armor* is used in Ephesians 6:11, it refers to all the weapons a soldier used rather than just the leather covering for his body.

Bows and Arrows were used for hunting animals for food, and also for war. Bows were made of wood; bowstrings were made of oxgut. Arrows were light wood or reeds tipped with metal. When bows and arrows were used as weapons of war, the bows were sometimes as long as five feet. Israelites from the tribes of Reuben, Gad, and Benjamin were famous for their skill with bows and arrows in warfare (I Chron. 5:18; 12:2).

Buckler (see *Shield*).

Club are mentioned as part of the weapons carried by the temple guard who came to arrest Jesus in the garden of Gethsemane. The clubs were probably something like the nightsticks carried by our police officers.

Coat of Mail (see *Armor*)

Dagger (see *Sword*)

Helmets for soldiers, during most of the Old Testament period, were made of leather; those for kings were of bronze. In New Testament times, soldiers' helmets were made of bronze.

Javelin, Spear, and **Lance** were roughly the same—long, slender pieces of wood with heads of stone or metal.

They were used in war either to thrust or throw at the enemy.

Sheath was the case or covering for a sword as it hung at the left side of a soldier.

Shields (sometimes called bucklers) were large or small objects that soldiers carried to protect themselves from the spears and swords of enemies. Shields were usually either wickerwork (thin, flexible twigs woven together) or leather stretched over a wooden frame. The leather was oiled before battle to preserve it or to make it glisten (Isa. 21:5).

Sling was a common weapon in early times for hunting animals and for war. It was not like our slingshots. Instead it was a band of leather that was wide in the middle to hold a stone. The soldier held both ends 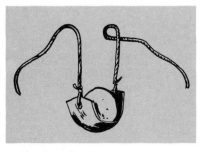 together in his hands, swung it around his head to get thrust, then let one end go to release the stone. Seven hundred left-handed men from the tribe of Benjamin were so skilled that they could "sling a stone at a hair and not miss."

This is the weapon David used to kill Goliath, the giant.

See Judges 20:16; I Samuel 17:40-50.

Spear (see *Javelin*)

Swords are the weapons most frequently mentioned in the Bible. Normally they were long, broad knives

369

with a handle. Some swords had two sharp edges, some only one. They were usually carried by the soldier in a sheath on his left side. A dagger is a smaller sword.

Sword is often used in the Bible as a word picture for the judgment of God or for violence of any kind. Jesus said, "All who take the sword will perish by the sword." *Sword* is also used as a word picture of the power of the Word of God.

See Matthew 26:52; Ephesians 6:17; Hebrews 4:12.

WELL

is a hole dug in the ground to find water. Since water was very scarce in dry Israel, wells were important for people and animals. Often people fought over wells.

When a well was dug, rocks were placed around it and a cover over it to keep animals or people from falling in. Some wells were shallow, others were

very deep. Sometimes dry wells or cisterns were used for hiding places. Joseph's brothers threw him in an old, dry well.

Among the famous wells in the Bible are the well where Jacob met Rachel (Gen. 29:1-10), the well of Bethlehem, and the well at Sychar, where Jesus met a Samaritan woman (John 4:5-15).

WHIRLWIND

is a violent storm with strong, gusting winds, sometimes like a tornado. Whirlwinds sometimes occur on the Sea of Galilee suddenly and without warning. Jesus once calmed such a storm. Elijah was carried to heaven by a whirlwind. It was also called a "tempest" in the Bible.

Whirlwind is sometimes a word picture for the judgment of God.

See II Kings 2:11; Job 38:1; Hosea 8:7; Zechariah 7:14; Luke 8:23, 24.

WIDOW *(WID-oh)*

is a woman whose husband has died. In ancient times, widows were usually poor because most women did not inherit anything from their husbands—all property was inherited by sons.

In Old Testament times, a widow wore special clothes to show she was a widow. The Old Testament Law said the Israelites were to use some of the Levites' tithes to feed widows. Hebrews also were to include widows at feasts and other happy occasions. God would punish any who cheated widows or harmed them (Exod. 22:22-24; Deut. 14:28, 29; 24:17).

In the New Testament, the early church in Jerusalem appointed seven men to see that widows had enough food (Acts 6:1-6). The Book of James says that visiting widows and orphans is part of true religion (Jas 1:27).

The apostle Paul wrote to Timothy that the church should make special provision for widows who were over sixty years old and had lived a good life, if they had no relatives to care for them (I Tim. 5:3-16). He advised younger widows to marry again.

WINE

is fermented grape juice. In Bible times, it was used as a drink, a medicine, and a disinfectant (Luke 10:34).

Wine was also poured out as a special drink offering to God, a symbol of thanksgiving or repentance (Lev. 23:13; Num. 15:5).

In the Bible, wine is spoken of both as a blessing and as a curse (Gen. 27:28; Prov. 20:1; 23:29-35; Hos. 4:11). Isaac blessed his son, wishing him plenty in grain and wine. But the prophet Hosea said wine takes away understanding. Proverbs calls wine "a mocker . . . a brawler; and whoever is led astray by it is not wise." The writer of Proverbs also gave a colorful description of a person who gets drunk on wine.

Jewish priests were commanded not to drink wine when they were on duty, and Nazirites were never to drink wine (Lev. 10:9; Num. 6:1-4,20).

In Old Testament times, wine was not diluted, but during the time of Jesus wine was usually mixed with water. The Pharisees complained because Jesus ate and drank with sinners (Luke 7:33, 34). He once turned water into wine at a wedding in Cana (John 2:2-11). At the Last Supper, Jesus said the wine symbolized His blood, which was to be poured out for sinners (Matt. 26:27-29).

Wine is sometimes used as a word pic-

ture for the wrath of God (Jer. 25:15; Rev. 14:10). It is also pictured as part of times of joy and love (Song of Sol. 5:1; Is. 55:1).

The apostle Paul told Christians not to be drunk with wine but to be filled with the Spirit.

WINEPRESS

was a large square pit or trough, often lined with cement. Workers put grapes into the winepress and then walked and stamped on the grapes to press out the juice. The grape juice flowed through a hole near the bottom of the winepress into a smaller vat. Then the juice was made into wine. Archaeologists have found some ancient winepresses in Israel.

The workers sang and shouted as they stamped on the grapes. It was a time of joy.

Winepress is sometimes a word picture for God's anger.

See Isaiah 16:10; 63:2, 3; Jer. 25:30; Revelation 14:19, 20; 19:15.

WINESKIN

was a leather bag for storing wine, water, or milk. Wineskins were usually made from goatskin.

Since fermenting wine creates gases, wineskins had to stretch enough to get larger. Jesus said that if you put new wine into old wineskins, the bags would burst. New wine must be put into newer, more elastic wineskins.

See Genesis 21:14-19; Matthew 9:17.

WINNOWING (WIN-oh-wing)

was the way farmers separated the good parts of grain (the kernels) from the waste parts (the chaff). Using wooden pitchforks or shovels, the farmers threw the grain into the air when there was a strong breeze. The wind would blow away the chaff, and the heavier kernels would fall to the ground.

Winnowing is mentioned many times in the Old Testament. In Psalm 1 evil people are compared to worthless chaff.

See Ruth 3:2; Psalm 1:4; Isaiah 30:24.

WISDOM (WIZ-dum)

in the Bible means not only learning, but also skills, common sense, and good judgment.

A skill such as weaving or building was considered wisdom (Exod. 28:3 (KJV)).

The Old Testament Book of Proverbs applies wisdom to daily life situations such as rearing children, handling money, telling the truth, and controlling anger. In Proverbs 8, wisdom is described as a woman who invites people to listen to her wisdom and live by it.

Some parts of the Old Testament are called Wisdom Literature. They include Proverbs, Ecclesiastes, Job, and Psalms 19, 37, 104, 107, 147, 148.

In the beginning of his reign, King Solomon asked God for wisdom, and God gave it to him (I Kings 3:9-14; 10:23, 24).

Solomon became known as the wisest king on earth.

God is the source of wisdom (Job 28:20-28). Job told some examples of the wisdom of God. Fearing or honoring the Lord is the starting point of wisdom for people (Deut. 4:6; Ps. 111:10). Following God's commands is a sign of wisdom.

In the New Testament, Christians are told that If they lack wisdom, they may ask God, and He will give it generously (Jas. 1:5). Paul wrote that Jesus is both "the power of God and the wisdom of God." He said that all wisdom and knowledge are found in Jesus Christ (I Cor. 1:24, 30; Col. 2:3).

WITCHES

are persons who do supernatural things by the power of the devil. Witches use evil spells, potions, and curses. The Bible forbids witchcraft (Lev. 19:26; Deut. 18:9-14). Witches, sorcerers, soothsayers, wizards, magicians, enchanters, and diviners are very much alike.

Witchcraft was common in ancient Israel, Egypt, Assyria, and Babylon. Queen Jezebel was involved in witchcraft (II Kings 9:22).

In the New Testament, Simon Magus (or "magician") practiced witchcraft, and so did Elymas on the island of Cyprus (Acts 8:9-24; 13:6-12). Paul called Elymas a "son of the devil."

WITNESS (WIT-nuss)

in the Bible usually means a person who tells the truth no matter what it costs. The word *martyr* comes from the Greek word meaning "witness."

In the Old Testament, the Law of God was called a witness to God's holiness and the people's sins. The tabernacle was called a witness to God's presence (Num. 17: 7, 8; Deut. 31:26).

The Ten Commandments include a rule that "you shall not bear false witness against your neighbor" (Exod. 20:16; Deut. 19:16-18). False witnesses were severely punished.

The men who told lies at Jesus' trial were false witnesses (Matt. 26:60).

God calls His people to be His witnesses—to tell His truth no matter what it costs. The disciples were witnesses to the death and resurrection of Christ, and they told about it (Luke 24:46-48; Acts 2:32). When Jesus was taken into heaven, He told the disciples that they were to be His witnesses to the end of the earth (Acts 1: 8).

The Holy Spirit is a witness to Christians.

WITNESS OF THE SPIRIT

refers to the Holy Spirit as a true witness—someone who tells the truth.

Jesus told His disciples that the Spirit would be a witness to the world about sin, righteousness, and coming judgment (John 16:7-11). The Spirit would remind Christians of Jesus' words and what He did (John 14:16, 17, 26; 16:12-15).

The apostle Paul wrote that the Spirit tells believers they are the children of God (Rom. 8:15-17). He also helps believers understand God's thoughts (I Cor. 2:11-13).

John told Christians that the Spirit of God witnesses that Jesus Christ, the Son of God, became a man with a human body (I John 4:2).

The writer of Hebrews illustrates that the Spirit sometimes tells believers truths about God through writings in the Bible—in this case through something written in Jeremiah (Heb. 10:15-18).

Sometimes the Spirit witnesses about something very specific. Paul said the Spirit told him he would face imprisonment and suffering (Acts 20:22, 23).

WIZARD (see *Sorcerer*)

WOLF (see *Animals*)

WOMAN

according to the Bible, is half of humanity, or mankind. God created the first man and the first woman, both in the image of God (Gen. 1:27, 28). He gave to them—man and woman together—dominion over His creation. He told them to multiply and to subdue the earth. They were to be "one flesh."

Sin destroyed the relationship God had meant for men and women (Gen. 3:1-19). In the Old Testament, the Israelites, like some of the pagan people around them, often treated women as possessions of men rather than as equal partners. In spite of this, many women in the Old Testament showed outstanding leadership ability and were used by God (Exod. 15:20, 21; Judg. 4:4—5:31; II Kings 22:14-20). Deborah was a skilled Old Testament judge. Miriam, Deborah, and Huldah were called by God to be prophets. The picture of a good woman in Proverbs 31:10-31 shows a woman who is a capable leader both in her home and in the community.

When Jesus came to earth, He showed clearly by His actions that He believed in the dignity and equality of women (Luke 8:1-3). He commended Mary for her desire to sit at His feet like the disciples and listen to His teaching (Luke 10:38-42). He made His first announcement that He was the Messiah to the woman at the well; He included women in the group of those who traveled with Him. Women were the first to receive the news of the resurrection and were told to make it known (Matt. 28:1-10; Mark 16:1-8; Luke 24:1-11; John 20:1-18). Women prayed and prophesied publicly in the early church (I Cor. 11:5). Phoebe was an early leader in the church at Cenchreae (Rom.16:1).

WORD

in the Bible sometimes has special meanings different from our usual use of it. Here are some of its special meanings:

1. *Word* sometimes means God's truth as it is now found in Old Testament writings. "Thy word is a lamp to my feet and a light to my path" (Ps. 119:105).

2. It sometimes means the Gospel, or the Christian message, as in "Be doers of the word, and not hearers only" (Jas. 1:22).

3. *Word* (with a capital letter) is sometimes a name for Christ, as in John 1:1, "In the beginning was the Word, and the Word was with God, and the Word was God." Using Word as a name for Christ shows that Christ was revealing God and His truth to people, just as we use words to show others our thoughts.

WORD OF THE LORD or WORD OF GOD

is a phrase that appears nearly 400 times in the Old Testament. It was used when God gave His prophets or other leaders a message that they were to give to other people. *The Word of the Lord* meant that this was truth from God that was absolutely sure, and the people could depend on it (Isa. 40:8; I Thess. 4:15).

Many of the Old Testament books of prophecy, including Jeremiah, Hosea, Joel, Jonah, Zephaniah, Haggai, and Zechariah have in the first verse something like "The word of the Lord came to . . ." to show that the message was from God (Jer. 1:1; Hos. 1:1; Joel 1:1; Jonah 1:1; Zeph. 1:1; Hag. 1:1; Zech. 1:1).

The Word of the Lord involves not only a message, but also power to do the thing mentioned (Ps. 33:6; Heb. 11:3). "By the word of the Lord the heavens were made" is the way the psalmist described Creation.

WORLD

has several meanings in the Bible:

1. The planet earth (I Sam. 2:8). Genesis 1 and 2 tell about the creation of the world, or earth.

2. Wherever people live (Mark 16:15). Jesus told His disciples to go into all the world and preach the Gospel.

3. The Roman Empire (Luke 2:1). At the time of the birth of Jesus, Caesar Augustus wanted "all the world" to be taxed.

4. Greek culture (Acts 19:27). When Paul preached in Ephesus, a silversmith said that "the whole world" worshiped the goddess Artemis.

5. The world to come (Heb. 2:3-9; 6:5; Rev. 11:15). This involves not only a new physical place, but also a new way of life.

6. The people who live on the earth (John 3:16; 7:7). This is the meaning in John 3:16, "For God so loved the world that he gave his only Son, that whoever believes in him should not perish but have eternal life." Jesus told His disciples that the "world" hated Him because He pointed out their sins.

7. The world system ruled by Satan, who wants disobedience and rebellion against God (John 8:23; Gal. 6:14; Eph.

2:2; Jas. 1:27). Jesus told the Pharisees that they were "of this world" but He was not. Paul said he had died to this world's ideas of doing whatever pleases self. True holiness is to keep oneself unstained from the world's basic idea of "me first."

WORSHIP

means to honor, praise, and adore someone who is worthy of such high honor. The English word was originally *worthship* to show that the one being honored was worthy of praise.

True worship involves not only things we do but also our thoughts and feelings as we do them. The Old Testament prophets said that acts of worship meant nothing unless the thoughts, feelings, and lives of the worshipers were controlled by God.

Only God fully deserves our worship. When Jesus was tempted by Satan, He said, "You shall worship the Lord your God and him only shall you serve." (Matt. 4:10).

The Book of Revelation says that John once began to worship an angel (Rev. 19:10). However, the angel cried out, "You must not do that! I am a fellow servant. . . . Worship God."

People can and should worship God both publicly and privately. After the Hebrew people came out of Egypt, they worshiped God publicly at the tabernacle set up in the wilderness. Later, when the temple was built in Jerusalem, the Israelites worshiped together in a more highly organized way. The people sang many of the psalms as part of their worship in the temple (Ps. 135:1-6).

Scholars believe that during the Exile in Babylon, the Jews began to meet in synagogues for worship and instruction.

Eventually, synagogues were built wherever Jewish people lived. The temple sacrifices were not carried on in the synagogues, however.

The early Christians met in homes to worship God (Acts 2:42; I Cor. 14:26; Eph. 5:19, 20). Their worship included preaching, reading the Scriptures, praying, singing, celebrating the Lord's Supper, and using other gifts the Holy Spirit gave them.

Today, Christians meet in church buildings and other places to worship God publicly.

WRATH OF GOD

means God's anger with sin. The Old Testament prophets talked often about the wrath of God and the judgment that would come upon His people if they turned away from Him (Num. 11:1; Deut. 1:26-28).

The Bible makes it clear that God's anger or wrath is caused by His people forgetting Him, turning away from Him and His commands, and despising His love and care for them. When God's people acted this way, they began treating each other unfairly, they trusted in their own strength instead of in God, and they began to worship other gods. God's judgment followed, and that included the destruction of Israel as a nation. The people were sent into exile in Assyria and Babylonia.

Because God is holy and because He loves us, He is angry when we turn away from Him and fail to become all He meant us to be. If God did not care about us, He would not be angry when we follow the destructive path of sin.

Jesus Christ came to die for our sins and to free us from the punishment of God's wrath (I Thess. 5:9; Rev. 5:9). Those who do not trust and obey Christ cannot have the reconciliation with God that Christ made possible, because they have not obeyed the Gospel.

In the final judgment, all people who refuse Christ's way of salvation must face the wrath of God (Ps. 110:5-6; Isa. 2:20, 21; Rom. 1:18; John 3:36; II Thess. 1:8, 9; Revelation 14:9, 10).

WRESTLING

was a popular game during New Testament times. Paul may have watched wrestling matches in Corinth. He used *wrestling* as a word picture of the way Christians must struggle against Satan (Eph. 6:12).

The most famous wrestling match in the Bible was between Jacob and God's angel (Gen. 32:24-30).

WRITING

probably began in Bible lands about 3500 B.C. Early writing was something like very simple pictures or lines. Gradually, over a period of many hundreds of years, these pictures developed into other symbols that were more like an alphabet.

So far as we know, the Hebrew language always had an alphabet. Many Hebrews knew how to read and write before 1000 B.C. (Judg. 8:14).

Hebrew (the original language of the Old Testament) is written from right to left and from the "back" of the book to the "front"—just the opposite of our kind of writing. The Hebrew alphabet had no vowels—only consonants. The vowels had to be supplied by the reader (see *Hebrew Language*).

The Greek language (of the New Testament) had both vowels and conso-

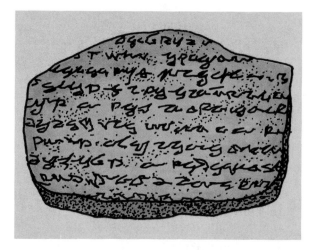

nants and reads from left to right, like English. However, Greek and Hebrew were both written at first in all capital letters, with no spaces between words and no punctuation marks. John 14:1 would look something like this:

LETNOTYOURHEARTSBETROUBLED
BELIEVEINGODBELIEVEALSOINME

So Hebrews and early Christians had a harder time than we do learning to read!

There was no such thing as paper in Bible times.

What did ancient people write on?

1. Stones were used for permanent records (Exod. 24:12; Deut. 27:2-8). When Moses received the Ten Commandments from God, they were written on stone tablets. Sometimes people covered stones with plaster and then wrote in the plaster while it was still soft.

2. Metal was used for writing. Engraving on gold is mentioned in Exodus 28:36.

3. Wood was sometimes coated with wax or clay and then used as a writing tablet (Ezek. 37:16, 17; Luke 1:63). This is probably the kind of tablet Zechariah used to tell that his son should be named John.

4. Potsherds, or pieces of broken pottery, were used for ordinary writing purposes. People could write on them with ink and then wash the writing off and use the pieces again.

5. Clay tablets were commonly used throughout the Middle East. If people wanted to make the writing permanent, they baked the clay in the sun or in an oven.

6. Papyrus was used very often for important letters or documents. Papyrus was a tall plant that grew in water and swampy places. Ancient people took the inside of the papyrus stalks and cut them into thin strips. They glued these strips on top of each other crisscross and left them under something heavy to make them stick together. When the sheets were dry, they were polished with stone and glued together to form long strips (scrolls) for writing. People could use pen and ink to write on papyrus. Probably Jeremiah's scroll that King Jehoiakim burned was made of papyrus (Jer. 36:23).

7. Parchment was an excellent but expensive writing material. It was made from the skins of sheep or goats. People removed the hair from the animal skins, soaked them in lime, and then stretched them on frames. When the skins dried, they were rubbed smooth with chalk or pumice stones.

Parchment lasted much longer than papyrus. Scribes often used parchment to make copies of the Old Testament writings.

What did ancient people write with?

1. Chisels were used to engrave stones or metal.

2. Styluses—pointed pieces of bone, wood, or metal—were used for writing on clay or wax. The Old Testament mentions "iron pens" that were probably metal styluses (Job 19:24; Jer. 17:1).

3. Pens were made from the stiff stems of plants. They were cut diagonally on the end, and the ends were then frayed to feel like a brush. These pens were used to write on potsherds, papyrus, and parchment.

4. Ink was made in two colors—black and red. Black ink was made by mixing soot with a thin solution of sticky resin from trees. This was dried and formed into cakes. When a person wanted to write, he moistened the cake of ink with water and dipped his stylus or pen into it.

Red ink was made like black ink, but with red iron oxide instead of soot.

How were books formed?

Early books were written on long scrolls. These were formed from sheets of papyrus or parchment glued together. Most scrolls were about nine to eleven inches high and about thirty feet long. Sometimes the scroll was written on both sides (Ezek. 2:10; Rev. 5:1). Scrolls were usually stored in pottery jars (Jer. 32:14).

XERXES I *(ZERK-zees)*

was the king of Persia from 485 to 465 B.C. Most scholars believe he was the King Ahasuerus who made Esther his queen. The Book of Esther describes events very similar to those in Persia's historical records of King Xerxes. See Esther 2:16, 17.

YOKE

was a wood frame that harnessed two animals together for heavy work. Oxen were often yoked to pull a plow, wagon, or other farm equipment.

The yoke was also a symbol of obedience for people. Jeremiah told the Jews to put yoke-bars on their necks as a symbol that they had to obey King Nebuchadnezzar of Babylon (Jer. 27:2, 6-8).

The Israelites told King Rehoboam that his father's "yoke" (meaning his demands) had been too heavy (I Kings 12:4, 14). But Rehoboam followed the foolish advice of his younger advisers and told the people, "My father made your yoke heavy, but I will add to your yoke."

In the New Testament, *yoke* is usually a word picture that means demands, requirements, or burdens. Jesus invited people to join themselves to Him and His work (Matt. 11:28-30). "Take my yoke upon you, and learn from me . . . for my yoke is easy, and my burden is light." He meant that loving and serving Him may look hard, but it is really easy because He makes our lives so different.

Other passages speak of the yoke of slavery, or the yoke or burden of trying to keep the Old Testament Law (Acts 15:10; Gal. 5:1; I Tim. 6:1).

YOUTH

in the Bible seems to refer to a broad period of time. Although no clear statement is given, it probably includes persons up to age twenty or twenty-five. A man was counted in the census for army service at twenty. A Levite could begin service in the tabernacle at age twenty-five. So the upper age limit of "youth" is not clear. See Exodus 30:14; Numbers 1:1-3; 8:24.

Jesus called Zacchaeus down from his tree and headed toward his house.

Jesus as He walked past.

Jesus surprised Zacchaeus by stopping beneath the tree to say He'd be staying at Zacchaeus's house. The crowds were surprised that Jesus would go to the house of a tax collector. But Zacchaeus was overjoyed. He said he would give half of his riches to the poor and repay those he had cheated with four times the original amount. It was his way of showing he was sorry for his sins.

See Luke 19:1-10.

ZACHARIAH, ZACHARIAS
(see *Zechariah*)

ZADOK *(ZAY-dok)*

was a priest who was loyal to both David and Solomon. When Zadok was young,

ZACCHAEUS *(zak-KEY-us)*
was the chief Jewish tax collector in Jericho. Men such as Zacchaeus were hated because they worked for the Roman government and were not always honest.

Zacchaeus was so short he had to climb a tree to see above the crowds and look at

379

he joined David in his war against King Saul.

Later, when David prepared to bring the ark of God into Jerusalem, he asked Zadok and other priests to sanctify themselves and carry it.

When King David's son Absalom revolted and tried to take over his father's kingdom, Zadok fled with David, carrying the ark (I Chron. 15:11-13). David told Zadok and Abiathar and their two sons to take the ark back into Jerusalem and act as his spies (II Sam. 15:24-36; 17:15, 17-21). Zadok stayed loyal to David.

When Zadok was old and David was dying, Zadok anointed Solomon king as David told him to do (I Kings 1:18-45). Solomon soon made him high priest (I Kings 2:35).

ZEAL (zeel)

means an eager interest and determination. David said he had a zeal for God's house. Paul said the Jews had a wrong kind of zeal. They were determined about the wrong things.

Paul admitted with sorrow that he once had zeal to persecute the church. However, Paul praised the Corinthians for their zeal in giving to needy Christians.

See Romans 10:2, 3; II Corinth-ians 9:2; Philippians 3:6.

ZEALOTS (ZEL-uts)

were a group of Jews at the time of Christ who were so determined to overthrow the Roman rulers that they sometimes used violence.

One of Jesus' disciples, Simon, was once a member of this group. He is called Simon the Zealot. He is not the same person as Simon Peter.

The work of the Zealots eventually helped to bring about the terrible war with Rome in A.D. 68 that destroyed Jerusalem and the temple.

See Luke 6:15; Acts 1:13.

ZEBULUN (ZEB-you-lun)

was the tenth son of Jacob and the sixth and last son born to Leah (Gen. 30:19, 20).

His descendants became the tribe of Zebulun. When Moses counted the men over twenty years old who could go to war from the tribe of Zebulun, the number totaled 57,400 (Num. 1:30, 31; 26:27).

Later, a second count was made in Moab. By this time, the number had increased to 60,500 men.

When the Hebrews got to Canaan, the tribe of Zebulun was given a section of land between the Sea of Galilee and the Mediterranean (Josh. 19:10-16).

When Jesus visited the territory of Zebulun, he fulfilled a prophecy recorded in Isaiah 9:1, 2. "The land of Zebulun ... the people who walked in darkness have seen a great light" (Matt. 4:12-16).

ZECHARIAH (ZEK-uh-RYE-uh)

was the name of twenty-eight people in the Bible. Five have some importance—one king, three men who were prophets and priests, and the priest who was the father of John the Baptist. The Old Testament Book of Zechariah is named for one of the prophets.

1. Zechariah, the priest and prophet whose prophecies are recorded in the next-to-the last Old Testament book, was from a family of priests (Ezra 5:1, 2; Zech. 1:1-3). His family returned to Jerusalem from the Babylonian exile to help rebuild the temple.

He began prophesying about 520 B.C. and may have continued on and off for many years. The first part of his ministry was during the same period as the prophet Haggai. He helped encourage the people to rebuild the temple.

2. Zechariah, the fourteenth king of Israel, reigned about six months in 753 B.C., about thirty years before Israel was conquered by the Assyrians (II Kings 10:30; 15:8-12). He sinned against the Lord like the kings before him.

After six months as king, Shallum murdered Zechariah and became king in his place.

Zechariah's short reign fulfilled a promise the Lord had made to King Jehu, his great-great-grandfather. The Lord had told Jehu that four generations of his sons would be kings after him. Zechariah was the fourth and last king related to Jehu.

3. Zechariah, a priest and prophet during the reign of Joash, king of Judah, told the people God had forsaken them because they had turned from God (II Chron. 24:20-25; Matt. 23:35; Luke 11:51). King Joash commanded that Zechariah be stoned to death, and he was killed in the courtyard of the temple. This may have been the Zechariah that Jesus mentioned as the last martyr in the Old Testament.

4. Zechariah was also the name of a prophet during the early days of Uzziah, king of Judah (II Chron. 26:5). (Uzziah is called Azariah in II Kings.) Zechariah instructed him in the fear of the Lord, and "as long as he sought the Lord, God made him prosper." Uzziah later (perhaps after the death of Zechariah) turned away from God and did great evil. Eventually God struck Uzziah with leprosy.

5. Zechariah, the father of John the Baptist, was a priest during New Testament times (Luke 1:5-25, 57-80). He and

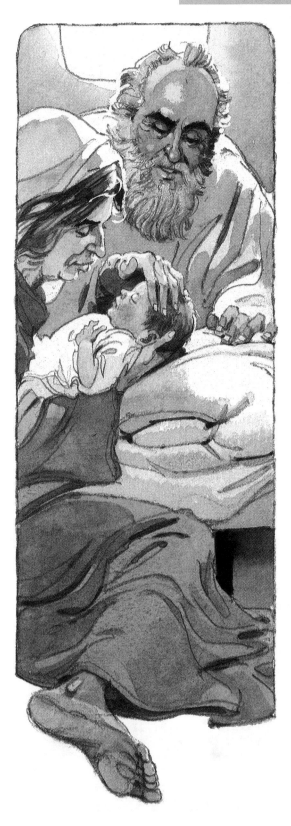

his wife, Elizabeth, both followed God's commands, and they were childless until their old age.

One day while Zechariah was burning incense in the temple, an angel appeared and said that he and Elizabeth would have a son. Zechariah couldn't believe it, so he asked for some sign that it would happen. The angel told him he would not be able to speak until his son was born.

When the baby was born, friends and relatives came to congratulate the parents. They thought the boy should be named Zechariah after his father. But Elizabeth said, "Not so; he shall be called John."

Then they gave Zechariah something on which to write what the baby should be named. He wrote, "His name is John" —and suddenly Zechariah could speak again.

Zechariah and Elizabeth's son, John, was a cousin of Jesus. John was the prophet who helped prepare the way for Jesus' ministry.

ZECHARIAH *(ZEK-uh-RYE-uh)*, BOOK OF

includes the prophecies of Zechariah to the group of Jews who had come back to Jerusalem after seventy years of exile in Babylon. Their goal had been to rebuild the Temple. However, soon after they began, the work was halted by the king of Babylon.

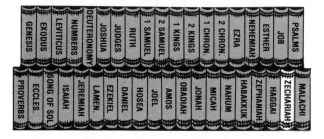

Twenty years later, in 520 B.C., Zechariah began to prophesy. He and another prophet, Haggai, encouraged the Israelites to go back to their work on the temple. Four years later, in 516 or 515 B.C., the temple was completed.

The Book of Zechariah contains five prophecies:

1. The first prophecy called the people to repent (Zech. 1:1-6).

2. The second prophecy encouraged the people to complete the temple (Zech. 1:7—6:15).

3. In the third prophecy, gold and silver were fashioned into a crown for Joshua, the high priest. This pictured the Messiah, who would be both priest and king to His people . Zechariah called this Messiah the Branch (Zech. 6:9-15).

4. In the fourth prophecy Zechariah urged the people to be fair and honest with each other (chapters 7 and 8).

5. In the fifth prophecy, the prophet looked into the future and made many references to a coming Messiah (chapters 9-14). Pagan nations were to be destroyed. The Shepherd-King would be rejected, but would return victoriously. God's triumphant kingdom would be set up.

ZEDEKIAH *(ZED-uh-KY-uh)*

was the name of the last king of Judah.

After King Nebuchadnezzar of Babylon captured Jehoiachin, the previous king of Judah, Nebuchadnezzar appointed Zedekiah to be king.

Zedekiah was twenty-one years old at the time, and he ruled for eleven years. He did not follow God's commands, nor would he listen to the advice of the prophet Jeremiah. He permitted Jeremiah to be placed in an empty cistern with muck at the bottom.

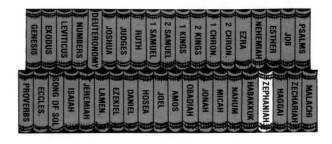

After Jeremiah was rescued from the cistern, he told Zedekiah that the Lord wanted him to surrender to the Babylonians so the city could be spared from destruction. The Babylonian army had surrounded the city, and all food supplies were cut off. Instead of following Jeremiah's advice, Zedekiah and his soldiers tried to flee. He was captured and his sons were killed. Zedekiah was blinded and the city was destroyed in 586 B.C.

See II Kings 24:17—25:7; Jeremiah 34:1-22; 37:1—39:7.

ZEPHANIAH *(zef-uh-NY-uh)*

was a prophet and great-grandson of Hezekiah, king of Judah. His prophecies are in the Old Testament Book of Zephaniah.

He lived in Jerusalem and prophesied in the royal court of Josiah, king of Judah, between 641 and 609 B.C. His prophecies seem to refer to the time before Josiah tried to turn his people back to God. Other prophets during his time included Nahum, Habakkuk, Huldah, and Jeremiah.

Zephaniah fearlessly denounced the evils of his time and told of God's approaching judgment. His prophecies also spoke of the hope that Israel would be restored as a strong nation.

ZEPHANIAH *(zef-uh-NY-uh)*, BOOK OF

was written by the prophet Zephaniah during the reign of King Josiah, probably about 625 B.C. Perhaps Zephaniah's prophecies helped urge King Josiah to make some of his reforms.

When Zephaniah prophesied, Assyria had been a world power for fifty years. Josiah's grandfather, King Manasseh, had paid tribute each year to Assyria. He encouraged idol worship and even persecuted those who worshiped God. Josiah's father, Amon, did the same things.

Zephaniah prophesied judgment for Judah and for other countries that ignored God's demands for righteousness. He also offered hope for Israel after the judgment that was coming.

Zephaniah spoke of God's judgment as the "day of the Lord" (Zeph. 1). This judgment would affect not only Judah, but also Philistia, Moab, Egypt, and Assyria (Zeph. 2). He said the Israelites perhaps could escape judgment if they would seek God and do His commands.

The last section of the book describes the glory that would belong to Israel when God restored His people and saved them from their oppressors (Zephaniah 3:9-20).

ZEUS *(zoos)*

was the chief of the Greek gods. The Romans called him Jupiter. His sign was a thunderbolt, and the rainbow was supposed to be his messenger.

In 168 B.C., the Syrian king Antiochus Epiphanes IV dedicated the Jewish temple at Jerusalem to Zeus. The Jews were outraged at this idolatry, and it became part of the reason for the Maccabean revolt (see *Maccabees*).

When Paul and Barnabas were on their first missionary journey, they healed a

crippled man in the town of Lystra. The people were so amazed they said, "The gods have come down to us in the likeness of men." They called Barnabas "Zeus" and Paul "Hermes." The priest of Zeus wanted to offer sacrifices to them, but Paul and Barnabas made them stop.

See Acts 14:8-18.

ZIKLAG *(ZIK-lag)*

was a city in southern Israel where David lived for sixteen months while hiding from King Saul. Achish, king of Gath, told David that he and his men and their families could live in the city.

Once while David and his small group of warriors were gone, the Amalekites raided the town and captured all of their-wives, children, and possessions. David and his men went after them and rescued their families and their possessions.

David was still living at Ziklag when he received word that King Saul had been killed in a battle.

Ziklag became one of the cities of Judah.

See I Samuel 27:1-7; 30:1-26; II Samuel 1:14; I Chronicles 12:1-20.

ZION *(ZI-un)*

is one of the hills on which Jerusalem stands. At one time, a Jebusite fortress stood on the hill (II Sam. 5:6-9). David captured the fortress and called it the "city of David." After David brought the ark of God to Zion, the hill was considered sacred.

When King Solomon moved the ark of God into the temple on Mount Moriah, the name *Zion* was extended to include the Temple hill.

Later Zion came to mean all of Jerusalem (Ps. 48:1-3). Zion also became another word for Israel (Ps. 126:1).

Finally, in the New Testament, *Zion* came to mean "heaven." Hebrews 12:22 says, "You have come to Mount Zion and to the city of the living God, the heavenly Jerusalem."

ZIPPORAH *(zih-PO-rah)*

was the wife of Moses. Her father was Jethro, a priest of Midian.

Moses met Zipporah after he fled from Egypt. She and her six sisters were drawing water for their father's flock, but some shepherds drove them away. Moses protected the sisters and helped them. Their grateful father invited Moses to eat and live with them and eventually gave Zipporah to Moses as his wife (Exod. 2:15-22).

Zipporah and Moses had two sons, Gershom and Eliezer.

When Moses returned to Egypt after forty years in Midian, Zipporah and their two sons went with him. However, at an inn along the way, Moses became very sick. Zipporah realized that the reason for his sickness was that they hadn't circumcised one of their sons as God had commanded (Exod. 4:24-27). So Zipporah circumcised her son.

Sometime during the conflict with Pharaoh or the beginning of the Exodus, Moses had sent Zipporah and their two sons back to her father's home. After Moses and the Israelites crossed the Red Sea, Zipporah, her two sons, and her father came to the Israelite camp near Mount Sinai. The Bible states that after a short visit, Jethro returned home (Exod. 18:1-7). It does not say whether Zipporah and her sons stayed with Moses or went back to Midian.